SELLING WAR

SELLING WAR

A Critical Look at the Military's PR Machine

STEVEN J. ALVAREZ

POTOMAC BOOKS

An imprint of the University of Nebraska Press

Library of Congress Cataloging-in-Publication Data

Names: Alvarez, Steven J.
Title: Selling war: a critical look at the military's PR machine / Steven J.
Alvarez.
Description: Lincoln: Potomac Books, an imprint of the University of
Nebraska Press, 2016. | Includes bibliographical references.
Identifiers:
LCCN 2015037891
ISBN 9781612347721 (cloth: alk. paper)
ISBN 9781612348179 (ePub)
ISBN 9781612348186 (mobi)
ISBN 9781612348193 (pdf)
Subjects: LCSH: Iraq War, 2003–2011—Public opinion. | Iraq War,
2003–2011—Political aspects—United States. | Alvarez, Steven J. | United
States. Army Reserve—Officers –Biography. | United States—Armed
Forces—Public relations—History—21st century. | Public relations and
politics—United States—History—21st century. | Communication in
politics—United States—History—21st century. | Mass media—Political
aspects—United States—History—21st century. | Information
warfare—Iraq—History—21st century. | Information warfare—United
States—History—21st century. | BISAC: HISTORY / Military / Iraq War
(2003–).
Classification: LCC DS79.767.P83 A48 2016 | DDC 659.2/935500973—
dc23 LC record available at http://lccn.loc.gov/2015037891

Set in Minion by M. Scheer.
Designed by Rachel Gould.

This book is dedicated to

all the U.S. military veterans who fought the war in Iraq; all these veterans' families who courageously waited for their return;

my Iraqi public affairs colleagues who daily tried to tell the story of their nation to a world that oftentimes could not hear them;

and the millions of Iraqis whose lives have been adversely affected by the U.S. invasion.

Above all this book is for my wife, Rosemary, whose enduring love and support filled my soul's rucksack and sustained me throughout my tour as she endured her own private, tortuous, and lonely hell for a year. To Cannon, Holden, McKenna, and Duncan, I hope someday your children will inherit a world far better and safer than the one I have tried to give to you.

—The Phoenix PAO

CONTENTS

PREFACE

I couldn't sleep early one spring morning in 2003. I was an Army Reserve officer sitting on the sidelines of my professional part-time military life, restlessly waiting to be called into the game: the war in Afghanistan and the pickup game the United States had started in Iraq. In the aftermath of 9/11, I knew going off to war was a question of when, not if. Even before 9/11 at the Defense Information School (DINFOS) at Fort Meade, Maryland, we were told by our instructors that if we were in the Army Reserve and serving as public affairs officers, we would likely deploy to operations in Kosovo or Haiti or to the Middle East in support of UN sanctions against Iraq. More than 85 percent of the Army's public affairs assets at that time were in the reserve.

I was a public affairs officer, known as a PAO in the ranks. PAOs are public relations (PR) guys in uniform. They are charged, in a nutshell, with selling war, although most of them would offer more glamorous job descriptions if asked. From the looks of things months after Iraq's "liberation," there'd be a lot to sell.

I sat in my home office grading papers from a college journalism course I was teaching as an adjunct faculty member. By the glow of the television I worked, occasionally looking up to watch the Fox News report that was on the air. Fox News war coverage was on at all hours of the day, so it was by default that it was on my television. Then I saw a familiar face on the television screen. It was Fox News reporter Greg Kelly, my classmate from the Defense Information School. We had attended PAO training together a few years earlier after Greg traded in his fighter-jet yoke for a handheld microphone. He decided to pursue a career in broadcast journalism, so he left the active-duty Marine Corps to become a Marine Corps Reserve PAO. The guy I knew as a Harrier jet aviator who wouldn't wear his uniform hat because it messed up his hair (something he readily admitted) was riding shotgun with U.S. troops as they crossed the border and fought their way into Iraq to depose Saddam Hussein.

There seemed to be on every channel an embedded journalist like Greg reporting from the front lines. Prior U.S. wars had seen problems between the press and the military, two professions rooted and protected in the U.S. Constitution. I hoped this war would be different, and days into it there were little signs of trouble. Politics aside and professionally speaking, the press had not challenged the call to invade Iraq, and they were along for the ride, literally and figuratively. That nonchallenging posture always made the jobs of PAOs much easier. The press was all over the battlefield, embedded with U.S. military units. Defense Department officials estimate that more than seven hundred reporters were embedded in the early days of Operation Iraqi Freedom.

Before long Hussein's statue was toppled in a dusty Baghdad square, and Iraqis danced in the streets. Coalition troops were heroes, and international press reports buzzed about the success of the liberation. The world was punch drunk that Hussein was on the run and Iraq was free. But by late 2003, a few months after U.S. president George W. Bush prematurely announced an end to major combat operations in Iraq on the deck of the USS *Abraham Lincoln*, attacks on coalition forces increased.

I watched from afar as the dynamics of the war began to change. Violence began to take a daily toll in Iraq on U.S. forces, and then as suddenly as a dust storm forms, the paradigm shifted and more Iraqi civilians were becoming casualties. An insurgency had formed, and anyone with a beef against the United States could come to Iraq and kill Americans. Ideologically motivated terrorists or anyone looking to earn a living as a mercenary found plenty of opportunity in Iraq if killing was their trade. Even Iraqis with no beef against the Americans could make a killing, no pun intended, by planting bombs, firing a mortar or rocket, or shooting at U.S. soldiers. We had unknowingly created a marketplace for mischief.

There was also a shift by U.S. communicators from tactical information management to a broader, more strategic operation. The journalists' embeds, a tactical information effort, had yielded remarkable strategic results, but in 2004, with little meaningful public relations products coming from the ranks, senior civilian leaders and U.S. military communicators centralized informational control in Baghdad.

Information would now be propagated from behind the blast walls of the Green Zone. For example, the capture of enemy forces might take place in the northern city of Mosul, but it was Coalition Provisional Authority (CPA) spokespersons in the Green Zone who would brief the press about the operation. Reporters were told about what happened; they were not shown what was happening. This was in sharp contrast to the embed operation that had reporters covering the war at the operational level where boots meet the ground. As the CPA pushed to control the U.S. military's public relations operation, gloomy news reports from around Iraq began to bubble up in nonmainstream media forums sharply contrasting the CPA's press conferences in the Green Zone, which were chest-beating, feel-good events designed to evoke feelings of U.S. accomplishment and progress in Iraq. Many Iraqis complained that security in Iraq had worsened since the U.S. invasion, and some studies indicated that at least one hundred thousand Iraqis had died between 2003 and 2004 as a result of the invasion.

Stateside, I wondered why the CPA wasn't informing Iraqis of the progress being made in Iraq. Something didn't seem right. The CPA was telling the world about all this great progress, yet there were images of squalor, violence, and dismay in just about every news publication and on every channel. In addition, why was the CPA hell-bent on selling progress in Iraq to Americans? It seemed like the CPA was briefing the wrong audience. I was starting to get a whiff of U.S. propaganda, but it never occurred to me the CPA was increasing their rhetoric about U.S. progress in Iraq to drown out the cries and concerns of Iraqis—nobody would do that, I thought. We have our flaws, but as Americans we'd never do that. I'd learn I was wrong.

Because information operations were centralized in Baghdad, the CPA had the floor and the microphone; they were in control. As U.S. forces ushered in 2004 in Iraq, the military slice-of-life news stories that had prevailed in mass media since 2003 were disappearing because of the CPA's tightly held rein on the communications operation. Small U.S. successes showcased by embedded press, and critical in maintaining public opinion, were all but extinct because the CPA had corralled reporters. If reporters wanted information about operations in Iraq, there was only one place to get it, in the Green Zone's convention center, where slick corporate-style contracted marketers, military PAOs, and administration cronies tried to convince the world that Iraq was in good hands.

Some Western reporters, having learned the lessons of a tightly regulated press corps in Operation Desert Storm, attended CPA press briefings but sent Arab stringers into the streets to verify the veracity of reports coming from the PAO or spokesperson at the podium. Most CPA claims were easily disproved. News reports began to reveal huge discrepancies between CPA assertions and Iraqi realities. The Arab media, distrustful of U.S. military PAOs and unimpressed with American reporters, whom they felt didn't show the Arab perspective in their stories, a belief dating back to Desert Storm, led the assault against the U.S. military's claims of utopia in Iraq.

From the start of Operation Iraqi Freedom the Arab media gunned for an unvarnished angle that focused mostly on Iraqi civilian deaths and on Arab suffering at the hands of U.S. forces. Arab suffering, an underreported issue in Western media, was the central theme. As the Arab press roused the Pan-Arab world with stories of Arab anguish, the CPA obsessively talked to the American press. PAOs were concerned more with improving U.S. public opinion about the war in Iraq and protecting the administration's reputation. PAOs and U.S. communicators were not concerned with using information to help save American and Iraqi lives by improving conditions on the ground in Iraq. While the coalition didn't ignore the Arab media completely, the bulk of the effort was directed at the Western press. The leftover scraps, I'd learn, would go to the Arab press.

Information could have served as a tourniquet in Iraq. With information an informed Iraqi people could have slowed, if not stopped, the societal and cultural violence in their world. There is a direct link between information operations and influencing public opinion. The U.S. Defense Department knows that information operations on the battlefield are critical to operational success in a fight against insurgents just as much as diplomacy is needed with military power. The Defense Department knows this and spent hundreds of millions of dollars trying to find the right public relations formula for Iraq, with very little success. While informing Iraqis certainly wouldn't have prevented an all-out insurgency, strong evidence suggests the lack of a sustainable contingency communications plan hastened the insurgency's ability to take root. U.S. military leaders have stated that successful information operations are critical to a counterinsurgency, but my time in Iraq showed me that few, if any, in the U.S. military and in the U.S. government understand how to successfully conduct information operations using factual, accurate information in public relations operations.

Journalist and media critic Walter Lippmann hypothesized that the bulk of a society is usually governed by an elite few who are educated bureaucrats with a bigger picture in their minds of what is best for the populace. Those who are governed are referred to as the "herd" and in essence are told what to think by the elitist class, who overlook local issues and strive for the better good of the collective mass. Lippmann believed that if 80 percent of the populace or the herd was not told what to do or how to think by the elites, the herd would develop its own opinions and chaos would rule.

Although a model like Lippmann's can be construed as outrageous and elitist, it is sobering, and his position is very much what American society has become in the millennium with its two-party system and politicos who are paid to vote their conscience and take liberties with their powers in the name of the people they represent. Americans are told what to think given limited choices on issues. Americans are mostly pro-this or anti-that, Left or Right. There are few options for Americans to truly develop and practice individualistic, independent, and moderate ideals. Marketers, public relations professionals, politicians, lobbyists, and communicators control American cultural habits. They tell us what to buy, how to think, and how to live, and they do it by spending more than $100 billion per year on advertising and public relations to sway and hold public opinion on everything from waffles to candidates for governors. Communications is critical for those who want power or to those who want to retain it.

In preinvasion Iraq Hussein controlled information, and Iraqis followed along because they had little outside information, but many more followed Hussein because they knew challenging the dictator meant dire consequences. Iraq controlled its herd by force. In the United States many Americans were manipulated to support the invasion of Iraq when they heard arguments for preemption based on a faulty connection to weapons of mass destruction or to the 9/11 attacks. As the war in Iraq progressed during its first year, the herd back in the United States was fed a steady banquet of information by CPA spokesman Dan Senor and Brig. Gen. Mark Kimmitt of the U.S. Army through the usual troughs of information, CPA press briefings. But Iraqi masses were famished and suffered from an information drought. To worsen the situation, they were infected with a viral strain of chaos caused by the insurgency. Lippmann's bewildered-herd theory had manifested itself in Iraq. Chaos, not democracy, had come to Iraq once the postinvasion dust had settled.

Communications is the cornerstone of all human actions; without it, we do not understand each other's intentions, motivations, and actions. Generally speaking, educated people cannot derive conclusions without first processing information, digesting it, and then formulating ideologies based on their personal bias, genetic makeup, education, and socioeconomic standing. Humans are hardwired to lean toward certain concepts and opinions, a genetic predisposition, but well-presented information can help people process events as the brain sends it into mental processing, sort of like adding salt or pepper to an entrée.

Communicators in academe no longer argue about objectivity in journalism. Lippmann believed that reporters processed events subjectively and that fairness and accuracy in the story were by-products of the personal beliefs of a reporter. He was a man ahead of his time, as increasingly in this political environment audiences are seeing press institutions taking sides, Left or Right, or, in the case of international media, the side of nationalism, meaning the media cover stories with news angles that connect to their audiences. This is nothing new but only now coming to light due mostly to the advent of communications technology and emerging media platforms.

Overseas, foreign media news angles often conflict with U.S. political and military agendas, and the conflict intensifies when news is compounded with graphic images or gory reports. "If it bleeds, it leads" is an old adage associated with the press. The more lurid the content, the more fascinating it is to consumers. There are many sociological and psychological reasons for this human obsession with death, and I'm certain part of it has to do with the fact that as mortals, it is captivating to be reminded of one's own mortality, but news also has entertaining human elements, including conflict, hope, and resolution, but across the board humans internationally cannot help but watch violence because the tragic fact is that another human somewhere is no more because of it. Conflict is why we buy books, watch movies, and listen to music. Without it, what is there? As inhabitants of this planet, our predecessors fought elements, enemies, disease, and nature to survive. Conflict is hardwired into us all, and as much as we may not like that, it's part of human nature.

The human drama can make public relations work harder or easier. In Iraq U.S. PAOs often joked about how hard it was to get positive stories in the press. They complained about trying to "sell" a war wrought with poor high-level administrative decisions. I joke about it, but the rudimentary mistake is that PAOs shouldn't fancy themselves salesmen marketing a product or concept, but rather they should be conveyors of facts that are carefully determined during operational planning. PAOs should be vehicles for truths that are created as objectives of broader civil and military operations. How PAOs approach their duties impacts the media's coverage of events. I too have joked about selling war, but the hard truth is that if PAOs fail to communicate effectively to a host-nation populace, people die and that is no laughing matter.

The insurgents with a small force of only about five thousand, according to U.S. military reports I read in 2004 shortly after I arrived in Baghdad, turned a nation of twenty-six million upside down. They used information on websites, notes left on front doors, flyers tacked onto street posts, pamphlets and newsletters, and broadcasts on Arab news channels to convey their objectives and beliefs. They followed up their statements with action.

They warned Iraqis not to help the coalition because the coalition's mission was unjust and unholy. Those who helped the coalition would be killed, and they backed this up by showing beheadings of coalition colluders. They warned towns not to allow coalition soldiers or Iraqi forces into their city's limits because doing so meant acceptance of coalition policies and would be viewed as cooperation. They supported their assertions by bombing a marketplace when instructions weren't followed. The insurgents communicated their beliefs and ideals and then showed they meant business by acting on their promises. They forcefully swayed Iraqi public opinion by denouncing the American system of Iraqi democracy, and they garnered Iraqi support through violence and fear, just as Hussein had done for decades.

The insurgency had gained a foothold in Iraq and forced support from Iraqis through aggressive intimidation and sometimes distortion of information, tactics that had worked well for Hussein. Iraqis increasingly began to allow insurgents to operate in their locales, fearing retaliation if they reported them because the coalition had disbanded Iraq's security forces and there was no internal defense or police force. But Iraqis also blindly followed the insurgents because there was no U.S. or Iraqi information provided to the Iraqi masses to counter what they were being told by the terrorists. The insurgents had their havens and a captive audience.

"Social reform is never popular in the victim country," social scientist Noam Chomsky wrote in *What Uncle Sam Really Wants* (1992). "You can't get many of the people living there excited about it, except a small group connected with U.S. businesses who are going to profit from it." Chomsky's words couldn't have been more apropos in Iraq. It was hard for Iraqis to get excited about their newfound democracy when violence and crime were rampant and living conditions had worsened throughout the nation since the U.S. arrival. The democratic experiment was failing not because of flawed ideals but because of flawed U.S. management. The only sources offering seemingly valid explanations to the Iraqi masses were the insurgents, and the Iraqis listened, maybe not believing what they were hearing, but they listened. The American government was too busy talking to the American media, and the Iraqi government was not talking to anyone.

I eventually got my number called as a reservist, and I was in the proverbial game. My assignment in Iraq was to support the U.S. exit strategy in Iraq by telling the world about the development of Iraqi security forces. Our unit was a multinational command composed of military advisers from the army, navy, air force, and marine corps from militaries all over the globe as well as civilian contractors and government officials from around the world. We were responsible for training, equipping, and mentoring Iraqi security forces. As the tip of the spear for U.S. foreign policy in Iraq, we had billions of dollars in our budget and priceless human capital.

Our mission was unique in that we weren't solely responsible for security and stability operations in Iraq like the bulk of the forces there. Our job was to prepare nascent Iraqi troops to someday provide security for their nation and defend it against attacks, including conducting intense counterinsurgency operations.

Days after arriving in Iraq in 2004, what I discovered was disheartening and discouraging, and it explained why the media's reportage had become what PAOs alleged to be "lopsided." Coalition PAOs weren't productive. CPA PAOs behaved as if they were at a frat party, and some were young, inexperienced civilians who treated reporters with contempt. They relied on a complex labyrinth of public affairs organizational charts to delay and confuse reporters on deadline. The military ranks weren't much better. People in key public affairs roles within the Green Zone weren't the very best the military had to offer, especially since President Bush had made Iraq such a highly visible priority in the U.S. War on Terror. Many military public affairs personnel had only one public affairs deployment under their belt, if any, and most didn't have wartime communications experience. Nobody knew how to conduct a communications campaign during an insurgency, including me. Fresh from the Cold War, PAOs were short on this kind of skill, and it seemed as if nobody had been paying attention to what had happened to the Soviets in Afghanistan or even to our own military in Vietnam. The Iraqi battlefield called for creativity, but what I found was a military entrenched in its conventional communications tactics, unwilling to leave its foxholes and try new strategies and take terrain from the bad guys.

For Green Zone PAOs evenings in Baghdad were a back-smacking good time. It seemed like there was a steady stream of incoming and outgoing PAOs, ticket punchers ensuring they got their war credentials so they could lock up careers and promotions. Those leaving the war zone were unjustifiably congratulated for "great work," and many PAOs who were now in the eye of the storm ratcheted up the antimedia rhetoric, firmly in control of information, as they ran the communications operation into the ground. Accountability, plans, strategy, and urgency were absent. There was no proactive connection between the operational forces on the ground and the communicators. There was only the usual reactive posture known to PAOs.

Poolside at Hussein's Republican Palace was the place to be seen for the CPA crowd. Meanwhile, infantrymen and combat support personnel turned riflemen were subjected to less than austere living conditions at forward operating bases throughout the country and performed nightmarish missions outside the wire that guaranteed someone in their unit would get hurt or killed. Those in the Green Zone lived a plush life, and the threat of mortar rounds and rockets kept life edgy under a romantic canopy of false bravado.

This is not to say that all public affairs personnel in Iraq were bad. There were a great many who did good work and tried to turn the tide. A few were bright thinkers. There were some who worked their tails off Stateside to support PAOs in Iraq too, and for the most part the majority of the enlisted personnel in the public affairs force braved the bullets, bombs, and chaos to capture the story of U.S. forces in Iraq. They did incredible work as they brought the war fighter's point of view to the rest of the world. But overwhelmingly, the collective public affairs force involved in the early stages of Operation Iraqi Freedom was an exceptional failure, and the efforts of a stellar few were overshadowed by the actions of a clueless many. While some PAOs can argue that they were just following orders, that tone is set at the top, and to the notion that things have always been done a certain way, I say, "Bullshit!" Anyone in uniform who is a commissioned or noncommissioned officer has a responsibility to be accountable and to speak up when things are running aground. I believe most PAOs said nothing about how screwed up the communications campaign was in Iraq because they believed they were doing nothing wrong; they were unwilling to analyze situations and examine problems thoroughly because they believed they were on a good path. Many thought they were doing things correctly, and when things went south the press was blamed. Rather than have deep professional introspection, or a careful examination of the stated mission and the environment, PAOs deflected the reality. I don't think many PAOs knew just how bad they were doing in Iraq. I use their actions as barometers. Emotionally, most PAOs running the communications war weren't connected to the real war in Iraq. It was evident by the hours they kept, the circles they ran in, and the amount of time they spent in safety. They were too close to the process and to the flagpole, and they couldn't critically review their operations because doing so meant taking a hard look at themselves and what they were failing to do.

I deployed to Iraq not as a war fighter in the traditional sense, but instead with a loosely assembled communications plan in my head and plenty of strategic concepts in hopes that my so-called combat reach would be broader than just the range on my rifle. My contribution to protect U.S. forces, my impact on the war, I believed, would come from my ability to sway and hold Iraqi public opinion through a graceful and transparent engagement of the Arab press. The insurgency was rooted in Iraq because of U.S. forces' and the Iraqi Governing Council's inability to talk to the Arab world. Iraqis had been ignored for more than a year, as the insurgency took away Iraqi public support from the Americans. The U.S. and Iraqi governments never deemed it important to communicate with the Iraqi masses, and I believed I needed to get Iraqi officials talking to the Iraqi masses to help calm Lippmann's bewildered herd in Iraq.

Iraqis wondered what their government was doing behind the high walls of the Green Zone, and as many PAOs sat comfortably in their air-conditioned offices enjoying the benefits of a headquarters assignment, coalition soldiers on the mean streets of Iraq paid the price for a reactive, poorly planned, and bungled war information plan. As a result of failing to communicate with the Iraqi masses and the Arab world, the U.S. public affairs community is partly responsible for the deaths and injuries of those casualties caused by the insurgency. The coalition should have fanned flames of Iraqi support, but instead it fueled an explosive insurgency by inaction and miscommunication.

I spent my entire tour in Iraq fighting my public affairs peers, their way of thinking, their adhesion to obsolete practices, their limitless patience for Iraqi bureaucracy, and their reactive posture. During my tour in Iraq we tried to paint a picture of what we saw. Like any other public relations professional, PAOs work to get information out to the public, and in Iraq that job included informing the Arab public as well as the American public, but most PAOs didn't see it that way.

Things were tough for me and my team, but our command was making strides and progress in training Iraqi forces and things were improving. That story reached many Iraqis and the Arab street during my tour as the chief PAO for the Multinational Security Transition Command Iraq (MNSTCI), and it reached many back at home and abroad. The insurgents took notice too and launched a violent campaign directly aimed at stopping our information flow to the Iraqi people. They attacked some of the Arab media contacts I worked with routinely and threatened my Iraqi public affairs counterparts. They even threatened me. It was a battle they would win in a war I am hopeful the United States won't lose.

Misdirected effort by the collective public affairs community in Iraq and Washington DC that includes the Coalition Provisional Authority, U.S. State Department, Defense Department and all its services, Iraq Reconstruction Management Office, Office of Reconstruction and Humanitarian Assistance, the multinational commands in Iraq, government contractors, and countless other agencies in the fray cost the military services of the coalition in human capital, the costliest of commodities; damaged the credibility of the nation in the region; and made the United States a spectacle in the Arab world.

While I may have faced frustrations and heartache in Iraq, my experiences and disappointments are minuscule when compared to what those under fire have survived. Their physical and emotional sacrifices can't be calculated. There is no scale to measure their devotion to duty or the cost of what they bear. My hope is that come what may in the publication of this book, the military changes the way it conducts its communications business and that PAOs come to understand that they need to be assertive on the battlefield. They can change conditions on the ground for our military personnel and not just be a reactionary force waiting to respond to incidents on the battlefield. If this book ultimately saves some lives, then I've accomplished my objective, something I failed to do in Iraq.

It is with an extremely heavy heart that I wrote this book because the U.S. military has been a part of my life longer than many of my personal relationships, and in many ways it was a surrogate family for me when I was a young man. New to the ranks in 1982, I was reared by tough Vietnam War noncommissioned officers who showed me how to grow a thick skin, how to lead from the front and find the strength to say things that are unpopular. My dirty-boot time during the Cold War was spent as an enlisted military policeman walking fence lines overseas with a military working dog, three hundred rounds of ammunition on my belt with an assault rifle slung across my back. I deployed to the field, lived in foxholes for days and weeks at a time, and prepared for a Cold War showdown that never happened. When I traded in my sergeant stripes for my second lieutenant butter bars and became an officer, I spent a short time assigned to an infantry battalion as a platoon leader charged with leading combat medics. I was fortunate in that the first half of my career offered me a small glimpse of how thankless some military professions could be, and I carried that with me as I became a PAO.

This book is part memoir, part public relations handbook, part after-action review, part white paper, part catharsis, and a firsthand account of my yearlong mobilization to support Operation Iraqi Freedom as an Army public affairs officer and as the first chief of public affairs for Multinational Security Transition Command Iraq. It was written using materials from my tour in Iraq, including thousands of conversations, interviews, e-mails, and unclassified documents that I was exposed to during that time. It is also peppered with supportive research.

Here is some information to process, digest, and formulate an opinion on, a story with an ending not yet written, but written with the belief that the pen indeed is mightier than the sword.

SELLING WAR

1

INSULATION

May 13, 2004: Attacks in Baghdad increased to 130 this week,

up from 81 the previous week.

—Office of Security Cooperation (OSC) unclassified intelligence report

My son walked next to me and held my hand as the creamy, sweet smell of jasmine drifted by us on a warm breeze. Occasionally, he glanced at me, mostly after thunder rumbled in the distance, well beyond the Spanish moss-covered oaks that canopied our neighborhood in central Florida.

"Don't be scared," I told him. "It's just thunder." But nonetheless we quickened our pace, his hand firmly clasped in mine, as the thunder roared again, closer this time, louder than before, shaking the ground beneath us. Then something I couldn't see began to pull at my leg almost like a cramp, and I heard a voice that was definitely not the soft voice of my two-year-old boy.

"Steve, get up!"

I looked around, and it was still just me and Duncan standing underneath the tall oaks. The tugging on my leg continued, but when I looked down, nothing was there. Then an extraordinarily loud sound enveloped me. Boom! A young man suddenly appeared and hovered over me. He was agitated. For a second I didn't know where I was or who he was, but as I rubbed my eyes I realized I was back in the shitty reality I had volunteered to join.

My roommate, John, a young Army Reserve lieutenant, was yelling at me. As I departed the clarity of my dream and entered the fog of war, his voice got clearer.

"Steve! Wake the fuck up, man!" John yelled. "Dude, get up! We're getting hit!"

Our camp along the banks of the Tigris River in the Green Zone was getting pelted with rockets and mortar rounds, and he had been tugging on my leg, trying to wake me. The thunder I had heard in my dream was in reality explosions from insurgent rounds angrily closing in on our officer quarters.

I was exhausted, a uniformed zombie propped up each day by the hope of our mission and propelled by shots of espresso and dozens upon dozens of cups of coffee and chai tea. Once as I waited for a helicopter at a landing zone (LZ) at Camp Liberty, desperate for a pick-me-up in the energy-sapping three-digit heat, I emptied a pack of freeze-dried coffee into my mouth and added a few gulps of water that had warmed in my canteen after a daylong trip to eastern Iraq.

My team had been working an aggressive media campaign for three weeks, sleeping about four hours per night, if we were lucky, and I was skipping meals, thinking about taking up smoking again after eighteen years, not calling or writing home, and putting my nervous system through hell with a steady drip of caffeine that kept me moving. When I was at the office I was often pinging off the walls. When we traveled my right leg twitched nervously, continuously, as if I were quickly stepping on a bass drum, keeping a steady beat of activity that was driving my dick into the dirt. That night the insurgents literally could have dropped a bomb on me and I would have slept through it.

John and I ran outside to watch the nearby British compound take a beating. The compound was just a few yards from our hooch, and the place had a pub and was one of a few mental-health havens within the Green Zone. Temperate British soldiers and overpaid American civilians enjoyed pints of ale and escaped the seemingly inescapable feeling of perpetual Groundhog Day syndrome common to those who spent their entire war tours under the long shadows of high concrete blast walls at the fortified Baghdad compound. A few of us congregated amid the camp's confusion, and we watched, stupefied, as the indirect enemy fire worked its way closer and closer to us. In between the mortar rounds, rockets exploded loudly around us, some closer than others. The rockets were being fired indiscriminately, and many simply whizzed overhead and impacted deeper inside the Green Zone, but the mortars were being slowly and deliberately directed toward our camp.

A small crowd of U.S. officers, including three West Pointers who moved closer from the other side of the camp to get a better look at the incoming rounds, all watched the attack like spectators. This was new to me even though I was a career officer, and there was something captivating and mesmerizing about people trying to kill us. Given the decades of training I had received, I think I would have had more common sense and an overwhelming drive to flee for my life, but no shit there I was, out in the open, watching the attack, failing to take cover, and getting sprinkled with a light dusting of powdery sand that had been pulverized by the exploding rounds.

For many that night the attack would be the closest they'd ever get to the enemy. For hundreds of thousands of "fobbits," as we were affectionately dubbed by the guys operating outside compounds known as forward operating bases, it would be the only way many remembered they were actually in a war. We were all morbidly fascinated by the attack. We had that luxury, unlike the soldiers who patrolled the streets of Iraq "moving to contact," militaryspeak for soldiers looking to brawl with the bad guys. They used themselves to draw the enemy out of hiding.

While there was a chance of getting killed or wounded by a random mortar round, rocket, or occasional suicide bomber in the Green Zone, most informed, professional, and pragmatic soldiers knew that the real threat was beyond the reinforced walls of the compound, and improvised explosive devices, known as "IEDs," were the leading killer of U.S. soldiers in Iraq.

There was a threat inside the Green Zone, and during my time in Baghdad several people died from lucky-shot mortar rounds, rockets, and even suicide bombers inside its walls, but given the fact that it had been raining mortars on us nearly every day for a month and only a couple of people had been killed, the real threat was outside the Green Zone's walls. Statistics showed the danger was elsewhere, and I suppose those figures gave us a false sense of security that night, but I think for most of us it was fascinating to be on the working end of a weapons platform. That changed when a round landed several yards from us.

"Get the fuck down!" John yelled as a round came screaming at us. We all hugged the ground as the round exploded, and a dusty cloud tinged with a burned gunpowder-like odor enveloped us. Another round came screaming in, and we finally did what we should have done minutes earlier: we ran for cover. An enemy spotter, it seemed, had our position locked.

I don't remember breathing, and my feet were heavy as if they were buried in wet sand. I couldn't move fast enough, although I knew mentally all pistons were firing and telling my body to run faster. As I ran away from the corner of the camp's perimeter, the rounds seemed to follow us. I was lost as I made my way, weaving in and out of the warren of trailers, trying to find someplace to put some concrete between me and the sky. The incoming shrieking rounds propelled me. I felt if I could outrun the sound, I would be okay. I looked around as I sprinted to find no one near me; everyone had gone different directions. I have never felt so alone. It felt like I had gone the wrong way, as if there was a right way to run. As I moved I got my bearings, and I made a beeline to the only known hard edifice in the compound, a blown-out building one hundred meters from our trailer. It seemed as if it was twenty miles away. In the distance the rounds menacingly kept announcing their departure with a sound familiar to magic acts. Foom! Then almost magically, the rounds would explode in our camp. Off in the distance the CPA's loudspeakers warned, "Take cover! Take cover!" although the rounds had now been falling for several minutes.

It was the early summer of 2004, and there were no bunkers to protect coalition personnel from enemy mortar rounds and rockets. We had air-conditioning and running water in our quarters, but no bunkers to protect us from indirect fire. At least we'd die cool and clean, we always joked, but the fact that we had creature comforts instead of personnel protection measures was an indicator of how mismanaged U.S. priorities were in Baghdad. The camps were basically trailer parks. Each trailer, if you were not a general officer or high-ranking civilian or if you didn't have connections, was shared by at least four personnel. The trailers were divided in half by a common bathroom; two people occupied each side of the trailer, and four people used one bathroom.

Living conditions were good, and we had electrical power and heated potable tap water most of the time, although I do remember taking one shower that coated me with a slimy film and made me stink of fuel. My guess is that a contractor likely hungover from the previous night's partying at Saddam's pool mistakenly filled a fuel tanker with water, or vice versa, and dispensed the tainted water into the potable-water reservoir camp residents used for personal hygiene. I figured the fuel-enriched water would kill any Iraqi critters that had set up their own camps on my body, so that day I simply stayed away from smokers. In hindsight I think I lucked out. Somewhere, I thought, there was a convoy in Iraq with sputtering engines caused by water in their fuel systems, something that likely pissed off a group of soldiers who got attacked due to the slow speed of their convoy. I happily smelled like a gas station attendant for a day.

Home life in Baghdad wasn't tough at all. We had new furniture and beds, including televisions with DVD players. Toward the end of my tour we were even given satellite television connections. Things were certainly much worse elsewhere in Iraq, and the steady nightly flow of medevac helicopters mercifully ferrying wounded troops into the Green Zone's military hospital was proof of that. As they came in over the river on their flight path, sometimes their prop wash would churn up dust and vibrate our tin living quarters and remind me just how much worse it could be for me. Even if we didn't have bunkers and sandbags, I wasn't going to bitch. I could be sleeping and shitting in a hole somewhere, or, worse, I could be sent home in a body bag to fill one.

Our camps were comfortable but impractical and evidence that the U.S. government was catering to civilians who shared battle space with military folks. Somewhere along the way someone had forgotten that we were in a war zone. As civilian personnel flooded Iraq, camps in the Green Zone were built to house them. But the trailers provided as living quarters and as offices were nothing more than aluminum sheds. Having spent time in the field in military tents, I loved the sheds. They kept heat and cool in as needed and were comfortable, but they didn't keep anything else out. In fact, once as my interpreter sat at his desk working on his computer, an

AK-47 machine-gun round came slamming through the roof and bounced off his desk, ricocheted off of some lockers and the floor, and bounced into his hands.

"It is Allah's will I didn't die today, Captain," he said happily.

"No, you're simply a lucky motherfucker," I told him. I've since heard that story told many times by Iraq war veterans. I guess I was successful in telling at least one story in Iraq or there were many more lucky Iraqis who dodged a bullet.

Months after I arrived and after months of constant indirect fire attacks, someone, thankfully, finally found the wisdom to insulate our trailers with sandbags in 2004. Although I was thankful for the protection, I'm certain the sandbags could have gone somewhere else where insurgent activity was much worse. The bags weren't placed on the rooftops because the tin sheds couldn't support the weight of sandbags, but they did place them high around the walls, which was better than nothing. Later, thick concrete bunkers were placed around the camp so we could run into them should we come under fire. One was thankfully placed right outside our trailer not more than ten feet from my door, right near the spot where I was a spectator with the other dumbass officers. Attacks would become so regular that many soldiers would grab their laptops, music players, and handheld video games as they ran to the bunkers. They grabbed anything to help pass the time as we waited for the "all clear" from the loudspeakers under twenty-four inches of reinforced concrete. It was like waiting for a train or for the rain to stop. We were simply killing time while insurgents were trying to kill us, but most of us didn't romanticize it. Attacks were inconvenient and annoying, but a part of life in Baghdad. While the attacks were frequent, they were ineffective, and the odds were great that a person could spend several years inside the sprawling Green Zone and never get hit or even near an attack. My odds that night were simply not the norm.

The night I was dreaming of my son, we had nothing but half-demolished concrete-block buildings to flee to and the moon's warm glow to find our way there in the dead of night, but at least we knew where the mortar rounds were landing and logic dictated we'd run the opposite way. When I reached the virtual safety of the building, another round launched across the Tigris River. Within seconds it screeched down almost atop us. I jumped into the building headlong through a jagged hole that used to hold a door. Iraqis had long since looted the windows, doors, and frames in the days following the invasion. The round exploded within a few meters of us.

I looked up from the smoky rubble, and there were two senior noncommissioned officers sitting calmly in the dark, smoking cigarettes. Early on in the attack as they evacuated their trailer and ran for cover, they had seen me and other staff officers, mouths agape as the mortar rounds rained down in the camp next door. They had watched us almost buy the farm. I wondered instantly why we had more rank. It seemed to me the Army had commissioned the wrong people.

"Hi, sir," he said, smirking. "What the fuck were you guys doing out there, sir?" he asked sarcastically, the cigarette dangling from his toothy grin.

"Sightseeing," I answered as I finally took a breath. I realized just how stupid my actions had been. I was disoriented from the fatigue, still asleep when John dragged me outside, and I guess I made myself vulnerable because I needed to see what had pulled me away from my family and brought me six thousand miles to Iraq. To this day I can't definitively say why I stood there and watched the mortar rounds come in, but I can say with no hesitation that I was never again a spectator.

We huddled closely into the small space of the shattered building, and I thought about how good their cigarettes smelled and wondered when the attack would end and how many more attacks I would have to endure. I had been in Iraq a few weeks, and while I had heard car bombs, mortar rounds and rockets exploding, and small-arms fire in previous weeks echoing in the distance, this was the first time the war had gotten close to me.

At the time I was working in Saddam Hussein's Republican Palace, an immensely disgusting display of wealth and opulence within the Green Zone, so I felt doubly safe and disconnected from harm inside of our marbled military headquarters. Because of this insulation I was still not yet used to the incoming fire, but in the coming months I would grow accustomed to it and eventually become numb to its sound as it angrily fell to the earth in search of a target. It would become a part of daily life sometimes for weeks at a time, and we treated it like inclement weather. We would don our flak vests and helmets and go about our business as calmly as one opens an umbrella or puts on a coat. It was part of the elements in Baghdad. The attacks were more inconvenient than they were dangerous. Maybe that's what I convinced myself of as I walked passed coalition soldiers cannonballing into Hussein's pool as other soldiers who couldn't resist the palace chow hall's three hot meals per day bronzed their bellies on lounge chairs. It was almost as if there were an invisible bubble over Saddam's pool. Nobody there ever felt like they'd get killed, or maybe they just didn't give a shit.

The mortars that night stopped firing shortly after a U.S. Army Apache helicopter flew overhead and headed off toward the Baghdad skyline. A soldier, moments later, walked up with a smoldering piece of rocket he had found a few feet from us, and we all looked at it as if it were an ancient relic. We were fascinated by it and pushed and shoved each other like kids trying to see something at show-and-tell. I didn't feel like a professional soldier. I felt like an amateur, a moron, someone just making believe he was a soldier. We had heard the mortar rounds coming in, but in between the mortar volleys the enemy had also fired rockets at us that made no sound as they came to the earth until they exploded.

"Steve, you're bleeding," someone said, and flashlights began to click on and get passed around as people checked themselves and each other for wounds.

I borrowed a flashlight to illuminate my leg, and there were a few small trails of blood flowing down my knee to my shin. My leg was a little meaty, but it was nothing more than a few lesions. I've seen worse injuries on my kids' knees after they fall off their scooters and color our driveway with their blood and skin. I didn't need a medic, just a change of underwear, a children's chewable aspirin, and a stiff glass of bourbon.

I pressed my leg to see if I could feel anything underneath my skin, but the only thing I felt was my knobby knee. My leg was a little numb, and I had no sensation on my skin. The leg worked fine, but at that moment I decided I would take up smoking again while in Iraq, and the next day I bought a carton of Marlboros reds and became a closet smoker.

More than thirty minutes later we walked back to the trailer and collected some things. We simply couldn't sleep at the trailer that night. It was too risky. I cleaned up my knee with a first-aid kit and put some bandages on the wounds. As we walked to the palace, nearly forty-five minutes after the attack stopped, the loudspeaker in the distance echoed, "All clear! All clear!" into the warm night air. No shit, I thought.

John found a comfortable picnic table al fresco on one of the palace's patios and made himself at home for the night, and I slept inside the makeshift multidenominational U.S. chapel on an ornate couch for a couple of hours as people quietly entered the chapel throughout the night. One soldier entered and went to the front of the chapel to a table that was considered the pulpit, and he kneeled before it, bowed his head, and prayed. He had enough ammunition on him to sack a city, and by the look on his face when he turned around I could tell that wherever he was going, the ammunition wasn't enough to make him feel safe.

The next day as I and fellow fobbits talked about what happened that night, some of my fellow staff officers opined that I was likely hit by shrapnel from the rocket or by some other object that was sent flying by the exploding shell. An airborne infantry major who worked at our command watched me run for cover from the blown-out building where he had gone when the shelling began. As I ran toward him he said I ran right through the impact area and that he saw blood on me as I arrived at the building. He was convinced I had been hit. I don't remember details like where I was or where I ran, and if asked today to retrace those steps I could probably just offer the direction I ran. I do remember the loud explosions, percussions of the rounds, and a lot of dust. The T-shirt I had on during the attack had a giant dusty skid mark on the front of it from the collar to my belly. Another possibility is that I got my pulpy knee from hitting the rocky floor of the building when I dove into it. The only thing I know for sure is that I had some minor cuts, and for that I was thankful.

My knee had bubbled up about as big as a grapefruit, so I iced it, wrapped it, and ate plenty of painkillers. One of my teeth overnight had also started hurting, and I couldn't chew on one side of my mouth. The major and another officer I worked next to insisted I should get examined by medical personnel. They were smart. It was better to be safe than sorry. I reluctantly went to the combat support hospital (known as a CaSH) to get examined. As I waited to be seen by the doctors, helicopters landed at the hospital's landing zone. Staffers hurriedly wheeled in soldiers on stretchers and whisked them into curtained rooms, where medical teams converged with machinery and tools in tow to try to salvage and fix broken soldiers.

The hallways were filled with walking wounded, some with visible injuries and others who might be there to get treated for food poisoning, the flu, or some other ailment. The CaSH was like any other hospital. It had sick and wounded of all varieties in it. I watched a soldier get wheeled in while several medical personnel walked quickly alongside his stretcher, talking fitfully at each other and reaching across the fallen warrior urgently, like hungry kids at a dinner table. Across from me a sergeant sat in a blood-soaked shirt with his buddy. A couple of seats down from me a soldier complained about having difficulty breathing, while others just sat there and stared at the wall across from them, avoiding eye contact.

An enlisted medic ran out from the curtained room and sprinted down the hall and out of view. Seconds later he returned with several others running with him, and they all disappeared behind the bustling curtained area.

"Fuck this," I whispered to myself. I walked out of the waiting area, down the long straight hallway, and out into the hot, scorching Baghdad sun. I had no business being there. I had all my limbs and organs. I felt like a big pussy sitting in that waiting area, especially as wounded warriors were being brought in on stretchers. I couldn't get out of there fast enough, and I felt an overwhelming sense of shame come over me.

Getting explosives lobbed at you was a part of life in the Green Zone, and living in a trailer so close to the Red Zone (we were about twenty yards from the edge of the Green Zone) had its downside for sure, but when I first arrived in Iraq I was placed in a transient tent as I awaited permanent quarters that was much worse. It was filled with about fifty musty men and air-conditioned, and it had plywood floors and electricity. Lights went out promptly at 10:00 p.m., but most of us were kept awake by the explosions echoing in the Baghdad night or by the guys who watched black-market porn on their laptops.

Some of the guys, despite a ban on food in the tents, sloppily ate at their cots, and a couple of times I felt rats crawling on me in the middle of the night as they searched for food. These were some pretty ballsy rodents, and somebody got smart and attracted one of the many feral cats around the palace and turned him loose in the tent during daylight hours. The rats all but disappeared, but the gunfire and explosions didn't.

One night as I struggled to fall asleep, a guy burst into our tent yelling, "We're being attacked! They're coming at us from everywhere!" I was in my boxers and a T-shirt, and I jumped up; put on my boots, flak vest, and helmet; and loaded a magazine into my Beretta pistol. I ran outside into the darkness and ran for a corner of the property to a spot I had scouted out when I arrived in Baghdad. I was a new guy and had not yet realized that the Green Zone was probably safer than most U.S. cities, save for the mortar rounds and rockets.

I crouched behind a tree stump and looked around. My tent was the only one of three transient tents emptying gun-toting, flashlight-wielding morons into the hot, arid night. Men in their underwear ran around with no direction, while many of the civilians ran into the nearby palace, despite having weapons and ammunition they could use to defend themselves. Outside the night was alive with gunfire my music headset had muffled as I lay on my cot. In the sky tracer rounds gracefully danced against the smooth black canvas of the night. They were bright as they shot out from behind the shadowy skyline and burned out softly as they disappeared in the skies above Baghdad. In my underwear and boots, armed with a little pistol, I was ready to make my last stand. John Wayne had nothing on me.

A U.S. naval officer crept up alongside of me.

"You see that shit, sir?" I asked him. Baghdad looked like 1991 all over again when coalition forces bombed the city in what we in the military call Gulf War Part I. This time it was small-arms fire and not antiaircraft artillery illuminating the night.

"What the fuck are they doing?" he said softly.

What could they be shooting at in the sky? I thought to myself.

As we crouched defensively a guy walked out of the nearby showers. The open door of the shower trailer momentarily illuminated the dark grounds around us and cast a light on us and our position. He walked by us wrapped in a towel from the waist down, carrying his toiletry kit in one hand and a flashlight in the other, his toothbrush sticking out of his mouth.

"That's celebratory gunfire," he said as he walked by spitting, pointing to the light show in the distance with his flashlight. "Iraq's soccer team beat Saudi Arabia," he said, and he disappeared into a nearby tent.

The naval officer began to shout angrily. "Who said we were getting attacked?"

The darkness offered no answer, just the distant sound of rifle reports. Most from our tent had already realized it was a false alarm or a really good gag and had already gone back inside.

"It's going to be a long six months if this keeps happening," the officer said.

"Yes, sir," I said. "But I've got to be here a year, so it's going to be an extra-long time for me."

"You poor bastard," he said, chuckling. "You must be in the Army," he said, smiling underneath a thick mustache. I nodded. "Shit, you should have joined the Navy," he joked.

Ain't that the fucking truth? I thought.

In the distance around the corner of the palace, the loudspeaker blared, "Take cover! Take cover!" as we went back inside our tent, and everyone on the grounds ignored the orders. Later as I lay in my cot thinking about the night's comedic events, I could only think about my family and going home. Then in the darkness I heard the loudspeakers announce, "All clear! All clear!" and in the distance the celebration continued and the rifle reports were my lullaby.

2

THE COALITION PROVISIONAL AUTHORITY DAYS

June 2004: An intelligence briefer says since 2003 there have been 2,666 improvised explosive device attacks in Iraq, nearly 900 of them in Baghdad.
—Unclassified Multinational Force Iraq (MNFI) intelligence briefing, Baghdad, June 2004

In late 2003 I was at the Pentagon doing an Army Reserve two-week annual training tour as a military reporter for the Defense Department website Defend America. I had just covered a meeting between Deputy Secretary of Defense Paul Wolfowitz and Iraqi women in a Pentagon meeting room. My assignment editor had told me the Iraqi women had concerns about getting photographed given the security situation back in Iraq, so I did not take their pictures, but a staff photographer from Wolfowitz's office had no problem sticking his lens in their faces and making them squirm. I had no idea how much that one incident would go on to reflect the larger mission in Iraq.

It was my first time back to the Pentagon since 2001. I had left my Washington DC assignment just six months before the 9/11 attacks, and now I was coming back to a Pentagon that was healing. After I left the Wolfowitz meeting I joined thousands of people walking in the large edifice, each hall flowing with personnel dressed in woodland drab colors, spilling into stairwells, elevators, offices, and adjoining halls. As I walked amid the tree-colored masses, one person stood out, dressed in his class B uniform, moving against the flow of the walkers toward me, going against the grain of humanity that was slowly making its way through the building.

It was a colonel whom I worked with a few years earlier in Washington DC. He was now one of the guys charged with pulling individual reservists from their cozy civilian lives and mobilizing them for the wars in Iraq and Afghanistan. He was also a reservist, but since war had broken out he had keenly volunteered for an active-duty tour at the Pentagon, keeping him safely back in the States for a couple of years.

"I don't like bombs," he told me slyly as we caught up in one of the hallways in the outer rings. We talked about family and former coworkers, and then the conversation's tone turned professional.

"It is such an odd coincidence to run into you, Steve," he said. "I was just going to e-mail you." He told me I was on a short list of eligible public affairs personnel identified to deploy. A list, shit—there's always a fucking list, and most of the time in the military you don't want to be on one unless it is a promotion list. I didn't want to go to war, unlike the hundreds of thousands of motivated and brave souls who volunteered to go into harm's way when sabers first began to rattle. Early on after 9/11, I would have gladly gone to Afghanistan on a suicide mission, because like most Americans I was angry and like most U.S. military personnel I wanted to kick some al-Qaeda ass.

The mission in Iraq, however, was fuzzy like a rotting fruit, and while Iraq was at the time linked to al-Qaeda and weapons of mass destruction by Bush's administration, there weren't clear reasons to go into Iraq since Hussein had been kept in check for more than a decade with international sanctions. Containment had worked. I was close to retirement from the reserve, with a new kid, a young beautiful wife, and a shiny new mortgage. Afghanistan never came knocking, but now Iraq was coming up the walkway to ring the doorbell. The colonel said it was a matter of days before I would likely get mobilized if I didn't volunteer.

"My advice is to volunteer," he said. "At least you will get a chance to control where and when you go." I got a lump in my throat, but I didn't want to address the issue right then and there. I told him I would get back to him and let him know.

I took a couple of weeks to think about it, and the colonel loomed over me, regularly reaching out to me to remind me of the inevitable fate that awaited me. After some careful thought and discussion with my wife, Rosie, I volunteered for the war and took the element of surprise away from the Army. If I had to go, I'd try to make it on my terms at least. I learned from Army Pentagon staffers handling my mobilization that I would deploy to Baghdad and provide public affairs support to the coalition command training Iraqi security forces. That meant I'd work public relations for the Iraqi training mission, a little-known undertaking that hadn't received much media attention. I contacted the guy on the ground in Baghdad who was working as the temporary PAO for the command at the time to get information about the environment. He was an Army Reserve major on loan from Combined Joint Task Force 7. He was pinch-hitting at the Office of Security Cooperation, my new duty assignment in Iraq, until the command could build its own public affairs team.

Within thirty days I was gone. Mobilization processing at Fort Bliss in El Paso, Texas, was typical military. The most memorable part of the processing was the hour-long cultural-awareness block of instruction that in sixty minutes was supposed to prepare a soldier for a year of interpersonal interaction with Iraqis. It was nothing of real relevance, and the contractor who was training us was more of a standup comedian than a cultural expert.

I had travel orders from the Coalition Provisional Authority, known as the CPA, the bureaucratic goat fuck managing the U.S. occupation of Iraq. While I cannot think of many things that the CPA did well as it sucked up U.S. tax dollars and got Iraqis and Americans killed through its ignorance, one thing comes to mind that it did exceptionally well. It knew how to travel and spared no expense.

A CPA assignment in Iraq meant resort-like living conditions for a year and fringe benefits earned by getting chummy with the right civilians working in the Green Zone. It meant rubbing shoulders with high-profile politicos and senior officers and sealing your future by drinking coffee with the right people. Militarily, working at the CPA was like getting invited behind the velvet ropes of a VIP club. For many it was a dream come true; for me it was a nightmare. The CPA represented everything I hated about being a military officer. It was a "who you know, not what you know" organization, and from the stories I was hearing back in the States, it wasn't exactly where I wanted to be professionally in Iraq, but I would give it a shot and see if I could make a difference.

On May 7, 2004, we received our weapons, boarded a darkened bus at 2:45 a.m., and began a multilegged journey that would take us from Biggs Army Airfield, Texas, to Maryland, Germany, and Kuwait and into Baghdad. As we approached the terminal, a DC-10 sat quietly on the tarmac, illuminated ominously in the distance. Someone broke the sleepy silence and said, "There she is."

The flight was long, as expected, but I passed part of the time watching a sergeant use his best lines and charm to try to join the mile-high club with a pimply faced flight attendant. He came very close since we were seated in the back of the plane. It was easy for him to get some one-on-one time with her. I stopped listening and watching the entertaining exchanges once they disappeared behind curtains and the talk turned physical.

After a brief overnight stay at Camp Wolverine in Kuwait, we boarded a C-130 aircraft, and our friendly flight attendants were now replaced by U.S. Air Force crew chiefs and loadmasters. I experienced a roller-coaster-like descent in a Wyoming Air National Guard C-130 that flew us into the hellish city from Kuwait. We fell from the sky and sharply banked, turning hard over the airport as we spiraled our way into the war, a tactic executed to avoid surface-to-air missiles. It felt as if we were being flushed down an aerial toilet. Seconds before we landed the aircraft leveled off, and we slammed onto the runway. U.S. military pilots are awesome, and I cannot believe what that man did with that big-ass plane that day.

The rear of the aircraft unbuttoned as we taxied, and it was as if someone opened a furnace door. The blast incinerated our faces immediately. The heat in Baghdad was incredible. Within seconds the thirty-five pounds of protective body armor and field gear we wore felt like one hundred pounds. Salty sweat stung my eyes as I squinted through my sunglasses and deplaned. Above us U.S. Army Apache helicopters took to the air and flew fast and low over the airfield toward a dark plume of smoke in the distance. Nearby, an explosion rumbled through the buzz of the C-130's engines. The pilots had opted to do a "hot" unload of passengers out the rear door, meaning that we would unload the plane with engines running; seems the insurgents had been a little busy prior to our arrival, and it made the Air Force guys nervous to be on the ground. As we disembarked forklifts moved in to remove our palletized bags, and small-arms fire crackled far off in the distance. Welcome to Baghdad.

Within a few days of leaving home and training at Fort Bliss, I found myself at Baghdad International Airport. I transitioned from being a communications assistant vice president and adjunct faculty member with my civilian employers to a soldier in ten days. It was May 10, 2004, and my journey from the States had taken three days, but I was finally in Iraq. There were soldiers everywhere and private security contractors in heavily armored, banged-up sport utility vehicles (SUVs). All the contractors, it seemed, looked like Vin Diesel. They all had shaved heads, massive bodies, and a lot of weapons.

I found out we would not be able to travel to the Green Zone until the next day, so I found a spot on the dusty floor inside one of the terminal tents and tried to fall asleep. I couldn't. The place smelled like a giant sneaker. Most soldiers had their boots off, and the tired air-conditioning was simply recycling the warm, acrid air. An announcement was made about a flight headed to Balad, and it emptied most of the tent. I put my stuff on a cot and tried to sleep. I still couldn't. I stepped outside and found a spot on some rocks where a rare warm, steady breeze blew. I sat down and looked up at the star-filled night and thought about evenings back at home reading *Goodnight Moon* to my son. Good night noises everywhere, I thought as I sat underneath a sky patrolled by unmanned aerial vehicles. Their barely audible monotone buzz hummed above me that night, and that sound would be with me for hundreds of nights in Baghdad as I closed my eyes and fighting resonated far away, closer to me than my wife and son who were now the only thing in my mind and led me into sleep.

The next morning I piled onto a bus with no armor protection along with about twenty other military and civilian personnel, and we headed to the Green Zone. Just prior to leaving Baghdad International, an Army sergeant came on board and told us to don our helmets and body armor. He said we should keep the curtains closed inside the bus so the insurgents couldn't see us. The sergeant also reminded us that if we got attacked, we should use our weapons. No shit, I thought, not realizing that in a few weeks I would be sitting in wide-eyed amazement as mortar and rocket rounds came toward me. In hindsight maybe that sergeant knew just how silly FNGs (fucking new guys) could be when they first faced the enemy in Iraq.

We were sandwiched between two armored HMMWVs (high-mobility multiwheeled vehicles, also known as humvees), each mounted with a machine gun in the turret as we drove out the airport gates and began to speed down the roadway. I sat near the driver so I could see out the front windshield. Gunners spun their turrets around quickly as we drove underneath overpasses, tactical pirouettes in their daily dances with death as they protected convoys. They were ready to engage targets above us, and they leveled their guns on pedestrians walking over the highway. As we entered overpasses we quickly changed lanes to prevent insurgents from dropping grenades on us as we exited on the other side. At one point we drove by an on-ramp where an Iraqi driven car drifted over into our lane, trying to merge. The lead humvee accelerated and forced the car to jerk back into another lane. We continued on in silence, almost as if by staying quiet we would be undetected. We passed torched automobile carcasses, pockmarked buildings that had been peppered with gunfire, and bombed-out, partially destroyed buildings. The war on my television was now just outside the window.

The convoy troops got us to the Green Zone safely, and although I didn't enjoy seeing the disgusted look on the Iraqi driver's face, I was thankful the U.S. soldiers were willing to do whatever it took to deliver their human cargo safely to the Green Zone. Their mission, convoy escort, was to ferry people and goods from point to point, not public diplomacy. I'd later come to appreciate that every soldier, regardless of his or her role, was a diplomat in Iraq, and what we did there left a lasting impression, whether it was to open a school or cut off an Iraqi in traffic. The little things mattered, but at the time I was simply happy to have safely crossed Baghdad in my first convoy. The road to Baghdad International, known as Route Irish, averaged at least one attack per day during my tour in Iraq.

While I had doubts when I first raised my hand to serve in Iraq, when I arrived I regretted not having come sooner, given the miserable failing condition of the mission. Months later I would learn that there was no list of eligible reservists kept by the Army and that the combat-avoiding colonel at the Pentagon had lied to me just to get a slot filled. My name was not on a list, and when he simply needed a name for a position he used mine because I had been fooled into volunteering. What are friends for?

I reported to the unit once I got situated and quickly deduced our outfit was filled with a lot of "chairborne rangers," a military nickname given to folks who predominantly work office jobs. It was a great life these guys had, with all of the career perks of serving in a war zone. Some reported to work at about nine in the morning; some attended staff meetings if they wanted to; they had large hot breakfasts every morning with everything from pancakes to made-to-order omelets, chased down with gourmet coffee people sent them from back home; and they worked inside of Hussein's palace in virtual safety and air-conditioned comfort. They took long lunches and had nice dinners, which included lobster every now and then. Oddly, those who had risked their asses to escort the food into the Green Zone probably would not enjoy it since they were likely from another base and had to return and escort another convoy elsewhere, but the desk jocks in the Green Zone grew fatter by the day. I couldn't believe that war managers were putting soldiers in harm's way to protect convoys of lobster tails, steaks, and ice cream. In Fallujah, a month before I arrived, security contractors had been killed while they escorted trucks en route to pick up kitchen supplies, for Christ's sake. What the hell was going on here?

The Green Zone was something a person can't appreciate unless they saw it with their own eyes. It was a lavish debacle of U.S. overspending, but the soldiers stationed there loved it because they knew if there was a place to be "at war," this was it: free hot food four times daily, free phones and computers to call and write loved ones back home, and free laundry and housekeeping services in office and living quarters. We had several gyms,

Iraqi shopping bazaars, a pizza place, Chinese restaurants, movie theaters, bars, worship services, several massive swimming pools, and brand-new fully loaded SUVs. Most people worked five or six days per week and closed their office doors by six o'clock at night after talking to their spouses or families.

In many of Iraq's forward bases, life sucked for U.S. personnel. In some of the larger posts like Taji and Camp Liberty, the chow-hall food was great and the conditions equally as good if not better than within the Green Zone, but there were some posts in Iraq that were squalid and god-awful. Some places had no power, water, or sewage infrastructure. They lacked communications resources and hot food. The U.S. military personnel at these places endured bitterly rough tours.

I knew we had it made behind the Green Zone's walls, and maybe I wanted to somehow make my life harder while in Iraq. I had tasted what nondesk duty was like as an enlisted man, and while it was nothing close to the hard duty that is the infantry, I had empathy for the soldiers doing tactical work. Because of my military roots I suppose I had some level of professional guilt, since I had worked my way out of jobs where I had to stand on post. I may have been a headquarters staffer, but I didn't have to act like one, and I certainly didn't have to appreciate our plush lives in Baghdad. My job, I felt, was to support those fighting the bad guys and make conditions better for them using information.

The CPA PAO ranks were full of young, inexperienced, or politically loyal civilians who were cutting their bureaucratic teeth and would move on to bigger and better things once they returned from their adventures in Iraq. Many military officers who worked alongside them weren't different: career officers in their final years of service who had never done a "combat" tour and were scrambling to get battlefield uniform mementos. There were also those who intended on making the military a career and were ensuring they went home with the right tin on their chest. Many went home highly decorated heroes, having fought the war only in their overactive imaginations.

At the CPA and at the Office of Security Cooperation, many military personnel working with the Iraqi government lacked drive. Days were busy, a mirage knowingly and unknowingly crafted by officers to deceive, filled with meetings and briefings and reports, bureaucratic smoke screens that alleged progress but masked the truth. People seemed as if they were in motion, but they were not; many were simply on hamster treadmills, achieving nothing but a steady decline in forestation because of the amount of rosy reports they were publishing. The processes of action filled days, and there was a legacy of inaction in Baghdad handed down from wave after wave of desk jockey who arrived.

The CPA, a civilian-led Defense Department entity, clogged the reconstruction and training missions with bureaucracy that bogged down military progress. There were no diplomatic milestones to complement the military achievements. There was little synergy between the CPA and the military outside the walls of the Green Zone, and some in uniform who were a part of the CPA all but lost their military identities and service loyalties. They became part of the frat house. There was little creativity on the ground to resolve issues with resources that were on hand. I found it amazing that soldiers had enough ingenuity to scavenge metal to up-armor their trucks and humvees, motivated, I'm sure, by self-preservation, but U.S. officers complained they lacked funding to buy the Iraqi Army weapons and ammunition, while miles away coalition forces destroyed weapons cache after weapons cache of perfectly good weapons and ammunition.

After I arrived in May 2004 President Bush shifted the emphasis in Iraq to training and equipping Iraqi security forces as the CPA prepared to dissolve. At the tactical level adviser support teams (military personnel training the Iraqis to fight a counterinsurgency) were doing a superior job with the little resources they had. They were masters at improvisation and managed a nearly impossible mission that included huge cultural and communication barriers without real support from the administration and from the CPA. Not all teams were good. Some were run by soldiers who treated the Iraqis with contempt and ridicule, but most were compassionate and patient and knew the U.S. government had bitten off more than it could chew.

I attended our command's staff meeting for the first time on May 13, 2004. Maj. Gen. Paul Eaton of the U.S. Army, the commanding general of the Office of Security Cooperation, had oversight of training, equipping, and mentoring Iraqi police and military forces. The environment was very laid-back. Everyone got along famously, and civilian clothes were worn after duty hours, which usually ended a little after supper time. Soldiers were doing whatever they wanted; there was little order and discipline.

The war inside the Green Zone wasn't real. People took excursions into the war, but they got to leave it and then return safely to the Green Zone. Green Zoners could travel by air or land into the real war zone, but they were merely passengers and not fighters, travelers going from a secured point to a secured point. They weren't the guys clearing the roads of IEDs, hunting bad guys, disarming bombs, shooting it out with the enemy, or protecting shipments of supplies being sent around Iraq. They were people who worked at desks and every once in a while suited up and made believe they were fighting a war so they could take a picture to e-mail back to the States. They had a better chance dying a violent death in the States than they did in Iraq. Baghdad's Green Zone was like a base camp for those on a high adventure in Iraq.

It seems that everyone had time to do everything but work, yet many complained they had little time to work. If people weren't cruising around Iraq or partying around the Green Zone, they jumped on board helicopters just so they could see Iraq. Once I was getting ready to fly to Kirkush for an Iraqi military graduation, and to my surprise there was an Army Reserve colonel sitting in one of the two helicopters I had reserved to fly media to Kirkush that day. She was sitting there, strapped in, ready to go. I had given her a seat at the request of a colonel who said she had business at the training base. Curious, I asked her why she was going to Kirkush and why she was on my air mission.

"I've never been there," she replied.

"Uh huh," I said, and I waited for her to say something else. She didn't.

She had no official reason to travel there, no mission need. I asked her what her egress strategy would be if we crashed. If we were shot down and she was the sole survivor, what did she know about the air-support mission she was flying on? Where were friendly forces positioned between the point she was flying from and flying to? She turned six shades of gray. She didn't know her destination's grid coordinates on a map, or the Green Zone's; she had no satellite phone, no global positioning system, no map, and about ten rounds of issued ammunition for her sidearm. She didn't even have a supply of water. She did have clutched in her hand a small digital camera.

Even though the bulk of flights in Iraq ended without incident, many soldiers never prepared for the worst-case scenario in the event their helicopters crashed, were shot down, or were brought down by mechanical failure. Flying from secure compound to secure compound gave personnel a false sense of security. Was the risk marginal? Yes. But as soldiers we should always be ready and have plans to mitigate the risks as much as possible.

There was a tomboyish Army specialist who started her Iraq tour working administrative functions, the military job she was trained to do, but with an overabundance of paper pushers without enough to do, she was somehow given permission to carry an AK-47, not the weapon she was trained with as a U.S. soldier, and she was assigned to convoy duty, a job she was not trained to perform by the military. I remember once seeing her and her buddies on the streets of Baghdad as I traveled to the nearby Baghdad Iraqi Army recruiting station. She was hanging out the window of an SUV, yelling at Iraqis sitting frustratingly in snarling traffic because there weren't Iraqi cops to keep the traffic flowing and streetlights were not working due to power outages. Her rifle was leveled at the commuters as she barked obscenity after obscenity at the Iraqis. This can't be good, I thought, as we quietly sat in traffic and waited our turn, trying to keep a low profile among the Iraqi drivers. I was taking an American general to meet up with a CBS News crew; the tomboy and her buddies, on the other hand, were risking their lives and making sworn enemies all for a Whopper. She and her friends every few days made the trip from the Green Zone to Taji Military Training Base to fetch Burger King and Subway for the staff. I admired her chutzpah to pick up a rifle; it showed initiative while many others were content to just sit around, but her inexperience, immaturity, and lack of interpersonal skills hurt the mission more than they helped it.

The police training team in our command was one of the worst elements of the CPA, although it too had a few motivated, hard-charging people.

It was led by an emotionless British general officer who had impeccable military credentials and had spent time in Northern Ireland. Despite his dossier the police training team staff was ineffective when I arrived and remained so for many years.

The police team was an organization replete with contractors, and the team was immersed in controversy and allegations of corruption from its early days. In 2006 it was disclosed that one of every twenty-five weapons purchased for Iraqi security forces was missing; nearly fourteen thousand weapons were gone. The team also had problems with ghost police officers. Cunning Iraqis had used the names of the dead to join the Iraqi police force and collect salaries and then used their own names and joined in another city, collecting two or three police salaries since there was no oversight.

The police training team had many civilian contractors who, unlike soldiers, controlled much of their work performance. The team best reflected the problems of having civilians on the battlefield. It's important to note that I value what civilians bring to a war. Without them the military couldn't achieve many objectives. I think in some cases it frees up soldiers to perform key military functions when contractors are hired, but I draw the line when contractors are involved in security training operations in nation-building missions simply because there are limitations that are created by using contractors under fire.

I had a candid conversation with an Army officer who worked with the police training teams. He said he could come back to Iraq as a police training contractor and make at minimum more than $150,000 per year (tax free), much more than he was making as a junior military officer. The officer said there was no risk: if he didn't feel like it was safe to visit a police station and mentor the Iraqis on a particular day, he wouldn't do it, and either way he'd get paid. If the threat was present for weeks and months at a time, advisers simply stayed in the Green Zone until conditions improved.

In an October 2005 report to Congress titled *Measuring Stability and Security in Iraq*, contractor ineffectiveness in police training is clearly addressed: "Absent without leave rates are a significant problem in areas where there is considerable strife. . . . The situation is largely attributed to intimidation by the insurgents. Absenteeism in the Iraqi Police Service is difficult to quantify because the patrol, station and traffic police are operating without significant transition team oversight. IPS absentee data will be more precisely known when International Police Liaison Officers are more readily able to work at local police stations on a regular basis."

During my tour in Iraq I saw countless reports and heard numerous complaints about police training contractors who would not take the necessary risks to accomplish their mission. In one city as violence surged, the police adviser stopped visiting the police station entirely because it was too dangerous. The Iraqis went weeks without a visit from their police training adviser. When the adviser finally visited the station, he discovered that the police force had been overrun by insurgents, the cops had abandoned the station, and the insurgents had burned it down. There was no longer a police force.

There have been plenty of contractors killed in Iraq. Estimates vary, but they total more than fifteen hundred, and many of those worked in security operations. I'm not trying to discredit their work or say that they did not do a good job. In facility protection roles in fortified compounds, they perform an invaluable service by controlling access, but as police or military trainers, those roles, I think, should have been left to soldiers who have the tools needed to train Iraqis and support them once they become operational. Some of our command's civilian security trainers did great work, but others didn't, and in 2004 when I arrived, Iraqi cop training was a damn mess.

I met Sgt. Jared Zabaldo, a law student from Oregon who had enlisted in the Army Reserve in the aftermath of 9/11, on my first duty day at the command. He was an older soldier but very fit, exceedingly intelligent, motivated, and ready to work. I immediately noticed he had a very serious urgency about him. He didn't seem to take shit from people, and he didn't much care for red tape. Those last two traits I liked the most. He had not been in the Army Reserve for very long. He was the command's military journalist, and he would be integral to our team and the command. Jared and I got to know each other in the first few days of my tour, and we talked extensively about how bored he was and that the major didn't allow him to travel or do anything other than administrative work. That would dramatically change for Jared.

As military journalists it is enlisted U.S. military personnel who should travel the most in war because they are responsible for capturing U.S. military stories. They get the sexy work. The stories of a war cannot be captured from behind a desk, and as a PAO it was my job to be the "meeting bitch," as I called myself. PAOs manage programs, set objectives, strategize, and do boring desk stuff. Guys like Jared get to go out and create public relations fodder. They generate the tactical products that help fulfill the strategic communications objectives. Their role is critical and oftentimes overlooked. There were plenty of occasions in Iraq when I traveled and had to take pictures or write articles and serve as a journalist, mostly because we were short-staffed, but also because I was a trained journalist. I could not expect Jared to shoulder the entire mission without any help from me, and likewise there were times when he sat in boring staff meetings and had to do officer work, but overall it was Jared who was out there capturing the story of the Iraqi training mission. I just shared his work with the world.

It's important to note that PAOs serve two masters, a concept I have never liked but grudgingly accepted. They serve their chain of command, but they must play nicely with others in the broader public affairs communities. For example, in Iraq my actions and messages were not only governed by the leadership of the Multinational Security Transition Command Iraq and my commanding general, but also monitored and controlled by Defense Department PAOs, U.S. Central Command (CENTCOM) PAOs, and the Army's Office of the Chief, Public Affairs. All of these entities jockeyed for control of what we did, what we said, how we said it, and when we'd say it. It is a redundancy that brings staleness and stagnation to the field of public affairs. It also kills expediency. There are no tactical PAOs, and the Army wants them all to be strategic minded and centrally managed. I don't agree with this posture because a PAO on a battlefield in Fallujah in 2004 might not have the same perspective as a PAO in Kurdistan, where it is safer.

As the command's temporary PAO, the major was in charge of offering public affairs counsel on public relations and communications matters to the command and the general. But as I mentioned earlier, he also had to serve the greater public affairs community from the Defense Department and, as a soldier, from the Department of the Army. That meant that in addition to serving Eaton, the major also had to answer to Brig. Gen. Mark Kimmitt, then the coalition military spokesman in Iraq.

Kimmitt was a straight shooter who was hated and feared by many in the public affairs community. He demanded immediate action from public affairs staffers and justifiably so: he was, after all, the guy who daily was in the media crosshairs each time he stepped in front of the mic and held a press conference. It was obvious by his demeanor that Kimmitt wasn't running for office. He had a job to do, and sometimes he didn't have the time to say "please" and "thank you," and in today's ultrasensitive military that can make enemies, especially in the supersoft world of PAOs.

There was always something meganewsworthy going on in Iraq: prisoner abuse, combat deaths, collateral damage, Iraqi officials on the take, hard-to-find weapons of mass destruction, you name it. That meant that there was always a reporter working a story somewhere that was on Kimmitt's radar, and getting timely, accurate information was something that Kimmitt took very seriously. While I didn't know Kimmitt on a very personal level, aside from professional interactions I had with him, he seemed obsessive about doing things right.

He was incredibly demanding, according to my friends who worked for him, but he was an exceptional officer. He approached media issues like a warrior. I watched him prepare for press conferences a few times, and he examined things carefully and always planned for the worst. He didn't rehearse. He learned facts and got well versed on subjects so he could address questions intelligently. He was articulate and personable.

Did he do everything perfectly? No. He said things in Iraq in front of the cameras that as a PAO made me cringe, but overall he was a pretty good spokesman, considering he was not a public relations guy by trade. I sat in Kimmitt's office many times before he completed his tour in Iraq, and the guy had more energy than fifty PAOs. Televisions were constantly on in his office, monitoring Arab and Western press alike; various computer monitors filled his credenza and controlled a portion of his attention as numerous fact sheets and reports lay neatly placed across his desktop, awaiting review. His was a busy mind. I once met with him as he ate his lunch, and he answered e-mails, watched the news, tasked his aide with finding someone, tasked one of his staffers with finding some obscure factoid, took a media call, and in between all that talked to me about Iraqi security forces while he reviewed some documents to prepare for a press briefing. He was an energetic, hard-charging officer, and he was a good kick in the ass for an unorganized public affairs community.

I befriended a captain who worked for Kimmitt. Matt Yandura was part of a team Kimmitt had assembled to help him collect information. According to Kimmitt's staffers, he expected information to flow to him immediately as events unfolded in Iraq. Hot-topic issues destined to surface at press conferences should be expeditiously researched and prepared for public consumption by the public affairs community for Kimmitt. PAOs at the Combined Press Information Center (CPIC) and at the Office of Strategic Communication (STRATCOM) in the Republican Palace, just downstairs from Kimmitt, could not process the information fast enough for Kimmitt to effectively engage the press, so Kimmitt formed his own team.

There was also a lot of resentment toward Kimmitt because PAOs felt slighted when he was appointed the coalition's spokesman. Many PAOs believed that a military communicator, a PAO, should have gotten the highly visible job. While I think that's a valid point, I don't think it's a compelling position, because many PAOs, especially those in the Army, aren't truly professional public relations executives. Most have minimal training in public relations and mass communications, and fewer are skilled in managing complex international, intercultural communications issues like we faced in Iraq. In fact, the chief of Army public affairs is ordinarily a career combat-arms officer who has spent most of his years in uniform in infantry or armor divisions.

Kimmitt's team in Iraq hunted down information for him and cut out the middle man. Guys like Matt, workaholics with a good sense of humor who were fueled by a passionate dedication to duty, knew how to work issues and get everyone moving fast in search of facts. It helped that Matt had political savvy, but he knew how to talk with people, and he was an instrumental cog in Kimmitt's machine.

Kimmitt had alienated most of the PAOs in Iraq by the time I arrived in Baghdad; there wasn't a PAO I spoke to who didn't have a "Kimmitt story." I have them too. He once called me on my cell phone while I was in a meeting with my Iraqi Ministry of Defense (MOD) counterparts. Kimmitt asked me for some vague data on Iraqi security forces that I didn't readily have committed to memory or referenced in anything that I had on hand at the meeting. It wasn't for a press query, but he wanted to know some current numbers.

"I don't have access to that data right now, sir," I explained. "I'm at the MOD and in a meeting." I could get it to him in about an hour, I went on, when I was done with my meeting, which had taken weeks to set up. He asked me if there was anyone else who could get the information for me and forward it to him. I explained I had no one in the office. There was an inflection in his voice as my phone crackled. He hung up on me.

I explained the general's urgency to my Iraqi counterparts, who had heard Kimmitt's voice surge over the phone from several feet away and feared he might come to the ministry to physically accost me. Most of these guys were former military men from Hussein's army, which routinely beat soldiers because of lackluster duty performance or on the whim of a senior officer, so they were eager to save me from what they considered would be certain violence. I excused myself from the meeting and later submitted the information to Kimmitt. I think it showed him I was there to support him despite my responsibilities to my command, to my general, and to the Iraqis. I would make the time. Other PAOs didn't see it that way. They saw him as an egomaniacal general.

Kimmitt's ad hoc formation of a research team that also did other things for him was an example to me early on in Iraq that I would have to work beyond the PAO infrastructure to get things done. It said clearly that if he as the lead military PAO in Iraq wasn't given the respect and support he needed, I would certainly be in a world of hurt as a captain. We'd have to work smarter.

It's hard for me to pinpoint why PAOs took so long to get Kimmitt information. There was an overabundance of public affairs personnel in Iraq, so it was certainly not due to manpower issues. In addition, most PAOs sat around and waited for the press to call them. There was little proactive work. Matt said the major who was working at our command temporarily, like his PAO brethren, worked too slowly, and he added that since my arrival Kimmitt and his team had noticed that information was flowing to them much faster. Kimmitt and Matt liked how the information was moving.

As my relationship with Kimmitt's team strengthened, more and more the queries and requests for information from Kimmitt's team came directly to me. It was an awkward time. I worked for the major, and he was allegedly showing me the ropes, although he didn't really know much about the Iraqi training mission. Kimmitt and Matt continued to contact me for information as they needed it, and I explained to them after a few weeks that the major had instructed me to pass all of Kimmitt's queries to him because he wanted to handle all of Kimmitt's questions personally, despite the fact that Kimmitt's team didn't want to work with the major because of his slow reaction time.

This is probably a good time to mention that the major readily admitted that he lacked public affairs experience, which is why I find it odd that PAOs gave him the keys to a shiny new mission, training Iraqi forces, so he could manage its communications. It made absolutely no fucking sense, especially in light of the fact that the major himself had told me early on that he wasn't "too good at all that public affairs stuff." Whoever put this guy in charge of the training mission's communications effort, even temporarily, had their head rectally immersed. Don't get me wrong—the man was a supernice guy, but even he admitted that he lacked PAO skills, so I question the professional decision to assign him to lead the training mission's communications efforts.

One evening after being queried by Matt for some data, I relayed the query to the major and told him Kimmitt's team wanted information on the number of trained Iraqi forces. There were conflicting numbers being reported by the Defense Department, White House, and the U.S. State Department, and Kimmitt wanted clarification for the media. The major acknowledged the request. Within twenty minutes Matt called me, demanding the information.

"Matt," I told him, "I've informed the major of the request, and there is nothing more I can do. I've expressed to him that the general wanted this ASAP, and he said he will get back with you."

Matt sighed in frustration. "Steve, we need this right now," Matt said. "What's the deal with this guy?"

Matt was annoyed, as he sensed that the flow was again going to clog. Matt hung up, and more than an hour later the major showed up at the office and I again reminded him of the urgency coming from Kimmitt's office. I had researched the query for him and found the data, and I told him he could provide it to Kimmitt. The major told me that he didn't like the way Kimmitt's staffers demanded information. He'd get the information to Matt when he could.

Matt called me again and asked to meet me. We met moments later for a cup of coffee at the chow hall in the Republican Palace. He wanted to hammer out a solution for the communication problems between our command and Kimmitt. He felt the major was about to start clogging things up again, and he didn't want that to happen. It was a trend that Matt did not want to start again. We needed a solution.

I tried to remain loyal to the major, who was my temporary boss, but he wasn't seeing the bigger picture and was hampering the mission. He simply took too long to get information to Kimmitt, and based on what he had said, he was slow-rolling Kimmitt just because he didn't like answering to Matt. That went against our principles of information management that stipulates that PAOs need to expeditiously get information out when it is requested. That night as we talked over coffee, Matt and I decided the major had to go for the good of the mission. With the major gone information would flow faster to Kimmitt and to the press. We decided Matt would talk to Kimmitt and ask the general to place me as the chief of public affairs at the Office of Security Cooperation, using the carrot that Kimmitt would get information faster and be able to appease the press quicker.

With the major gone Matt would be able to improve his operation. If Kimmitt asked for something, Matt would get it quickly. I'm not innocent. On my end, if the major was gone, that would give me the public affairs mission for the command, albeit briefly, and buy me time to prove myself to the inbound general who would replace Eaton. More broadly, the overall mission would benefit because timely information would flow to the press and public via Kimmitt, so with those justifications we acted. Matt called our informal meeting that night the first organized meeting of the captains' Mafia Baghdad chapter, a group of captains who worked for high-profile officers in Iraq and tried to move mountains. I'm proud to be a charter member. I returned to my desk and worked a bit, and about an hour later I got a call from Matt.

"It's done," Matt said with all the melodrama of a Mafia movie scene.

I laughed but suddenly felt my stomach fall to my feet.

Shit, what'd we do? I thought as Matt hung up. The major sat innocently at his desk behind a big care package filled with candy and cookies, dressed in civilian clothes, poking away at his keyboard with extended digits, unaware that a coup had just been launched against him.

Matt told Kimmitt that there was an information flow problem at my command and that information would flow faster to Kimmitt from the Office of Security Cooperation if I was given control of the public affairs mission there. The next day Kimmitt summoned me to validate the claims that were being made to him.

Kimmitt was engaged in the issue of the day. I checked in with his aide, who announced my presence, and I got a wink from Matt as I walked into Kimmitt's office. Kimmitt continued to work as I reported. He barely looked at me.

"If he was gone, would you be able to handle the work?" Kimmitt asked me.

"Yes, sir, without a doubt," I replied.

"You know what's going on at OSC?" he asked.

"Roger, sir," I said. "I know that mission."

Kimmitt then yelled to his aide to have the major report to his office immediately.

As I sat nervously in front of Kimmitt's desk, the major arrived. Kimmitt explained to the major that he was needed back at his original duty assignment at the task force and that I was relieving him.

The major's face turned red, and I could feel my ears getting warm. The major countered that I had been there only a few weeks and didn't have a grasp on things yet. Kimmitt, who at the time was eating, reading, and e-mailing, stopped everything he was doing, wiped his mouth, and looked at the major and told him he was expected to return to the task force in twenty-four hours.

"Understand?" Kimmitt asked.

"Yes, sir," the major replied.

"Great, thanks," Kimmitt said.

I stared straight ahead as the major popped to attention, executed a right face, and left the room. I felt as if I were sitting under a broiler. I didn't think the major was fired because I'm certain I wouldn't have been asked to be there for a firing. I think he was merely ensuring the major understood that he had been replaced. I could feel my forehead getting velvety with beads of warm sweat. Kimmitt looked at me at long last as he munched aggressively on his salad.

"Do you have anything else?" he said as one corner of his mouth almost stretched into a slight smile.

"No, sir," I replied.

"Okay, thanks, Steve."

I stood, saluted him, and left the room.

It was May 30, 2004, and I had been in country less than a month. I wrote in my journal: "I was made the PAO today. Major was relieved by BG Kimmitt and I took over. We've a very long road ahead. We have a lot to do. I'm swamped in press activity and we have a lot of shortcomings operationally, but we'll get through."

Ironically, Kimmitt had no real authority to appoint me as the PAO for Eaton's command. Eaton was really the only one who could determine who would serve on his staff, and that had to be cleared by U.S. CENTCOM in harmony with the CPA. And the major's boss was the only one who could truly tell the major where and when to serve. But Eaton was on his way out, and Kimmitt had presence and a hardened demeanor that I think scared the shit out people. And Kimmitt's a general, and whether he was in someone's chain of command mattered not. If he said something, a soldier was expected to make it happen.

Kimmitt installed me as the PAO with no objection from Eaton. Thus would begin my journey in the most important, most coveted public affairs job in Iraq in 2004. I became responsible for the communications strategy of the multibillion-dollar U.S. exit plan in Iraq. Training Iraqi security forces would become the tip of the spear of U.S. foreign policy in Iraq, and I would be in the center of the political firestorm, from the Beltway to Baghdad. Our command would be our nation's way home, and the world would soon turn its attention to us and what we were trying to accomplish.

Iraq at the time was divided into three multinational commands, Multinational Corps Iraq, which had six subordinate commands and a corps of engineers division under it and executed the security and stability operations; Multinational Force Iraq, which managed all forces in Iraq; and Multinational Security Transition Command Iraq, which managed the training of Iraq's security forces after it transitioned from being the Office of Security Cooperation. MNCI had a colonel leading its public affairs mission. Beneath it the regional commands and the supporting commands in Iraq had colonels and lieutenant colonels leading their public affairs missions. MNFI had two one-star general officers leading its public affairs mission. MNSTCI had me, a lowly prior enlisted captain.

I would be the most junior-ranking PAO in Iraq, manning the highest-profile public affairs job in the entire theater. While only a captain, I filled a position intended to be staffed by senior PAOs in the ranks of colonel or general. As the chief of staff at our command would later say in my officer evaluation at the end of my tour, I would prove to be a "colonel in captain's garb," and with one great sergeant we set out to try to make a difference in Iraq and try to win our little piece of the war, one word at a time.

3

THE IRAQI FACE

June 2004: Average number of weekly attacks in Iraq
from June to November 2004 nears 550.
—Multinational Corps Iraq unclassified report, November 2004

There was a confluence of events all stirring in Iraq in the summer of 2004, and if we played our cards right the coalition and the Iraqi government would be able to entrench themselves and not lose further ground in the communications war. More and more reports of violence in Iraq were dominating the headlines, as reporters began to peel back the truth and reveal that progress was not truly being made in Iraq and was not as widespread as reported by the CPA. The occupation's first year was not a banner year, as touted by the Bush administration. Satellite channels like al-Jazeera fanned embers of dissidence throughout the Arab street by showing the world an unvarnished view of the American war in Iraq. Early U.S. diplomatic decisions made by the CPA were microanalyzed by Arab media, and support for the American presence in Iraq began to dwindle, crumbling like sand pillars not just in the Middle East, but also in the United States. While things were bad and quickly worsening, there was still time, I thought, to salvage the communications mission because of the many things happening in June 2004 in Iraq.

At this point the CPA's PAOs were doing too much talking. It was plainly evident to those of us in Baghdad that senior CPA officials were defensively justifying the past year of their lives. They desperately scrounged up metrics for reports, numbers, dollars, megawatts, anything that they could use to pad the stellar record of underachievement and hide the fact that a year of valuable time had like sand somehow slipped through their hands. An insurgency had gathered momentum, and Iraqi civil life had fallen into a horrid existence. Many in the media considered the CPA crowd unprofessional and immature, but many of us coming in from the outside viewed them as delusional.

CPA PAOs were on message, and if there is one thing government communicators are good at, it is staying on message. They are taught, as I was taught at the Defense Information School, to always come back to a key message or theme, whatever point they're trying to convey, no matter the question asked of them. For example, if I wanted to tell the world that Iraqi security forces were improving, I would creatively blend that message into my response, regardless of what a reporter asked me.

The CPA's problem was that there was substantial evidence, sadly, in the form of dead Iraqis and coalition soldiers, and legions of unhappy Iraqis, that countered everything that they were saying. The CPA's enduring theme, that progress was being made in Iraq, was refuted by the reality on Iraq's streets. Security was terrible, civil services were virtually nonexistent as sewers overflowed and garbage piled in the streets, and more jobs disappeared, crumbling Iraq's economy. Firmly, the CPA stuck to its guns and stayed on message as cries for help came from over the walls of the Green Zone from Iraqis living on the mean streets.

For example, while the CPA claimed in a 2004 report that it had created a "vibrant civil society" in Iraq, life outside the Green Zone was anything but vibrant for most Iraqis. In this report the CPA boasted that it had helped Iraqis maintain a high level of oil production and that five hundred thousand new jobs were created nationwide. It also claimed that electrical infrastructure was vastly improved and that the increased demand for electricity showed a "thriving economy emerging out from three decades of isolation." They even went so far as to say that Iraqi security forces were "protecting" Iraqis nationwide.[1] The report was nothing more than cheap public relations drivel assembled by government public relations lemmings in a desperate last-ditch attempt to stay on message and leave Iraq on a good note.

The truth is that prewar oil production was 2.5 million barrels per day, according to U.S. congressional reports, but more than four years after the start of Operation Iraqi Freedom, the coalition had still yet to achieve prewar oil output. As for new jobs, the Iraqis complained incessantly in the Arab media that unemployment in Iraq had reached a dangerously high level. Some CPA officials argued that unemployment rates couldn't genuinely be examined since there was no way to measure the joblessness among twenty-six million Iraqis, but weeks after the CPA's report was released the Iraqi newspaper *al-Mutamar* published a story that the Iraqi Ministry of Planning had reported that the unemployment rate in Iraq was 53 percent. Work was hard to find in Iraq, and on the streets shops closed, markets were empty, and commerce and the economy came to a grinding halt. The Iraqis I worked with were thankful for their high-paying U.S. contractor jobs because they said there was no work in the Iraqi economy.

The CPA's report used action words to evoke feelings of accomplishments and hide the fact that the CPA did very little in the arena of public works. The report was carefully but not skillfully written. For example, one sentence says, "The Ministry of Municipalities and Public Works has approximately US $3.2 Billion in over 100 projects potentially improving the water supply to 10 million urban and 2 million rural Iraqi people." In another statement the report says, "Over the past four months, more than $200 million has been obligated toward more than 200 emergency projects in nine different districts." Nowhere in this section of the report does the writer say plainly that construction on a project was started and completed. Instead, the writer leads the reader into thinking that progress is being made simply by stating that money has been committed or that projects have been initiated. "Initiated" can also mean that someone thought of a good idea and staffers talked about it, and that is not something tangible to document in a report that is showcasing accomplishments. To illustrate the creative use of language, consider this. On one page of the CPA report, the words "initiated," "obligated," and the phrase "will be" are used in seven out of ten bulleted accomplishments.[2] Simply put, it is greasy public relations, and the CPA did a lot of this in the short time I worked with them.

Iraqi security forces weren't faring much better than other things in Iraq led by the CPA. They had been neglected by Hussein after the 1991 allied onslaught, and there was little left of them not in dilapidated, antiquated, and demoralized condition. The straw that broke the proverbial camel's back came when Paul Bremer, the CPA's chief, disbanded Hussein's Iraqi security apparatus on May 23, 2003, and then did not establish a new Ministry of Defense for nearly a year, until March 22, 2004. The coalition then had to start rebuilding the Iraqi security forces from the ground up, which was no easy task, and the first one thousand trainees did not enter training until August 2, 2003, at Kirkush Military Training Base. In 2004, a little more than a year after they shut down the Iraqi military, the CPA closed its own doors for business and released its report card, *An Historic Review of CPA Accomplishments*. It also included a section on Iraqi security forces in its self-aggrandizing seventy-one-page report.

"Since the liberation of Iraq on April 9, 2003, Coalition Forces in close cooperation with their Iraqi counterparts have made tremendous progress in helping make Iraq a safer, more secure place for Iraqi citizens to live and work," the report said. Yet intelligence reports we received almost daily, Iraqis I worked with, coalition personnel on the ground, the media, and academics all stated that violence was increasing in Iraq and was far worse than when Hussein was in power. I didn't need anyone telling me things were bad. The daily barrage of indirect fire was proof enough, and steady incident reports about units getting attacked made their way to us. The CPA report also said: "Ramped up the [Iraqi Police Service] to over 78,000 police with an additional 5,000 in training, who are protecting Iraqi citizens each and every day throughout the country." What they failed to say was that thousands of these guys weren't working at all and were merely collecting a check for doing nothing. I learned this from plenty of discussions with advisers who worked with the Iraqis and from the Iraqis at the ministries. The report also stated that seventy-five thousand guards were protecting three thousand critical infrastructure sites throughout Iraq, but no mention was made that insurgent attacks had been instrumental in disrupting electrical service and oil production, so the guards, who were mostly unarmed, weren't doing too good of a job protecting their facilities.[3] They were outnumbered and outgunned. Every week we heard about infrastructure attacks on pipelines and the Iraqi grid at intelligence briefings.

The CPA reported that the Baghdad Police Academy had been renovated and updated to adequately train the police. It failed to mention that the U.S. government was in bitter dispute with the contractor for shoddy workmanship despite a price tag of $70 million. CPA reports boasted that 60 percent of all Iraqi soldiers had prior military service and that all of the officers and noncommissioned officers had prior service.[4] That might seem like a recruiting victory, but keep in mind that Hussein's military was known to sometimes surrender to news crews and lay down their arms when confronted by an enemy, even surrendering to an unmanned drone aircraft once. Hussein's army, now the new Iraqi Army, was known more for its cowardice than its fight.

By May 2004 American credibility was in a nosedive, as was American support for the war. According to Gallup polls 44 percent of those surveyed believed it was a mistake to have sent military forces into Iraq, a 22 point increase from about the same time in 2003.[5] The CPA wasn't making good on its deliverables to the Iraqi people, but we figured that wouldn't matter for too much longer since the CPA was soon leaving Iraq. With an interim Iraqi government recently seated and perched to take control from the CPA and a constitution on the way in the future, the coalition and the Bush administration determined that the priority would shift from building political infrastructure to stabilizing Iraq with Iraqi forces. Billions of dollars were rerouted from reconstruction projects and channeled into efforts to rebuild Iraq's police and military forces.

The primary concern for most Iraqis in June 2004 continued to be security. Polls and surveys all stated clearly that Iraqis wanted normalcy in their lives. Violence prevented many families from working and sending their kids to school; kids in some parts of Iraq couldn't even play in parks or on the streets anymore. Before anything else could be fixed, Iraq's security situation needed traction. A lack of infrastructure and services was merely inconvenient when compared to loss of life. Training and equipping Iraqi security forces had been under the public's and media's radar for more than a year. It was only when the Iraqi Ministry of Defense was created in 2004 that someone thought it was a good idea to have a PAO at our command. Eaton had not had a PAO until the major arrived to support him, and it was obvious by the command's nearly invisible media profile that the program was getting little, if any, attention.

The CPA's departure would enable us to shine a spotlight on Iraqi forces once the Iraqis were given sovereignty. Our plan was to rally everyday Iraqis and their political leaders around their new security forces. Our command, through the Ministries of Defense and Interior, could show the world Iraqi forces, their motives for serving, how they trained, and how they fought for and protected Iraq. When they died we'd make them, not the insurgents, the martyrs. With our Iraqi counterparts we would show the Arab street that Iraqi forces were more and more taking control of their nation with the support of the coalition, and we would illustrate to Iraq's neighbors that the new Iraqi military was about internal defense and not an instrument of outward aggression.

I do not wish to imply that Iraqis were capable of defending their nation at that moment in time—they were not—but with the support of U.S. personnel, we could deter some potential insurgent activity and Iraqis would gain confidence in their forces. At the very least there would be continuing communication about force development, and the Iraqi populace would not feel as if they were alone and at risk. They would know the cavalry was coming and that a security apparatus had been installed. For example, the Iraqi police had organized a unit that dealt solely with kidnapping crimes, an immense problem plaguing Iraq in 2004, and they had already been successful in finding abducted Iraqis and returning them to their families. There were also Iraqi special tactics teams in the Iraqi police that would go after insurgent cells. Iraqi Special Forces were an incredible deterrent to those up to no good, since they could swoop in and kill or capture bad guys without anyone knowing what hit them. The Iraqi Air Force was preparing for infrastructure patrols with reconnaissance aircraft that would detect sabotage before it damaged Iraqi resources. A lot of things were stirring that we could talk about and showcase.

The time was ripe, I thought, for the Iraqi police and military forces to appoint spokespersons to talk to Iraqis about developments in the training and deployment of Iraqi security forces. Because the coalition planned to hand over power to Iraq, we felt it was important for Iraqis to see that the Iraqi government was in control and taking steps to secure the nation and protect its citizens. Nobody could communicate that better than an Iraqi wearing a police or army uniform. There would be no better way to show and tell Iraqis that their nation was in good hands, or at least in hands that were trying to fight the insurgents, than to have the Ministries of Interior and Defense, the organizations charged with defending and protecting Iraq, brief the world and, more important, Iraqis about the progress of Iraq's forces. It would send a message to Iraqis that their government was addressing the security problem. There would be no bewildered herd, and things couldn't happen fast enough.

An Iraqi friend noticeably absent from his job in the Green Zone told me he had been away from his coalition job because his nephew had been kidnapped and held for ransom. His brother, the boy's father, sold his business to get his son back, but lost not only his business but also the earnings from its sale that he paid as ransom for his son. Police did not investigate the crime, and nobody was ever brought to justice for the kidnapping.

If we were talking about Iraq police development at that moment, the Iraqi populace could have known that the coalition had established tip lines along with the Iraqi government whereby citizens could offer anonymous tips about insurgent and criminal activity for a cash reward. When I asked my friend if he knew about the Iraqi police kidnapping unit, he said he wasn't aware of it and that they had gone to the local precinct for help, an organization not manned or equipped to do investigative work. With little options his family paid the ransom, but if the family had been aware of the resources available to help them, maybe the outcome would have been different. If we communicated the developments that were occurring, the Iraqis might not feel their only option was to allow insurgents and criminals to have their way. The hopelessness and permissiveness might not proliferate.

Public affairs guidance distributed in Baghdad by the U.S. PAOs as the

CPA began to prepare for its departure stipulated an "Iraqi face" would be put on every public relations effort flowing out of Iraq. Everywhere in the palace that's all people talked about as the transfer of authority neared in June 2004. A guy we shared office space with joked as he returned from using the bathroom that the feces he had just dropped in the toilet had an Iraqi face on it. At breakfast once a guy put syrup on his waffles and said excitedly, "Look, my waffle has an Iraqi face." While there were plenty of jokes circulating around the palace about the upcoming transition and transfer of authority, I saw it as an opportunity to put the Iraqi training mission on the map.

The coalition's communications plan was simple. The Iraqis would be expected to talk to the media and address the many problems facing their nation. The problem was that coalition PAOs never told the Iraqis about the new expectations, according to my Iraqi PAO counterparts, and the CPA had made Iraq such a mess that many Iraqi officials didn't feel it was their job to answer the many tough questions the CPA had ignored for more than one year.

As winds of change stirred in Iraq, back in Washington DC Lt. Gen. David H. Petraeus of the U.S. Army was selected by President George W. Bush to replace Eaton at the Office of Security Cooperation. The Office of Security Cooperation would become the Multinational Security Transition Command Iraq, and Petraeus would receive his third star. Bush told Petraeus the mission had his full support. The U.S. departure from Iraq hinged on Iraqi forces who were able to keep Iraqis safe.

Like most policies in Iraq, the new public affairs guidance for Operation Iraqi Freedom was written inside the Beltway by people with little understanding about conditions on the ground. A PAO at the Office of the Assistant Secretary of Defense, Public Affairs, penned the "Iraqi Face" public affairs guidance. It stated that the assembly and training of Iraqi security forces would be the focal point of the U.S. mission in Iraq, and local public affairs guidance from Multinational Force Iraq stated the United States would take a backseat in the media and push the Iraqis into the limelight. I felt that if along the way Petraeus got some exposure that improved public support for the war in the States, so be it, but it wouldn't be our focus; it would be merely a by-product. Our focus would be to lure the media to our command using Petraeus and then seamlessly and creatively redirect the press to speak with his Iraqi military and police counterparts once we hooked them. It would be our way to get the media to transition to Iraqi officials too.

Kimmitt could see the signs coming down the road long before most. While I thought we needed spokespersons from the ministries even before I set foot in Iraq, weeks before the transfer of authority and well before I was even mobilized, Kimmitt asked our command to find a suitable spokesperson for Iraq's security forces. We recommended to Kimmitt and to Multinational Force Iraq public affairs personnel that as the Iraqis took control of their nation, Iraqi spokespersons should hold regular weekly joint press conferences to talk about the development and deployment of their security forces.

The weekly press events we would save for later and hoped they would fill the void left by Kimmitt and his civilian Defense Department counterpart, Dan Senor. They would also help reassure millions of Iraqis and Arabs that the security situation in Iraq was a work in progress, that it was receiving money and attention by coalition planners, and, above all, that it was being managed by Iraqis, for Iraqis. We could, we hoped, calm some fears. For example, one of the first things municipal governments do in the States when disasters or civil unrest strike is get on the air and talk to the community via radio, television, newspapers, text messages, you name it, before and after catastrophic events such as hurricanes, floods, and tornadoes. They are a voice of calm and reassurance. They tell citizens that police are on the streets keeping order, they pass on information about curfews and safety notices, and they keep folks abreast of developments in the restoration of basic services. I couldn't help but notice that something that state officials in Florida, Oklahoma, and other disaster-prone states could do in their sleep was not being done by federal officials or the Iraqi government. As a former National Guard PAO, I wondered why my National Guard PAO brethren who manage stuff like this all the time were not being sought out to offer their input.

Aside from the void in communications addressing security issues, there was nobody from the Iraqi government talking routinely to the Iraqi masses about anything. In the buildup to Operation Desert Storm when the United States first squared off against Iraq in the early 1990s, the media were tightly controlled by the U.S. military, not surprisingly since many senior military leaders in Desert Storm were Vietnam War veterans and believed the press had been pivotal in losing the war for them by swaying public opinion, which eroded public support.

Gen. Norman Schwarzkopf and his PAOs (led by NBC News reporter Pete Williams, who was then the assistant secretary of defense, public affairs) aggressively controlled the media during the Gulf War, but in exchange Schwarzkopf would routinely brief the media and dazzle them with video footage from precision munitions. He was masterful at telling people what was happening and not really showing them the mayhem being caused on the ground by the allied air campaign. But by centralizing the information and the communications effort on one man, Schwarzkopf brought all eyes on him, and he became the face of Desert Storm: he personified the mission to expel Iraq from Kuwait; he was the allied forces incarnate.

Our goal was to deify the Iraqi spokespersons the same way and make them the face of the Iraqi security forces and the face of a struggling Iraq that would endure anything to be a new democracy in the Middle East. We would centralize the communications effort around the Iraqi PAOs, but instead of telling Iraqis about progress from behind a podium like Schwarzkopf told reporters about the Gulf War, we would couple press briefings with media trips and media embeds to ensure we were showing the press the progress and not just talking about it. Iraqis would have a familiar face they could associate with the Iraqi forces, maybe a Sunni and a Shiite, and those persons' names would be in the newspapers; their voices would be on the radio, their images in news publications, and their personalities on televisions.

The book *Taken by Storm* examines the press, public opinion, and foreign policy in the Gulf War. I think the book's findings are applicable for Operation Iraqi Freedom and can be applied to the Iraqi culture. Daniel C.

Hallin and Todd Gitlin, chapter authors in the book, state that the American media when they cover their troops at war tend to help the nation build "ties of sentiment between the soldiers in the field and the home front."[6] Hallin's book *The Uncensored War* also states that the misconception of the media's impact on the Vietnam War is off base. "Popular myths about the media and Vietnam, both liberal and conservative, die hard. But among the growing community of people who have systematically investigated the media's role in the war, there is an impressive consensus rejecting the notions that the media were adversaries to American policy in Vietnam or a decisive factor in the outcome of the war."[7]

These are important points because there is a phenomenon that occurs in strife between those in arms and those in the media. Research like Hallin's shows that American journalists sent to cover American wars, including Vietnam, have routinely repeated the military's enduring messages, and they have done little to explore stories outside of what is presented to them by PAOs. Think about the start of the war in Iraq. There were touching stories about U.S. soldiers and the sacrifices they make for their country. As they stormed into Baghdad, they were international heroes. The U.S. media covered the broader national objectives at a wider level, and within that realm local press focused on individual soldiers making contributions to the war. The American media at war, researchers say, serve as a tool that triggers a sense of community and nationalism in Americans. I simply call it press proximity.

From personal experience there is no U.S. reporter whom I know who would embed with military forces, enjoy their rations and protection, and then turn around and file a bad report about them even when grave mistakes are made on the battlefield. American reporters are Americans, and by that very association there are values and national connections that predispose them to present reports about U.S. service personnel in a certain way. They are hardwired, and ordinarily it is flawed policies that are attacked by reporters covering wars and not the soldiers themselves, unless of course the soldiers commit crimes and then they're fair game.

We wanted to use press proximity in the same strategic manner with

Iraq's domestic media and more widely the Pan-Arab networks. Aggressive Iraqi media engagement would enable Iraqi reporters to get to know their soldiers and share stories of Iraq's security forces with their Iraqi audiences on local and national levels.

Far-reaching satellite channels like al-Jazeera and al-Arabiya could be engaged to reach the wider Pan-Arab audience across Iraq's borders. With an Iraqi official talking to these Arab satellite channels, the press-proximity theory would work in our favor because those channels routinely reminded their critics they were Arab journalists reporting matters of interests for their Arab audiences. It was a no-brainer for us to engage them.

In 2004 the U.S. Defense Science Board released a telling report on strategic communication in Iraq. The damage inflicted by the CPA on the American image in the region was clear. "Thus the critical problem in American public diplomacy directed toward the Muslim World is not one of 'dissemination of information,' or even one of crafting and delivering the 'right' message. Rather, it is a fundamental problem of credibility. Simply, there is none—the United States today is without a working channel of communication to the world of Muslims and of Islam. Inevitably therefore, whatever Americans do and say only serves the party that has both the message and the 'loud and clear' channel: the enemy," the report said.[8]

Before I arrived in Baghdad Kimmitt and the major had found Col. Sabeeh Hussein Radhi, who had been "voluntold" he would be the first Iraqi PAO for the new Iraqi Army. He was a good choice. He was articulate and personable and spoke English fluently. He had learned English years earlier as a transport pilot in Hussein's air force, a position that enabled him to learn the universal language of aviation.

We didn't try to find a spokesperson for the Ministry of Interior. Their problems were so deep that the last thing I wanted to do was put some poor Iraqi in the spotlight of a problematic ministry and have his press conferences turn into a heat-lamp interrogation. Too many things needed to be fixed there, and while the Defense Ministry was no walk in the park, it lacked a lot of the drama that was stirring at the Interior Ministry. I figured some extra time searching for a spokesman for the Ministry of Interior would give the Iraqis and the coalition time to fix whatever deficiencies they had with police forces, and it would let us focus on the Ministry of Defense and getting their PAO up and running. Once we were done at the Ministry of Defense, we could take those lessons learned and apply them in the creation of a Ministry of Interior public affairs shop.

We were poised. Colonel Sabeeh began to shadow Kimmitt at work. He spent time with Kimmitt at press gaggles, informal on-the-record press gatherings that provided an intimate setting for the press to get to the heart of issues, and he also attended some backgrounders with him, press gatherings where information is given but not directly attributed. Sabeeh also watched me work with the press. He learned how to do interviews and how to answer questions, and he realized that he didn't have to be mechanical and formulaic with his responses. He could be conversational, but he had to be truthful.

In early June 2004 Kimmitt, our deputy commanding general Brig. Nigel Aylwin-Foster of the British Army, and I began the arduous process of convincing the Iraqi Ministry of Defense to finalize Sabeeh's selection as spokesman, since the process had been dragged out by the Iraqis and had included multiple candidates, most related to the defense minister. The problem the ministry had with Sabeeh wasn't that he was a bad candidate; it was that his initial selection wasn't properly vetted through the Ministry of Defense. Sabeeh had been recommended and approved by the coalition, but they didn't get senior-level Iraqis to buy in first. Decisions were made for Iraqis, not by Iraqis, and sometimes that was needed because Arab culture can voraciously consume time and make little progress. But those who routinely worked with Iraqis knew that if a decision was made for them, it required buy-in at many levels. The Iraqis were a little cold in their reception of the fact that a highly visible position in the new Defense Ministry had been filled by the coalition without Iraqi approval. Frankly, I think the approval had been given at lower levels; it had just not been granted at the minister's level, and if it was, the minister was now jerking us around.

Aylwin-Foster informed me and Kimmitt less than a month away from the transfer of authority that the Ministry of Defense would not be talking to the press until it developed its media policies. He had been told by the Defense Ministry that a plan was in the works, but until it was finalized, nobody from the ministry would interact with the media. Aylwin-Foster recommended the coalition support the new Iraqi defense minister's wishes. The Iraqi minister of defense, it was agreed, would develop a comprehensive Iraqi media plan, and Sabeeh would simply have to wait before speaking to the Iraqi and Arab masses. Things didn't smell right to me. I disagreed but figured the plan would be completed by the transfer of authority, though I heard rumblings from Iraqi peers that the minister had appointed a cousin to manage public relations and protocol issues for him, despite having a half-dozen civil service employees in the ministry already hired to manage the issues for him. I informed Kimmitt and Aylwin-Foster that Iraq's defense minister, Hazim al-Shaalan, was planning to replace Sabeeh with a relative. I told them I thought al-Shaalan was stalling.

Kimmitt and Aylwin-Foster agreed with me in theory, but they insisted we give al-Shaalan the time he needed to develop a plan. They also voiced concerns that Sabeeh might be replaced as we waited for the plan's delivery, and they joked that because they had worked so hard to find an Iraqi spokesman, the coalition should appoint someone to protect Sabeeh, a political bodyguard of sorts, a watchdog. Kimmitt and Aylwin-Foster appointed me Colonel Sabeeh's mentor so I could train him but also protect him from professional fratricide.

"Steve's the right guy to be the junkyard dog," Kimmitt told Aylwin-Foster, and with those simple words I earned my Iraq nom de guerre.

Sabeeh spent his days shadowing me, but with my workload it was something I could not manage. Jared and I were traveling a lot, sometimes in different directions, and that made it hard to have steady mentorship for Sabeeh. With the transfer of authority weeks away, I contacted Kimmitt and informed him that I was swamped with work and needed help with Sabeeh. We couldn't provide the sustained mentorship Sabeeh needed. Weeks earlier when he relieved the major of his duties and made me chief PAO, Kimmitt told me if I needed support that all I had to do was ask. STRATCOM and the press center had an overabundance of personnel, he said, and their role was to support the commands, so all I had to do was ask. I did what he said, contacted STRATCOM, and asked them for help in training Sabeeh. They declined my request, citing a lack of available personnel. I contacted Kimmitt and explained that I had asked for help but was rejected, and I inquired if he had any other recommendations I should explore.

We needed help, so Kimmitt contacted Col. Jill Morganthaler of the U.S. Army Reserve, who was the PAO at the task force that was running the mission in Iraq at the time. Kimmitt informed Morganthaler that she would have to loan me personnel so I could train Sabeeh or her team would have to assume mentorship of Sabeeh. He told her that he needed her to work to solve the issue. He had looked at the workload at our command, and he said there was far more work there than at the task force or STRATCOM and we had far fewer people.

It was an energized period in Iraq. Everyone in country knew that our mission was now the priority, according to the president and according to recently released PAO guidance. Despite a presidential proclamation, congressional budgetary shifts to fund our mission, Kimmitt's request, and public affairs guidance that stipulated the Iraqi training mission would be the main thrust in Iraq, the manpower never came to our command and responsibility for Sabeeh was never assumed by anyone else. Once Kimmitt left Iraq the issue was never resolved. We needed a seasoned PAO (someone other than the self-admitted inexperienced major) to help train Sabeeh, and we never found one.

I continued to work with Sabeeh as best as I could and try to encourage the ministry to assume a proactive posture as the transfer neared. Al-Shaalan insisted his staff would deliver a communications strategy that would be implemented the day after authority was transferred. As we neared sovereignty I pushed the ministry harder for a policy that Sabeeh could use, but by then I knew I was getting played.

One morning I learned that al-Shaalan had fired Sabeeh before he could ever take the podium, days before the transfer of authority. Al-Shaalan hadn't even had the decency to call Sabeeh to the ministry or to even speak to him. Sabeeh had learned about his dismissal from other ministry employees.

When I contacted the ministry I was told a new gentleman had been assigned to handle public affairs, but he would not be talking to the press. The minister had signed a directive indicating he was the sole authorized mouthpiece for the Ministry of Defense. Nobody was authorized to speak to the media. The minister's media plan was complete, and we had waited weeks for a one-paragraph document.

I would spend the next nine months battling and circumventing al-Shaalan's policies and trying to convince disjointed coalition PAOs that the ministries needed to communicate to the Iraqi populace. The coalition, as it had planned in public affairs guidance, backed away from the media spotlight as the press conferences from the CPA ended and Iraqis embraced their sovereignty. Al-Shaalan did not talk to the press, nor did anyone from his ministry. The problem-plagued Ministry of Interior did not talk either. They were busy fending off charges of corruption, police abuse, and secret prisons. There was only silence from the Iraqi government and the usually loquacious American military amid the ongoing violence.

Strangely, as Sabeeh had prepared to talk to and engage the media, some coalition PAOs began to argue with me that Iraqis weren't willing to talk to the press so we shouldn't try to push them. Kimmitt, they said, was asserting himself on the Iraqis at the expense of the Iraqis. I'm sure there were Iraqis who didn't want to talk to the press, but Sabeeh was ready to take the plunge, and many of the Iraqis I had contact with were more than willing to tell their stories. I felt compelled to ask the PAOs, "If the Iraqis aren't willing to talk to the media and everyone thinks it's such a bad idea, then why did the coalition write public affairs guidance that says everything will have an Iraqi face? Why did we plan for the Iraqis to talk?" Nobody had an answer.

I pointed to plenty of Iraqis willing to talk. Jared dug up incredible stories within our command of Iraqi bravery and commitment to a new democratic Iraq. We used Iraqis' names in our stories, and some agreed to have their images published too, despite warnings from us that they could be targeted by the insurgents. It was mixed: some Iraqis demanded anonymity, but many others didn't. Like the Iraqi women at the Pentagon whom I did not photograph, if an Iraqi asked for anonymity, we complied, but in the eyes of some of my public affairs peers, I was callous and so was Kimmitt. Some coalition personnel accused me of coercing the Iraqis to talk to the press, which was wholly untrue.

Shortly after 9/11 many U.S. Air Force airmen, including members of the Air National Guard, referred to themselves in news stories by rank and first name only, and they didn't show their faces to news cameras. The U.S. Air Force feared terrorists might still be on the ground in the United States, and they didn't want to put their airmen and their loved ones at unnecessary risk as they flew combat patrols over the United States. They protected their identities. The Iraqis were doing the same thing in 2004 and 2005, and we respected that, but if some were okay with using their names, we were okay with it too.

The CPA also used the fearful-Iraqi excuse for the two months I was there prior to their shutdown, but a CPA PAO later admitted to me that the CPA had intentionally kept Iraqis away from the press because they didn't want the Iraqis to appear unrefined and unpolished. They were afraid the Iraqis might say inappropriate things to the media.

"Like what?" I asked.

"They might not appropriately express their appreciation for what we've done for them," the young CPA PAO said.

"Oh, like, 'We want the Americans to get the fuck out of Iraq because they've fucked it all up'?" I joked.

"Exactly," the twentysomething staffer replied.

It was a valid point. I had heard some Iraqi soldiers bitch and moan to the press about not getting paid, not having uniforms, getting sick from bad Iraqi military food, and a host of other issues. Then again, I could also pick up any American newspaper and find stories about U.S. soldiers bitching about not getting paid, long deployments, lack of armored vehicles, short-notice mobilizations, you name it. The Iraqi complaints weren't flattering to the new Iraqi government or to the coalition, but sometimes there were valid complaints, and simply because the coalition didn't want to hear them, or share them with the world, didn't mean the Iraqis should be sequestered from the media. I have always been a fan of airing operational dirty laundry in the media.

Remember that National Guardsman who asked Donald Rumsfeld why his unit had to use "hillbilly armor" to protect themselves? The soldier was referring to the lack of armored humvees in Iraq, and he exposed that soldiers were finding their own way to armor their vehicles since many lacked armor protection. Had this soldier not publicly asked the question, and had the media not been there to capture the exchange, the interaction might not have been the catalyst it became for improving the safety of our road warriors in Iraq. Embarrassment aside, there is good that comes from allowing people to show their ground-level truth.

I was leaving a meeting at STRATCOM once when I ran into two PAOs I had briefly met who were somehow connected with the Iraqi public affairs effort. One was a U.S. civilian, the other a U.S. military officer. I explained that we needed to assign a point person to get in front of the Iraqi government and explain the value of communications. I didn't think anyone had told the Iraqis that they would be expected to fill Senor's and Kimmitt's shoes. They replied that there were Iraqis who knew how to talk to the press, and when they were ready they'd engage. We didn't need to push and rush them.

We needed to devise a communications strategy, I explained, which would help curb the death rates of U.S. troops and of Iraqis. We needed to get information out to the Iraqis and the Arab world that would empower the people and Iraqi forces, but at the same time educate the average Iraqi to such a degree that they would not tolerate insurgent activities on their street corners.

I'm sure my comments were far less eloquent and included ample doses of profanity, but I was passionate about this point and truly believed that if we were to be successful counterinsurgents, we needed to sway the Iraqi populace. We needed an Iraqi public affairs team that was dedicated to providing a sustained information stream; a steady communications drum needed to be beaten. We had to move beyond reactive informational exchanges between Iraqi officials and the press.

"The coalition reaches out to the Iraqi community now," the civilian said. "And [interim prime minister Ayad] Allawi's going to deal with all that. Their government's forming a communications directorate, I believe."

I agreed that the coalition talked a little to Iraqis, but, I countered, we needed the Iraqis to do it. It wouldn't be perceived as an occupation if the Iraqis were controlling things and doing the talking, I added.

"Sounds great," one said, smiling. "Good luck with that, and let us know if you need help."

Fuck, I thought, we are alone in this and surrounded by a sea of clueless motherfuckers. Nobody saw things the way we did. What was scarier is that nobody, I mean nobody in the coalition, saw the connection between communications and violence. If they saw it, they did nothing to remedy the communications clog because there was no information flowing; there was violence.

Iraqis did have some press interaction between 2003 and 2004, but most of what was published by the press was well rehearsed and tinged with coalition flavor. The few times an Iraqi government official expressed something candidly or was critical of the coalition or the Iraqi Governing Council, they were categorized as paranoid conspiracy theorists. For example, in 2004 there were allegations floating around that al-Shaalan, the minister of defense, had embezzled millions of dollars. While many Iraqis accused him of the crime, the accusers were written off or discredited by guys like Iraq's prime minister, Ayad Allawi, and the allegations were avoided by refocusing the media's attention on the fact that Iraqis were now free to criticize the government, and the fact that Iraqis could level such accusations in the first place was the real story. An elected Iraqi government in 2005 would publish a warrant for al-Shaalan's arrest, accusing him of embezzling billions of dollars. He was eventually convicted in absentia and fled Iraq. Guess those conspiracy theorists were right.

Petraeus and Lt. Gen. James N. Mattis of the U.S. Marine Corps years later would coauthor a new counterinsurgency field manual for the U.S. military. In their final draft they wrote:

Insurgents have an additional advantage in shaping the information environment. While the counterinsurgent seeking to preserve legitimacy must stick to the truth and make sure that words are backed up by appropriate deeds, the insurgent can make exorbitant promises and point out governmental shortcomings, many caused by the insurgency. . . . Insurgents can lie at will, while governments must continuously maintain their integrity to be credible. This often gives the initiative to the insurgents and puts the host nation or COIN [counterinsurgency] personnel on the defensive in the information fight. Understanding the information capabilities and vulnerabilities of insurgents is the first step to effectively counter insurgent information activities and take the initiative away from them.

These were concepts we tried to convince the coalition of in 2004. The Iraqi government needed to talk to the Iraqi populace and dispel rumors and put out accurate information about government progress.

As Eaton prepared to leave and hand over command of the training mission to Petraeus in 2004, he conducted a series of media interviews in which he told reporters the training mission under his management could have been better. He took blame for Iraqi military desertions in April 2004 when a small group of Iraqis were asked to fight but refused. Eaton gave Jim Krane from the Associated Press an interview I had set up that was smeared with accountability. Eaton, in my view, was falling on the sword and making his tenure a low point so anything that would happen in the training mission after his mea culpa would show progress and hope. He was being a good soldier, I think, considering many in the Iraqi Army called him "the father of the Iraqi Army." The CPA public affairs community lost its mind when Krane's article hit the wires.

A CPA staffer sent me an e-mail and questioned Eaton's actions. Seconds after I got the e-mail, I shared it with Jared, who calmly got up and very purposefully walked out of the office. Minutes later I got an e-mail from the CPA staffer, a young kid with some low-level Republican Party connections. He ran back to Dan Senor like an elementary schoolkid and ratted on Jared in an attempt to get him in trouble. He had copied me on an e-mail to Senor that outlined what Jared had done.

Jared had stormed into STRATCOM, and by accounts I received from witnesses (and from this kid's e-mail) he asked for the guy aloud, almost like a Wild West gunfighter looking for a fight in a saloon. When the staffer identified himself, Jared walked over, got in his face, and quietly whispered something menacing into his ear. I told the CPA PAO next time to keep his brawls on the playground instead of bothering senior people with petty bullshit. Jared was being protective of his general, and despite the fact that his actions were a bit unorthodox in the eyes of some college boys, in my book he was simply being a loyal, good soldier. His actions showed me that Jared had gumption and fortitude to stand up for what was right and most of all that he was protective of our unit.

It would be our last real interaction with the idiocy of the CPA. They would leave Iraq soon after that, their indelible mark left on the bloody streets of Iraq. But the run-in would set a tone and send a message as rumors of the event spread. It clearly let PAOs know that we took our mission seriously, that we were territorial about our command and those in it, and that we didn't want to be fucked with. We weren't part of the public affairs clique, and we didn't want to be associated with what was known widely as a broken public affairs machine. We had tried to work with PAOs to get information to Kimmitt, to train Sabeeh, and to improve the way public affairs did business, but we had been unsuccessful. So rather than waste any more time, we pissed on the proverbial tree, marked our territory, and realized that we could rely only on each other. That day Jared and I learned that junkyard dogs run in packs.

The Iraqi face that the coalition wanted and waited for never happened, and it's no wonder: the public affairs guidance from the Pentagon that called for the Iraqi face was signed, approved, and published on April 1, 2004—April Fools' Day.

4

THE BLOG OF WAR

Average casualties in Iraq start to grow significantly in July 2004 through
November 2004, averaging 28 coalition and 40 Iraqi casualties per day.
—Multinational Corps Iraq unclassified intelligence report

I have always had issues with the way the military does business, particularly
the Army. If there is a complex and inefficient way of doing something,
they will find it, and many commissioned officers are programmed to first
say no to new ideas and then look for ways to impede methods that can
improve a process. The Army is an organization that loves to get wrapped
up in processes.

I've always tried to eliminate red tape and find the fastest and most effective way to do things while trying to improve the way I do my job along the
way. Part of this is due to the fact that I am an immensely impatient person
when it comes to all things bureaucratic.

I do things differently, and in saying that I don't necessarily mean that
when I do things my way, it's done better; sometimes my way has sucked,
but most of the time the military improves a process when a soldier thinks
outside the box and does things differently. Trying a fresh approach shouldn't
be a crime, and in the military it is often not welcomed, at least not in the
world of desk jockeys.

As a PAO I had taken notice that military communicators hadn't truly
embraced emerging technology and social media to disseminate information in 2004. Changes were occurring all around within the news and
public relations industries, but the military wasn't keeping up. Newspaper
readership was declining, and the broadcast mediums all had a limited

shelf life. News delivery in the modern era was evolving. News posted on the Web could go viral and have an expanded shelf life. Individual news consumers could more easily share news. Little did I know the transformation the news industry would undergo as cell phones proliferated and social media exploded.

In 2004 the strategic communications effort of the U.S. military focused too much on the traditional media, and the military ignored nontraditional avenues. In addition to lacking creativity in disseminating information, in previous military assignments I came to realize that a large portion of the public and even many in the media didn't really understand how the U.S. military was structured and how it operated—a significant informational shortfall for a military at war.

In 2004 down the street from me lived Anthony Moor, at the time the editor for the *Orlando Sentinel*'s online newspaper and website. The *Sentinel* was my hometown newspaper, and Anthony was a neighbor. Prior to my departure Anthony asked me if I'd be willing to keep a blog of my tour in Iraq. The blog would be published on the *Sentinel*'s website as often as I could write it. I knew no other PAOs had embraced blogs as a way to communicate with the masses. There were some instances when soldiers were maintaining blogs on their own, and some of those were problematic because some of the troops were bitching about stuff and putting too much information on the Internet that put operational integrity at risk, but none of those blogs were "official," and they did not represent the official views of their commands or of the U.S. military. My blog would be an official source of information.

In essence, the public would be virtually embedded with me in Iraq, and they would get information firsthand from the front lines. Information would flow from the battlefield to the public through me. My audience would be primarily American, and this would be an easy way for me to talk to the home front without expending too much effort and without neglecting what I believed was my real mission: talking to the Arab world. I knew I had to talk to our U.S. stakeholders to ensure they knew what their military was doing in Iraq. Through the blog a small group of Americans from my hometown would learn about their military, its soldiers, and Iraqis.

Prior to his departure from Iraq I met with Eaton briefly one evening, and he approved my keeping the blog. I needed his approval to maintain a sustained media presence of an official nature, especially since I represented his command.

The blog was a brilliant idea by Anthony, and from a public affairs perspective there was no question the blog would add value to our mission. I had the necessary approval needed to keep an official account of my time in Iraq, and the blog was incorporated into my duties as the PAO. I didn't seek approval from Multinational Force Iraq, the Defense Department, the Army, or the Army Reserve because I knew the blog would be composed of mostly public information already disseminated in our command's press releases. I had authority from the commanding general of our unit, so I didn't require outside approval from lesser-ranking PAOs two grades below.

The blog was first published on the *Sentinel*'s website on July 4, 2004, long after Eaton was gone. I submitted entries from a journal I kept, starting with the day I left home.

May 2, 2004: Leaving for war

Rosie and I have never left Duncan with a sitter, but now I am on a plane, prepared for a yearlong absence from my son. And I have never left Rosie (we're one of those couples who make other couples sick, we do everything together), but now I sit in this plane, and cruelly replay the memory over and over again of Rosie and Duncan standing in front of me at Orlando International Airport, surrounded by hundreds of travelers bottlenecking through a checkpoint, none aware that my family is about to endure a hardship that millions of families have endured before, but even more millions have never had to experience themselves.

Rosie was crying and Duncan looked around at the people bustling about the terminal. I kissed her and told her everything would be okay, and that I loved her. I touched her one last time, kissed Duncan and walked away. I looked through the crowd and lived a moment I will never forget, but I'm sure each day I will wish I could. I looked back and waved at them as I walked deeper into the terminal, until finally I couldn't see them.

I boarded the plane and left for war.[1]

Within weeks we had thousands of hits on the blog. It was an instant success. There was so much happening within our command that I opted to write a daily blog entry. Regardless of where I was or what had happened, I wrote something for the blog and sent it to Anthony whenever I could. What I was saying in the blog was far different from what my PAO counterparts were spewing. It was balanced, and I included both good and bad news in the blog. I didn't paint a rosy image in the blog. When things were tough, I said so, and this wasn't what PAOs in Baghdad had been doing for the past year.

I didn't focus on the bad news flowing from Baghdad and ignore the small developments and strides we were making and that the Iraqis were making. I wasn't exaggerating things like the CPA; I kept things honest. Some of the stories that I put in the blog went on to be covered by some mainstream media outlets, so some of our milestones were getting coverage.

The *Sentinel*, then owned by the Tribune Company, weeks later began to publish my blog in their sister newspapers and websites all over the country. Anthony had cleverly titled it *Dispatches from Iraq*. I started getting e-mails from people and reporters nationwide, asking me questions about Iraq and thanking me for giving them what they considered an unvarnished view of the war.

As readership grew the *Sentinel* began to publish my blog as a regular column in the Sunday edition of the newspaper. Now the diehard newspaper crowd that might not be fans of online news would be reached too. According to Anthony, that meant more than three hundred thousand readers of the weekly hard-copy Sunday edition would have access to my blog columns, and online the blog was getting roughly twenty thousand hits per month at the *Sentinel*'s website. We couldn't track the visitors throughout the Tribune's other websites, but the blog was on many Tribune-family news sites, including most notably the *Baltimore Sun*, the *Los Angeles Times*, *News Day*, and the *Chicago Tribune*.

Back in the States the blog had blossomed from a hometown war report for readers in central Florida into a national news source about the war. People and press from all over the nation were reaching out to me. It came as no surprise then that PAOs in Georgia and at the Pentagon discovered it.

One afternoon I got a surprising e-mail from Morganthaler at STRATCOM about the blog. While I thought we had done something good by publishing the blog, apparently many in the Army public affairs community thought it was a bad thing.

Morganthaler forwarded me an e-mail thread that started in Georgia somewhere in the gaseous bowels of the Army Reserve's public affairs offices and worked its way up to the Pentagon and eventually over to Iraq. Her e-mail was direct and in essence said that based on the e-mail traffic in the thread, I was to immediately stop writing the blog. Some public affairs staffer safely in the States had come across my blog. The staffer who discovered it forwarded a link to my blog to a superior within the Army Reserve. The superior then forwarded it to counterparts in Georgia and to Washington DC at the Department of the Army, Public Affairs.

The e-mail made its way to PAOs throughout the Defense Department within a couple of days, and anyone and everyone seemed compelled to jump on the pile and offer critical remarks about the blog. The e-mail then traveled throughout the public affairs community in Iraq. True to form, many PAOs had their say, and they all said the same thing: shut it down.

The PAOs who called for the blog to be shut down believed, erroneously, that the blog was being written to draw attention to myself. I think most of them were simply projecting, and cries to close it down were more about controlling people and getting a nonconformist to conform. Admittedly, I hadn't gone around and asked for everyone's permission, and that type of action wasn't tolerated in the zero-defect, zero-tolerance, ask-for-permission-to-wipe-your-ass world of PAOs. The PAOs in the e-mail thread were angry that I hadn't "cleared" the blog or gotten permission. That was untrue. I simply didn't ask them for permission; I asked those in my chain of command, and they supported the blog. It had been cleared by those who mattered in this issue.

I ignored Morganthaler's instructions for a day or so since Eaton had approved the blog, but I had not gotten approval from Petraeus, who had months earlier replaced Eaton as the commanding general. Noting the objection from the PAO community, I thought it would be prudent to get approval from Petraeus. I met with the general late one night in his office, and I informed Petraeus that I had a blog on the Web through my hometown newspaper. He enthusiastically supported it. His only instructions, interestingly enough, were to "keep it honest." Petraeus never asked to see the blog. He never once reviewed it, nor did I have to seek regular approval from him to publish it. This was a vastly different management method for me, because I was used to working with PAOs who have immensely overbearing approval processes.

After I left the general's office I stopped by to speak with our chief of staff about the e-mail thread that Morganthaler had forwarded to me asking me to shut down the blog. Col. Pete Henry of the U.S. Army was an armor officer, a tanker with a "go through the problem and not around it" disposition. I informed him that PAOs were calling for the blog to be shut down. Henry asked me if keeping the blog violated any public affairs rules. I explained it didn't. There were no regulations governing blogs, since they were relatively new.

Some PAOs accused me of exclusivity, I told him. I was a public official, and providing content exclusively to one press organization, other media outlets could argue, was unfair, but the *Sentinel* agreed that if another press organization wanted to publish my blog entries, I would make them available. What we created for the blog was public information. I was surprised that many in the public affairs community argued this point, considering it was common practice for senior officers to write editorials exclusively for civilian publications. In my case it would be a protracted professional relationship, but it was still based on the same premise and precedence. Others questioned my ethics, I told Henry. Many PAOs in the e-mail chain falsely accused me of getting paid for writing the blog, in direct violation of military joint-ethics regulations. None of these people had ever even talked to me. I didn't even know them. They were wrong. I was never paid a dime or compensated in any way for writing the blog.

Henry looked at me and said, "Who do you work for?"

"General Petraeus," I replied.

"There's your answer. Just ignore her when she writes you again," Henry said.

That night I returned to my office and hammered out another blog entry.

Days later I would receive another e-mail, asking me yet again to shut down the blog. As instructed by the chief I ignored Morganthaler, and the blog continued. The PAOs took no action against me, which sent me a very clear message that the PAOs calling for the blog's termination didn't have a legal or ethical justification to shut it down. They never gave me a lawful order, and they never charged me with violating anything. That spoke loudly.

Rear Adm. Greg Slavonic was the U.S. Navy Reserve's chief PAO and the number-two PAO for the U.S. Navy. He was supposed to be the spokesperson in Iraq, but somehow the coalition hired Brig. Gen. Irwin Lessel III of the U.S. Air Force, so Slavonic helped where he could and rode shotgun with Lessel. I asked Slavonic for an assessment about my blog. Days later we met outside of STRATCOM, and he told me he saw nothing wrong with it. In fact, he commended me for it and said he could see why Petraeus liked me so much. He recommended that I "keep charging!"

I next approached our public affairs educators. A small cadre from the Defense Information School had deployed to Iraq for a couple of months. The crew included the commandant of the school, Col. Hiram Bell of the U.S. Army. Bell and his team concluded there was no precedence for a blog. Nothing in the military's regulations or field and training manuals offered any words about blogs. The term was in fact not even in the military communicator's vocabulary. There was nothing in Defense Department doctrine to govern my actions. Therefore, they concluded, I should shut it down until they could further review the issue.

I continued to pen the blog, and soon after I began to get pressured by STRATCOM to complete a report that I publicly and loudly decried as a worthless bureaucratic time sucker. As PAOs we were required to submit reports to operational leaders that showed our past and planned media activity. I always felt it was a way for PAOs to say, "Look at how busy we are, and look at what we're doing." They were justifying their existences.

The reports were pointless, because PAOs would run media searches and track this information at the Pentagon and at other major commands, so why the duplication of effort? As for the future interviews I simply didn't have the manpower to track this information, package it, and disseminate it. The PAO reporting requirements were ridiculously time consuming, and I felt the reports served no meaningful purpose. And, frankly, if the PAOs wanted reports, they could send someone to augment my team so the reports could get completed. As I prioritized work the reports simply were not a priority for me or my team because they didn't impact our mission or objectives.

However, one late evening I had a lull in activity, and I wanted to extend an olive branch to Morganthaler because I thought our relationship might be going down a rough path with the whole blog thing. I submitted a report to her to try to at least seem compliant and cooperative, and she in turn forwarded my report to Lt. Gen. Ricardo Sanchez of the U.S. Army, then the ranking officer in Iraq, and she copied Kimmitt. The e-mail distribution also included other high-level senior executive service personnel in the Defense Department public affairs community and key Army public affairs players. My report informed her of past and future press activity. Morganthaler also copied PAOs at U.S. Central Command and the Joint Chiefs public affairs team and others in the Multinational Force Iraq. However, for some reason, although she copied seemingly everyone, I was not copied on Morganthaler's forward of my report.

Her e-mail advised everyone that I had submitted the media report to her, and she added that as a young PAO I now knew I had to inform her of Petraeus's media interviews. Kimmitt copied me and Petraeus in his reply to Morganthaler and also all the others she had copied, and he complimented me, using the term "young PAO" as she had referred to me in her e-mail, adding that I was doing a great job and working ahead of my contemporaries.

I thanked Kimmitt for his support, and he replied that some people were taken aback by Morganthaler's e-mail. He wanted to ensure that the record was straight in case anyone took it the wrong way.

Kimmitt that day showed me something I had not seen from officers in nearly twenty years in the military: the general openly and strongly backed me. I think the endorsement from him hurt my standing with the PAOs, since they didn't like him, but I appreciated that he had my back. I was guilty by association, but, as I said, I liked Kimmitt, so when he took up for me, I relished it. Now, I was in a key position as a captain, something many PAOs hadn't achieved yet. Morganthaler was a PAO for a three-star general in Iraq. So was I, but I was doing it as a captain and she as a colonel. I had gotten to that career point much faster and with less rank.

Days later I briefed Sanchez on my team's mission and manning-increase request as part of a joint manning document review before we submitted personnel requests to U.S. Central Command. When I introduced myself, Sanchez said, "Wait, what's your name again?"

"Captain Steve Alvarez, sir. I'm the PAO."

"Oh, okay, I've heard of you," Sanchez said, smiling sneakily. "Go ahead, young PAO," he said sarcastically as he smiled.

Former Defense Department chief PAO Torie Clarke recommended in her 2006 book that public affairs personnel use multiple tools to reach people. However, while she stated that blogs have impact and influence, she also admitted that she was not yet sure what their "real, long-term role will be."[2]

I think PAOs in the defense industry looked at blogs as something done by hacks. There was an influx of freelance journalists in Iraq telling unfettered truths about the war via blogs. Some were fantastic and had high-quality writing and photography; some were bad and amateurish. Some in the mainstream media tried to write off bloggers as people who lacked journalistic credibility in a move to discredit and silence bloggers and remove competition. The Pentagon also tried to silence military bloggers who weren't thoughtful in their blog entries and violated operational security rules by posting sensitive information on their blogs. Some had administrative punishments leveled against them.

About one year later after I rotated back to the States and two years after I first penned my blog, I would learn that the public affairs office at U.S. Central Command had established a dedicated public affairs blog team that provided information to bloggers. The team engaged bloggers with information as they did the mainstream media in an effort to get information to blog readers. In conversations I had with the CENTCOM blog team in January 2006, the team estimated that their blog-team initiative had reached more than twenty million in the blogosphere. Blogs, they said, were critical information mediums, and the military realized the importance of these forums in the information war. Senior defense leaders, including most general officers in key positions, at one point kept blogs on official military websites. Many more have embraced social media forums such as Facebook and Twitter. Bloggers are now referred to as influencers within the communications industry, and they are often trusted information sources.

A month after talking with Central Command's blog team, then U.S. defense secretary Donald Rumsfeld would say in a speech to the Council on Foreign Relations:

> Government public affairs and public diplomacy efforts must reorient staffing, schedules and culture to engage the full range of media that are having such an impact today. Our U.S. Central Command, for example, has launched an online communications effort that includes electronic news updates and a links campaign, that has resulted in several hundred blogs receiving and publishing CENTCOM content. The U.S. government will have to develop the institutional capability to anticipate and act within the same news cycle. That will require instituting 24-hour press operation centers, elevating Internet operations and other channels of communications to the equal status of traditional 20th century press relations. It will result in much less reliance on the traditional print press, just as the publics of the U.S. and the world are relying less on newspapers as their principal source of information.[3]

Really wish he would have said that about two years earlier and saved me the headache of justifying my blog with PAOs.

More than two years after my blog was published a U.S. military PAO who served in Iraq would write a white paper and present it at a U.S. Army public affairs symposium. He would admit, despite his earlier calls for my blog's termination, that blogs add value to the public affairs mission, and he encouraged his peers to embrace the concept.

It is amazing how some of our PAOs will follow the leader once a concept is embraced from above, but they lack the stones to boldly step up and forge a new path when something is not tried and true. They are immobilized by a fear of failure, I suppose. It takes no courage and requires no boldness to vocalize support for blogs once the secretary of defense has stated support for it or after the chief of public affairs for the Army has said it is a good idea. PAOs should be driving change from their level upward and not the other way around.

Interestingly, Morganthaler was also a blogger during her tour in Iraq, although she didn't make it a part of her official public affairs duties. Instead, she used it to write about what she called her adventures in Iraq. She wrote about things like how great it was to have air-conditioning at her quarters and office and about how good the food was at the chow hall, but she also covered the personal challenges she faced serving in Iraq, like when she complained about living too far from the pool and how the gym was smaller at Camp Victory than in the Green Zone. Morganthaler wrote in her blog that she was the only alabaster strawberry-blonde colonel in Baghdad. She also talked about how she didn't like getting challenged by security personnel who were simply doing their job when they asked her for identification.

The Defense Department in 2004 would issue a report that said, "The U.S. needs trusted, reliable web sites conducive to dialogue on political, intellectual, and cultural levels. The impact of digital convergence is only beginning to be understood by political and military leaders. U.S. strategic communication has not evolved in ways to coordinate and leverage the potential of Internet-centric information dissemination."[4] Based on my experience with the blog, all I can say to that is "No shit!" And I didn't need to convene a board to arrive at that conclusion.

A month after I left Iraq in 2005 the Defense Department would begin to crack down on bloggers as public opinion of the war plummeted. Military bloggers, even those maintaining a personal, unofficial blog, were required to ask permission from their commanders to keep blogs, and they had to register with the U.S. Army's Web Risk Assessment Cell or the Defense Department's Joint Web Risk Assessment Cell. The cells monitored blogs for operational security violations. As a PAO it smelled like military censorship.

Sometime later, CENTCOM would create and publish the *Blogging*

Handbook for PAOs, which described in depth how to use blogs to communicate with the public and the information viral effect they can have in the communications sector. Morganthaler would have benefited from reading the military's blog book and registering her site, though on her blog I found a picture of her with NBC's Tom Brokaw. In the photo she is violating a basic security tenet that stipulates military personnel should hide or remove their restricted access and security badges when being photographed. The logic, security experts told me, was that they didn't want the insurgents to create a likeness of access badges by using images found on the Internet.

My blog, after all the professional pissing and moaning, would go on to be one of the most successful initiatives from my time in Iraq. More than one year after I returned from the war, U.S. Central Command officials stated that my blog was the inspiration behind the creation of their strategic blog initiatives and the reason they assembled a blog team in Tampa. *Dispatches from Iraq* made the public affairs community rethink its approach to blogs and appreciate the viral affect the forums offer the online world. It made the Defense Department look at nontraditional communications mediums and embrace electronic forums.

Although there may have been blogs kept by military personnel prior to my blog, Anthony's idea would be historic in that it was the first time a military official was a blogger in his official role. Most important, *Dispatches from Iraq* would be the first-ever official military blog in U.S. military history.

I guess you can teach an old Army new tricks.

5

DAVID VERSUS GOLIATH

80 percent of all attacks launched by the insurgency are against coalition forces, but 80 percent of the casualties are suffered by Iraqis.

—U.S. congressional report, October 2005

In May 2004, a little more than a month before the transfer of authority, I sent an e-mail to then U.S. Army major general David H. Petraeus. It was about nine o'clock in the morning in Baghdad, which meant it was around two o'clock in the morning back in the States. I introduced myself as the current PAO for the command and gave him a short update about press activity surrounding his arrival in Baghdad. Within minutes of my sending the e-mail, I got a reply from him thanking me, and he said he looked forward to getting a full briefing when he arrived. Little did I know that his immediate reply was a harbinger of the pace he would set for the command during his tenure as our commanding general.

Petraeus was an unbelievably energetic man. He had an internal power source that enabled him to operate at almost full throttle all the time, but his professional pace wasn't reckless and visibly hyperactive, as is sometimes seen when people do too much at once. He was steady, calculated, and calm yet fierce in his devotion to his duty. Although he was juggling about a trillion things, remarkably he did all of it well, and everything seemed to get a healthy dose of his attention. Although he was competitive it seemed he was most competitive with himself. His brain was constantly processing things. He had the most acute attention to detail I have ever seen in a military officer, but he didn't come across as being a micromanager, anally retentive, or an obsessive compulsive, and I've seen him do on-the-spot corrections on soldiers who were wearing the uniform incorrectly. He once gave an Army Reserve colonel a lesson on how to properly wear her Kevlar helmet, and he helped her adjust it and properly fit it on her head so it wouldn't look like she was wearing a yarmulke. I didn't escape his keen eye. Months after we started working together he asked me why I wasn't wearing shoulder-sleeve insignia, also known as a "combat patch." Back then soldiers who served in a combat zone for thirty days could permanently wear their unit's insignia on their right uniform sleeve. I had earned the right to wear the U.S. Central Command patch on my right sleeve because I had been in Iraq for a few months, but I was so busy I had not really given the patch any thought.

"You should be proud of that. You've earned it," Petraeus told me.

I acknowledged him and offered no excuses, but I admit that once I walked away from him I forgot all about the patch. Several days later I suspect my grace period had expired because he brought it to my attention again. There would not be a third time. That night I hand-sewed the patch onto my uniform.

Petraeus had plenty of other things to worry about, and the way I see it is that he cared enough about people to make those adjustments. Army leaders have an old adage that says mission first, but people always. I think he lived by that, and I enjoyed the fact that he noticed stuff like that and made the corrections.

We once published a story in our command newsletter about an Iraqi unit that had completed training and was starting to go out on operations. Jared had embedded with these guys, and he took some pictures while out with the Iraqis. The picture accompanying the news story that Jared wrote was of an Iraqi soldier with ammunition belts stretched across his chest like Pancho Villa, sporting a rag tied around his head like a pirate.

Within minutes of sending out the newsletter electronically, I got an e-mail from Petraeus that he wanted to see me. I paid him a visit that night, and he told me he did not like the image we had selected for the newsletter. The Iraqi did not look like a professional warrior. I agreed and apologized for using the picture, but I added that that was what the Iraqi soldiers in this unit looked like and that the image we had used was the best in the bunch. They had very loose uniform standards, and there was little military discipline being applied to their attire.

Part of the problem was the supply system that we managed for the Iraqis, and the other part of the problem was that there was no Iraqi military uniform regulation. If he wanted Iraqis to look more professional, the problem wasn't the picture; the problem was the reality on the ground. The Iraqis needed uniform rules and standards. My visit that night turned into a realization for the general, and rather than chew my ass and focus on something my team had done, he used the opportunity as a way to fix a problem that had received little attention until we printed a picture of an Iraqi Pancho Villa. He focused on the positive.

I've worked for a few generals in my time, and most kept us guessing. We couldn't really figure out their intent, and they were moody or hard to read. Petraeus routinely talked to his staffers, making it easy to determine what he wanted. He didn't have to spell things out for intuitive staffers. If they were perceptive, they fed off of his comments and moved ahead accordingly. During my professional relationship with him, I never once asked for his permission to do my job, which is rare in an Army officer, at least in my experience. Most Army officers I had served with up to that point were incredibly controlling and demanded approval and review for even the smallest of projects. In garrison (meaning a unit is not deployed or out in the field) officers don't seem to have enough to do, and they cultivate a zero-defect environment that prunes creativity and initiative. In Baghdad the Iraqis weren't the only ones experiencing newfound freedom, so I spread my wings and enjoyed some breathing room. We launched the command's newspaper and website, two very public projects without his input, and Petraeus was ecstatic about it and told us the products were "Super!"— which, if you speak Petraeus, means that he was extremely satisfied. He never reviewed prior to public release a single press release, article, video, or photograph we disseminated, and he never once read one of my blog entries before they were published.

When Petraeus assumed command at the unit, he also assumed the role as chief of the NATO training mission in Iraq. On June 7, 2004, I met with Petraeus late one night. I remember after he shook my hand he offered me a chair and looked me over as I sat down. His eyes were scanning me up and down, and he did not seem too impressed. His first words were a little grainy and hard to swallow.

"I don't need a PAO. I am my own PAO," he said as he slid down into an ornate chair in the middle of his office. I acknowledged the remark and continued with my media briefing, but as I spoke my mind wandered, and sometimes my expletive-laden thoughts were getting much louder in my head than the words coming out of my mouth. I struggled to stay focused after the remark, and I immediately disliked him and his ring-knocking, arrogant, ivory-towered demeanor.

We couldn't be more different. He was active duty; I was a reservist. He was a field grade officer; I was a company grade. I had gone to college after serving my first hitch in the enlisted ranks on active duty; he was a West Pointer. I had gotten commissioned late in my career; he earned his right after he finished West Point. I had a master's degree; he had a doctorate. He seemed worldly and refined; I was street smart and rough.

You don't fucking need me? Fine, send me the fuck home, I thought, as I made recommendations concerning whom I thought he should interview with and why. I explained that a press trip to visit Iraqi security forces might be good since he was taking over the training mission. It would be a good opportunity for him to see the Iraqi forces, meet the advisers, and get some exposure as the man taking the helm of the training mission. His eyes continued to scan me as I handed him a recommended press interview schedule, and he leaned back in his chair and sighed.

"Look, Steve, you can handle my public affairs logistics until you earn my confidence," Petraeus said. Although I had more to discuss with him, I felt that was the silver-spoon way of saying that he was done listening to me.

Earn your confidence? I got your confidence right here, I thought to myself. I immediately started thinking maybe the major would like his job back. Needless to say, I was disappointed. This guy, I thought, was going to be just another Army officer. What was it that was causing him to take this position? Was it that I was a reservist and he didn't care for reserve officers? The military preaches that active duty, the reserve, and the National Guard are one team in one fight, but part-time warriors are often looked down on by their active-duty counterparts, and there are stereotypes and prejudices. In fairness, some reserve and National Guard officers aren't that great. They are bloated, unmotivated opportunists who climb the ranks by checking boxes, keeping their noses clean, and outlasting those who grow sick of the reserve system. Then again, I have seen some active-duty officers who wouldn't know what leadership was if it bit them in the ass, so I think there is no component free of poor officers.

Maybe the general thought that I didn't have the experience based on my rank. It could be that he equated capability with rank, and because I was a captain he suspected I would not cut it. Professionally, I had a lot more experience as a communicator than many of those who were senior PAOs. He did not know I had almost twenty years in uniform and that I was about the same age as, if not older than, some colonels. Could it be that all he was seeing was my rank? In fairness, he knew nothing about my educational credentials, my civilian experience, and the fact that I was a mustang (what naval personnel call a prior enlisted officer).

Honestly, the comments bothered me for about ten minutes. In a very public profession like public relations, you have to have thick skin and be open to very heavy and sometimes ungraceful criticism. Petraeus's remarks weren't too bad, and they certainly weren't disabling, so I moved out. In hindsight I think he wanted to let me know that I needed to earn my spot on his team. I was happy for the chance to try out, and his comments did not impact anything. I came out of the gate charging just as hard as I would have had he given me a gift basket to greet me. What he thought of me didn't matter. I had a job to do.

Over the next three weeks Petraeus had several interviews per day with key media players. I often joked with Petraeus that I had him on "three-a-days." It was a busy press schedule for him as he squeezed in media interviews between his meetings and trips, but he was the most accommodating officer I've ever worked with as a PAO. If there was something on his calendar that I could make media worthy, we did it.

In addition to having interviews with some of the news industry's biggest names, Petraeus spent part of his first few weeks traveling around Iraq with the media, showcasing the Iraqi training program. As he traveled I sent with him a small entourage of press. We did a media blitz, a concentrated, intense media campaign that got his name and face everywhere. We worked eighteen- to twenty-hour days, seven days per week, during this period, and we kept the pace for about a month, and with each interview Petraeus was fresh and crisp as if each one was his first. Sometime during our campaign Petraeus learned about my civilian academic and professional credentials, and he began to ask me questions about his media interactions. How did he come across, what did I think, and what recommendations did I have?

We were gelling, and our work during his first few weeks in Iraq proved to him I could easily handle the job. In fact, he was so impressed with our media campaign that he surprised us when he pinned medals on me and Jared just a few weeks after our initial meeting, awarding us with an impact medal. Days later via e-mail he would tell U.S. Central Command and other military leaders at the Pentagon and in Baghdad that I was his PAO and that he was retaining me on his team. He reached out to CENTCOM and told them not to think they needed to send someone more senior while I was there.

I felt relieved after reading his note, but I felt good because I had not set out to impress Petraeus or convince him of anything. I was only doing my job and by doing that earned a spot on his team. Despite his proclamation and endorsement of me, though, several PAOs, including a one-star officer, would try to replace me as the command's PAO during my deployment, and Petraeus would turn them all down. He stuck by me, and that earned my loyalty, trust, and respect for eternity, and he earned his spot on my team, which truth be told I think has more rigid acceptance standards.

Petraeus was then widely considered the most gifted U.S. military officer in service, and he had given me his stamp of approval. Rather than view that as a sign that maybe some introspection was needed, that maybe they should rethink their feelings toward me, and that I wasn't a bad guy after all, some PAOs circled their wagons. It made me a moving target, and I wore a scarlet letter during my tour. While the Baghdad and Pentagon PAOs could pick fights with me, they knew Petraeus and Kimmitt were in my corner, and that, I think, is what truly angered them.

I should note, though, that Petraeus was right: he doesn't need a PAO. When reporters e-mail him he responds back to them personally; he doesn't pass the e-mail along to a PAO or a staffer and have them respond. I have seen the man respond to Podunk newspaper reporters and individual citizens just as quickly as he has responded to a foreign affairs columnist from a newspaper of record. He understands the value of being accessible and answering to the media and the public. He is a one-man communications dynamo, and he is like this because he understands the importance of public relations in his role. Petraeus values communication.

Many senior military leaders make themselves inaccessible, and their PAOs filter their access. What separates Petraeus in the communications arena is that he is approachable and responsive. In Baghdad he understood that communicating was critical to the command, to the mission in Iraq, to the Army, and to the administration. Our war was one of perception and ideology, not territory or real estate. We could take territory whenever we wanted to, but holding that land harmoniously without excessive force was a different story. To succeed we needed to win hearts and minds, and he knew that.

When Petraeus arrived in Iraq the training mission he took over had received little media attention. In fact, the most popular story at that point was Eaton's interview with the Associated Press, so having hit that low point, we had no place to go but up in the media. The training mission lacked a face, and the broader mission in Iraq had become its own entity, represented by snippets of catastrophic violence and burgeoning bureaucracy. Petraeus's star was rising in the ranks, but he wasn't widely known to the American populace. An author had written about him in a book and covered his work in northern Iraq as a division commander, but overall he was not a household name, though many soldiers had heard of him.

I made it my goal to make his name and face synonymous with success in Iraq, very much like Norman Schwarzkopf had been in the Gulf War.

There isn't an American who was an adult during the Gulf War who does not know Stormin' Norman. The guy personified the coalition effort to expel Iraq from Kuwait. Americans watched him talk about military operations, and they knew he would bring home a victory. We needed a calming, reassuring, and confident face to achieve the same thing, and I intended to make that face Petraeus's.

The plan was simple. We would saturate the Western media with information about our mission, and the information would be delivered by Petraeus. This would put a face on our mission and offer a charismatic general the opportunity to speak to the Western masses through the press. We would engage all of the major news organizations and on-air personalities to reach this objective. In addition, we would get Petraeus in front of Arab media and have him build trust with them and try to repair some of the strained relations that the Defense Department had caused. The difference was that as we engaged the Arab media, we would have Iraqi security force leaders there to speak to the Arab press. After several weeks of media trips, interviews, and backgrounders, we would fade Petraeus slowly to the point where only Iraqi leadership would be talking to the Arab press. This would be a gradual scaling back of Petraeus's media footprint, but it would be done steadily as the Iraqis grew accustomed to interacting with the media and as they managed more of the security of their nation. The plan included weekly joint press conferences with Petraeus or his senior leaders and Iraqi leaders from the Iraqi Ministries of Defense and Interior.

Like other things we executed on our team, I never told Petraeus about my plan to make him the next Schwarzkopf. I had to be careful in my marketing of him because I do not think he would have supported such a plan had he discovered I was going to make it about him. While I think he would have done anything reasonable to help me communicate about our mission, making him the face of the U.S. mission in Iraq was something I simply do not think he would have knowingly supported. With this plan in my head I moved forward and engaged the media. Tom Brokaw, Dan Rather, Geraldo Rivera, Christiane Amanpour, Anderson Cooper, and Peter Jennings, just to name a few, were all willing and eager to interview

Petraeus. *Time, Newsweek*, the *New York Times*, the *Washington Post*, the Associated Press, and other major publications and outlets all agreed to interview him and cover our mission.

By the early summer of 2004 *Newsweek International's* Rod Nordland wanted to interview Petraeus. We took Rod and his photographer to some Iraqi training bases, and they attended meetings with us and got some great information about our mission. After spending a couple of days with us, Nordland and I spoke about putting Petraeus on the cover of *Newsweek*. I thought it was a great move, and it would satisfy an informational void in our mission. It would certainly serve as a propellant when done in unison with all of the other media efforts we were pushing with Petraeus.

I was wrong.

On July 5, 2004, *Newsweek* put Petraeus on its cover with the words "Can This Man Save Iraq?" sprawled across it. With the help of the busy media schedule we had placed him on, he was literally everywhere: on most of the networks, in most newspapers of record, in Europe, in the Middle East, in most newsmagazines, on the radio; we left no forum uncovered. We had an articulate, charismatic, and confident general officer telling people the way ahead in Iraq was going to be rough, but there was reason for optimism. He had a calming effect in his interviews; reporters told me they walked away feeling everything was going to be okay after talking to him. He wasn't grim or defensive, but he wasn't overly optimistic, either. He set just the right tone needed in Iraq, and it was unlike anything anyone had done since we invaded. He wasn't confrontational. There were no promises being made, and he often said that the mission to train Iraqi forces was "like building an airplane in flight." We had succeeded in saturating the press with Petraeus. Now we simply needed to measure what the result of that saturation would be and how we could move forward with it.

The *Newsweek* article along with all of the network coverage caused a massive demand for Petraeus. My phone rang about every fifteen minutes with a new request from the press. I received hundreds of e-mails from media, and it got to such a point that I had to pick which interviews would best give us a return on investment of our time. I didn't need to make phone calls any more to market Petraeus and our mission; instead, our media-blitz campaign had put us on the map, and my phone and in-box were exploding with activity. He was like a rock star. Everywhere we traveled soldiers wanted their pictures taken with him, and even the press took personal photographs with him. Slavonic even asked me for an autographed copy of the magazine, as did other PAOs. Days after the magazine hit the streets I met with Petraeus about the additional media interviews I needed to schedule.

"Seems we got a little too much attention, Steve," he told me as I entered his office.

I had been so caught up in the euphoria of the plan and how smoothly it was working that I hadn't thought about the potential threats. I hadn't considered the political ramifications of oversaturation, and I hadn't thought about mitigating risks. *Newsweek* certainly built up Petraeus's role in Iraq. I think they were spot-on: he was our way home, and he was due this type of attention. Any reasonable person who understood the mission and the climate in 2004 knew the article was fair. Inside the magazine the article was the centerfold, with a large photo of Petraeus sandwiched between two Iraqi officers, and it was titled "Mission Impossible?"

The article did not sit well with U.S. leaders in Baghdad. Gen. George Casey of the U.S. Army, the ranking military officer in Iraq and the man who became Petraeus's boss when he took over as commanding general of Multinational Force Iraq, took issue with the article. Joining Casey in the unhappy ranks was Ambassador John Negroponte, who replaced Bremer as the chief U.S. administrator in Iraq.

Nordland's article made Petraeus look like he was fighting the war single-handedly. The article did not mention Casey or Negroponte, and it had some philosophical shifts from the current command culture. Petraeus was focused on quality and not quantity of Iraqi forces, and he made it clear in Nordland's piece that Iraqi sovereignty might place pressure on the Iraqis to field a force too quickly. The Iraqis needed time to develop their forces. In addition, in some parts of the piece he was painted as bubbly and seemed aloof in regards to the deaths of some of his men, but I understood the context of what he was saying and how he meant it, and that just didn't translate too well in the article. However, it was still a very good article. Maybe it was the honesty that came out in the article that caused the fallout, but it shouldn't have. We needed this kind of candor and transparency in Iraq. Our mission demanded it.

The article made Petraeus and our command look like we were the way home when, in fact, we were, so we had achieved our objective, but I had fucked up recommending that Petraeus do the *Newsweek* cover story. I fucked up big time because I had not taken egos into consideration when I did my threat matrix. Shit, friendly fire was not even part of the equation. I honestly did not think anyone could ever have a problem with the attention we were getting the U.S. mission in Iraq. My inexperience working at such a high level in such a complex, politically charged environment cost us deeply. I had walked us into a political minefield, and we would be forced to stop our march forward because we didn't want to step on any more.

Casey, a four-star general, had taken command as Iraq's ranking officer, and it wasn't so much as a blip on the media's radar screen compared to the amount of attention we were getting Petraeus upon his arrival. Similarly, Negroponte didn't make a big splash with the press when he arrived in Iraq. Although all three men were interviewed and got media attention, it was Petraeus who commanded the spotlight. During our blitz period I reviewed a public affairs report that tracked media story lines and subjects. A table showed the number of press reports done on the war's leaders. The table included Negroponte, Bremer, Sanchez, Casey, Petraeus, Eaton, Kimmitt, and others. Petraeus was mentioned in hundreds of news reports per week, whereas the sum of all the others was hundreds less. Collectively, Casey and Negroponte weren't in the media as much as we had gotten Petraeus in the news with our media campaign. Jared and I had managed to do what a small army of U.S. PAOs located in several countries couldn't accomplish for Casey and Negroponte.

Casey asked Petraeus to ratchet back the interviews, and Petraeus complied. Prior to his gag order Petraeus had about fifteen to twenty interviews per week with major media outlets such as ABC, CNN, CBS, NBC, the *Washington Post*, the *New York Times*, and the like, but we cut back to three or four interviews per week after Casey's order. After a few weeks of ratcheting back, Petraeus told me we needed to cut back on the interviews even more. His leaders were still complaining, and they didn't like seeing him in the headlines. Soon Petraeus was averaging only a couple of interviews per month.

Weeks after the initial request for suppression Petraeus completely shut down, and he was precluded from interacting with the media. Petraeus, a three-star general leading the exit strategy in Iraq for a multinational command, a man who had the president's highest confidence and endorsement, and a man who routinely communicated with former secretary of defense Rumsfeld, would now spend the next seven months in the most visible role in Iraq, conspicuously quiet, muted, all because his bosses would not allow him to talk to the press.

Casey's PAOs were oblivious to the gag order because they bombarded me for months with interview requests they had received from the media. I responded that the general had a busy travel schedule and couldn't accommodate the interviews. I wouldn't tell anyone the truth about what was happening. It would embarrass my boss, and it would show disharmony in the upper echelons of the coalition. I had screwed up enough, and I certainly wasn't going to let this get out.

Our campaign hit a wall, and while I felt it was a wasted opportunity, I felt worse for Petraeus. Shortly after we were muted by Casey, the Iraqi-face phase of the mission kicked in, and that solidified our fate. Media relations at the command would come to a virtual standstill as the war entered a violent 2004 fall season. Attacks in Baghdad reached more than one hundred per day, and as the din of the violence got louder, the coalition grew quieter. The insurgents were talking loudly through their fiery rhetoric and through their actions. Oddly, although Petraeus had been muted, Casey didn't jump in and fill the void immediately created by Petraeus's silence. For that matter, neither did Negroponte, and the new coalition spokesperson, Lessel, was absent from media circles too. They all waited for the Iraqis to talk and took no steps to help the Iraqis step up to the microphone.

Because we could not talk to the media I redirected press queries to the

Ministries of Defense and Interior and offered the Iraqi PAOs guidance, data, and information so they could respond to the queries, but the Iraqi chains of command refused to allow press interactions, and the silence continued. The only voice that was heard was that of the insurgents and those against the coalition; they were the only people talking. Where once there were stories about our mission, media reports again began to show a trend toward violence. While stories in the international press had for weeks been about turning a corner in Iraq and a hopeful future, focused on the Iraqi forces and on Petraeus, they were now starting to slump back into stories of the sad U.S. slog.

I was responsible for our command's silence. I could blame it on Casey and Negroponte, but the bottom line is that I never took them into consideration as I conducted my media blitz, and I should have thought about Casey's perceptions. It was a huge lesson learned for me. It was immature of me to think a professional military officer like Casey would accept that a mission he was leading was getting extraordinary press coverage it had not received since we had ousted Hussein. Not since the end of the reporter embeds had this much good press been circulating throughout the world about Iraq. I could have easily avoided all of this had I simply briefed Casey and outlined the plan for him or recommended to Petraeus that he brief Casey on our press plans. Instead, I didn't take anyone but Petraeus into account, and now the command and my boss were paying for my error.

I'm not a big fan of rigidity, so while the instructions were clear (Petraeus could not do interviews), I found loopholes. In the months that followed Casey's gag order, we embedded reporters and columnists alike throughout our command. We had reporters shadow the general and be "flies on the wall" during his staff meetings and as he traveled to meet with Iraqi leadership throughout the country. We had one ground rule for the press: Petraeus could not be quoted in any story or be the subject of any news item. All the reporters and columnists we hosted, guys such as Dave Ignatius, Greg Jaffe, Fouad Ajami, and Dexter Filkins, to name a few, all agreed to abide by the ground rules. Al-Arabiya, a Pan-Arab satellite news channel, traveled with Petraeus extensively in a deal I had set up with them, and they too agreed to keep him off their videos. Luckily, policy coincided with our silence at that time. I explained to the media that the Pentagon wanted U.S. forces to take a backseat to the Iraqis in the press to save my boss and the U.S. military the embarrassment of admitting what had truly transpired.

For months there was nothing but silence. A couple of times in the fall of 2004 Petraeus was directed by senior civilian PAO officials at the Defense Department to interact with the press. Once he was asked to write an editorial for the *Washington Post*. Another time we did a press conference with the Pentagon press pool via video teleconference. We also hosted several media military analysts, and he had very frank discussions with them. All three interactions were conducted in response to critical media reports and to help the administration shore up public support. They were all reactive solutions orchestrated by Pentagon types who had no idea one of their media darlings had been forced to be quiet.

Months after a prolonged silence I launched a two-pronged attack to get Petraeus back into the media in hopes we could get the Iraqis talking. I explained to Petraeus that we had lost a lot of ground in the information war because of our prolonged silence and that our media absence was hurting the mission. We needed to get him and the Iraqis talking, and we couldn't wait another minute.

Petraeus asked me to move forward with my plan but to keep his "fingerprints off of it." I understood what he meant. We needed to do what was good for the mission, but he could not be perceived as being insubordinate. The mission simply couldn't sustain a high-level story line of contempt. I moved forward with the plan.

A friend who was a PAO at the Pentagon would tell some high-level PAOs that he had heard rumors Petraeus was silenced by Casey. Simultaneously, as my buddy worked his magic inside the Beltway, I confided in a friend who was a member of the press about our media ban. He said there was a lot of speculation about why Petraeus wasn't talking, considering the splash he made when he arrived in Baghdad.

As we had planned my reporter pal sent me an e-mail requesting an interview with Petraeus. I responded, as we had outlined in a conversation, that we could not do the interview. I offered no explanation, and I was dismissive in my response. My friend put on a front in an e-mail response to me and acted annoyed, and he forwarded his request, and my flippant reply, to some senior PAOs in Baghdad, complaining that I was a bit brusque for his liking, and he asked them to encourage me to grant the interview.

The PAOs contacted me. They explained the value of the interview and said they appreciated the fact that Petraeus was busy but that he was an essential cog in Iraq, and they wanted him to consider the interview. I pushed back softly, and without offering much of an explanation I declined the interview, as I had been declining them in previous months. I ignored subsequent calls from the PAOs and let their e-mails sit in my in-box for a couple of days.

I knew the PAOs in Iraq would escalate the situation and get the Defense Department involved, and I also knew they'd circumvent me. There were a few exchanges between public affairs staffers in Iraq and Washington DC, and before long Petraeus was contacted and directed to do the interview. We had leveraged the power of the Pentagon's PAOs and PAOs in Baghdad against Casey's media-ban order. All of these PAOs thought they were making us do something we did not want to do, but little did they know we had just manipulated them to do exactly what Casey did not want. Because it came from the top at the Pentagon, there was little Casey could do but just watch and agree to let Petraeus do the interview.

When the interview directive came around from the Pentagon, I don't think Petraeus realized I was the one behind it, and I never told him. I think he thought he was being asked to do something by the Pentagon, and he complied with their directives. I not only kept his fingerprints off it, but kept my own off it as well. Even though the directive to engage the press came from the Pentagon, we still asked Casey to approve the interview, and because the request was coming from the secretary of defense's office, one of Casey's bosses, there wasn't a lot he could do but approve it.

Casey acquiesced, and we did the interview. The interview shook Petraeus loose a little bit. Eventually, U.S. Central Command leaders figured out Petraeus had been noticeably quiet. I'm not sure how Gen. John Abizaid found out, but he knew that Petraeus wasn't talking to the media. Abizaid told Petraeus he couldn't be quiet forever, and slowly we began to thaw from our deep freeze. We were still expected to ask for permission to do interviews, and we complied, but we had been quiet for seven months, and now the insurgency was in full swing.

In early 2005 we began to step out of our fog, and Petraeus was able to talk again because the Iraqi elections were approaching. Our press activity picked up right where it had left off, and as the Iraqi elections neared Petraeus, according to my media friends, became the most-sought-after interviewee in Iraq. The Iraqi training mission was still considered critical by the public and the press. It had been several months, and the world wanted to see what progress had been made. I had been bugging Petraeus to talk for a couple of months, and now that the Pentagon and CENTCOM were encouraging him, he came out of deep freeze.

"Okay, you're grinding me down. Start bringing them on. With whom do you want to start?" Petraeus told me as we ramped up for another go-round with the media.

I had a list, and it included plenty of high-profile Western press to appease the Pentagon cronies and enough Arab media to satisfy me. Dan Rather was coming back for another interview. Brian Williams from NBC was making his first trip to meet Petraeus. Geraldo Rivera was also coming back for another visit, and the list went on and on, but a lot of time had been lost. We had been quiet for seven long months, and thanks to that silence the U.S. exit strategy and the man leading it had been kept out of the public eye.

As the 2005 elections were under way we conducted interviews with CNN, Fox, NBC, CBS, ABC, and other major news organizations. One interview from that time stands out for me. I took Fox News' Dana Lewis to meet members of the Muthana Brigade, a well-oiled Iraqi unit in Baghdad that was going to be a backdrop for Lewis's preelection report about Petraeus.

As Petraeus visited with the Iraqi brigade, fighting erupted nearby, and explosions and gunfire echoed off buildings as Lewis conducted his interview. As Lewis continued his interview, Petraeus started walking toward the fighting. In tow was the Muthana Brigade.

Where in the fuck is he going? I thought. Petraeus's security detail looked at each other and reacted, fanning out, scanning the buildings, and eyeballing cars as they approached. We walked out of a little-known Green Zone gate and onto the streets of Baghdad, continuing to move toward the sounds of the fighting. I wasn't too thrilled with the point he was trying to make, considering what I knew, but this was the kind of balls this man had.

As shots grew louder in the distance and the sounds of explosions intensified, Lewis winced and flinched and asked Petraeus if he trusted the Iraqi soldiers. Petraeus responded that he had been in Iraq so long that he not only trusted the Iraqi soldiers, but could sometimes barely tell them apart from U.S. soldiers. He was right—these guys looked pretty tough, and in the few months we had been silent, they went from looking like Pancho Villa to looking like professional warriors. What Petraeus didn't know was that an Iraqi sergeant had approached me minutes before the news team arrived and told me that they didn't have enough ammunition to be effective on patrol. He said for weeks we had been sending them out on missions with very little ammunition, and he wanted someone to help them. Weeks earlier the unit had come under heavy fire on Haifa Street, and many Iraqi soldiers were killed, the sergeant said, when they ran out of ammo. The soldiers had been given only one magazine of ammunition for their weapons.

I told him I would look into it. I asked him not to share the ammo issue with Lewis. He should give me a chance to resolve it. Besides, if he did say something to Lewis, the information might give the enemy intelligence about the combat power of his unit, and that could be bad, since the Muthana Brigade routinely patrolled Baghdad. He agreed. I tipped off our supply folks about what I had learned, and I was told that within days the soldiers were given more than enough ammunition and even had a surplus to refit themselves after operations. Luckily, that day the Iraqis didn't need any ammo. We walked back into the Green Zone without firing a single round, but it was a low-risk, highly visible gamble, and for Petraeus it paid off.

With that interview and the others that followed, our trajectory started upward again, and Petraeus sent me a note. "Look's like you're in business again, Steve!" Petraeus said. It was a bittersweet moment, because I was glad to see him talking to the press and doing what came very naturally to him, talking passionately about our mission, humanizing Iraqi and coalition soldiers, and offering perspective to a task that seemed daunting.

Deep down I knew it was just too late, seven months too late, and the mission had suffered a huge setback, one we'd never recover from while I was there, a setback that would cost a lot of lives and enable an insurgency to entrench itself in Iraq.

The airplane we had been building in flight had crashed and burned.

6

IRAQI MEDIA TEAM

In a twelve-month period in Baghdad 4,279 deaths are reported in the city of 5.6 million. This is an average of 357 killings per month in Baghdad. The figure excludes deaths due to accidents.
—Daniel Cooney, Associated Press, May 23, 2004

Early in my tour in Iraq after the coalition failed to help us train Sabeeh, I knew I wasn't going to receive additional personnel, despite the fact that we needed a team of at least eight public affairs soldiers. I had contacted a short list of people I considered to be public affairs thoroughbreds shortly after I took over as the chief of public affairs for the training mission. Many volunteered. I asked Jared if he could recommend any military journalists to come support us, and he gave me names of people he knew and considered to be studs. I contacted the soldiers, and they quickly agreed to serve in Iraq. I had six volunteers who were ready and willing to come to Iraq.

The initial joint manning document, a personnel roster created for our command by civilians at the CPA, stipulated that my office was to have a senior civilian public affairs chief, a captain, and sergeants assigned to it. Once it was determined I'd stay on as Petraeus's PAO, I scrubbed the document and changed the manning requirements based on what I believed were the future manpower needs of the command's public affairs office. When Petraeus took command, the Multinational Security Transition Command Iraq was reorganized, and it would take some time to implement the joint manning document. That meant I likely might not see any fresh public affairs troops assigned to us during my tour, or, as our chief of staff would say, "You're building the team for the next guy behind you." To get the help we needed, I had to be creative. I knew that there was no way Jared and I would be able to juggle the public affairs workload for a year with just the two of us assigned to the team. Most three-star commands in Iraq had a headquarters public affairs staff of three or four personnel and also had multiple public affairs units of twenty or more personnel scattered throughout the country. We had two people, and we were supposed to cover nearly 170,000 square miles. I asked Petraeus to reach out to U.S. Central Command for assistance. I knew people there, and they told me they had an overabundance of underutilized personnel, and many of them wanted to deploy.

In the interim I submitted the names of the potential recruits we had found to our J-1 staff, the human resources department of our command, in hopes they could send us reinforcements. I also submitted an updated joint manning document, which was the new blueprint of what I wanted the public affairs team to look like in the future. Petraeus reviewed the document and approved my piece of it after chopping the manning to eight from twelve. He told me he had to "spike" my manning requests over concerns about the command's size. I understood what he meant. If all the section chiefs were bloating their staffs, the command would explode with growth, and as it was the command was going to more than double in size. I felt Petraeus was also gun-shy about building the public affairs apparatus in our command because of the *Newsweek*-article backlash. Casey's command also reviewed and had input into our manning documents, and if Casey saw that Petraeus was trying to build a large public relations team, I think that would have added to the developing tension. Personally, I think asking a man to keep his face out of the news is one thing, but condemning a military command into media obscurity is another, and that is exactly what happened when we didn't receive personnel to support our mission.

In response to Petraeus's personal plea for help, U.S. Central Command sent us a U.S. Navy journalist for a little more than two and a half months. He was a nice addition, and he got to travel quite a bit, including a trip to Jordan with Petraeus, but he was forced to return to the States and his tour was cut short almost four months. Our command's personnel section was unable to get the service branches to mobilize reservists whose names I had provided. With few meaningful solutions coming from the public affairs community and from human resources, Petraeus and I spoke about my team's composition, and given our need to communicate with the Arab masses we decided to focus our energy on hiring Iraqis. We decided to hire an Iraqi media team, a contracted group of public relations hired guns who could help with the public affairs mission.

They would fit nicely into our mission. They spoke the language and had the necessary skills to independently work with Iraqi security forces and create public affairs products for the Arab and Iraqi press. The contracted Iraqi public affairs team would take pictures, write press releases in Arabic, and capture video of Iraqi military and police operations, training, and key security events. Their news releases and photographs would be disseminated to the Arab and Iraqi press for their consumption the same way PAOs engaged the Western press, and the team's video footage would be offered to networks as pool footage, accompanied with a news release so Arab networks could voice-over the video. Interviews of Iraqi security forces leaders would also be offered in raw, unedited form for use on Arab newscasts and also accompanied with a news release. The team would be in essence Iraqi PAOs working with our office.

We thought the idea was a good workaround for several reasons. First, because the Iraqi government wasn't actively talking to the press, this was a good way to engage local and Arab media by creating accessible public relations products that would help get information flowing to the Arab street. Al-Shaalan had prohibited personnel from conducting media interviews, but his directive said nothing about interviews conducted by Iraqi public relations contractors employed by the coalition. He could not control what our contractors were doing since they worked for the U.S. government. Second, it helped us publicize events that might not ordinarily have been covered by our busy team of three. It would also serve as a force multiplier for my Iraqi PAO counterparts, who had no staff.

The grandest plan for the Iraqi team was the creation of an Iraqi *Cops* reality show. We'd embed our Iraqi media team with Iraqi cops, and as the cops worked the beat, went on tactical operations, and made arrests, the team would be there, capturing it all. The challenge would be finding a network to air the program, but first we needed to assemble a team.

I met Fahmy al-Jaff while visiting the press information center. He would become the team's manager and had worked at the press center as a translator, but he was looking for more challenging work. He was an Iraqi Kurd, Christian, and he had degrees in media arts and spoke five languages. Iraqis could say anything they wanted about their qualifications and credentials since there was very little we could do to prove them right or wrong. If we asked for transcripts or diplomas, they could say that records at the university had been looted or destroyed during the invasion and reference checks simply weren't possible, or they could create their own documents and we had little to validate their veracity. Fahmy was a nice guy who looked like an Iraqi Wayne Newton. He loved to smoke and always was quick to offer me a cigarette. He would give me great insight into the Iraqi mind and culture. I had little choice but to trust the man. He would go on to hire Iraqis from different tribes, genders, and religions. The team would consist of interpreters, writers, photographers, videographers, Web-content editors, and reporters, most of whom were former stringers for al-Jazeera, al-Arabiya, and Reuters.

One of the guys on our team was a young Muslim named Assad who dressed and spoke like he could have been from New York or Chicago. When I first met him I thought he was a Hispanic American.

"Bullshit, you're not an Iraqi. Are you former U.S. military? Army, Marines, what?"

"Sir, no, I'm telling you, I am an Iraqi," Assad said.

"Bullshit!" I replied.

"Yes, motherfucker!" he said, and I knew he'd fit right in. He cussed a lot. I suspected he picked up the habit in 2003 while working for U.S. Marines as an interpreter.

We hired Ahmed, a cameraman and friend I knew from al-Arabiya who had quit his job with the network in fear for his life after two separate violent events came very close to him. Ahmed had a baby girl several months old and didn't want to risk making her an orphan. Our second cameraman was former al-Jazeera stringer Oula, who always called me "Sherif." He was a kindhearted young man who got jittery easily. He looked like an Iraqi version of Curly from the Three Stooges. The other Iraqis on the team often poked fun at him because of his nervousness, but I understood his concerns. Iraq was incredibly violent at the time, and there had been many Arab journalists killed in Iraq covering fighting between U.S. and insurgent forces. Oula had quit his al-Jazeera job because of pressure from his wife, who was at home with small kids and said it was too dangerous for him.

Iraqis working for the coalition were in considerable risk too, and retaining Iraqi media-team members was hard. Insurgents would threaten our workers, leaving notes on their doors, and as the threats and violence increased, the team would get immobilized. Some on the team never returned, their status unknown to me and Fahmy, and they were simply replaced.

We used a pot of money known as the Commander's Emergency Response Program, money invested at the local level by commanders in the field that helps kick-start local economies. Petraeus had a pot of it, and if we could employ some Iraqis, help their economy, and at the same time gain something from it, CERP was the way to go.

In my statement of work, a memorandum that in essence captures the reasoning for the funding request, I wrote that the Multinational Security Transition Command Iraq had established a need for an Iraqi media team. The team, composed of ten Iraqis, would provide broadcast and print journalism, Web communications, and photojournalism services to the command. Their products would be distributed through the Arab press to provide Iraqis a better understanding of what their security forces were doing in posttransition Iraq.

For about $3,000 per month the command would employ ten Iraqi personnel. As I submitted the statement of work to create the team, I also prepared the needed documentation to purchase their equipment. Jared got online and did some price checking. He made a wish list of professional equipment that he and the Iraqis would use and then got prices from three different vendors online who sold photojournalism equipment. All of the places we selected offered no-fee shipment because we were spending a little more than $50,000, and we could have the gear in a couple of weeks. Because they knew we were ordering from the war zone, they would rush it to us at their expense. But as I prepared to purchase the gear, I was told by a U.S. officer at the contracting office in Baghdad that we were required to draft more paperwork and hire a local Iraqi contractor who would supply us with the equipment we needed. We would have to open the contract out for bids.

I played the game and did what he asked, and within days the contract was bid on and accepted by an Iraqi lady who had relatives who worked in, of all places, the coalition's contracting office. I felt it was a conflict of interest, but I was reassured by the contracting office that everything was done legally and that she had bid on the contract to supply my team with gear just like any other contractor. In the new Iraq, as in the old, those with ties to the government got ahead. She promised she'd have our equipment in about eight weeks. The cost? Nearly double the price we found online, $96,000. I contacted the contracting office.

The items had to be purchased in other countries in the Middle East and then shipped to Iraq. Logistical ground travel was risky and expensive, the contracting officer added. True, I thought, but double the price? There was no outrage over a $46,000 overcharge in Iraq because millions were being squandered all over the country, so a paltry sum like ours wasn't something that raised eyebrows. In 2006 the special inspector general overseeing Iraq reconstruction stated that more than $9 billion was unaccounted for in Iraq. With contracting practices like this, it's no wonder why. I saw the value in pumping money into the local economy, but it wasn't working, and the money wasn't being used to help the economy; it was being hoarded by a few well-connected Iraqis who would get rich and get out of Iraq.

I argued with the contract officer. I could buy the matériel for half price, a fair price, and shipping would be free. The shipping risk being leveraged to justify the higher prices would be eliminated if the items were sent via U.S. mail to my office. We'd save the taxpayers nearly $50,000. But the rules were in place: the Iraqi would get the contract, and the equipment would arrive more than three months late. When it finally arrived we traced the purchases through documents that accompanied the equipment. The gear was purchased in the United States using online e-commerce and then shipped to the Middle East, the very method we wanted to employ from the start. In the meantime, Fahmy's team sat around for three months collecting a paycheck with no equipment to use and, worse, no place to work.

In the early days of the Iraqi media team, as we waited for the team's equipment to arrive, I looked for ways to keep the team busy. They would gather at the press center, drink a lot of coffee and tea, smoke, and wait for us to give them something to do. We thought that the equipment's arrival would coincide with their hiring, but using the contracting office delayed our deployment of the team. I couldn't really put any of them to work because they lacked computer workstations, cameras, and other tools needed for their trade. In addition, it took us a couple of months to get them cell phones, so even communications was an issue.

Even if they had equipment, I had no place for them to work. Work space at our command was tight. We had roomy office space at the palace, but Casey's bloating team pushed us to Phoenix Base. There we shared space with multiple other command sections, but eventually we would have our own space, two sheds, located in the courtyard. Until then the Iraqi team lacked gear and a place to work, so I asked them to go fishing for news in hopes that they could churn up something for the coalition, the Iraqi government, or our command to share with the Iraqi populace.

The press center was hosting sporadic press conferences, so I asked the Iraqi media team to attend the pressers in hopes that they might catch some tidbit of useful information and use it to develop a story line. One day I met Fahmy at the convention center, and he said that he and others on the team had been refused access to a press conference by press center personnel. In addition, Fahmy said, he and his team were accused of unethical behavior, and they were asked to leave by a crotchety U.S. civilian public affairs employee. Some of the Iraqis on the team were being accused of maintaining their employment with their previous employers, the news organizations. According to Fahmy and his team, they were called names and yelled at and were shooed away like stray dogs. That further upset many on the team, who already had strained relationships with the coalition because they were former members of the Arab press and had been treated poorly by PAOs and folks at the press center.

When they were hired the team agreed to sever ties with their old employers. I could not have a contractor double-dipping and working as an Arab journalist. They all signed written agreements as a condition of employment, so I was surprised by the accusation that was being leveled.

I contacted the press center to inquire about the expulsion. I was told that the Iraqi media team could not attend press conferences because they were contractors. I chuckled and then explained that they were U.S. government contractors working as public affairs personnel for our command and that they had the endorsement of Petraeus and Casey. But the PAOs at the press center argued that press conferences were only for the media. This was a shallow argument, considering the U.S. government was employing several American contractors to help support PAOs, including one at the Ministry of Interior and another on the coalition police training team, and many others who were working for the coalition at Multinational Force Iraq.

I asked the director of the press center if he was implying that our Iraqi media team didn't have the right credentials to enter the press conferences and if the team could get press credentials issued to them so they could access media events because they were serving as journalists for the command. The director countered that he would not issue contractors media credentials, that they were considered either contractors or media, but not both.

Asking for contractor access to press conferences wasn't completely new to the press center, and in my view it was no different from what al-Iraqiya or *al-Sabah* newspaper was doing. These Iraqi "media" organizations were part of a media network funded and operated by the U.S. government. American companies such as the Harris Corporation hired Iraqis as U.S. contractors, and they operated under the umbrella of the Iraq Media Network. To me it was a scary notion for the U.S. government to underwrite host-nation media and journalists, but it was being done in the same manner in which other state-funded media programs, such as Great Britain's BBC, had been done.

But whereas the Brits paid for programming that was targeted at Brits, the problem with the Iraq Media Network was that it was funded with American dollars and the programming was targeted at Iraqis. The network had an almost instantaneous lack of credibility in the eyes of most Iraqis, who saw the network as a mouthpiece that pushed a coalition agenda. Many Iraqis I knew referred to it as the "Propaganda Channel." The Iraq Media Network was just another extension of the public affairs infrastructure.

As far as credentials were concerned, considering the Iraq Media Network and its contracted employees were given press credentials and media access to coalition press events, I argued it made sense to credential Fahmy and his team because he was an Iraqi contractor running a team of public affairs journalists. In principle, it was the same thing. The Iraq Media Network was credentialed as press, so why not our guys who were public relations types and working for U.S. PAOs? Shouldn't they be considered a part of the team? Additionally, Iraqi contractors employed by the press center routinely attended press conferences. If Fahmy and his team members attended a briefing, in essence it was as if a PAO was in the briefing. He was a representative of our command and merely collecting information. A press conference is a forum to share public information, so it wasn't like there was a concern for information security.

As U.S. contractors Fahmy's team had U.S. Embassy identification cards that granted them access to 90 percent of the facilities in the Green Zone. They could travel in U.S. vehicles, on U.S. aircraft, and on U.S. vessels, so why couldn't they access a place where public information was being disseminated? The press center team knew Fahmy worked directly for me and for Petraeus, they knew Fahmy worked there as a translator, and they knew him before he joined my team, but they wouldn't budge.

In April 2005, months after I argued for access to pressers with the press center bureaucrats, Ahmed al-Rubai'i, a reporter with the U.S. government–funded Iraq Media Network's *al-Sabah* newspaper, was killed in Baghdad after being abducted. His press center media credentials were found in the possession of a group of men later captured by Iraqi police who admitted they had killed al-Rubai'i for being a traitor. His body was never found.

Keep in mind that the press center would not issue Fahmy's team press credentials because they were contractors and couldn't be both journalists and PAOs, press center officials said; they had to be one or the other. However, al-Rubai'i was not only a contracted journalist, like our Iraqi reporters, but also the PAO for the Media Department of the Iraqi National Assembly, a role he had been in since November 2004. How can an allegedly independent member of the media from *al-Sabah* newspaper also be employed as a PAO for the Iraqi government? Doesn't this represent a conflict of interest? Isn't this precisely what the press center accused my team of? Al-Rubai'i was a contractor and a PAO, and he had press center credentials and access to press briefings, information our team was denied despite the fact that they worked for the exit strategy in Iraq.

I moved on. The story of Iraq wasn't within the walls of the safely insulated press center, and I was merely trying to give my guys something to do. If the press center didn't want to give my team access to the pressers, it was no big deal, and I mention the anecdote only to illustrate the pettiness that went on in Baghdad. The real story of Iraq wasn't at the cozy press center amid the hundreds of care packages, air-conditioning, satellite television, and tasty lattes where it was hard to remember that a war was being waged just outside the walls of the Green Zone, although some officers who served there said they served in "combat conditions" solely because the buildings' windows shattered once from an IED attack outside the Green Zone.

The press center's unprofessional expulsion of the Iraqi media team and a few run-ins with U.S. military patrols on the streets of Baghdad had pushed our staff photographer to a breaking point. Some on the team had shared with me that he had stated a few anticoalition remarks during his few months with the team, but I admit that I disregarded those comments as Iraqi paranoia. Many Iraqis I worked with lived a rough existence where they couldn't trust people and were always looking over their shoulder. Such is life in a lawless land, but tension on the streets and the recent event at the press center had pushed him too far.

We finally got our equipment for the team, so I sent the team's photographer and Assad to Kirkush Military Training Base to cover an Iraqi military graduation. That same day some of our military advisers were going to be awarded the Combat Infantryman Badge for some fighting they had done alongside Iraqi troops. I asked the photographer to take pictures of the ceremony for a short news article we'd include in the command's newsletter, the *Advisor*.

As the photographer took the photos of the U.S. soldiers getting their badges awarded to them by a general from our command, he told Assad, my translator, that the soldiers were being decorated for killing women and children. They weren't heroes, he said; they were murderers. Assad said nothing and waited for a chance to talk to me alone once he returned to Baghdad. He told me what had happened at Kirkush and said that for weeks, the photographer had been expressing anticoalition statements and complained that the Americans were rude and overly aggressive with Iraqis. Assad didn't want me to confront the guy because he was afraid the photographer might do something to hurt him or his family. Assad admitted that many Iraqis, away from the company of their American employers, expressed resentment toward the U.S. occupation. Many Iraqis who worked in the Green Zone could be heard after hours badmouthing the coalition. He was brutally honest, and while I didn't like hearing what he had to say, I didn't doubt it was the truth.

I approached Fahmy about the issue, and I didn't tell him that Assad had tipped me off. Fahmy asked the photographer if the accusations were true. When he confronted the photographer Fahmy made up a story that one of the U.S. soldiers he was photographing was a fluent Arabic speaker and had understood what the photographer had said. The photographer didn't deny the allegations and began an anticoalition rant. Fahmy asked him to surrender his equipment and contractor identification card on the spot, and he was escorted out of the Green Zone. When we checked his camera's memory card, he had erased all of the pictures of the soldiers receiving their badges.

Months of sitting around with no place to work and no equipment to use had taken their toll on the team. In addition, in about six months our public affairs team was relocated five times, the Iraqis three times. Once we finally settled them into Phoenix Base, the violence outside the Green Zone hampered their efforts to become serious contributors to our mission.

A surge of violence in late 2004 caused curfews to be implemented nationwide. Most of our trips outside the Green Zone lasted only a few hours. Black Hawk helicopters ferried us to our destination and back, and we ordinarily were back by late afternoon or early evening and would use the rest of the evening to write stories and news releases, prepare news imagery we had captured, and update our website about whatever event we had just covered, whether it was a patrol, convoy, operation, training mission, graduation, leader meeting, you name it. For me and Jared, it was no problem because we worked late and then retired to our trailer camps. For the Iraqis on the media team, this posed a serious problem, because they had to fly back to the Green Zone, clear security checkpoints into our compound, and then complete their work—edit video, write releases, download photos—and then try to get back home, all before dark. It was impossible to do most times. There were a few times that due to flight delays, they could not clear the Green Zone in time to make it home before curfew. All but one of these men and women had spouses and small children, and they didn't want their families to be alone at night in a lawless country where electrical power was absent. And they had no quarters in the Green Zone because their identification cards couldn't get them access to sleeping areas in the compound. Several times they were trapped in the Green Zone and slept on cots we kept at the office. Fahmy voiced concerns that it would be harder to perform their mission with the tighter security. He was right.

As the country ramped up for its first-ever elections in January 2005, it became harder for Fahmy to make it to work, and if he didn't come in, none of the team came to work. Fahmy began to ask for time off. A relative had been kidnapped, and the family needed to pay ransom. The power in his neighborhood had been cut and was turned on only a couple of hours per day. His children were sick because of lack of heat, so he couldn't work and had to care for them. The reasons were many, and so were my frustrations.

When the team did come to work, they were routinely late, citing long security lines as their reason for being tardy. They would miss flights and convoys routinely because of the security problems plaguing Baghdad outside the Green Zone. Things had deteriorated in Baghdad so badly that now something else was impacting our mission. I understood what Fahmy was going through. If the roles were reversed, I doubt I'd ever leave my family for a job, especially in the violent climate of a place like Iraq. I'd likely hole myself up in our house with as much ammo and weapons and canned food as I could find. Iraq was a miserable place to be if you were an Iraqi. I knew what he was risking, but what bothered me was the fact that Fahmy had knowingly signed up for this job and knew there were risks involved, but now those risks, once manageable obstacles, had become excuses. While thousands of Iraqi contractors managed to find their way to the Green Zone each day to work and help their country rebuild, despite the risk Fahmy stayed at home, rarely answered his phone, and hardly ever sent me e-mails. We were paying them, again, to do nothing, and while he and his team had valid reasons to not come to work, I simply couldn't see beyond the fact that thousands of other Iraqis did still come to work. I felt guilty judging him like this, but that was the complexity of the situation.

I didn't know what lay between Fahmy's home and the Green Zone, and I didn't really know what was happening in his personal life. I was insulated in the safety of Phoenix Base, and even if I did travel outside the wire, I was protected by aircrews and convoy soldiers, and we had a whole bunch of weapons that would help sway our fate a bit. I'll never know what it is like to walk as an unarmed man affiliated with the coalition through the streets of Iraq as Fahmy and his team did. That in and of itself takes huge balls, and I'll forever believe that Fahmy told me the truth, that things for him and his team were dangerous and unsafe. I'll also know that for months I had Iraqi contractors who were itching to do great things, but instead they sat and waited for an overburdened government contracting office in Baghdad to finalize the contract between our command and Fahmy, a process that took two months, and then they again sat on their hands while they waited for us to find them equipment, and then waited yet again because they had no place to work, and now, months later, after they had worked collectively only a few weeks, they were sitting around again, waiting for a lull in the violence. More than five months had elapsed, and they'd not been able to contribute steadily and significantly to our mission. They were becoming a logistical burden and not a force multiplier.

During the escalated fighting Assad, my interpreter, did report to work regularly and helped us create Arabic press releases. I wondered how he could make it to the office, while the rest of the team did not. Was he braver than them, or was he connected to the bad guys? The violence did not seem to impact his mobility, but these were some of the things I was forced to think about in Baghdad. History proved Assad was a loyal friend, but the environment in Iraq forced you to think about the worst someone might have within them. I hated that part of our mission because I wanted to help my team and the Iraqi people build a better nation. I truly believed in what we were doing, but when you've seen a beheading, that makes you consider things much closer.

Assad grew to be a trusted friend, and he also got to travel to Jordan with Petraeus, a trip he wouldn't have made on his own. While in Amman he went out to eat at an Italian restaurant with our temporary military journalist from the Navy. Assad asked the sailor what he recommended on the menu. The sailor was perplexed, and he explained that he had never eaten at the restaurant before. Assad then clarified that he wasn't seeking recommendations on what was good to eat on the menu; he was seeking recommendations about Italian food. He had never eaten it before. The sailor recommended the tortellini, and Assad, a man well into his twenties, had Italian pasta for the first time in his life.

Assad was a nice young man and what I considered to be a good, balanced Muslim. He prayed several times each day, and our office would grow quiet as he busted out a piece of cardboard, faced Mecca, dropped onto his knees, and did his business. When he first started working with us, he asked me if he would be allowed to pray. "It's your goddamn country, hell, yes," I told him.

Assad was young and therefore prone to do young-man things. During the few periods of downtime at the office, he would surf the Internet and look at pictures of bikini-clad women and Corvettes. We all knew what he was doing when he'd turn the computer monitor toward the wall, but we never said anything. There were worse things he could be doing, but he was a decent guy and with aspirations that his nation would someday be like the bustling and healthy Jordan he had visited with us. He hoped to someday own an eatery. Guys like him kept me going in Iraq.

While Fahmy and I drifted apart professionally, we got closer personally. Issues aside, we were both in hard places at that point in our lives. He became a leaning post for me. As a company-grade officer most of my staff-officer peers in the Green Zone didn't have the same level of responsibility that I did. I was filling a colonel's billet as a captain, so I couldn't necessarily find sympathy with those of similar rank because they didn't understand what I was enduring. Professionally, my peers were colonels, and they wanted nothing to do with me. As an officer I couldn't complain to my team about my doubts and frustrations because that might impact morale. Did I go on rants and cuss to high heaven in front of my team? Hell, yes, and I did show my frustrations and anger toward PAOs and to stupid things in general, but I never showed my soft underbelly. I never let them see that I had all sorts of doubts about where we were going in Iraq and how we were executing things as a nation. I did, however, share that with Fahmy. As the murderous onslaught continued outside the wire, I began to express my doubts to Fahmy.

"I wish we could do more for you guys, Fahmy," I told him one day as we smoked some of his foul-smelling cigarettes that seemed to choke my throat shut. "My hands are tied, and I can't do shit! The fucking PAOs don't listen to me. The military doesn't seem to know what the hell it's doing. I don't know what to say. I don't know what to do. A lot of people are dying out there," I said. "I'm really sorry for fucking up your country, Fahmy. I hope we can fix it and make it what you guys want it to be."

He looked at me with tears welling up in his eyes. "How will you spend Christmas?" he asked.

"Here at work," I told him.

"You will not be home?" Fahmy asked.

"No, I was just home for Thanksgiving."

He embraced me. "Thank you, amigo," he smiled, continuing, "for being here with us."

"We're fucking this up, Fahmy," I said.

"Take it easy. You worry too much," he said, putting out his cigarette in the butt can outside our office. He joked that I should leave the Green Zone and come to his house to celebrate Christmas. I looked enough like an Arab that he could get me to his house and back without detection.

Aside from letting me vent, Fahmy was also a phenomenal source on all things Iraqi press. He knew what networks Iraqis were watching and what newspapers they were reading. As Multinational Force Iraq in the Green Zone generated analytical reports about the Arab press, I found that Fahmy countered everything they asserted. He was the one, in fact, who tipped me off that al-Arabiya was being well received by Iraqis, and that encouraged me to build rapport with them. I wanted to work with al-Jazeera, but Fahmy thought they were too ostracized by the coalition and would be harder to work with, and some Iraqis were finding al-Jazeera repulsive, so he recommended that we engage al-Arabiya, whose viewership ran a close second to al-Jazeera's.

I followed Fahmy's advice, despite U.S. intelligence telling me otherwise. In Baghdad a then unclassified open-source intelligence document known as the *Baghdad Mosquito* was created and distributed on a regular basis. In it there were abstracts of what was being said by Iraqi and Arab media, and there were in-depth analyses of media content. Most of the time what the *Mosquito* said countered what was Fahmy's reality.

Fahmy not only proved useful in directing our information to those media outlets deemed credible by Iraqis, but was also instrumental as a public opinion sensor. He was out on the streets and lived in the society, and while the coalition was great at collecting the opinions of surveyed Iraqis associated with the coalition or the Iraqi government, it lacked the ability to get an honest sampling of Iraqi public opinion from deep within the Iraqi culture's pool. Fahmy, in a very crude and unscientific manner, could do that for us. He was also the one who recommended that we engage tribal sheikhs, community leaders, and religious men with accurate information about Iraq's security forces. He felt local Iraqi leaders were key to getting Iraqi troops accepted in societal circles in the locales, and part of that was due to his understanding of the Iraqi rumor mill.

The Iraqi rumor mill was the most prolific informal communications network I had ever seen. News and disinformation alike spread like a virus within Iraqi circles faster than it could travel using electronic devices. Fahmy said the network was strong because many Iraqis during Hussein's reign communicated only through familial and tribal lines.

The strength and accuracy of the Iraqi grapevine were proven to me one day when Fahmy asked me to meet him at the convention center. Fahmy said there was a rumor on the street that U.S. military officers were paying Iraqi journalists to publish procoalition stories in their newspapers. Through the rumors Fahmy had identified reporters who said soldiers were paying cash for editorial space in the Iraqi publications and paying for procoalition coverage. The soldiers, Fahmy continued, weren't giving the journalists news releases as PAOs do in their job duties; they were giving the Iraqi journalists payment to prominently place articles written by the coalition in Iraqi publications. They were paying Iraqi newspapers to run positively slanted stories. Fahmy said it would hurt U.S. credibility. I agreed and asked him to put me in touch with the reporters or to get me the names of the U.S. soldiers who were paying.

Fahmy days later connected me with an Iraqi newspaper reporter, and we met at the convention center and talked about what he knew.

"Ask him if its *al-Sabah*, the U.S.-funded paper. If that's the case, then this doesn't matter because the paper is filled with propaganda anyway," I told Fahmy. The fat Iraqi listened attentively to Fahmy, and he shook his head. It was not *al-Sabah*. It was another Baghdad newspaper, independent from the Iraq Media Network. The reporter who had boasted about his firsthand knowledge of the payments was suddenly unsure which newspaper was accepting money from the Americans. He squirmed in his seat, didn't look at Fahmy as he talked to him, and was sweating even though it was cool outside. He and Fahmy exchanged words for several minutes, and I remained quiet, listening, examining the guy. He was hiding something. I could tell he was lying. He told Fahmy that he didn't have all the information and that he wanted to collect his facts and then meet with us again. We agreed and said we'd link up with him in forty-eight hours. He never showed, we never heard from him again, and because of Fahmy's sporadic work attendance, it became a back-burner issue.

More than a year later, in 2005, the Pentagon announced it was investigating reports that the U.S. military was paying Iraqi journalists to print positive stories. The Lincoln Group, a public relations firm contracted by the Pentagon for $100 million, an investigation revealed, paid Iraqi news outlets to publish positive articles about the coalition. The American contractor gave Iraqi journalists stipends in exchange for favorable exposure. The Pentagon said the program was designed to counter false enemy information. I guess my question is, why not just use truth and engage those same outlets with factual information? Why was there a need to spin it?

The company was exonerated in 2006 of any wrongdoing and was found to be operating within the boundaries of its contract, but the media payola scandal further damaged American credibility in Iraq. Regionally, it cemented in the minds of many Arabs that the Americans didn't want a true democracy; they wanted a society and a press that could be controlled, just like Hussein's.

The Iraqi media team, despite their initial challenges, managed to capture video footage that we did get aired on al-Arabiya, and some of the team's news products were published in *al-Furat*, *al-Sabah*, and *al-Dustor* newspapers as well as by al-Sharq and al-Awsat news services, just to name a few. Our pictures too had managed to make it onto newspaper pages, but overall I considered the team about as successful as the overall U.S. public affairs effort, which meant that while there was visible success, the impact wasn't very deep and therefore was not very good. It was a fantastic idea, but it just never got the traction we needed. We never launched the Iraqi *Cops* show as we wanted to, and the media team would not be granted the access it needed to Iraqi security forces thanks to oppressive leadership at the Ministry of Defense and ignorant public affairs advisers at the Ministry of Interior. We were prevented from capturing the essence of the new Iraqi military and police forces.

In early 2005 we moved yet again to another workspace. This time we were placed in shipping containers, the kind that are hauled by 18-wheelers on the interstate; they had been fashioned into office spaces. We were given two trailers with air-conditioning and wooden floors. They got a bit cold in winter, but I wasn't going to bitch about it. My concern as always wasn't where we worked and whether we had air-conditioning or heat, but whether we could survive a direct hit from a mortar or rocket round. As soon as we moved in I began to ask the chief of staff for sandbags because a bullet had punctured the thin skin of one of our huts and scared the shit out of Assad as he worked.

One day Fahmy showed up to work with one member of the team. It had been raining heavily, and our compound was covered in thick claylike mud. Iraq's rain was dirty, seemingly grainy from the dusty air it fell through. Our trailers were located in a dirt parking lot, so we created plywood walkways to keep from sinking into the mud and covered the area with rocks to facilitate movement around the base. It was a temporary office, and we would likely move again in about two months.

Fahmy was visibly disgusted by the conditions. He was a professional and often dressed in slacks and a blazer. As he tried to move around that day, it was hard for him to keep his well-polished shoes clean, and he wiped them constantly with a tissue. It was the first time he had seen our new office space, which we had been occupying for several weeks.

"This is where we work now?" he said, pointing to the trailers.

"Yeah," I replied. "Where's the rest of the team?"

"I cannot work in such a place," Fahmy said. "You are a soldier and you have to, but I do not have to do this."

"What's wrong with this place?" I said innocently, knowing Fahmy's pride was interfering in what should have been a pragmatic matter.

"This is how you treat animals. Do you know where others like me are working? They are in nice, clean offices in the palace, at the convention center, at the ministries, and I am here, in a box used to transport supplies, thrown away like an animal," Fahmy said.

Suddenly, all of the frustration Fahmy had been internalizing for months finally got released on me. I knew he had been boiling over and had taken a lot of shit from us and from the coalition for months. Frankly, I was surprised he lasted this long, but he was loyal to me and the command, and I think he really wanted to make things work. But like the other Iraqi who left our team, he too complained that the Americans at the press center treated him rudely and like a terrorist, which hurt him deeply because he had once worked there for them. Fahmy said he thought they were his friends because they had worked together, but when they kicked him out of the convention center and then refused to credential him, he said he felt he was risking his life for people who didn't care about him. He also complained that many Iraqis believed U.S. soldiers should not be entering Iraqi homes without permission or damaging personal property as they were doing. He felt he was treated badly by coalition guards at checkpoints, too. He stood there and went off on me.

"Fahmy, I can't imagine how hard it is for you. I know it is hard for you to work here and then have those CPIC folks treat you poorly, but I hope things will get better someday. I don't know what to do for you," I said.

He seemed to ignore what I said. He kept his diatribe going where he left off. "Other Iraqis have nice phones, laptop computers, new desks. They drink tea at work, and they are happy to come to work. I waited for many months, and this is what I get for waiting? No, sir!" Fahmy said.

He was right to a degree, but I think everyone, Iraqis and Americans, assigned to comfy staff duty at the FOBs needed to make more sacrifices and do what was needed to get the job done. Security had gotten so bad in Baghdad that the team was rarely capable of completing its projects in a timely manner to inject its products into the Iraqi news cycle.

"Many on the team, I'm sorry to say, sir, have found other jobs, and I have been offered something else too that pays more," Fahmy said.

I wasn't shocked, but I wasn't happy about his handling of the whole ordeal. Before he could finish I said what should have been said months earlier. "Fahmy, if you have something better, that will pay you more money as you said, then you have to worry about you. Take the other job and no hard feelings," I said. "You have to think about yourself and your family." I extended my hand, and he shook it.

"It's what I have to do, sir," Fahmy said.

"No worries. Then do it," I said.

We smoked and talked a little longer, and we set a date he would return all the equipment I had issued to him. The last time I saw him he gave me a huge hug, complete with man pats on the back, and he said his good-byes. It was one of those dying good-byes, the kind you give someone you will never see again. I do not think Fahmy thought he was going to die, and I do not believe he thought I was going to die, but it was just a very final moment for us both. The relationship had reached its terminus, and we both knew we would likely never see each other again.

"I will be okay. Do not worry about me," Fahmy said.

Oddly enough, I never did worry about him. He would always find a way to make it through things. The Iraqi media team would come to an end in 2005, just months after it was formed, another solid command public affairs plan driven into the wall by the forces of war and the forces of public affairs inaction and dysfunction.

Fahmy within days of leaving the command said he became the bureau chief at al-Arabiya. I've not heard from Fahmy since. I kept in touch with Assad, and years later when I told him that Fahmy had gotten a job with al-Arabiya, he was shocked. He said Fahmy never told him about the al-Arabiya job and said that Fahmy had told the Iraqi media team that I had dismantled the team. All of the team members thought I had put them out of work, which was not true. In addition, Assad told me that when the team dismantled, he missed the money he was making with us. We started talking about salaries, and then Assad volunteered what he and the others were getting paid by Fahmy. Needless to say, I was shocked that Fahmy was paying them all half of what we agreed to pay each member of the team. When I told Assad how much he was supposed to be earning, we sat in a long, uncomfortable silence. Assad never spoke to Fahmy or the other members ever again.

For months as I tried to stand up and gainfully employ the Iraqi media team, I pressed U.S. Central Command, Multinational Force Iraq, STRAT-COM, and our personnel section for personnel to staff our team from 2004 to 2005. The Ninety-Eighth Division finally sent a large contingency from the Army Reserve to Iraq to help train Iraqi forces and to provide logistical and administrative support to the command. During the course of two months as the division trickled into Iraq, several personnel walked into the office and said they were being "detailed" to public affairs. None of them had public relations, mass communications, or journalism experience.

I sent most of them away except for one noncommissioned officer who had been mobilized involuntarily just a month from retirement. He expressed concern for his safety, and I couldn't blame the man. Why the Army would mobilize a guy one month shy of retirement and put him at risk is beyond me. I promised I would keep him inside the safe confines of the Green Zone if he managed our logistical and administrative issues for a few months. He agreed. There was also a well-qualified man from the Air National Guard from California who did some great work for the command, but he spent only about a month with us and then was asked to return to his post in Qatar, and there was a guardsman from Florida who arrived as I was leaving and went on to do great things too, but unfortunately for me I wasn't there very long to work with her.

There were a couple of other mobilized National Guard and reserve soldiers who did some time on our team in 2004–5, but there is nothing notable to share about them. One was with us a very short period of time before I sent him back to the States, and the other stayed a little longer but had no significant military PAO experience and made little impact on the mission while I was there. I worked only briefly with both of them before I completed my tour.

It baffled me that I had willing, trained, qualified professional personnel willing to get into the fight and do great things for the command, but the military sent me personnel (not the good ones previously mentioned) with no public affairs knowledge, skills, experience, or training. I have to wonder if the military PAOs thought our mission was as important as the Bush administration thought it to be. While the president said the training of Iraqi security forces was the way home, U.S. Central Command and the services offered only patchwork support, but staffs ballooned at CENTCOM, the Pentagon, Army, Multinational Force Iraq, and other public affairs offices worldwide.

I had asked everyone in the public affairs universe for assistance. I e-mailed personnel back in Washington DC at the Department of the Army and at the Office of the Assistant Secretary of Defense, Public Affairs. I also contacted the public affairs office at U.S. Central Command. I petitioned U.S. PAO leaders in Qatar and Kuwait. I asked the press center, STRATCOM, Multinational Force Iraq, and public affairs personnel scattered throughout Iraq. Interestingly, most of the enlisted people wanted to work with us, but all of their officers said they couldn't afford to lose anyone. Military journalists at the press center were eager to join our team, but when I asked if I could have them on an extended temporary basis I was told I could "borrow them" to cover stories, but temporary assignments were out of the question because there was too much work for them at the press center. I found this comment comical, considering Army journalists at the press center told me they were bored out of their skulls and would welcome a temporary assignment to our command. The few times we did use press center journalists, they loved the missions we gave them and did not want to return to their desk jobs.

I was even approached by several officers from the press center who wanted to work with us. They told me if I could make it appear as if they had been involuntarily reassigned to my team, they would help make it happen, but they could not appear as willing participants because "that would be bad."

Those from the press center and other Baghdad public affairs shops who wanted to work with us said that most of the PAOs in Baghdad spent their time shopping, eating pizza, and enjoying time off. One soldier I ran into, excited about our missions, said he worked "banker's hours," went to the gym several hours per day, and got at least one day off per week (sometimes more when he was given passes). But, he admitted, "I have it made. I don't want to stir things up, sir."

Meanwhile, his peers, like Jared, worked seven days per week, eighteen hours per day, for months on end, simply because it was what we had to do to make the mission successful. Luckily for me, I was given the good fortune to work with Jared. Anyone else would have broken under the weight of the workload, but Jared just carried the load on his shoulders every day. The lack of support for our command from PAOs was so regular, I simply stopped asking for help. It was what Kimmitt had experienced before me and the reason he assembled his own team.

STRATCOM had public affairs personnel, military journalists I desperately needed, assigned as part of a personal security detail (PSD, bodyguards) for Lessel, the coalition spokesman who replaced Kimmitt. One of the Marines guarding him was a trained military journalist, and I certainly could have used his skills in the field embedded with Iraqi forces. The public affairs community would not release him to me (despite his admitted desire to be assigned to us). He was protecting Lessel, who spent the bulk of his time behind the secure confines of a compound. Who was he protecting him from? It was just a huge waste of PAO talent. As a military journalist that man could have reached millions, and anyone could have taken his place as a PSD.

Slavonic had a qualified PAO lieutenant whose assistance I could have used, but he was kept with Slavonic and worked as an aide-de-camp. Certainly, someone else could do that job. Why were qualified public affairs personnel being misused?

U.S. Central Command also had excess public affairs personnel in Tampa and in Qatar. In conversations with the enlisted staffers there, they all told me the same thing. They wanted to get into the fight but weren't being allowed to move forward. They too were bored out of their minds and were looking for more ways to contribute in a meaningful manner. They had asked their officers if they could go to Iraq and fill manning requests being made by our command, even if temporarily, but instead they were kept in office jobs capturing data to pad PAO presentations delivered to senior officers and making little, if any, impact. I can say this confidently because public opinion of the war hit rock bottom by 2006 in what started as a steady spiral and downward trend in 2003.

If PAOs were doing such a great job directing press centers, performing as spokesmen, leading engagement teams, and executing media relations, then why was public support so horrible, and why did it remain exceedingly low until U.S. troops pulled out? Why did we waste manpower staffing teams that were ineffective and could not capture and hold public opinion? It was obvious U.S. Central Command was being used as a public relations firm to help the Pentagon and White House maintain a firm grasp on public opinion where it mattered least, in the United States.

I continued to petition U.S. Central Command for my entire tour in hopes of getting additional manpower assistance. CENTCOM said they would work the issue. Months later, I still had nothing, only temporary personnel who rotated through, so I got Petraeus involved, again. This time, we found the problem or at least part of it.

An officer in our command told me why my team's manning requests were going unfulfilled for so long. We were routing our manning requests through Multinational Force Iraq, Casey's command, which was in our chain of command. The requests were being reviewed by Casey's team prior to getting sent to CENTCOM. According to the officer in our command, Casey's team had been rejecting all of my requests for manpower, and his team had never told me or given me the courtesy of offering an explanation. I was incensed at the revelation, given that we had been dealing with this bullshit for months. I told Petraeus what I had discovered. Seven months after I arrived in Iraq, we still didn't have the team the command needed, despite my incessant manning requests and pleas for help to various personnel throughout the public affairs community in Iraq, in theater, and in Washington DC and Tampa. We had tried to supplement our manning by hiring the Iraqis, but there too the PAO community put up obstacles that prevented us from succeeding. I started to think that someone on Casey's team might be rejecting my manning authorizations because they knew about Petraeus's gag order. I had no proof. None of it made any sense.

I talked to Petraeus and told him that for months, the public affairs office had tried to fill public affairs billets. We had six quality Army and Navy volunteers, all of whom were willing to serve for six to twelve months, fall away because of problems getting them on board. None of the problems were related to the candidates themselves; the issues were all bureaucratic.

An officer from our command said he exchanged e-mails with a PAO from Casey's command about my staff requirements. The officer said this PAO rejected the increase in manning at our command's public affairs office and offered no explanations. I explained to Petraeus that a PAO had made recommendations within the public affairs and personnel community, opting not to staff our positions even though we had submitted a request for forces with complete justifications. I reminded him of our many manning requests to the various PAO entities who said they were stretched too thin and couldn't spare personnel. I added that I did not understand why the decision to staff our public affairs team was in the hands of an entity outside of the command, but I thought I should make him aware of what was happening on his PAO team. We were the exit strategy, and we had a critical need for public affairs personnel to support the mission, including an adviser support-team role at the Ministry of Defense.

Petraeus quickly sent an e-mail to Lessel and copied me. In it he asked Lessel to support our filling of PAO positions. Lessel replied that he would be happy to help.

I sent Lessel my approved manning document that outlined the manning requirements we had. He confirmed receipt of it. Nothing happened, and three months later I would leave Iraq. The command's public affairs team would swell to eight people after I rotated back to the States, the same year Petraeus left Iraq. A lieutenant colonel would replace me, and later the job would be filled by a colonel and the staff would swell to eleven people. The personnel clog opened once Petraeus and I were gone.

Jared and I as the only assigned personnel to the command managed to do the work of eleven for nearly a year. With some temporary help we got thanks to Petraeus, we made ends meet. It had taken the military more than a year to fill the manning needs on our team, a huge mistake given our mission as the exit strategy. In 2005 after I had rotated back to the States, the director of Defense Department websites at the Pentagon would tell me that Jared and I created more usable news content for Defense Department websites during our deployment than all the PAOs in Iraq combined. During our tour our newsletter and website were composed of 100 percent original content. After we left Iraq the amount of original content being written by the command dropped considerably, despite the fact that the staff had grown nearly six times larger. We had worked our asses off, especially Jared, who did 95 percent of the writing and journalistic duties. We simply lived for our mission and lived a busy life, while most of our counterparts went shopping, went to the gym, and even got to go on three-day passes to Qatar to golf and swim.

After my tour I examined a public affairs duty roster and some news data I collected about the press center. According to a news report and a manning roster, the press center had 66 personnel assigned to it; according to the roster, Multinational Force Iraq public affairs office, which includes STRATCOM, had 12 public affairs personnel assigned to it (the number does not include American and Iraqi civilians who were assigned to the U.S. Embassy public affairs staff); Multinational Corps Iraq had 10 PAOs on their team; a small public affairs team at nearby Camp Victory had 7 public affairs personnel; and U.S. Central Command had 22 public affairs personnel assigned to it. Our command, the Multinational Security Transition Command Iraq, the command made the focal point of the exit strategy in Iraq, the command personally recognized by the Bush administration as the single most important mission in Iraq in 2004–5, was given 2 personnel, me and Jared, to perform the mission. In all, there were 129 personnel committed to the public affairs mission in Iraq, 95 of them in Baghdad alone; combined, there were more than 300 PAOs supporting the war in Iraq around the world in various locations. Yet nobody could be spared to support the president's main objective, our mission.

The press center had two positions on its roster that I found interesting. One was an officer's billet that was the chief of Iraqi media engagement, and another was a sergeant's position titled "MOD/MOI Trainer." In other words, there was a sergeant categorized as someone who trained the Iraqi ministries on public affairs matters, and there was an officer who worked with Arab media. But when I spoke to my Iraqi PAO counterparts at the Ministries of Interior and Defense, neither Radhi, the Defense Ministry's media relations director, or Col. Adnan Abdul-Rahman, the Interior

Ministry's spokesman, had ever known or seen a U.S. sergeant who trained them or anyone in their ministries on public relations. Both men said only our office had helped train them. For that matter, nobody had ever trained Sabeeh, so what was the sergeant doing instead of training the ministry PAOs? As for the officer who worked Iraqi media engagement, members of the Arab press credentialed by the press center, which includes the Iraqi media, denied there was a U.S. officer engaging them and helping them get information. Nobody, they said, actively and regularly engaged them from the press center. On the contrary, they argued, getting information from the press center was difficult.

By January 2005 the PAO roster had grown to more than 165 PAOs involved in the war in Iraq on the ground, but the roster did not include public affairs staffs at Headquarters, Department of the Army, or the Office of the Assistant Secretary of Defense, Public Affairs, at the Pentagon. Nor did it include U.S. Naval, Marine, and Air Force public affairs personnel stationed in the Middle East who could have been temporarily assigned to our team to help.

We fought our own manpower-augmentation system more than the enemy. But the mystery that I came home with is still unsolved. Why did so many people reject our pleas for help? Why did so many people ignore the president's wishes and public affairs guidance and not support our mission?

I always maintained that if I was doing something wrong, unethical, immoral, or illegal as I did my job in Iraq that I would have been relieved of duty or brought up on charges. That never happened. Was support being kept from my team intentionally to prevent Petraeus from having another *Newsweek* moment? Did someone or some people have it in for him? For me? Years later, as I see Iraq in turmoil, the answer to my question still evades me, but after serving in Iraq as a PAO I can't help but think that we commission and promote military officers too easily.

7

TRAINING THE IRAQI MINISTRIES

The Green Zone averages three mortar or rocket attacks per day.
—Multinational Force Iraq report, October 2004

On October 23, 2004, soldiers from the Iraqi Army graduated from basic military training at Kirkush Military Training Base, just several miles from the Iranian border. After graduation ceremonies they donned civilian clothes and boarded buses and vans on their way home for a few days of leave before reporting to their assignments. U.S. trainers from our command said the mood was jovial as forty-nine of the Iraqi soldiers headed south from Kirkush near Baladruz through desolate desert roads in Diyala Province in several small buses.

The next time anyone saw the soldiers was on the side of the road about thirty miles from Baquoba. It is believed their buses were commandeered by insurgents who set up a checkpoint and were dressed like Iraqi policemen. The unarmed soldiers were lined up and executed along the roadside. This was the single worst violent military loss the coalition had experienced.

I contacted Radhi Badhir, my Iraqi public affairs counterpart at the Ministry of Defense, minutes after I learned about the attack. I asked him what he planned to do as the ministry's media relations director, and he said he had some ideas he was working on. He would get back to me. I had ideas too, and I was certain we could take this horrific situation and use it as leverage against the insurgents.

I informed Petraeus that I had reached out to the Ministry of Defense and started working a reactionary plan with Radhi to try to use the attack's energy against the insurgents and to try to make the Iraqi soldiers martyrs instead of just helpless victims strewn on the side of a dusty road. Martyrdom, or some degree of it, was popular with many Arabs, so our effort would be a strategic maneuver to get the populace to rethink its perception of Iraq's security.

We believed that with a sustained media-saturation campaign, starting with Iraqi prime minister Ayad Allawi and filtering down through the Ministry of Defense and local commands, and, as a reinforcement, through our command, we could cause the Arab populace to recognize that Iraqi security forces were trying to do something good in the name of Iraq, and therefore their deaths should be heralded. This is important because without support for security services in Iraq, the insurgents would continue to thrive. We could use this tragedy as a springboard to get the Iraqi military in the news in a different light. Thus far, they were known for desertions and for being kidnapped or killed.

Our plan called for the Iraqi government to claim a national day of mourning within forty-eight hours after the killings to recognize the sacrifices being made by Iraqi security forces. It would let the Iraqi populace know that their government felt the soldiers were important enough to be heralded as heroes for choosing to wear the cloth of their nation, and it would place the families of the fallen in endearment with the culture. No longer would dead Iraqi soldiers be faceless and nameless, as they had been for decades; like other successful cultures in world history, the Iraqis would pay homage to their warriors.

My team crafted a plan for review by Radhi for a memorial event in the Green Zone, and the guests of honor would be the families of the murdered soldiers. The Iraqi prime minister, minister of defense, president, and other dignitaries would attend. The Iraqis had thus far been silent for several months. The death of the forty-nine soldiers would enable us at long last to put a face on the Iraqi military. We worked feverishly into the night and well into the next morning, planning all the details.

The day after the killings Radhi called me about the plan and the recommendations I had sent him. He said he spoke to the defense minister's office and that they didn't intend to talk to the press about the deaths of the forty-nine soldiers. They were treating the killings of the fallen forty-nine like other Iraqi soldier killings, inconsequential and routine, part of the cost of doing business in a postoccupation state. For months I had watched as the Iraqi government sustained human loss after loss and said and did nothing about it. Their civilians were violently and indiscriminately killed, and they said nothing, and now, their soldiers, who volunteered to serve their nation and protect its people, were killed en masse, and the sense of outrage escaped the Iraqi leadership completely. Radhi said the ministry would issue a written statement on behalf of al-Shaalan, and that would be it. I lost it. I grabbed my gas mask, which I kept in a desk drawer, and left the office. I went around the corner of the building and stuck my face inside the gas mask and screamed as loudly as I could, so loud, in fact, that I almost passed out. Nearby, Iraqi gardeners stared at me as I continued to release my frustration into the sound-muffling gas mask. Because there were no weapons of mass destruction, I instead used the mask to counter my reaction to the mass stupidity coming from the Defense Ministry.

Meanwhile, my phone lines and my e-mail were jolting with activity. The media wanted comments about the deaths, and now with the bad news from Radhi the mounting interest was annoying me. I delayed them and told them the Iraqis would likely have an official statement soon. American PAOs at Multinational Force Iraq contacted me and asked me for a position on the issue. What happened to the Iraqi face? I thought. Why were we being thrust into the spotlight all of a sudden?

One of the many calls and e-mails I received in the course of a few hours after the killings was from Jane Arraf, who at the time was with CNN. She asked me for comments about the killings.

Jane said she knew we were doing our best with the Ministry of Defense, and she understood what she called "a very Iraqi response." She knew they were scared to talk and that the Iraqis thought that if they didn't talk about it, the whole matter would just go away. Jane was spot-on.

There was a lot of reactive language by the Iraqi government when insurgent attacks happened, but there was never really anyone who stepped up to offer something more palatable and in-depth. In the States after hurricanes, tornadoes, earthquakes, whatever, usually there are press conferences before, during, and after these events to help quell concerns and offer information to people that help is on the way or to deliver critical information about utility services, emergency operations, and recovery efforts. In Iraq the Iraqi government offered no information, so naturally Iraqis felt they were alone and that nobody was protecting them. If they lashed out against the insurgency, they would be taking on the insurgents, one on one. In the case of the forty-nine soldiers, there might be outrage within the populace, but that outrage would turn to fear because if soldiers could get murdered, what would prevent the same fate from finding Iraqi civilians? With nobody from the government talking, the murder would take on a life of its own in the bewildered herd, and if bad guys came around asking for support, like in the Saddam era, Iraqis gave it out of fear.

Jane said she knew the intent was to let the Iraqis talk but that the Iraqis were unwilling or incapable, and with no one on the U.S. side stepping in to fill the breach, she said, an information vacuum would inevitably be filled by people substituting opinion for fact. She'd prove to be right. Jane was not only a hard-nosed news professional, but in my opinion she was probably one of the more culturally knowledgeable Western correspondents in the region. At that point in 2004 a Defense Department report said that many in the Middle East had anti-American attitudes, including 98 percent majorities in Egypt, 94 percent in Saudi Arabia, and 88 percent in Morocco. Even Jordanians, a people whose government was supporting the U.S. occupation by providing personnel, money, and resources, were tired of the violence, and 78 percent expressed anti-U.S. views. About 85 percent of Iraqis, according to Defense Department reports, didn't approve of the U.S. management of the war. In addition, a U.S. State Department survey of editorials and opinion articles in seventy-two countries uncovered that nearly 83 percent of all commentaries expressed some negativity about the U.S. presence in Iraq. Things weren't good. The Iraqis really needed to talk. Their silence had gone on too long.

Sensing Radhi would get no traction on the issue with al-Shaalan, I contacted Alaa-Eldin A. Elsadr, the communications adviser to Prime

Minister Allawi, to try to encourage them to pressure al-Shaalan. I tipped him off that al-Shaalan was not talking to the media and would issue only a written statement. I said that an Iraqi government official needed to talk about the dead soldiers beyond issuing a statement.

Alaa, or "Al," as he was called, said that Allawi had requested al-Shaalan respond as quickly as possible to the attacks. He added that Allawi would say something only after al-Shaalan addressed the issue with his ministry. Allawi might follow it up and strengthen any message put out by the ministry.

Radhi asked his boss to write a statement that would be released to the media later in the day, twenty-four hours after the event. Salih Sarhan told him that he "would get to it tomorrow," meaning the statement would not be released for at least two days after the killings. Meanwhile, al-Shaalan invited a local television news team to the ministry, and they recorded a short interview that aired the day following the attack. The news crew was from al-Sharqiya, Iraq's first satellite channel and the third most watched station in Iraq, but the channel had credibility issues with the majority of Iraqis because it had ties to Hussein's Ba'ath Party.

According to Radhi, al-Shaalan picked al-Sharqiya because the station employed one of his relatives. There would be little media impact by using al-Sharqiya, especially by offering them an exclusive. The short interview aired without much fanfare. I contacted Al again once the Ministry of Defense had done its interview to gauge the administration's reaction to the broadcast and to determine if that would spur them into doing something else.

Al told me he appreciated all the efforts Radhi and I were exerting, but Ramadan was described in the Arab world as the month of laziness, Iraq could not afford any slow-paced movement, and government officials need to understand that. Despite his words, Allawi's office did nothing to push al-Shaalan or Sarhan to do more, and Allawi himself did nothing. At the time, I should note, Al was being touted as an Arab national, and everyone who worked in PAO circles thought he was a local national. I would later learn that he was a U.S. contractor who had worked for the CPA and worked his way into a U.S. State Department job and later became a U.S. Defense Department employee. So much for an Iraqi face, but I guess Al had an

Arab face and name, which was close enough for the coalition, even though he wasn't Iraqi and was a U.S. government employee.

The killings would be just another atrocious act, committed by a faceless foe upon a faceless nation. At the time, it was the single most important news story in Iraq, but the Iraqis weren't talking. I received at least five dozen press calls from all the major networks and key international print publications in the hours following the roadside execution of the fallen forty-nine, at least a hundred in the days that followed. There was a media expectation that the coalition or the Iraqi government would step up and address the tragedy that had occurred.

Having Sabeeh trained, mentored, and in place at the ministry would have certainly helped the Iraqis manage the aftermath of this attack. Other Iraqis had received a bit of public affairs training, but voids like the one created by this murder could be filled by mentorship, which is what I was trying to offer Radhi. However, a huge failure by coalition PAOs in Baghdad was the lack of follow-up mentorship for Iraqi PAOs.

At our command we helped recruit Iraqi soldiers, we trained their trainers, and then we guided those Iraqi trainers as they trained Iraqi troops. When the Iraqi forces graduated from training, coalition soldiers would mentor them as they entered the operational phase of their professional development. Even after many operations, Iraqi military units had to be validated before becoming fully operational and before conducting operations on their own. The formula worked well because there was sustained training and mentorship throughout the professional development of the Iraqi military force. But even with sustained mentorship Iraqi soldiers still had operational problems, and their performance was less than exceptional, many advisers told me. The forces would need years, not weeks, in order to become a strong fighting force. This to me was a strong sign that only intensive, prolonged mentorship would get Iraqis operating to acceptable standards in any of their endeavors, including public relations.

I took notice early on and knew that the Iraqi security forces' public affairs apparatus would work only if it had a similar sustained training and mentorship program in place. I didn't understand, despite my barrage of requests and pleas, why the coalition did not follow this proven doctrine within the Iraqi public affairs community. There were plenty of PAOs in theater. The intent was obviously there because the public affairs guidance clearly stipulated it, but there was no action by the coalition to prepare the Iraqis to handle their own communications program, and it was obvious by what had just happened with the Iraqi response to the fallen forty-nine. Throughout Iraq our command was helping the Iraqis transition into the lead. We helped the Iraqi security forces assume control of areas. We taught them how to do it. But the coalition did not transition the Iraqis and teach them how to assume high-profile stewardship of their communications mission, and when I tried to mentor and help Sabeeh and Radhi, we were not supported.

The death of these soldiers was personal for our team. We covered the Iraqi military extensively, and we got to know a lot of them. Our advisers patrolled the dangerous streets with them on foot, rode shotgun with them as they rolled through Iraqi cities in convoys, flew as their copilots in Iraqi skies, and were vigilant aboard Iraqi naval vessels in the Persian Gulf with them. My team was no different, and we were along for many of those operational milestones and became connected to these men and women as we tried to tell their stories to the world. The day they died a U.S. Navy journalist traveled to Kirkush to cover the graduation of the battalion, taking pictures and writing a news release about it. It was a mission that had become routine for us, as the pace of Iraqis completing training quickened under Petraeus. The journalist referred to the digital images stored in his camera as "ghosts in the machine." The images are haunting and show the young soldiers caught in a happy moment, smiling from inside of a computer screen as if they are in some type of portal, alive somewhere else, suspended in time. He captured them for a brief, joyous second of their lives. For many it was the first time they had been photographed. The next time a camera would take their pictures was on a roadside in the desert when news photographers arrived to capture the grisly scene of their demise.

Although al-Shaalan wasn't talking and it seemed the issue of the murdered forty-nine soldiers would simply fade away, Radhi and I kept the pressure on the ministry to get someone to talk. Our ace in the hole at the ministry was always Gen. Babekir Zebari of the Iraqi Army, the chief of the Iraqi Army Staff, an equivalent to the American chairman of the U.S. military's Joint Chiefs. Babekir was always receptive to our media advice. He liked and trusted Radhi, and because I was Petraeus's PAO he trusted me too. I had started working with him shortly after Petraeus arrived, and I helped Radhi prepare him for interviews with Western press well before the media suppression of the ministry.

Babekir had indirectly spoken with the press in the past. He didn't violate the minister's rule knowingly. Radhi and I would invite press to a graduation or a training exercise, and the media would capture video of Babekir as he spoke to Iraqi troops or addressed them at graduations or prior to operations. It was a way of circumventing the minister without getting the general or Radhi in trouble.

Babekir declined to comment. Radhi told me that Babekir blamed the Americans, particularly our command, for not having armed escorts with the soldiers as they traveled home. Babekir felt that the Americans had put his soldiers on a bus, without weapons or armed escort, and put them at risk by sending them out of the gates of a military base. He left for a long holiday weekend in Kurdistan after speaking with Radhi.

I visited my gas mask yet again.

What highlighted the differences between the United States and its Iraqi hosts was the Iraqi government's response to the killings. It was obvious the government did not value its soldiers, and that was the larger problem. Iraqi soldiers knew nobody gave a shit about them, so why should they get hurt or give their lives when Iraqi leaders didn't give one squat about them?

If forty-nine U.S. soldiers had died in an attack, there would most certainly be some sort of recognition or memorial ceremony and a serious tactical response. During Desert Storm soldiers from a U.S. Army Reserve quartermaster unit died when an Iraqi Scud missile hit their quarters. The Army Reserve still observes the anniversary of that tragic event in Pennsylvania where the unit was stationed. Similarly, the U.S. military marks tragic events each year around our country, and Americans value these ceremonies. They help us understand the sacrifices made by military personnel, but they also help us heal. U.S. government components working for the coalition failed to communicate that value to the Iraqi government in the aftermath of the killings of the fallen forty-nine. That's not to say that we should have tried to instill our values on the Iraqi government, but we should have had a very frank and professional conversation at a high level to let them know that humanizing the attack and the loss would be valuable for them as a nation.

It was no secret in Baghdad that when U.S. personnel traveled in buses to and from Baghdad International Airport, they had several gun trucks protecting the mostly armed occupants. Toward the end of my tour we rode in Rhino buses that were fully armored. The poor fallen forty-nine didn't have shit, just the promise of a regular paycheck. Somewhere, collectively, a ball had been dropped. The coalition should certainly take part of that blame, but not all of it.

Throughout our compound U.S. soldiers wondered why forty-nine soldiers didn't try to overpower a few insurgents. U.S. soldiers applied American logic to an Iraqi scenario. Certainly, some Iraqis would die as they tried to overpower the insurgents, Americans argued, but many others would live if they succeeded, and that was worth a try. It was the glaring difference between the Americans and the Iraqis. Americans would fight to the end for each other, but most Iraqis left their fate in the hands of Allah. I can say with certainty that had there been forty-nine unarmed U.S. soldiers roadside that day, some might be dead or wounded, but I guarantee that most if not all of the insurgents would be dead, and in the aftermath the U.S. military would be handing out medals for bravery.

I should note that not all Iraqi soldiers surrendered their fates to Allah like the fallen forty-nine. I met hundreds of exceptionally motivated and inspiring Iraqi leaders and soldiers who wore the Iraqi military or police uniform and were warriors in every sense of the word, but they were the exception, not the rule. There were plenty of Iraqis who could look beyond their family and tribal lines and see that they needed to do something for the good of their nation, but there were just as many who were loyal to family and tribe first.

Days later I arrived at the office early, trying to get a jump start on returning e-mails. As I sipped my first cup of coffee I reviewed an e-mail from one of my colleagues. The situation would change considerably and turn from national tragedy to a diplomatic nightmare as the American and Iraqi governments showed disharmony.

"There was major negligence by the multinational forces," Allawi told the Iraqi National Assembly.[1] The comment was picked up by the media, and his comment was now swirling around Baghdad coalition staffs like a dust devil.

Allawi set the tone for the rest of the Iraqi government, and rather than try to leverage the tragic event to gain ground on the information campaign of the insurgency, instead Allawi chose to give the coalition a black eye. Petraeus, who had reviewed our fallen-forty-nine media plan, said it was "brilliant" and added that Allawi's comments were "unfortunate." He understood that we would not be able to take action due to the climate Allawi had created. The Iraqis had run the course on the issue. Radhi shamefully admitted to me that he shut off his phone and stopped responding to press e-mails the day after the killings because the media overwhelmed him and he had no answers to offer them. I knew how he felt, and I didn't blame or judge him. Some days I wished I could just turn off the war and go home.

In return for the Iraqi inaction I leaked to the media personal phone numbers to al-Shaalan and those of his personal staff. I also released their e-mail addresses in addition to Al's personal phone number and e-mail address. To ensure the media reached someone, I also released contact information for other players in Allawi's office. If the Iraqis weren't going to talk, they could tell the press themselves. It was apparent to me, and to many, including those in the press, that Allawi was trying to distance himself from the coalition right before the first round of Iraqi elections in hopes of garnering Iraqi popular support and not appear as a Bush ally.

Eventually, al-Shaalan and the Ministry of Defense would release the following statement to the press. The English version read:

PRESS STATEMENT 12: In this honorable and blessed month of Ramadan where God forbid the fight, the terrorists never stopped from taking the religion as a cover to commit the most horrible crimes which target our sons from new army. So Iraq's enemies prove their blind hate upon this institute and their clear fear from the cultivation of its size and its threat against their wicked cancer existence over our beloved country. And these coward and treachery actions will not stop our fighters of the courageous army from carrying on to purify the soil of Iraq from the criminal and terrorism groups.

At 2000 p.m. on October / 23rd / 2004 an armed terrorist group killed 49 unarmed soldiers on leave heading to their families along with 3 other civilian drivers and burned 3 vehicles on road Karkush–Jassan. As we condemn this criminal action, we promise our patient people to make the criminal terrorists get the fair punishment for their crimes against our people and against the sacredness of Islam and Muslims. PRESS OFFICE MOD.

Months earlier I had befriended CBS News producer Andy Clarke, who had come to Iraq to produce Dan Rather's segment with Petraeus in the summer of 2004. Andy was back in Baghdad for a few days and was one of the many who contacted me about the killings. I asked him to meet me at the convention center. By then stories in the press had shifted from forty-nine dead Iraqis to theories about what led to their demise. Since the Iraqis and the coalition had chosen not to focus on the heinous act, the media focused on the conditions that led up to the attack.

The coalition was being blamed for the deaths but also being questioned about the vetting process of Iraqi security forces. There were reports in the press that internal sources in the Iraqi Army tipped off the insurgents about the forty-nine soldiers and their route, bringing into question infiltration of the Iraqi military ranks, in addition to infiltration of police ranks. Security was also an issue with the press. Why hadn't the coalition protected them? The bulk of these press queries were coming to me, and we were still waiting for the Iraqi-face plan to kick in.

For months Lessel and the PAOs in Baghdad had encouraged everyone to be patient and give the Iraqis a chance. The Iraqi public affairs response to the fallen forty-nine was evidence that giving the Iraqis several months to formulate communications strategies without coalition mentorship was a mistake. The public affairs leadership in Baghdad who had not given the Iraqis the mentorship they needed and the guidance they required was now scrambling to get me to respond to the deaths of the Iraqi soldiers. I remained silent.

Advisers and staffers from our command felt especially betrayed by Allawi, as our command more than any other U.S. entity in Iraq had worked closely with Iraq's forces. The blatant public inaction by the Iraqi government was more and more being perceived by the media as a cover-up. In the press it was rumored that the Americans had fucked up and gotten forty-nine Iraqi soldiers killed, and now the coalition was telling the Iraqis to be quiet and that's what had caused Allawi to lash out. I asked Fahmy how the average Iraqi on the street felt, and he said, "Most think the Americans should have protected the soldiers, amigo. They think the Iraqis are just doing what the Americans have told them to do." The Iraqi government's lack of reaction was so blatant that even Iraqis couldn't believe their government was silent. Naturally, because many Iraqis blamed the Americans for the poor conditions in the country, this, too, had to be our fault. That, of course, wasn't true, so I asked Andy to meet me for some off-the-record discussions.

I met Andy and gave him an earful. I explained there were problems between the coalition and the Iraqis. I focused the conversation on issues that were higher level, how U.S. soldiers were given a hard mission to execute and lacked the backing of U.S. and Iraqi political leaders. There was an expectation from Rumsfeld's corner that the Iraqi soldiers would get trained quickly, and there was a big focus on the numbers—quantity, not quality. We were reporting the number of trained Iraqis directly to Rumsfeld weekly. At the ground level Iraqi soldiers were being held to a very high American standard by operational coalition forces, and the two militaries were very different. Our advisers were doing incredible work and understood the Iraqi mind, culture, and work ethic, but there was a really long way to go, and I felt that we needed to be in Iraq for at least another twenty years (based on what advisers were telling me). The demands from the Pentagon were unrealistic, and the lack of urgency from the Iraqi leadership was borderline dangerous. Ancient tribal hatreds were preventing progress in Iraq, and coalition leaders like Petraeus were working hard to build trust and make strides, but the Iraqis needed to step up and cut the shit. They needed to unify, but that wasn't happening. U.S. military personnel were like kids stuck in the middle of an ugly divorce, their parents using them as fodder in the no-man's-land of a fallen relationship. In this case the U.S. government was on one side, the Iraqi government on the other.

I explained that the Iraqis were really the gist of the problem. Yes, the coalition had made mistakes early on, but now we wanted the Iraqis to step up and take charge and show some initiative, and they instead did nothing but line their own pockets.

Andy and I talked for about an hour, and while much of what I told him he and others in the press already suspected, he was hearing it firsthand from someone on the inside with access to senior leaders in Iraq. American and Iraqi camps were at odds with each other. It was cathartic to get the real picture of Iraq off my chest because for so long I had been selling the war, trying to create an environment on the ground that was conducive to safer operations for our ground pounders, but by that point I was a little tired of the Iraqi bullshit, their government's lack of drive, and the lack of vision and strategy of our politicos in Baghdad and our senior military leaders. I had been living in political purgatory for months, and letting a third party know that although the coalition had done almost everything wrong during the first year of occupation, the coalition couldn't progress in Iraq without Iraqi help.

A week after the killings Allawi spoke at a press briefing. Andy was there, armed with all the information I had given him. An Iraqi friend captured this quote for me: "I haven't blamed, I don't blame the multinational force. I said there has been negligence that has occurred, whether it is by the multinational, or part of the multinational force, or whether by the Iraqi Ministry of Defense is not clear. I have ordered an investigation, the investigation is under way, and we should be getting the results very soon. And then we will make a public statement out of this. This is again a murderous attack, attempted to undermine Iraq from developing its own security forces," Allawi said.

Allawi was asked a pointed question. Was the relationship with the U.S. military command still good?

"I just answered your question, sir," Allawi said.

His deflection of the issue spoke volumes, and everyone in the press knew it. There were a lot of issues that needed resolution between the two sides, and without addressing those issues little progress would be made.

There would be no public announcement made later by the Iraqi government about the deaths of the fallen forty-nine. There was no investigation made into the matter that was ever publicly released, but I took every chance I could to speak to the media off the record and get the heat off of the coalition and put it back on the Iraqi government where it belonged since Allawi was casting blame. Redirecting the media back to them wasn't right, diplomatically speaking, but it was the least I could do to save face for our command and its people who had busted and risked their asses to build the Iraqi forces. I wasn't going to let Allawi or anyone tarnish us simply because they wanted to save their political asses. Needless to say, I was happy when Allawi was not reelected.

I have always thought that had we had dedicated PAO mentors in the ministries, individuals with actual political and military muscle, maybe the communications mission would have gone a better route than it traveled while I was there. Certainly, the fallen forty-nine murders would have been managed much differently. I should note that there were plenty of coalition PAOs and diplomats offering tidbits of communications advice during my time in Baghdad, but there was not a single voice directing the ministries regarding ministerial communications. Nobody wanted to offer mentorship full-time, but PAOs from various entities felt compelled to offer communications advice that usually confused the inexperienced Iraqis since everyone was offering different advice.

Opinions on communications matters were fed to the ministries from the

1. NPR contributor Ben Gilbert interviews me moments after a mortar and rocket attack at Taji Military Training Base, Iraq, January 6, 2005. Photo by Andrew Hughan.

2. Iraqi soldiers and I gather around a two-foot-deep crater caused by a mortar shell at Taji Military Training Base, January 6, 2005. Minutes earlier, insurgents had launched an indirect fire attack, using mortars and rockets. The attack injured several Iraqi soldiers. Photo by Andrew Hughan.

3. I stopped to say hello to some kids in Baghdad who were playing on the burned and twisted carcasses of automobiles, a battlefield playground. Days later I would leave Baghdad. Photo by Lorie Jewell.

4. Sgt. Jared Zabaldo, the hardest-working military journalist in Iraq, enjoys a couple of minutes of downtime with Iraqi soldiers at Camp Fallujah, Iraq, prior to the launch of Operation Phantom Fury on November 7, 2004. Photo courtesy of Jared Zabaldo.

5. Dan Rather, Lt. Gen. David Petraeus, and I pause for a moment shortly after we finished an interview in the Republican Palace in Baghdad, summer 2004. Photo courtesy Steve Alvarez.

6. Lt. Gen. David Petraeus and Brian Williams from NBC News prepare to do an interview in the courtyard of Phoenix Base in Baghdad, January 2005. Behind the photographer were at least one hundred coalition military personnel watching the interview. It was the best media training I could ever offer as a PAO. Photo by Andrew Hughan.

7. Maj. Gen. Abdul Qader Mohammed Jassim al-Mifarji of the Iraqi Army briefs the media during a press conference at Camp Fallujah, Iraq, during Operation Phantom Fury, November 2004. Photo by Steve Alvarez.

8. Radhi Badhir, the media relations director for the Iraqi Ministry of Defense, stands in the foreground (with crutch on his right arm) near an international press corps at Taji Military Training Base. Photo by Andrew Hughan.

9. Visiting Iraq's Tomb of the Unknown Soldier in Baghdad, Iraq, in the spring of 2005. The day we visited two disrespectful U.S. civilians were mountain biking down the tomb's steps and all over the memorial while Iraqi facility protection guards watched. Photo by Lorie Jewell.

10. Geraldo Rivera and I joke over the often contentious relationship between the media and the military at Phoenix Base in Baghdad, Iraq, January 2005. Photo courtesy Steve Alvarez.

11. Iraqi Army soldiers celebrate the graduation of the Iraqi Army's Seventeenth Battalion at Kirkush Military Training Base on October 23, 2004. Hours later, forty-nine soldiers were lined up and executed by insurgents on the side of the road as they traveled home for leave. Photo by Joe Kane.

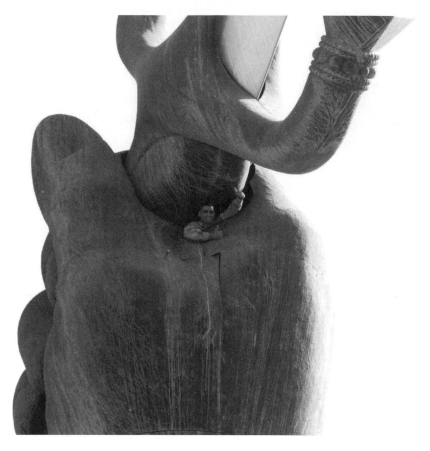

12. The Swords of Qadisiyyah in Baghdad memorialize the Iraq-Iran conflict. Saddam Hussein's hands served as the model. Nearby, helmets of Iranian soldiers are strewn so Iraqi troops trample them as they march under the crossed swords. The Iraqi guard on watch charged me three dollars to show me how to climb to the top. There isn't a GI who served in the Green Zone who didn't visit this site and do the same. Photo by Jared Zabaldo.

13. What is left of the Green Zone Café, a few blocks from our headquarters, after it was bombed on October 14, 2004. Bombings at the popular eatery and a bazaar killed ten people, including four Americans. I took this picture while giving Ben Gilbert from NPR a look at the devastation. Photo by Steve Alvarez.

U.S., British, and Australian Embassies and from our command, STRATCOM, NATO, the Iraqi Reconstruction and Management Office, Multinational Force Iraq, a few contractors, and anyone else who happened upon the ministry and decided to throw in their two cents. A bunch of PAOs, contractors, and political advisers had their hands on the ministries' communications rudders, and none could agree where the Iraqis should be going. Even when they did agree, nobody did anything to help get them there. We all wanted an Iraqi face to be out front, but nobody, it seemed, wanted them to step into the spotlight on their watch. I knew they could manage it with a little help from us, but the rest of the PAO community was reluctant, so they whispered in their ears and let them sit in the corner.

Radhi was a motivated PAO, and I felt bad that he had to endure the revolving door of advice. Frankly, he was more knowledgeable and hardworking than most of the coalition PAOs hanging out in the Green Zone. He had heart and knew the value of talking to the press. Had he had more support, more manpower, mentorship, and diplomatic power, he would have won the information war with a little help from his friends. Most of all he was a cultural expert because he was from the Iraqi culture. While the coalition spent a small fortune hiring contractors, including Al, to educate them on the Arab culture, I could just plunk down in Radhi's office and learn more from him in five minutes than from a so-called cultural adviser. He was the best Iraqi cultural and historical source I knew.

I met Radhi a couple of months after I had been in country. Radhi had contacted me weeks earlier with a plea for help. He said he had worked with public affairs personnel at the press center, but since being appointed the media relations director for the Ministry of Defense, nobody had helped him and offered him further guidance. Radhi had no staff and no guidance, and he had been appointed to a key position in the Ministry of Defense.

The coalition public affairs community referred Radhi to me, not surprisingly, when he was looking for help. Coalition public affairs staffers at STRATCOM and at the press center had told me shortly after I arrived that working with the Iraqis was not something they were fond of, so I wasn't surprised when Radhi contacted me and asked for help.

I was glad he contacted me, and it gave me the ability to advise the Iraqis on a critical piece of their security puzzle, strategic communications management. It also allowed me to serve as an adviser, the very mission our troops were performing. I was more than happy to help even if we lacked the manpower to support him. I'd at least try, whereas overstaffed public affairs teams in Baghdad hell-bent on engaging the Western press did little, despite knowing there was a need. I can make that statement confidently because in the months I worked with Radhi, our team was the only one who worked with him regularly. Radhi and other Iraqi PAOs told me they saw coalition PAOs only a handful of times in the months I worked with them, whereas I interacted with them daily.

I found the Iraqi work culture fascinating. It was not uncommon for me to be able to contact Radhi and ask to meet with the secretary-general of the Ministry of Defense or a high-ranking military leader without having an appointment. They had an open-door policy for my team. I found many patriots within the walls of the Ministries of Defense and Interior, idealistic men who knew they could bring about change to their country. Many had stories that strengthened my resolve to help them, like Mustafa al-Doujaily. He was a teenager when Hussein's troops surrounded his town of Dujail, killing, kidnapping, and jailing hundreds in response to an assassination attempt by the Dawa Party. Hussein was convicted of crimes against humanity in 2006 for the Dujail murders and hanged for the killings. While I found many patriots in the ministries, I found even more opportunists who were lining their pockets and doing whatever they could to advance their personal agendas. Guys like Radhi and Mustafa simply were not the norm.

The first time I went to see Radhi at the Ministry of Defense, I surmised quickly, based on the condition of the military headquarters, that if the nerve center was in poor condition, the rest of the military body must have been in dire straits. The Ministry of Defense was about a block away from our headquarters at Phoenix Base, and I walked over to meet Radhi, who would become not only my counterpart but my good friend as well. As I approached the ministry Iraqi soldiers sat around outside, smoking cigarettes. Some had on complete uniforms, and others were in mismatched uniforms, camouflaged pants with button-down business shirts. Most looked like they were playing dress-up, pretending to be soldiers for Halloween or wearing their dads' clothes. They all looked at me suspiciously. Few Westerners back then came to the ministry, and even fewer had the same dark Arab features that they had.

"Marhaba, shlo-nak," I told them. "S'allah me lekum."

They smiled and uttered some words, of which I understood one, "shukran," meaning "thanks." The courtyard and parking lots of the ministry were packed with damaged cars. Some were sharp-cornered masses of steel and rubber that barely resembled cars after IEDs had destroyed them; others were peppered with shrapnel or bullet holes; few had windshields or windows intact.

Inside Iraqi men lined the hot, darkened hallways, smoking and talking as heavy dust frolicked overhead in sunbeams that penetrated some of the glassless windows of the building. In the cavernous building there were hundreds of men sitting around talking as if they were in a giant barbershop wasting time, waiting their turn. A wing that had been rumored destroyed by a U.S. cruise missile was being slowly rebuilt, so the sounds of machinery every now and then muffled the steady groan of mumbling men. Just inside the front entrance of the ministry was Radhi's office.

Radhi was a short man with two wives who was not a fan of working with women. He spoke exceptional English. He was unemployed prior to the liberation, something he attributed to Hussein's culture, which viewed handicapped people as second-class citizens. Radhi was physically disfigured and needed a crutch to walk, but what he lacked in physical prowess he made up for in attitude, intellect, and work ethic.

Radhi was sitting busily working at his desk, located in front of a large broken window. The room was full of people doing nothing, and when I walked in all eyes were on me—all eyes except Radhi's, who kept working until he heard other Iraqis in the room muttering about my presence.

"Please come in," he told me. "My name is Radhi Badhir." I firmly shook his hand as a wrapped crutch dangled from one of his wrists. He shooed away a few Iraqis sitting around his work space and offered me their warm seats.

"I know you see someone with a handicap, but I can do this job," Radhi told me urgently.

"I don't doubt that," I told him as I looked beyond him and noticed the shattered windows that were his office's backdrop.

"Rockets," Radhi said as he looked at the window, answering the questions my eyes must have been asking. We exchanged a few pleasantries, but as we spoke I could tell that he was uncomfortable talking to me in front of all of the men in his office. The room had at least thirty men in it, all of them attentively listening to and trying to comprehend our conversation. Radhi then asked me to step into the hallway, and I followed him.

"The man I share an office with is trying to take my job," Radhi said. "I have told him we do two different things."

Mohemmed H. Salih, the man Radhi shared an office with, was the community relations officer for the ministry. He was a liaison for the Defense Ministry and the populace. His job was to engage tribal, political, and religious Iraqi leaders in dialogue and garner community support for Iraqi military policies and plans. Instead, he spent his days sucking on hard candy and sipping tea. The guy didn't do shit, but he had a title, director for the public relations directorate, that could threaten Radhi's position in media relations. Stateside, use of the term "public relations" would likely mean Radhi would work for Salih, but in Iraq the term "public relations" as it was used in the ministry meant "tribal liaison."

Radhi painted a very glum picture as we conversed in the hallway. He said al-Shaalan did not want anyone talking to the media. Al-Shaalan believed that most Iraqi soldiers weren't eloquent enough to properly convey thoughts to the media, but beyond that he simply believed it wasn't a soldier's place to speak to the media. Al-Shaalan believed they were "too low class." The spotlight was reserved for Iraqi officials, and only al-Shaalan and his inner circle could do that.

"We have a grave problem here, Steve," Radhi said, as I noticed that a man with an abnormally large forehead had passed by us at least four times in the span of about three minutes, and each time he did Radhi's voice got lower until it became a whisper.

"Who's that guy?" I asked. "What the fuck does he want? Why does he keep looking at us?"

"He is the assistant to the man who is trying to take my job from me," Radhi said.

"Do you outrank him? Is your position here greater than his?" I asked Radhi.

"Yes, he is an administrative aide. I am a director," Radhi replied.

"Then ask him what the hell he wants. Don't let him intimidate you," I said. "Tell him to get the fuck out of here."

Radhi unleashed a forceful barrage of harsh-sounding Arabic that sounded like he was going to cough up a lung and go into a seizure. The guy avoided eye contact and tried to find an escape route, apologizing repeatedly in Arabic as Radhi madly motioned with his hand, his crutch swaying underneath his arm like a bingo wing. Once the man left the hallway, Radhi smiled.

"Oh, I liked that, Steve," Radhi said, grinning and chuckling.

"Don't take shit from these guys. You're a director; they need to respect you. Sad-ass motherfuckers! What did you tell him?"

"I told him to find something better to do than hang around the hallways," Radhi said, laughing.

"I recommend next time you throw something to let him know you mean business," I said, and we shared a hearty laugh as our bromance began.

I got to know Salih a little better once I started working with Radhi. He was a former officer in Hussein's military, a real gem who claimed to have commanded thousands. In one of our meetings he explained he was trying to consolidate his office with Radhi's. I read between the lines, and that meant he was trying to get Radhi to work for him. I simply couldn't trust the guy. He rarely looked me in the eye when he spoke to me, and he obsessively wiped his hands with sanitized wipes after we'd greet each other. He was a typical arrogant Iraqi bureaucrat who fancied himself a prince because he had an office job in one of the ministries. He rubbed me the wrong way from the onset.

He told me in one of our meetings that he had some communications ideas, many of which sounded like ideas Radhi had shared with me. I told him, as I had Radhi, that I was happy to support him. I wrote Petraeus about our developing relationship.

I told him that I had I met with the Iraqi communications director and his PAO staff at the Ministry of Defense and that they were in desperate need of mentoring. I explained that the Iraqis asked me for assistance, and based on our command's doctrine of "train, equip, mentor," I felt obliged to offer assistance. I added that I had asked the press center and Multinational Force Iraq PAOs for help with mentoring the Iraqis months ago, but it seemed that I would have to get in this fight and just do it myself.

I began to notice things as I hung around Salih and Radhi. They were vastly different. Salih surrounded himself with a group of brownnosers who served him as if he were a king. They'd fetch newspapers, tea, dates, pastries, candy, you name it, at his beck and call. I could tell by the way he dressed and acted that life wasn't too hard for him. He knew the right people and was getting away with doing nothing. One of the guys who worked with him said he was married to a physician.

Radhi was aggressive and hungry to make things work, and he had an incredible work ethic. I think being handicapped during Hussein's era had left a big chip on his shoulder and that the weight of it forced him to push harder. I remember one morning he sent me a text message at 4:00 a.m. I was supposed to meet him at his home inside the Green Zone so we could pick up a press pool at the Green Zone's Assassin's Gate by 5:00 a.m. The gate was appropriately named because of the many suicide attacks that occurred there.

That morning as I shaved, to my surprise, my phone beeped. It was Radhi, sending me a text message.

"Wake up. It is time to meet the press," he wrote. That might not sound like a big deal, but that was not normal for a Green Zone Iraqi. Frankly, it wasn't normal for most working in the Green Zone, Iraqi or coalition. I was so impressed I took a picture of the text message. It gave me hope in the slow-moving environment.

The bulk of Iraqis I worked with were being given a shitty example to emulate by coalition PAOs. The coalition wanted Iraqis to have a sense of urgency, and they criticized them for their lack of it, yet many coalition PAOs didn't nurture that climate by displaying urgency themselves. As the coalition made itself at home in Iraq and prepared for a long, uninvited stay, it brought with it the fruits of its labors, the spoils of successful societies sent to the front lines to accommodate staff weenies, high-ranking civilians, and contractors.

In Iraq I saw money being spent at an incredible pace. It's estimated the U.S. government spent more than $300 billion in Iraq in the first three years. By 2006 nearly $9 billion could not be accounted for.

There was too much work to be done in Iraq, and it seemed that most coalition PAOs in the Green Zone didn't have a problem taking time off, either. I heard people argue, "If you burn yourself out, you won't be useful to anyone." That was a lame excuse for people who failed to see that if everyone let their guard down even for just a minute, collectively, we lost traction in the war. We were in an informational tug-of-war, and resting meant defeat.

Recreational activities were a distraction and enjoyed only by the underworked. If a person had time off, it meant to me that they could have devoted more time at their job or helped someone else with their duties. I wasn't one to subscribe to the notion that "work will always be there tomorrow." We worked as if there might not be a tomorrow, and we crammed as much as we could into each day. Time off to me was something reserved for fighting forces. Our quality of life was much better than that of combat personnel, and staff pukes like me and other PAOs needed to reserve those privileges for those who earned them. We should not use them just because they were available to us. A twenty-hour day behind a desk is still much less stressful than a two-hour convoy across Baghdad, but the Green Zone was considered a "war zone," so people flocked to it. It was war lite.

A few weeks after I arrived in country, a small cadre of instructors from the Defense Information School, where military PAOs are trained, including the commandant himself, Col. Hiram Bell of the U.S. Army, flew to Baghdad to train Iraqi public affairs personnel. I found it interesting that the school's commandant would travel so far to train Iraqis when he was an administrator at the school, but Bell would say in a military news article that he deployed to support his team and to provide assistance to senior public affairs officers.

The deployment of the information-school instructors was very out of the norm, and it got a lot of attention on the ground. It was weird that the U.S. military at that time would send the head of the military information school to teach Iraqis about public relations and communications but didn't send the heads of the infantry, armor, flight, and police schools to teach Iraqis how to fight and protect themselves. Why weren't instructors or the commandants of the U.S. infantry, armor, artillery, logistics, Special Forces, or other schools mobilized with their own teams and sent to Iraq on rotations to train Iraqi forces? It was the first time an information-school training team had deployed to a war zone, and all I could think about was why, especially given the quiet climate.

Like many public affairs problems in Iraq, deploying a public affairs mobile training team made little sense if the Iraqis weren't talking. DIN-FOS would train them to talk while they were silent. Imagine deploying instructors from the U.S. Navy's Top Gun school to teach Iraqi pilots how to dogfight, but the Iraqis aren't flying any planes. It makes no sense. It was like teaching someone to walk who was bedridden.

I thought the cadre should wait. They should come to Iraq when the Iraqis were actually engaging the media and prepared to put their Iraqi face out there. Once the ministries were allowed to speak, then the Iraqis could be taught and then mentored, but at that time it made little sense to train people on perishable skills. The Iraqis had no concept of public relations or military public affairs. A crash course wouldn't help them in the middle of an insurgency.

Before DINFOS instructors departed I was contacted by Colonel Bell. He knew I was working with the ministries, and he asked me to help him fill seats for his proposed Iraqi public affairs courses. I explained that I thought it was a bad idea for them to come. The Iraqis had no knowledge of public affairs operations, public relations theory, or effective use of a free press at wartime. Culturally, they were not ready for something like this, the timing wasn't right, and the climate wasn't conducive to deploy public affairs instructors. The Iraqis needed sustained mentorship, not some days-long public relations course.

I offered that the school should deploy a group of advisers that would offer a training course but then embed with the Iraqi ministry PAOs and spend as much time with them as possible, maybe a year or so, teaching, mentoring, and guiding the Iraqis as they embraced military public relations. It was the same adviser-support model our command was using to train Iraqi troops. Bell's team didn't have a year, he said; they had only a few weeks.

I warned Bell that while his course might be a good foundation, without continued mentorship after they completed the course, the Iraqis would quickly forget their lessons. I also explained to Bell that the Iraqi ministers of interior and defense prohibited anyone from speaking to the media. Overall, the Iraqi government was not talking to the press. The cadre would be training personnel who could not perform the tasks they had been trained to perform. It would be a waste of taxpayer money, resources, and time.

Bell responded that after the two-week course that would cover topics like press release writing, how to respond to media queries, and how to set up press conferences, the Iraqis would be mentored for another two weeks. He said the course was for all Iraqi ministry PAOs and not just for those at the Ministries of Defense and Interior. With a team of six people he would be awfully busy, as there were at least thirty Iraqi ministries and only fourteen days to mentor them. The quality of mentorship, if it happened at all, based on that short time line, would be poor, I thought. It would not be meaningful.

I repeated to Bell that the coalition had issued public affairs guidance that directed PAOs to find opportunities to put an Iraqi face on things. I explained that I was working with Allawi's office, the highest Iraqi governmental office in the nation, and that they were refusing to proactively talk to the media and that Allawi had set a tone at the top for the ministries to remain silent, but I would not sway them. The school deployed a six-person team, despite my warnings and recommendations. In new stories published on U.S. military websites, the team boasted that they had been flooded with more students than expected. In reality, the team had asked everyone in Baghdad to find people to fill the seats. The ministries sent a lot of administrative personnel who needed something to do. Any Iraqi with a pulse was sent to fill an empty seat. I visited the class once while picking up a news crew at the convention center. I approached one of the Iraqis I knew who was attending the course. He worked as an admin assistant in one of the ministries.

"What are you doing here?" I asked him.

"I am training," he replied.

"What are you training for?" I asked.

"I do not know," he replied. "I was told to come here today, so I did."

When I told him he was receiving training to be a PAO and to speak to the press, his face became ashen.

"To speak to media?" he asked.

I nodded yes. Minutes later I saw him load his pockets with food and juices and haul ass.

The cadre may have been able to tout afterward that they had trained a particular number of people (and they did, "more than thirty," they claimed), but did they succeed in their mission? Even if the classes had a robust curriculum and interested students, the Iraqi government was not letting anyone talk to the press. The Iraqis who were trained by DINFOS within weeks were doing non–public affairs jobs at their ministries or, if they had public affairs titles at work, were doing something other than public affairs duties.

After a few weeks the DINFOS instructors got their short war tours under their belts and headed home. I should say that the training-team concept is good in theory, but Iraq back then was a mess. The collective PAO community on the ground did not need more PAOs to train folks who weren't doing the work; they needed mentors to educate and advise the Iraqis. Those mentors could also have been used to unify Iraqis who were infighting within the ministries.

Not surprisingly, less than three years later, the coalition reported in a January 2007 military news article that previous coalition public affairs training had not made an impact. The Iraqis attended another public affairs workshop, and an Iraqi deputy media-operations director for the Iraqi joint headquarters said that there was little knowledge at the ministry in regards to public affairs.

"Before the course, we never knew how to deal with the media," the Iraqi PAO stated. This is what I had warned against.

Radhi and Salih's friction would lead to plenty of problems and melodrama, most of it caused by the coalition, but we made some strides with Radhi. Under our team's strong urging Radhi wanted to establish a command information newspaper for the Iraqi troops. He had told me that there were many rumors circulating throughout the ranks of the Iraqi military. Many were outlandish, like how some soldiers feared they would not be paid because the government had run out of money and that Americans were shooting deserting Iraqis on the battlefield. There were many rumors afoot.

We felt it would be a good idea to launch an Iraqi military magazine to counter rumors and keep the Iraqi force informed. Because the average Iraqi *jundi* (private) back then didn't have Internet access, and if he did probably wouldn't know what to do with it, we thought we could create the newsletter with a desktop publisher and print it. We could distribute hard copies at all training posts and help quell rumors and distribute the electronic copy to those Iraqi soldiers and officers with Internet and e-mail access. Our command could help with distribution through our well-connected adviser network. We made enough trips all over Iraq that we could carry hundreds of these things, and we would also e-mail it to our advisers, who could print them at their outposts. It would be unsophisticated, but if the primitive distribution model worked for U.S. troops during the Revolutionary, Korean, and Vietnam Wars as well as World War II, the distribution system could work for us until we developed something better. We also planned to hang the newsletter up on the Ministry of Defense's website.

Because Radhi had no staff and so as to be inclusive of his office mate, we borrowed two Iraqis from Salih's fat team and trained them on how to lay out the magazine, work with images and graphics, and do a little article, caption, and headline writing. It was Newspaper 101, and the guys trained with us for a few weeks. A U.S. Navy journalist led most of that effort, and we were making good progress when Salih began to reel them in and the pair showed up less and less at our office. They soon stopped coming.

I called Aqeel, one of the guys we were mentoring who had become a good friend, and I asked what was wrong. His job was being threatened by Salih, and he couldn't come to Phoenix Base anymore.

During our mentorship of Salih's men, I had continued to push for Radhi's control over the public relations directorate. Some of my comments to some of the coalition PAO leadership, like the fact that I thought Radhi worked harder and was more dedicated to the mission and less to kissing ass, had made its way back to Salih, thanks to gossiping coalition PAOs, Radhi said. In response to learning about my opinion, Salih quickly reneged on the offer to help with the newsletter. I didn't care that Salih knew that I thought Radhi was better qualified to lead the directorate. I was paid to give my professional opinion about what was right for the ministry communications team, and it wasn't personal. The best man needed to be given the job, but I wanted to be diplomatic, so I scheduled a time to visit the nepotistic egomaniac, Salih, to see what was going on.

When I arrived we went through the slew of greetings, and I shook hands with what seemed like twenty men. At long last I sat down with Salih and Ziad, the guy with the big forehead, after being served candy and chai tea and some pastries. I got through the pleasantries quickly.

"Sir," I started, "I understand there is now some resistance to publishing the soldiers' magazine. Why?"

He spoke in Arabic to me, the whole time looking me square in the eye, as if he were trying to address something inside of me. Ziad stammered as he tried to listen, translate, and speak to me at the same time.

"Mr. Salih was a general in the great Iraqi Army," Ziad said. "He is a man who has been commander to many. He appreciates your advice, but he does not need to be told how to do his job."

I wanted to reach across the table and pull Salih out of his seat. But because he was a former general officer, even if he was from another nation, I wanted to show respect for his rank, despite not having any for him personally. I let them continue and spoke once they were done and only after asking if I could reply.

"Sir, if I somehow gave you the impression that I was telling you what to do, I apologize," I told Salih. "I know you are a man of respect and stature in the Iraqi military community, and it is my privilege to work with you, but I was merely training your personnel, something you asked me to do, by showing them how they should publish and distribute the newsletter. I didn't mean for that to be construed as me overstepping my position."

Despite my diplomacy Salih was hot. Ziad said I had insulted him by telling others he was not qualified to be a PAO and that his people now felt he was not knowledgeable and had contempt for him. Coalition PAOs, Ziad said, had told Salih I was pushing for Radhi's appointment as chief PAO, and he didn't like the way I operated. I continued to slather on the apologetic bullshit, but Salih kept coming at me as if he were some god whose wrath I somehow needed to feel.

"Okay, I've apologized, sir. I am entitled to my professional opinions, and as the chief PAO adviser for the Ministry of Defense, I think Radhi, not you, is better to lead. As a former soldier you of all people should understand professionalism and not take things personally. I don't know what else to tell you or what else to do," I said.

Ziad translated what I had said. "There is nothing else to say," Ziad said.

I stood up and extended my hand. Salih didn't shake it and looked away from me.

"Actually, there is one more thing to say," I said. "Fuck you, asshole." I turned and walked out of his office and nodded at Radhi on my way out. As I walked down the hall I could hear Salih's voice get louder as Ziad tried to finish the translation.

"Captain!" Ziad shouted. "Captain!"

I might as well walk straight to Petraeus's office, because when he hears about this one, he's going to send me home in cuffs, I thought. Nothing ever happened. Nobody said anything to me about the incident, not even Radhi, who had never seen me lose my cool.

I had shared my thoughts about Salih in the strictest professional confidence with Multinational Force Iraq, British and U.S. Embassy PAOs, and political advisers, but Salih had lied and told them he had been appointed the PAO chief by al-Shaalan, because he sensed I was gaining ground on getting Radhi appointed as the PAO boss. Naturally, what Salih said the coalition PAOs took as gospel, despite the fact that al-Shaalan's office denied Salih's assertions. What made the chain derail off the sprocket, so to speak, was when my peers told Salih that I was trying to get Radhi the job Salih wanted to take from Radhi, a job Salih thought he had locked by working with me and lying to others. My PAO counterparts made me look like a backstabber, when the truth was that I was helping Salih get something constructive done. As the lead public affairs adviser at the ministry, Radhi, I believed, was the smarter choice to lead public affairs at the Defense Ministry. It wasn't gossiping. I was weighing in professionally by stating that the ministry would be better served by Radhi. As a coalition adviser I shared my professional assessment of Salih and offered my opinion based on the good of the mission.

Salih's beef with Radhi was because Salih didn't think Radhi could be a good PAO because he had no military experience. One of Salih's men once told me, "How could a handicapped man possibly know anything about the army?" Radhi was right. There was discrimination in pockets of the Iraqi culture toward handicapped people. But aside from the prejudice, Salih simply didn't like Radhi.

I would later learn from a British senior Ministry of Defense adviser that as I petitioned to have Radhi take the lead for public relations, he had been proposing to al-Shaalan that the public outreach and media-relations offices be rolled into one and that Salih direct both under one roof. Problems at the ministry with the PAO hierarchy were further complicated because al-Shaalan had created a job for Sarhan, one of his relatives, which added a third wheel to the mess, and Sarhan, along with Salih and Radhi, was bucking to be the big boss of the consolidated public affairs directorate. It was a political mess and one that was agitated when guys like the Brit "adviser" offered advice without first getting an understanding from guys like me who were daily working with the Iraqis.

The Brit said the Iraq Reconstruction Management Office had a PAO mentoring program that was covered by a pricey media-training contract that would be coming online soon. I was flabbergasted. I had sought someone to train the Iraqis in public affairs for months. I had been bounced around by the coalition as I tried to find the Iraqis mentors and permanent trainers, and now this. For that matter, why had the school of information bothered to come out if there was a contract to provide what they supported? The fact still remained, the Iraqis were not talking. Why did we bring the U.S. information-school trainers to Iraq, and now why were we dumping money into a contract that would offer services that could not be used?

Salih and Sarhan would both eventually convince everyone that they were Radhi's boss, everyone except me and Radhi, and control of the public affairs office was given to them by the coalition (so much for sovereignty) but never by al-Shaalan. Radhi's office became sort of like the divided Korean peninsula: there were some in Salih's camp and others in Sarhan's. Radhi and I mostly stayed away from them and continued to work with Babekir, getting stories out as best we could about the Iraqi security forces, engaging the Arab media directly under everyone's nose with limited success. Like the coalition PAOs who actively impeded my progress, Salih and Sarhan expended their energy to stop Radhi, but Radhi and I were too busy and worked around the lot of them to try to develop command information products.

Command information, what the military calls its corporate internal communications, is meant to inform the military masses or internal audiences. Initially, military corporate communications was limited to command newspapers, which were mostly read by military members and their families at a particular location. Homestead Air Force Base, for example, had its own newspaper for that community. The introduction of the Internet as it transformed the news industry also changed military newspapers because it enabled local military news to have far-reaching readership to include the general public.

Command information is an important element of any military command because it is a forum for a commander to communicate mission-related information to a unit. Military news products inform readers about command-related topics that impact command personnel, but also those in the command's community. These products also help control rumors, and that is the value I saw in the Iraqi military magazine.

One day Radhi told me that the ministry had heard rumblings of the plan to publish a magazine. I knew that some in the ministry knew about it and supported it, but I wanted to fly underneath the minister's radar because I knew he would squash the initiative if he learned about it.

Weeks later the Ministry of Defense published a glossy magazine that would be distributed only at the ministry building. I guess all those guys sitting around needed something to read. Iraqi soldiers in the field were precluded from reading it because it had been created exclusively for Iraqi military leaders, exactly the crowd who didn't need a publication. It was a piece of crap and had no command value for the average Iraqi soldier we were trying to reach.

The weeks we had spent on the magazine were wasted. The minister shut down our magazine effort. He viewed the soldiers' newspaper as a redundancy because he had published the glossy magazine, and the coalition diplomats who had supported the publishing of a magazine (something they didn't relay to me) also recommended we shut down our publishing efforts. We had planned to publish a monthly magazine titled *Jundi*, the Arabic word for "private or common soldier," but a political IED ended that effort.

Meanwhile, the Iraqi ranks swelled with rumors. There was a serious desertion problem, and the Iraqis were losing around 25 percent of their forces, advisers told me. (Some sources estimated the percentage to be as high as 80 percent; by comparison, the U.S. military in a four-year period starting in 2003 had about eight thousand desertions, according to the Pentagon.) But the rumors that were circulating indicated that tens of thousands were deserting, and that was wholly false. There were a lot of rumors to combat, and now we had no way of fighting those rumors. But command information is not just a tool to dispel rumors; it is also a way to improve morale.

An Iraqi military newspaper would have also shared stories of Iraqi military heroics, and there were plenty of stories, like that of Qassem Mohammed, who died in the line of duty. Mohammed was manning a machine-gun emplacement protecting a military compound when a homicidal car bomber drove at his position. Mohammed fired at the terrorist and caused him to lose control of his vehicle. When the car crashed part of the bomb exploded, killing Mohammed, who died manning his gun, though he had succeeded in repelling the attack. Stories like this would inspire esprit de corps across Iraq's army.

Stories of successful Iraqi military operations would also motivate Iraqi units. As Iraqi forces read about their brethren's successes, it would reinforce the point that Iraqi soldiers had made the right choice to serve in Iraq's military. Like U.S. command information programs that had now started to inform the public and press alike, our team envisioned the same thing happening in Iraq. As the information was disseminated, it would inevitably make its way to the Iraqi and Arab press and eventually to the Iraqi masses. Iraqi command information newsletters would become yet another prong in our approach to inform Iraqis, and the news would have an impact on the enemy because we planned on disseminating electronic versions of the publication via the Web. There would be a level of deterrence delivered by the newsletters.

I viewed the termination of the Iraqi military newsletter not only as a huge defeat for our mission, but also as a very obvious indicator of a need for a mentor in the Ministry of Defense. If we had a mentor in the ministry advising leaders about the importance of building morale, informing forces, and educating the masses, maybe the publication would not have been shut down. It seemed to me that had the landscape been examined more carefully by Defense Information School cadre, PAO leaders in Iraq, contractors, and interloping politicos, we could have trained and educated Iraqi leaders on the importance and strategic relevance of communications instead of training technicians to execute a mission they were not allowed to perform. Money would have been better spent educating Iraqi societal leaders on the value of communication. Instead, we prepared underlings to do a job their bosses believed they had no right to perform.

I was so convinced Iraqi public affairs mentorship was critical to achieving mission objectives in Iraq that I asked Petraeus to allow me to serve as a full-time public affairs adviser at the ministries. I was willing to relinquish my position in the most coveted military public affairs position as Petraeus's PAO and as the PAO to one of only a handful of general-officer commands in Iraq. I had my dream assignment, but I felt I could do more meaningful, longer-lasting work at the ministry than as his PAO. The mission demanded it.

"Would hate to lose you," Petraeus told me, and he said he'd think about it. I never broached the topic again, and Petraeus never brought it up. I took that as a no and moved on. We simply did what we could with what we had.

On the other side of our counterinsurgency communications plan was the Iraqi police training mission. Since I had arrived the Iraqi police were selectively talking to the press, but it was mostly reactive commentary after attacks, confirming the number dead and what had happened at the scene of a crime. There was no constant proactive Iraqi police media presence, despite the fact that public-order battalions had been deployed, police commandos were on the streets kicking ass, Iraqi highway patrolmen were cruising long stretches of highway on the frontier of Iraq's badlands, and border forts were being erected around the country. There were good strides being made, but nobody really knew about them. Iraqis didn't know there was anyone trying to protect them by the latter part of 2004. Moreover, all of the rumors of police corruption were overshadowing any small gains we were making with the Interior Ministry.

The Coalition Police Assistance Training Team was the second of two training teams in our command (the other was the Coalition Military Assistance Training Team), and they were charged with training Iraqi police forces, which reported to the Ministry of Interior. The team was composed of mostly contractors, some ex-military and former, or current cops who served as international police trainers and advisers for the Iraqi police. The Ministry of Interior when I first arrived in Baghdad had a young, brand-new college graduate serving as the lead public affairs adviser for the ministry. She was a journalism school graduate, and her job in Baghdad was the first she held after graduating from college. A few months after I arrived the college grad was replaced when she left Baghdad with her CPA buddies. Another young lady replaced her, and she too had little professional experience and lacked what was needed to be a lead communications adviser in the Ministry of Interior. In fact, she had little to no experience in international public relations and no experience working in a foreign environment. At least military personnel had experience working with foreign forces. Personally, during my years with the military I had worked with forces from Korea, El Salvador, Germany, Australia, England, Italy, Spain, Mexico, Honduras, and several other countries.

While Iraqi police made strides to keep Iraq safe, these "communications advisers" were not doing anything notable to get the word out. I never saw a news release about the ministry's activities, and I didn't see the Ministry of Interior in the news other than just the reactive commentary to an attack or crime. They never held a press event or a press conference to showcase anything being done by the Iraqi police service. The ministry had yet another PAO in a city filled with PAOs who collectively weren't accomplishing any communications objectives. The Ministry of Interior was lost. While things were bad at the Defense Ministry, the Interior Ministry was much further out of touch. They weren't doing anything meaningful, but they were spending money.

The Coalition Police Assistance Training Team in 2004 had a $400,000 media contract. As the command's PAO I didn't know what that money was used for. I had discovered the figure as I reviewed the police team's expenditures. I asked the police training team's chief of staff, the former commanding general of the team, and the contracted PAO, and nobody knew what the money was for or who was getting it. Worse yet, nobody ever tracked down why and how the money was spent.

Shortly before the fallen forty-nine were killed, the Ministry of Interior wasn't doing anything proactive with the press. Again, it was only responding to media queries and not actively engaging the press. The proof, as always, was in the pudding. There was little mention of the Iraqi police in the press, which is why I was perplexed when Slavonic approached our command about sponsoring and paying for two communications-related contracts. The first contract would remodel a conference room, so the ministry could conduct press conferences, $195,000. The second was to pay for a $1.5 million media-engagement program. He said if we funded the engagement contract, the ministry could underwrite the Iraqi *Cops* show I so badly wanted to create.

"What do you think, Steve?" Petraeus asked.

I gave him an earful. I didn't see the need for a room that would not get used. Did the Ministry of Interior have a busy press schedule? If the ministry committed to the plan we were proposing, weekly joint press conferences with the Ministry of Defense and their sustained involvement, we should revisit the issue once they proved their commitment to press relations. Building a facility when there were no press briefings seemed wasteful. I found it strange that proposals had already been assembled for these two projects (complete with bids) and that we knew nothing about it. I wasn't trying to be difficult, but the truth was that the Interior Ministry wasn't doing anything proactive in the press that justified building their own press center. As for the $1.5 million media-engagement plan, I didn't see why we needed to spend more money when we had everything we needed to engage the media already in Iraq. We had hundreds of PAOs, a press center with a press briefing room, a ready and willing Western press corps that was bored and tired of reporting from the Green Zone, and an Arab press corps that had long been ignored and was waiting to be engaged. Above all, we had more material than we could use each week to feed pressers. Each week, on average, our command had at least thirty to forty meaning-ful and marketable stories we could use to engage the press. We had all the necessary elements, but the public affairs community was convinced that it needed to add another layer of bureaucracy by hiring more contractors to do work that could be done by military PAOs and federal civil servants. It seemed like PAOs wanted to spend more money so contractors could do their jobs for them. Above all, I believed that because Iraqi political leaders had a history of appointing people loyal to them to high-profile positions, there was nothing to stop them from rewarding individuals with large contracts to build things that weren't needed. It was a big money grab, and I didn't support it.

I hired our Iraqi media team simply because the coalition wouldn't give us the personnel we needed, and I was able to employ ten people for less than $40,000 per year. Once I equipped them they would be able to capture the footage we needed to create the Iraqi *Cops* show, but it never came to fruition because the Ministry of Interior made it difficult for us to send our team to cover their forces and refused to grant us access to police personnel. Now the ministry through Slavonic was using the show as leverage to get what it wanted. We already had a contracted Iraqi media team that could provide support to the Interior Ministry, so why the need for more contracts? They wouldn't even use what was already in place.

When Slavonic pitched his contracts in September 2004, it was a particularly violent time in Iraq, and because I had delivered the ultimatum of starting press conferences to Slavonic in exchange for contractual support, I wanted to test the waters to see how committed the ministry was to proactive communication. If they really wanted and needed these contracts, they would jump on my recommendation to start the joint Iraqi police and military pressers in exchange for our underwriting their pet projects. I pitched it to Lessel and Slavonic via e-mail. I knew it would go nowhere.

Lessel wanted me to wait. He said the Iraqis had just hired a communications director (yes, yet another communicator to add to the fray) and were beginning to formalize their process for getting information out. Lessel said he was working with Allawi's office to get the ministries and Allawi's office working together to put out consistent messages on security.

Slavonic, who was pushing to get the contracts funded, disagreed and wanted me to move forward, saying that we should not wait and that we needed to continue to move forward and ensure we kept everyone informed as we went. I agreed with the admiral and pushed for Lessel to reconsider. Waiting, I said, leads nowhere. We needed to be more aggressive, I told Lessel.

Lessel said I had done some great things with the Ministries of Interior and Defense, but he said if we moved forward we absolutely had to coordinate press conferences. Lessel was concerned that the Iraqis would all be saying different things or wouldn't be on the same sheet of music, and my concern was that they weren't saying anything at all. I moved ahead and started coordinating the press conference, keeping everyone informed, as we had discussed.

In early October 2004 I called a meeting at the Ministry of Defense, between Radhi, the Defense Ministry's PAO; me; and Col. Adnan Abdul-Rahman, the Interior Ministry's spokesman. Our first goal would be to schedule a regular weekly joint-forces press conference where the Iraqi military and police forces could interact with the media on a regular basis. There would be opening remarks from each ministry PAO, and then there would be a question-and-answer period for the press. Our first conference would be on October 11, 2004.

We agreed that field soldiers and police officers would be brought to the press briefing to showcase heroics or successful stories of Iraqi security forces in action. There were plenty, Radhi and Adnan said, and they were excited at the prospect. They liked that we were leaning forward in the foxhole. The soldiers and police officers would talk to the Arab and Iraqi presses about their duties, missions, experiences, and, of course, success stories. We all agreed that we needed to put a face on the Iraqi security forces and let the Iraqi public see their forces for themselves, in their own words. I briefed Petraeus, and Radhi and Adnan said they would coordinate and inform their ministries. Petraeus was excited about it and encouraged me to "keep pushing."

Days after briefing Petraeus about the joint press conference, who in turn briefed Casey (who supported the idea), our idea for the joint weekly press conference was shut down by STRATCOM and by the Iraqi government, citing a lack of coordination.

Lessel said he understood what I was trying to do, but he hoped I understood what the Iraqi government was trying to do. He said that I had been pushing them forward and making some solid gains in the public affairs arena, but cancellation of the presser was done by the Iraqis because of a lack of coordination.

Sabah Kadhim, known as Dr. Sabah, was the Interior Ministry's communications director, and like Salih he liked to be the center of attention. He rarely traveled anywhere and stayed holed up at the ministry, safe behind its walls. In talking to Radhi and Adnan after the press conference was canceled, I learned Adnan had not yet briefed Dr. Sabah about the presser. When Sabah learned about it he rushed to shut it down before being briefed by Adnan. Learning of his misstep, Sabah, Adnan said, would happily allow us to turn it back on. The coalition PAOs advised against it, Adnan said.

Radhi had scheduled Iraqi soldiers to attend the briefing and had already locked his plan and told Salih and Sarhan about it. When asked about it by coalition PAOs, they played dumb and said they were not informed about the presser and called for it to be shut down. Radhi couldn't believe Salih and Sarhan were lying right to his face.

Lessel said that the whole thing could be frustrating but that it should resolve itself, as the Iraqis established their coordination process and improved communications. Given the history, though, I didn't think it would resolve itself, like al-Shaalan's media plan, which never came to fruition, and just like how we waited for them to put an Iraqi face on everything and their response to the fallen forty-nine. I had been trying to get the ministries to do weekly press conferences for months, and this would be my final try. I was sick of pushing the boulder up the hill.

In 2006 Petraeus coauthored the U.S. Army's newly revised counterinsurgency field manual. In it there was a theme that resonated with those of us who worked hard to get the Iraqi security forces into the public forum, starting with joint press conferences.

"Weekly press conferences might be held, particularly with host nation media, to explain operations and provide transparency to the people most affected by counterinsurgency efforts. Such venues also provide an opportunity to highlight the accomplishments of counterinsurgency forces and the host nation government." We may not have succeeded in getting the Iraqis to do the joint press conferences, but there was validation for my team in 2006 when this statement was published in the U.S. forces' counterinsurgency field manual two years later. There was meaning and purpose in what we were trying to do in 2004.

Communicating to counter the insurgency had been our goal, yet the coalition public affairs community prevented it from happening. I tried my entire tour to bring both Iraqi police and Iraqi military forces to engage the Arab and Iraqi press, but it would never come to fruition during my tour, at least not in the manner I envisioned it. We did set a high-water mark with one particular effort involving our Iraqi media team, but that would end almost as quickly as it started.

Despite overwhelming support for the Iraqi *Cops* show from Petraeus, Casey, Lessel, Slavonic, and the Iraqi government, including Allawi, we were unable to accomplish anything because we could not clear low-level hurdles at the Ministry of Interior and because the coalition PAOs and politicos were unable or unwilling to help us. Why as the lead nation and government in this operation we stood idly by and watched our own people impede progress is beyond me.

"The right messages can reduce misinformation, distractions, confusion, uncertainty, and other factors that cause public distress and undermine the COIN [counterinsurgency] effort. Constructive and transparent information enhances understanding and support for continuing operations against the insurgency," the U.S. military's counterinsurgency manual reads. These are things that could have been achieved through the joint press conferences, through the Iraqi soldiers' magazine, and by sustained mentorship in the ministries.

The many good things being done by Iraqi forces would mostly go uncovered by the press, and news from Iraq transmitted around the world would go into a steady morbid drumbeat once my team left the country. Radhi e-mailed me after I left to say that the public affairs community was more lost than ever once I was gone and that he had no allies. He missed working with me. I think of him daily, and I miss the man who became an emotional crutch for me. I keep a picture of the two of us on my desk and often think about how he and one of the leaders in the ministry once referred to me as "a friend of Iraq."

The last time I saw Radhi he was walking into the Defense Ministry after he gave me a memento and we said our good-byes. I keep the brass plaque on my office wall as a daily reminder of the battles Radhi and I fought to try to do something good for his country, and it reminds me of my dear friend who is still in danger every day. We fought an enemy, and we fought our own people. I routinely send him e-mails to ensure he is okay, e-mails that since the U.S. military pulled out of Iraq in 2011 have gone unanswered. He is my friend for life even though I do not know if he has given his.

Surprisingly, despite having civilians identified as public affairs advisers, there was no public affairs advising going on at the military or police training teams. Even though the press center had personnel assigned as ministry advisers on their personnel rosters, the ministries did not have anyone from the press center who provided steady, meaningful public affairs counsel. In fact, Radhi said that nobody from the press center ever went to the ministries to work with him.

The last time I saw Salih was at Landing Zone Washington in the Green Zone in late December 2004. Radhi and I had multiple Black Hawk helicopters reserved for a press trip traveling to Basra; it would be Radhi's first solo press trip without any of us there to help him, and we were starting to engage the press more as the Iraqi elections were coming. Suddenly, the Iraqi politicos thought it might be a good idea to talk to the press, and the defense minister was away on holiday, so we took advantage of things.

Radhi and I helped load the helicopters with Iraqi government and military officials and a small group of Arab press people. I was worried about Radhi, not professionally but physically. At the landing zone he routinely had to hold onto me, and I had to embrace him when Black Hawks landed and dusted off everything in sight with strong gusts of wind pushing off their blades. To get into larger vehicles he needed help, and even walking with him took considerably more time because of his physical limitations. Radhi could definitely handle the mental rigors of the job, but physically the smallest demands of being a wartime PAO pushed him hard, but I'll be damned if he didn't try.

I helped Radhi aboard the Black Hawk and helped him get buckled in when a crewman approached me from another aircraft.

"You guys got too many people, sir."

"What?" I replied.

"Too many people!" I had heard him the first time, but I was surprised.

We had organized the manifests and counted each passenger at the landing zone and matched a name with a body. Now, as we were loading, there was no room.

I helped Radhi down off the Black Hawk as the engines ran on four helicopters, waiting for us to figure out what was wrong. We went chopper by chopper and counted and reviewed each manifest we had made. When we got to the last one, there were Iraqi government guys in suits looking disdainfully inside their bird. Seated inside along with some of his pals was Salih.

"What the fuck are they doing here, Radhi?" I asked.

Radhi leaned into the belly of the bird and asked him, and Salih replied that he was going on the trip.

"What for? He has no business being here," I said. "This is a media trip."

Radhi explained it to Salih over the din of the engines that the mission was a media-relations trip, not a public-outreach mission, and Salih offered a short reply and then looked straight ahead. On his lap was a gift basket full of flowers and goodies to eat.

"He needs to get off this helicopter, Radhi. This is my aircraft mission, and he's not authorized to be on the aircraft," I said.

Radhi explained this to Salih. If he and his buddies went on the sightseeing trip, people with valid missions to southern Iraq would not get to fly and complete their work.

Salih wouldn't budge.

"Sir, please get off this helicopter now. You are not authorized to fly on this mission. Tell him that, Radhi," I said.

Radhi tried again, and Salih looked forward and ignored us.

We walked over to General Babekir's helicopter. He asked what the delay was, and we explained what was happening.

"We need for you to tell Salih to get off the helicopter, sir. He won't listen to us," I pleaded.

Babekir looked at us and said, "Tell him I said to get off the helicopter."

Crap, I thought; that's not going to work. As we walked back the flight lead's crew chief came to me and said that they needed to take to the skies.

The crew chief gave me one minute. Something was strange. Back then when Iraqis flew on U.S. helicopters, they had to have been properly vetted and cleared. I had not cleared Salih and he was not on my manifest, but someone had obviously done it because the aircrews weren't complaining about the passenger changes. They were just worried about keeping their scheduled flight time.

I walked back and found the men who were supposed to be going on the trip arguing with Salih, punctuating everything with heavy hand motions. Salih continued to look forward and ignore everyone. I had become so sick of Salih that for a moment he became the personification of everything that was wrong in Iraq: the bullshit tribal connections, the lack of energy in the Iraqi ministries, the overwhelming sense of individual entitlement over nationalism, the arrogance of the Iraqi leadership, the lack of direction of PAOs, the endless violence, the senseless loss of life, the sheer folly of it all. I fantasized about pulling my pistol and shooting that fucker right where he sat. Then I clicked that thought down a few notches and thought I could force him off the aircraft at gunpoint. I could use security as an excuse. He wasn't supposed to be on the aircraft and his insistence made me nervous, so I could draw my weapon and challenge him and physically remove him. Would it work?

About a thousand different scenarios played out in my head if I started down that road, and none of them ended well. Then I could hear Radhi calling my name just barely over the thumping of the helicopter blades. I looked at him.

"Steve, what are you doing?" Radhi said.

My hand was on my holstered pistol and I didn't even realize it.

My inability to get anything done in Iraq thanks to the international cluster fuck that we had created in Baghdad right at that point started to take its toll on my morale and on my personality. What had once been sarcastic and comical edginess that I could always use to deflect the stupidity of some PAOs had turned into bitterness. I really fucking hated it there because just beyond all of our headquarters bullshit, miles from our lobster tails, near beer, warm glistening pools, Friday-night parties, shiny medals, false bravado, and ivory towers, our soldiers and Iraqis, women and children, were dying barbaric deaths and nobody seemed to give a shit.

Imagine if you knew people were in danger and you had the proven ability to help save hundreds if not thousands of them, but there were people that were doing things to prevent you from helping others. This is what my tour in Iraq had become. I had deployed with the hope of helping improve conditions on the ground, and somehow my life, my mission, had taken the directionless and dysfunctional form of the U.S. mission in Iraq. The abysmal failure of our mission at that point started to pull me down almost as if a hand were reaching out from hell itself, through the scorched, bloody earth, pulling me down. I was no longer a part of the failing mission in Iraq. I was the failing mission in Iraq.

The months of relentless shelling, the constant negativity and lack of cooperation, the unprofessionalism, pettiness, immaturity, the sheer depth of how little PAOs knew about counterinsurgency, the seemingly endless obstacles placed before us had not beaten me, but it had all finally, eight months later, gotten my attention, and now this son of a bitch was sitting in my helicopter, refusing to look at me or talk to me, and I had a loaded gun. The rage coursed through me quickly, and somehow I found solace by looking at Radhi.

"Steve!" Radhi shouted again as the crew chief walked up to me and started talking. His lips were moving, but I couldn't hear a word he was saying.

I could feel myself surrendering to the tension, not giving up, but embracing the frustration and wrapping it around me like a blanket. I took off my helmet, looked at a picture of Rosie and Duncan that I kept inside, and leaned into the bird as my sweaty hand slid off the pistol grip.

I got as close to Salih as I could and spoke into his ear. Salih understood English, Radhi had told me, and he was allegedly a retired two-star Iraqi general who had been a pilot, but I didn't know how much of that was true. He always chose to speak through translators, I assumed so as to not degrade himself by speaking English.

"I would fucking love to shoot you right now, you piece of shit. Hopefully, this insurgency will fucking kill you," I said. He ignored me and sat motionless.

I turned and told the few gentlemen who had been bumped off the flight to meet me at my truck. Radhi repeated my instructions, and they shouted some more. I told the crew chief to close the door to the Black Hawk, and I walked Radhi back to his bird and helped him aboard. I strapped him in, and he apologized repeatedly. He was embarrassed and kept saying he was sorry, over and over again.

I grabbed him by the back of his head and made him look into my eyes once he was strapped in and seated. "No, brother, I'm the one who is sorry," I told him.

I backed off the bird, and the crew chief came in quickly and closed the door. I walked away from the chopper and then stood there as one by one all four birds took to the sky in a sequence that made it seem as if they were attached by an invisible chain.

As the dusty rotor wash hit me, so did the realization that I would never be able to accomplish anything in Iraq, and as I turned to walk back to my truck, the Iraqi men argued about who would ride in the front seat.

8

ARAB MEDIA

More than 50 Iraqis die each day in Iraq November 2004–February 2005.
These figures include only reported deaths.
—**Multinational Corps Iraq**

Iraqi journalists had little professional credibility in the eyes of American PAOs while I was in Iraq. In speaking to PAOs who had experience dealing with Iraqi press, many said they were unrefined and unprofessional. Part of the problem, I suspect, is that journalism in the Pan-Arab world is much different from American journalism. Most Arab news agencies ordinarily are no more than public relations mechanisms for their nations. They file reports that are rarely critical of their governments and serve the interests of their administrations or kingdoms. There are exceptions, of course, such as al-Jazeera and al-Arabiya, the top two satellite news channels that have built their empires on government criticism, but even al-Jazeera has been criticized for not looking too deeply into the Qatari government that funds it and for turning its cameras on all other nations but never on Qatar.

Under Hussein's dictatorship the Iraqi press lacked editorial freedom. Iraqi reporters I spoke to in Baghdad said Hussein controlled editorial content through his Ministry of Information. Foreign press in Baghdad was tightly controlled. After three decades of Hussein Iraqi reporters suddenly found themselves in a state of journalistic atrophy in 2003. Many weren't accustomed to asking questions and demanding answers and accountability from government officials. Some, having spent an entire career as part of Hussein's propaganda branch, didn't have basic journalism skills, such as how to verify facts, properly attribute information, and assemble a solid news story. There were no journalistic standards, no codes of ethics, and no libel laws similar to those in the United States. The Iraqi journalists reported whatever government officials had told them to report.

I should note that many media scholars opine that the U.S. media parrot whatever they are told by government officials with little investigation, so the American media are not free from this categorization too. From my end I can say that's slightly true. If I give a reporter a figure on the number dead at a bombing site or my official account of what happened at a particular event, reporters ordinarily quote me verbatim without cross-checking my data with a coroner or with witnesses. Because I was a government official there was an assumption that the information was accurate, but sometimes PAOs give information that isn't wholly accurate or even true. Take, for example, how at the onset of operations in Fallujah in 2004, a U.S. PAO stated that operations had begun when they had not. The announcement was to trick the enemy into movement in hopes that the coalition would be able to see what the bad guys were doing to respond to our battle plan. It was a smart move, but when the U.S. military uses PAOs to deliver false information, it hurts the credibility of PAOs who are supposed to deal in fact, not fiction. Beyond that there is also a nationalistic connection that U.S. reporters have as Americans that influences how they report.

In the ramp-up for war with Iraq the American media overwhelmingly supported President Bush's claims that Iraq had weapons of mass destruction and that there was somehow a tie to al-Qaeda. They, much like administration officials, beat the drum for war and also said it was time for America to deal with Saddam Hussein. Many media experts in that region made statements in their news reports that helped convince Americans that Iraq needed to be dealt with militarily. We all now know those statements were inaccurate.

In Iraq there was hope for a democratic media. A U.S. Congress report indicated that while there were no independent media under Hussein, in 2005 there were forty-four commercial television stations, seventy-two commercial radio stations, and more than one hundred independent newspapers and magazines in Iraq. But the Iraqi press corps initially wasn't assertive, and they were nonconfrontational. As the Iraqis spent more time around Western-trained and -educated reporters from al-Jazeera and al-Arabiya, they realized they could ask hard questions and demand answers from the Americans and the Interim Iraqi Government.

The coalition's primary media engagement target in Iraq was the American press. There was no denying that the American press corps came first. The unspoken and unwritten logic was that if the press was actively engaged with good news coming out of Iraq, U.S. public opinion would be secured and the administration could continue to push its Iraq agenda to the American people. It seemed that based on their actions, PAOs in Iraq were concerned more with the legacy of the president's administration than they were with turning the tide of the war. That's not to say that PAOs sat around and thought of ways to get Bush reelected, but the public affairs and communications policies being driven by the Pentagon were focused primarily on garnering American public approval, and PAOs in Iraq ensured they were being executed accordingly. Keeping the American people informed and creating conditions that led to confidence in America's Army were, and still are, the public affairs mission statement.

The plan was flawed in a very simple way. The coalition communicated with people who cast votes and not with those killing U.S. soldiers. Had the coalition focused on working more with the Arab press and providing them with the kind of access that it gave the American media, it's very likely things would be different in Iraq.

I talked to dozens of PAOs who served in Baghdad between 2003 and 2005, and each had a horror story about the Arab media. Most PAO criticism surrounded al-Jazeera and its reporting tactics and allegedly slanted news stories, although many of the PAOs I spoke with admitted that they had never seen an actual al-Jazeera news report or website. They had heard it was bad. When I asked the same PAOs if the Arab media might be justified in reporting the way they were, every PAO I spoke to attacked their veracity.

"They sit on street corners with video cameras and wait for us to get attacked. They're terrorists," one STRATCOM PAO said.

I countered with a question: "Then what are they called when they embed with the U.S. military, as they did in 2003, and wait in ambush with U.S. forces who are going to kill insurgents?" I asked.

He stared blankly at me and smiled. "That's a damn good question," he said. I never got an answer.

At the highest levels of the Pentagon and throughout the U.S. government, al-Jazeera had become a communications challenge. At the tactical level in Iraq, it was a battlefield obstacle; strategically, it was a problem the coalition never professionally and effectively addressed. Al-Jazeera's assertive posture showed normally passive Arab journalists that they could push around the most powerful nation in the free world and force them to deal with tough questions about the human condition in Iraq.

PAOs, ordinarily devoted to the American press corps during peacetime and short on international media experience, found the return on investment with Arab press to be small. PAOs might devote a lot of time to showcase something, but the Arabs would find the sole blemish and make that the focal point of a news story. Above all, engaging the Arab press would not have any impact on the American audience or on public support for the war, so why bother?

The intense Arab scrutiny of American operations in Iraq is likely due to four things. First, the Iraqi press had been suppressed for a long time and was now overzealous in its role as a free press once it realized it could be aggressive after 2003. Second, the Arab media was pandering to its Pan-Arab audience the same way American media feed American news consumers what they think the culture wants. Third, there was a true revolution occurring in Middle Eastern media, and for the first time in history an Arab news organization was a powerful force in the region. Unfortunately, its rise came on the back of the U.S. mission in Iraq. Fourth, knowing that PAOs were pitching news stories to the American media, the Arab press went looking for its own stories around Iraq and found them because it had free-roaming, unlimited access. It could offer the Arab audience unfettered information from the Arab perspective, not sanitized story lines presented by PAOs.

PAOs had little to show for their efforts with the Arab press. There was no tangible American impact, and the Arab audience didn't care to hear about what good was being done in Iraq when al-Jazeera could show how many bad things were happening. While the majority of deaths came at the hands of insurgents, many Iraqis blamed the Americans for the insurgents' presence in Iraq. The insurgents had come to Iraq to fight U.S. forces, and now the U.S. government couldn't contain them. The Arab press highlighted this dynamic.

If a PAO was able to plant a great sound bite in a news broadcast or get a solid quote in the newspaper, this made bosses happy. Good news stories influence public opinion, and the more good news flowing from Iraq, the higher the presidential and public opinion ratings. With those high numbers public fiscal and moral support increases, and a war is successful on the home front even though it may be violently failing on the front lines.

In Iraq the CPA kept telling the American press that things were progressing and that Iraqis were happy, but the truth spoke louder. The Arab news organizations, much to the dismay of the CPA, were there to counter happy claims made by the CPA, and they were the first ones to really expose the violence that was occurring in Iraq. As more accurate pictures of Iraq began to trickle back to the United States, the PAOs had little room to wiggle. U.S. PAO resentment toward the Arab press was under way.

Many PAOs felt that they shouldn't help get Arab media information and cooperate with them because they weren't reporting what PAOs were presenting, but instead they were finding all the skeletons in the closet. Because they were straying from the U.S. company line, they gave the PAOs license to be uncooperative and unprofessional. Rumsfeld and other top defense leaders had in no uncertain terms labeled al-Jazeera and other Arab media "anticoalition," so there was a natural inclination by most PAOs to write off the Arab media entirely since that message was being delivered by top defense leaders.

Controlling the media during U.S. military embeds as Operation Iraqi Freedom started in 2003 yielded high public opinion of the war. Some introspective American reporters have criticized the U.S. media for being lazy and for shallow news coverage in Iraq, and while journalists can argue about the professional drive of their peers, Arab media did have an ethnic advantage over their Western counterparts on the ground. American reporters couldn't independently travel around Iraq to get the complete war stories, because if captured by insurgents they faced certain death, whereas most Arab reporters working for Arab news groups had nationalistic ties and safety since they were Arabs. They could report safely from both sides of the story.

PAOs knew they had an upper hand in Iraq and used that as leverage. They could pitch stories and tell the press about things without having to show them. American press could travel around Iraq, but usually only with U.S. personnel, so the stories were always controlled by the U.S. government somehow, and the angle was distinctly American. Some U.S. reporters took the risk and tried to report independently, but overwhelmingly most didn't. And some Arab reporters working for Western media were sometimes captured and killed by insurgents.

The Arab media didn't need a U.S. escort and sniffed out stories of despair, struggle, and violence. While the U.S. PAOs were talking about free elections to the Western press, the Arab media were uncovering stories of sectarian violence. While the PAOs talked about a children's vaccination program and the American media covered it, the Arab press talked about how children were being killed by American firepower in collateral-damage incidents. The Arab media was a pitch the U.S. military never learned to hit.

The Arab media had by 2004 been ostracized, and they alienated themselves as they showcased Iraq's human drama. PAOs publicly denounced them, as Rumsfeld did to al-Jazeera, and refused to develop a relationship with them simply because their story lines differed from what the U.S. military wanted to push out to the public. The harder the U.S. military tried to use data to counter strong Arab news imagery and stories of violence and misery in Iraq, the more credibility it lost on the streets of America, as more and more Western news groups began to use Arab media footage or stories compiled using Arab news sources.

The Americans, like other things in the Iraq war, miscalculated the impact of the Arab press. By dismissing them as hacks simply because some seemed to lack the professional refinement of American reporters, like the shoe-throwing Muntadhar al-Zaidi, who chucked a shoe at President Bush in 2008, PAOs underestimated their value to the Arab culture. What most PAOs didn't realize in their ignorance is that many al-Jazeera reporters were trained by British journalists, and many Arab journalists knew more about being reporters than PAOs knew about being public relations professionals. Simply because the Iraqi press corps wasn't polished or maybe was a bit out of practice didn't mean that all Arab media should be disregarded.

In Baghdad I noticed that most press junkets and media opportunities were ordinarily reserved for Western press and included a couple of token Arab press personnel. The small Arab media presence was ordinarily the hired guns from the Iraq Media Network, the U.S.-funded Arab news network. I even catered to the American press once early in my tour before I realized that I should not stray from my focus of engaging the Arab press. Once on a press trip I had planned for Petraeus, I had invited an Arab news crew for a trip to Tikrit. I had told them they would be the only broadcast news crew on the trip, but at the general's request at the last minute I added Jane Arraf and her crew from CNN. When Arraf arrived at the landing zone, she was surprised to see another news crew and was not happy about it. When I explained they were Arab media and that their audiences and markets were different, she cooled a bit, but I could tell she was annoyed. The Arab crew, on the other hand, was gracious and did not complain about Jane's presence on the trip, despite the fact that CNN was encroaching on their scoop. For one of them it was his first time on a coalition press trip, and for the other it had been months since an American PAO had even talked to him.

Petraeus's travel party ballooned with the addition of some Iraqi officers, which meant some folks from my press group were going to get bumped. I took myself off the manifest, and I bumped off the Arab news crew because I believed Petraeus would want Arraf on the trip with him, as they had history in northern Iraq from his days with the 101st Airborne Division. The Arabs were pissed.

I didn't make the right call that day. The Arab television crew had been invited first, and I should have had the balls to tell the general that Arraf was getting bumped because we needed the room and it was the right thing to do. My first interaction with the Arab press was off to a poor start. Had I been smarter, I would have acted on my idea that Arab journalists talking to Iraqi officers in Tikrit would have more tactical and strategic communications value, but now my credibility with the Arab crew was not too good. What message was I sending? I didn't pull Arraf off that flight because my relationship with Petraeus was still new, and I didn't want to make waves and bump a friend of the commander in order to do the right thing. It was chickenshit. As the Black Hawks lifted off the ground, I came to the sickening realization of what I had done. I owed the Arab news crew a favor. I promised them I'd make it up to them. After the trip I told Petraeus I felt horrible about bumping the Arab press and candidly told him my motivations.

"I bumped them because Jane's a friend of yours, but it wasn't right. I need to know the next time this happens if you'll support my doing the right thing," I told him. Petraeus said I should have let the Arab news crew stay on the trip and that he would have understood had I explained things to him at the landing zone. He asked me to contact the Arab network and apologize again and let them know that he was furious with me. Most of all he asked me to ensure I made it up to them. I did exactly what he said, and from that moment I began anew with the Arab and Iraqi press and knew that my boss, like me, valued them for the stories that they could tell and for the professionals that they could be.

After a few short weeks in country I saw Arab news-agency requests for information ignored. When they asked for media interviews, they were usually ignored by U.S. officials. Coalition PAOs were not actively engaging the Arab and Iraqi press corps. They did cater to the Western media, and that continued for most of 2004–5. If there were Iraqi "journalists" on trips, most of the time they were from the satellite station al-Iraqiya, the newspaper *al-Sabah*, or Radio Sawa, all U.S.-funded operations; two of them, al-Iraqiya and *al-Sabah*, were part of the not-so-credible Harris Corporation's Iraq Media Network.

I worked briefly in Iraq with an officer who later became the chief of public affairs at U.S. Central Command, Col. Jerry Renne of the U.S. Air

Force. Back then he was a PAO for Multinational Force Iraq. Renne was a nice guy, plainspoken, and hardworking, and he tolerated me and tried to help me, but I mention him because I think he best illustrates the mistakes we were making in Iraq by focusing on American audiences.

I informed Renne in 2005 that Greg Jaffe with the *Wall Street Journal* wanted to talk to Petraeus and embed with us for a week and be a "fly on the wall" in our command. I was seeking Renne's approval, as he was a PAO in Casey's command and Petraeus was still on mute. I usually didn't engage American press after the *Newsweek* debacle, but if they came knocking, I supported their visits.

Renne was supportive, and his reply clearly shows the problem that plagued communications operations in Iraq and reveals the misguided motivations of PAOs at the heart of the public affairs operation in Baghdad.

Renne said that having Jaffe embed with us was an outstanding opportunity. He said that the *Wall Street Journal* reached the nation's top-tier decision makers and had a daily circulation of about 1.9 million. He said that story placement would reach influential congressional, business, and military audiences and that given current events, my timing was perfect to leverage the power of the *Wall Street Journal* to reach key audiences and leaders with our command's message.

Renne's recommendation and assessment were spot-on if I wanted to get Americans behind us, and that, I think, was the PAO mission in Iraq and hence why Renne was so jubilant about Jaffe's embed. I saw my role, however, as one of trying to save American behinds by informing Arab masses, so Jaffe's embed really wasn't that big of a deal for me (although Greg did write some good stuff from his time with us).

Surrounded by formidable press challenges caused mostly by inexperienced, unprofessional communicators, the U.S. military and government found themselves in a predicament. They recognized that communicating with the Iraqi populace was important, yet they did little to make that happen. I say this not because any PAO ever said that engaging the Arab media was important. During my time in Iraq and in subsequent discussions with PAOs who served in Iraq, not one admitted that engaging the Arab press should be the focal point of U.S. strategic communications or even that it was important. They would, of course, change their minds once Petraeus published his COIN manual after leaving Iraq, and it was fun to watch all the nonbelievers quickly become converts and Petraeus disciples just because they wanted to align themselves with the views of a popular U.S. general. When it mattered in 2004, they made us feel like we were lepers, but years later they were all suddenly acting as if they had been in our house all along.

I really enjoyed watching the hard-liners flip. I'm not ragging on them because they flipped—I'm glad they changed their minds—but I am razzing them because they are ignoring the fact that they were once on the other side of the fence, arguing that the Western media were the priority and that there was no connection between the duties we performed as PAOs and violence on the ground. They have selective recollections. Philosophically, PAOs didn't care if al-Jazeera got an interview or if al-Arabiya got questions answered. However, strategically, somebody in the Defense Department recognized the value of communicating with the Arab masses or saw an opportunity to get their buddies rich with fat contracts and dumped millions of dollars into contracts with the Harris Corporation and the Lincoln Group because they thought it was important. What these companies failed to do is communicate with the Arab media and the Arab street. They instead tried to become the Arab media by establishing the Iraq Media Network rather than focusing on engaging organic Arab media that were already in place and established. The American companies' lack of success isn't because they didn't spend enough money. It's because Arabs don't want to hear from Americans; they instead want to hear from Arabs. Think I'm kidding? How many Americans watch BBC America or al-Jazeera America? Americans don't want to hear their news from foreign sources, and it is no different for other nations.

I came across a report created by a U.S. contractor in Baghdad that noted that the challenge facing the U.S. military in Iraq was not removing or restructuring the way the Iraqis got their information. Instead, the U.S. military needed to find a way to influence Iraqis in such a way that the U.S. military became a trusted cultural insider, like al-Jazeera, al-Arabiya, clerics, and other Arab sources of influence.

The report went on to say that in order for the coalition to get this cultural prominence within the Iraqi culture, it needed its own media outlets to ensure its messages were being disseminated to the Iraqi people. This couldn't be further from the truth. Commissioning this report is like asking a carmaker to study the reasons people need cars. Arabs want to hear from Arabs. Rather than dump resources, money, and time into trying to create a communications vehicle from the Americans to the Arabs and Iraqis, the coalition should have focused those resources on helping Arabs talk to other Arabs.

The American government formed the Iraq Media Network to pump out the information it wanted to feed to Iraqis. As the coalition argued with the Arab media about their newsgathering practices, the tone of their content, and their questionable sources, the Iraq Media Network was born. Many Arabs deduced rather quickly that because the coalition had been unable to control what the Arab media was doing and saying, it simply created its own national media to control the message. The Iraq Media Network was instantly labeled a mouthpiece for the occupation and a propaganda tool of the Americans. Few Iraqis watched al-Iraqiya, and fewer read *al-Sabah*, the network's two anchor mediums, according to my Iraqi counterparts, friends in the media, and Iraqis I spoke with in my travels. The Iraq Media Network was mostly watched by Iraqis connected to the coalition. What most Arabs didn't realize or ignored is that al-Jazeera is a state-funded media group, like the state-funded al-Iraqiya. But the money trail leads to two different pots, and that makes a difference. Al-Jazeera is Qatari funded, and al-Iraqiya at the time was paid for by U.S. taxpayers. It would have probably been a good idea to help the Iraqis start their own national network, but using Iraqi dinars, not U.S. dollars.

In order to succeed in Iraq all PAOs had to do was tweak their audience, their messenger, and their message. PAOs could have helped the fledging Iraqi press corps by hosting regular media roundtables or meetings that encouraged dialogue between Iraqi government officials and the Arab press so they could better understand their relationship and their roles. Media academics from around the globe, including media advocacy groups, could have been brought in to mediate the meetings, sort of on-the-job training for the Iraqi press. Instead, the U.S. government paid $82 million to Science Applications International Corporation and later handed off the job to the Harris Corporation, which charged more than $95 million to train Iraqis how to be reporters (or at least reporters who behaved how the U.S. government wanted them to). Had independent media organizations or think tanks been approached by the U.S. government or military and asked to help train a core Iraqi press corps, they likely would have taken the offer. But the goal does not appear to have been to train Iraqi journalists to be true journalists; the goal, it seems, was to teach them to support the U.S. mission.

Iraq was a complicated scenario. Iraqis were either forcibly supporting the insurgency or voluntarily supporting the insurgency. There was no gray area. Some had little choice and passively supported the insurgency in fear of retaliation for aiding the coalition. They were afraid to speak out against the insurgency because there was little protection for citizens. Others had been forced to work with the insurgency, their families and property threatened if they did not assist monetarily or through some other method. Still others simply hated us and what we had done to their country. Famed Arab expert T. E. Lawrence explained it best, I think, in his *Seven Pillars of Wisdom*: "The guerrilla must have at least the passive support of the populace, if not its full involvement."[1]

The coalition failed to monopolize on the tragedy of insurgent cultural captivity. By showcasing acts of valor and operational success of the Iraqi security forces, Iraqis would see that there was progress being made, albeit slowly, and that maybe they too had a chance to overcome the violence. Likewise, if the Iraqis showcased instances of civic and government cooperation to clear a particular city of crime, it would let Iraqis know that systems were in place and that the government had plans to address violence. If Iraqis could have seen their forces in action, arresting thugs, sentencing them, moving through cities, killing insurgents, and protecting their infrastructure, things would not have been so hopeless in the average Iraqi heart. If every day, on many channels, in many news publications, on many airwaves, the successful stories of the Iraqi security forces were repeated, the information saturation would have dislodged the communications foothold the insurgency had in Iraq. Truth cannot be ignored or disproved. But the information must be plentiful, well organized, factual, and not gold plated. Above all, it must be backed up with visible and tangible deliverables. People don't want to be told things are good; they want to experience it. The insurgency took root in Iraq because the insurgents stated their views, made their threats, and then delivered upon them. To remove the insurgents, the coalition would have to function the same way, only in reverse.

On a smaller scale, I suppose, we experimented with counterinsurgency public affairs, to coin a phrase. We had pockets of media engagements. We were fed information from our embedded advisers around the country, and we disseminated the information to the Arab media through our Iraqi PAO counterparts and our Iraqi media team. It wasn't a full-scale effort, but Radhi made some calls here and there and planted information, and the media in turn shared that information with the Iraqi populace and the Arab street. I also engaged Arab press when I could. The results were encouraging on a local level, so I never found much use for all of the big-money information contracts the Defense Department was awarding in Iraq. I can't imagine what we could have accomplished had we been given support.

By the fall of 2004 I knew Casey showed no signs of relenting on his media ban on Petraeus, and I came to the realization that the Iraqis would not be talking at all. I looked at our options as I continued to rally for joint press conferences for Iraqi spokesmen to talk to the Arab media and for other objectives we felt were vital. Al-Jazeera was immersed in controversy. The Defense Department clearly didn't like it and the way it did business, and I would likely run into resistance if I tried to work with it. I knew I needed to talk to the Arab populace through the Arab media, but I wasn't sure whom to use. I needed a television channel, because most Iraqis back then got their news from television. There was the added appeal of visual stimulation in televised news reports, something that can work favorably for a PAO. After consulting with Fahmy and Radhi, we made a choice.

Al-Arabiya was the second seed in Iraq network news and had Pan-Arab reach, but it had recently fallen out of favor with the coalition because it too, the coalition would argue, was "anticoalition." In addition, Abdul Rahman al-Rashed, al-Arabiya's director and a Saudi journalist, penned a column saying Muslims had to recognize that all terrorists were Muslims. This showed critical introspection. Al-Rashed had also lived in the United States and attended a U.S. college, so I decided to engage al-Arabiya, since it seemed the network and its leadership could be critical of its own viewership. My logic was if they could look inward deeply into their own culture, they would likely be fair.

The Iraqi Air Force was getting ready to spread its wings and begin reconnaissance operations in the southern city of Basra in the latter part of 2004. I had traveled earlier in the year to Jordan, where Iraqi pilots trained on the Seeker aircraft, and I got well versed on their mission. The Seeker could track enemy activity and help protect oil lines and infrastructure. The small two-seat aircraft used forward-looking infrared radar to detect ground activity even in the darkest of nights. The Iraqi pilots, some of them former MIG jet fighter pilots, were preparing to start routine operations.

I asked Fahmy to get in touch with al-Arabiya and invite it to Basra. Al-Arabiya sent a very popular reporter for our trip to Basra, who my Iraqi public affairs partners said was the "Iraqi Peter Jennings." We had invited it exclusively. Everyone knew this guy, Fahmy told me, and by the reactions of Iraqis as he passed, I believed it. People flocked to him, shook his hand, touched him, and wanted to talk with him.

The next day after traveling to Basra, I arranged for the al-Arabiya crew to meet some of the pilots and ground crews from the Iraqi Air Force at Basra's airfield. As we approached the hangar, the reporter smirked as he saw the modest Seeker airplane on the tarmac. An interpreter was between us to help us communicate with each other.

"This is the mighty Iraqi Air Force?" he said. "This is a joke, this little plane. They used to have MIG fighters, and this is what you've given them?"

So much for objectivity, I thought. But he was right. Hussein had built what was once the fourth largest army in the world filled with tanks and fighters and missiles, and now the Iraqi Air Force had a little propeller airplane with a mighty strong camera.

I spent about ten minutes giving the journalist a good backgrounder on the aircraft and the air force's new mission, which was all fresh in my head from my trip to Jordan. Iraq needed reconnaissance platforms right now, not offensive or defensive capability in the skies. It needed detection capability to help stem the flow of attacks on Iraqi oil pipelines and electrical grid infrastructure and to help protect the borders. I also told him that in the coming months C-130s would be joining the Iraqi Air Force's fleet. Helicopters would follow. Iraq's air force was going to do good for its nation, whereas before it was an instrument used against its neighbors.

By then a senior Iraqi pilot who recognized the reporter nonchalantly came over and introduced himself. He had flown MIG 23s in Saddam's air force for more than twenty years. The colonel echoed my comments without any prior orchestration with me, and he added that although the aircraft may not look like much, it was ideal for the internal security mission the air force now had. As soldiers the colonel and I both knew the new mission of the Iraqi military was to secure its people and its infrastructure. The facts spoke for themselves, and we didn't need talking points and messages. I walked away, and the two began a deep dialogue and talked around the aircraft as the cameraman recorded.

I never worried about getting Iraqi soldiers who were posted far from the Defense Ministry into trouble for violating al-Shaalan's media ban because I had tested the waters all over Iraq and learned that al-Shaalan hadn't sent his directive nationwide to his troops to keep them quiet. Most didn't know about the order, and, strangely, when al-Shaalan saw the few reports about his forces that included commentary from Iraqi officers, he did nothing about them. It seemed he wanted those closest to the flagpole to keep quiet. Baghdad had a lot of media, and that was generally his enforcement radius.

Nearby on the tarmac Brig. Gen. James Schwitters of the U.S. Army was talking to a U.S. Marine adviser. Schwitters was the commanding general of the Coalition Military Assistance Training Team, which was the lead unit that trained Iraqi military forces. He had commanded the military's Delta Force. His call sign, some said, was "Flatliner," but he had the disposition of a friendly farmer.

"Sir," I told him, "I'd like to put the al-Arabiya cameraman in the aircraft and let him capture this first solo flight." As I started to try to sell the idea to him, he interrupted me and said, "Good idea. I've got no problems with it, but ask the pilots."

The Iraqis had flown solo before (without coalition advisers), but this would be the first time their air force was conducting operational missions, not training missions, with an all-Iraqi crew. I checked with the Iraqi pilots, and they gave it a go.

As the Iraqi Seeker pulled chocks, taxied, and lifted off the ground on its first-ever solo operational flight over the skies of Iraq, there was a member of the Arab press aboard, an Iraqi named Ahmed. It was the first time a member of the free press was given access to an operational Iraqi Air Force mission. It would become, in fact, the new Iraqi military's first Arab media embed and the first for the new Iraqi Air Force.

The next day I had the same news crew fly out to the port of Umm Qasr from Basra. They would board an Iraqi Navy ship and cruise on a routine patrol to some oil platforms a few miles offshore. This was another first. Al-Arabiya had in two days embedded with Iraqi naval and air forces on operational patrols. Though the missions were limited in duration and scope, we were still showcasing the Iraqi military and giving Arab press first crack at the scoop. Most U.S. advisers stayed off camera. This was a pure Iraqi military experience. We helped get the media to Basra and Umm Qasr and then stepped out of the picture and let the Iraqis do the talking. This is what I had wanted to do all along, and it worked well—so far.

Back at the British base in Basra after spending the day in the Persian Gulf, the al-Arabiya crew was very happy. The reporter leaned over and told our interpreter something, and I saw him putting his hand over his heart, which meant something meaningful was coming. Ahmed and Hassan, the soundman, nodded their heads and chimed in with agreement.

"I have never in all of my years as a journalist been treated like this by the United States," our interpreter told me he said. He complimented us for the unprecedented access to the Iraqi Air Force and Navy and ended it with a very humble, "Shukran," Arabic for "Thanks."

When we returned to Baghdad I waited impatiently for al-Arabiya's report. I was scanning an unclassified media-monitoring service for it, and I also had Fahmy glued to the television night and day, waiting for it. Days later it finally aired, and Fahmy gave me the rundown. The story began by offering comparisons of Iraq's new air force to its old air force.

Shit, I thought. He's going to screw us based on his previous comments. I began to worry.

But then the story turned to the air force's new mission, its equipment, and the spirit of the pilots. It had interviews with the Iraqi pilots and ground crews. Fahmy said as we watched the report end that the reporter said in a voice-over that Iraq's air force, long missing over the skies of Iraq, was now again flying over its people, protecting them from harm. The footage was from inside the aircraft as the Seeker banked softly over Basra's landscape and flew into the setting sun.

Just like that our command's fruitful relationship with al-Arabiya took off. I knew that if we could give them access, they would be fair. Whenever Petraeus traveled I reserved seats to accommodate al-Arabiya. Al-Arabiya assigned Ahmed and Hassan to cover our stories because we had all enjoyed each other so much in Basra. When they returned from trips with us one of the al-Arabiya reporters would do a voice-over report using information I had given them through Fahmy's team to make it appear as if he or she had been at the event. I was happy with that. The reports were solid and factual, and the footage Ahmed captured complimented the voice-over well. Ahmed did interviews and asked some good questions, usually to high-ranking Iraqi military leaders or Iraqi politicos whom Petraeus was meeting with throughout the country.

Over the next couple of months we had al-Arabiya with us on press trips about three times per week. We had a steady beat of stories airing on their network. When Petraeus convoyed to a meeting with a local police chief, al-Arabiya was there to talk to the Iraqi cops. If there was a new initiative launched in the Iraqi military, al-Arabiya covered it. When Iraqi commandos trained in Jordan, al-Arabiya was there to report it and to cover meetings between Petraeus and the Jordanians. When we flew to Kurdistan to meet with Kurdish president Jalal Talabani, they went with us.

Al-Arabiya knew to stay away from Petraeus. They could talk to him, of course, and ask him questions for background, but on-camera interviews were forbidden, and nothing was on the record with Petraeus since he was still banned from the press. They could film him or record what he was saying as he conducted his business with the Iraqis, but interviews were a no-no.

Al-Arabiya reported facts without a negative or a positive spin, and that is all we wanted. There were a couple of things that surfaced in the reporting, like the time soldiers complained about the Iraqi Army's food, the living conditions, and the lack of equipment, but luckily some quick-witted Iraqi sergeants jumped in and said, "Low pay, bad food, and bad equipment is the life of a soldier anywhere," and it offset the remarks of the *jundis*, who I'm certain later got their teeth kicked in by the sergeants. Their comments never made it into the story.

When I befriended al-Arabiya, their name was mud to U.S. PAOs. Al-Arabiya, founded in March 2003, had once been the most-watched satellite news channel in Iraq. In 2004 in the heat of competition for ratings, al-Arabiya began to air insurgent-recorded videos and expressed what could be classified by the ultradefensive public affairs community as "anticoalition" views.

The U.S. government in Baghdad monitored the Arab and Iraqi press aggressively. It published the *Baghdad Mosquito*, which offered a snippet of what was being said in the Arab press. It offered Iraqi and Arab media summaries and reports examining Arab media trends. There were analyses of the press activity and its context and content.

Al-Arabiya was working with us and regularly airing reports about Iraqi security forces. We helped connect them to stories on everything from the Iraqi Army's armor brigade to stories about how thirty insurgents were captured by Iraqi forces in Babil. That's why I found it peculiar when the *Mosquito* wasn't listing all of the stories I knew al-Arabiya was airing about Iraqi forces. They were absent from the report. Even stranger was the fact that the *Mosquito* even after more than a month of steady stories from al-Arabiya that were fair and showed no "anticoalition" slant still listed al-Arabiya as having "anti-coalition bias." Their classification included this brief summary: "Anti-Coalition Bias. Al-Arabiya has increased its criticism of the U.S. and the Coalition since the U.S. Deputy Secretary of Defense accused the network of inciting their audience with anti-Coalition reporting. Al-Arabia has used the term 'Enemy Broadcast' when referring to Coalition-controlled media sources."

Despite the noticeable absence of good stories al-Arabiya had aired about the Iraqi forces and their inaccurate classification, I was struck by the fact that the *Mosquito* boldly stated that al-Arabiya was also in the doghouse because it criticized the Iraq Media Network, something the coalition insisted was independent, but for the internal audience it was known as "coalition-controlled media sources."

A lot of PAOs read the *Mosquito*, and I was convinced that the *Mosquito*'s inaccurate classification of al-Arabiya was contributing to its alienation. I had spoken with a few al-Arabiya crews and Baghdad's office manager, and all complained that the coalition was ignoring them (except for us). Fahmy too told me that the Baghdad bureau manager had complained to him more than once that the coalition would not return his calls and would not grant his interview requests. As our relationship with al-Arabiya blossomed, I received complaints from al-Arabiya several times as they sought information on deadline and the press center and STRATCOM didn't get them the information they requested. Several times I had to retrieve answers for them and work with Fahmy to get them what they needed, and many times it had nothing to do with the Iraqi training mission, which was my mission.

Being an Arab journalist in Iraq was fraught with challenges. Not only was the Arab media treated poorly by PAOs, but on the streets their lives were also in danger (as were the lives of all Iraqis) because of insurgent violence. Coalition operations also added a layer of complexity. Al-Arabiya in 2004 lost three members of news crews due to U.S. firepower. Ali Abdel Aziz and Ali al-Khatib both died in March 2004 in Baghdad after being shot by U.S. soldiers.

In September 2004 al-Arabiya reporter Mazen al-Tomaizi was reporting in Baghdad, covering the aftermath of fighting between U.S. forces and insurgents. A battle-damaged U.S. Army Bradley armored vehicle was quickly surrounded by celebrating Iraqis once it was evacuated of wounded

U.S. troops. As al-Tomaizi reported from the scene, U.S. helicopters fired missiles and killed al-Tomaizi as he reported. The attack and his death were videotaped by his cameraman.

I informed Petraeus about al-Tomaizi's death, and Petraeus dispatched me to deliver a handwritten note to al-Arabiya's bureau chief in Baghdad, Haidar al-Wattar. I apologized to Haidar and regretted what had happened, especially now that we had gotten close to his team. The apology from Petraeus, by the way, although meant to be a personal gesture of sorrow to our friends, was reported in a local Baghdad newspaper.

"A U.S. general apologized for this week's killing of an Iraqi journalist," the paper reported (even though al-Tomaizi was Jordanian). It was the only public apology for that event from the coalition. Haidar was very upset, and I told him I'd look into the attack that killed Mazen. It was a tough time for al-Arabiya. The coalition was classifying it as an element that nurtured insurgent activity. The coalition had killed a few of its reporters, and on top of all that, the coalition was giving al-Arabiya a really hard time as it tried to do its job as a news organization. When I asked him if there was anything I could do, Haidar gave me an earful.

His reporters could never get access to Multinational Force Iraq spokespersons. He knew because Western news bureaus told him they could reach PAOs anytime at will, but he was never able to reach them or get past administrative personnel who answered the phones. He was especially incensed at Lessel's office. Al-Arabiya's calls routinely went ignored by Lessel's team, Haidar said.

I recommended to Haidar that rather than try to contact Lessel, who was the coalition spokesman, he should call the media officers at the press center. It was their job to work media calls. There, too, Haidar told me he had access problems. He said he had been experiencing problems with the public affairs community for months.

I told Haidar that in the future, if he had problems communicating with U.S. spokespersons, he should call me, and I'd help him get in touch with people or go on record for him and hunt the information down myself, as I had in the past. Weeks later, in October 2004, the coalition launched offensive operations in Samarra. Haidar wanted a coalition source to answer questions about the operation on an evening news show. He had placed numerous calls to Lessel's office and had tried the press center for days. Neither was helpful, and neither returned al-Arabiya's calls. He called me and asked for help. I explained that he should be calling the Iraqis. He laughed, and then I joined him in the laugh after I thought about what I had just recommended.

I contacted the media situation room at Multinational Force Iraq, and a U.S. Air Force major told me they were aware of Haidar's request. He offered nothing else.

Later, the coalition public affairs community became enraged when al-Arabiya reported that the Iraqi National Guard had experienced two hundred desertions at the onset of operations in Samarra. The PAO community got busy trying to refute the report.

Haidar said in his defense that he had tried to reach coalition personnel to verify the desertions report before the network aired it. He had even gone so far as contacting the Iraqi ministries, but because the Iraqis weren't talking and the coalition didn't return his calls, he aired the piece and cited "reliable sources." Haidar had tried to confirm the desertions with officials at higher levels, so he used information from tactical sources on the ground inside Iraqi units. Al-Arabiya was again in the doghouse.

The coalition criticized the Arab press for its unrefined reporting, but how could quality reporting be accomplished without fact verification? How can reporters do their jobs correctly if PAOs don't do theirs?

I contacted the guy at the *Mosquito* who e-mailed the report regularly and asked him how he and his team determined the classifications of the Arab media. I explained that our command had developed a solid relationship with al-Arabiya and that it had blossomed into the most rewarding public relations relationship I had experienced in my career. I needed to know why the stories we helped al-Arabiya get on the air weren't being analyzed in his report, and I needed to know why if the command charged with the exit strategy in Iraq was benefiting from a good relationship with al-Arabiya, the channel was still categorized as unfavorable.

I reached out through the generic e-mail address for the *Mosquito*, which I think could be accessed by multiple people because I interacted with a chap named Tom Johnson and later with a guy named Bill Putnam. They said the classifications were done based on current reviews of the media in question and on historical data, but they added that they'd have a look at al-Arabiya to see if anything had changed. Several weeks went by, and I noticed that al-Arabiya's Iraqi forces stories were still not included in the report and that the network's classification had not changed.

Al-Arabiya is a massive network with reporters all over the Middle East. I knew ours weren't the only stories airing, and I admit I didn't see what else al-Arabiya was broadcasting, but I was alarmed that reports about the training mission, which had been superb and fair, were not being analyzed by the *Mosquito*. I contacted the *Mosquito* again and reiterated my concerns. Review of al-Arabiya's Iraqi forces stories would make the *Mosquito* more comprehensive and might elevate the rating of the network to "unbiased." I was concerned, I explained, that the rating was unfairly classifying these guys as enemies of the coalition and subsequently causing them to be blacklisted by PAOs, just like their competitor al-Jazeera.

Days later I got a response that said the *Mosquito* had not seen al-Arabiya's reports on the Iraqi forces I was talking about. They didn't have proof al-Arabiya was being unbiased. If things changed, they said, they'd make a note of it in the *Mosquito*.

I offered to bring al-Arabiya's stories, which I had on tape, to their office. I also asked if they worked for the same company that operated the Iraq Media Network, Harris Corporation, but I never heard back from them. I would discover after I left Iraq that Putnam was a U.S. military officer and that Johnson worked with the Iraqi ministries and also had U.S. military connections.

I started to think that the *Mosquito*, a tool of the information-operations community, was somehow linked and trying to help another tool in the information-operations community, the Iraq Media Network, which was having a hard time getting off the ground. Considering that the U.S. military paid independent Arab media to publish procoalition news, I didn't think the coalition was beyond unjustly categorizing al-Arabiya and leveling the playing field for U.S.-funded al-Iraqiya to take flight. With al-Jazeera and al-Arabiya, the top two networks, out of the way, guess who was now running the roost with exclusive stories—the Iraq Media Network.

Al-Arabiya's stories about the Iraqi security forces eluded the *Mosquito's* staff for months, but they were carefully watched by another group when they aired. Like the *Mosquito's* staff, they too analyzed Arab media material, and this group found the al-Arabiya reports to be unfriendly and contradictory to their agenda.

On a beautiful fall day in October 2004, insurgents drove a car to the al-Arabiya office in Baghdad and calmly blew it up, killing seven people and injuring nineteen. Seven of those injured were journalists, and 80 percent of the station's equipment was damaged. A group calling itself the Jihadist Martyrs Brigade claimed responsibility for the attack and said on a website, "The building collapsed on the spies, the Americanized journalists . . . mouthpiece of the U.S. occupation." The insurgents said that al-Arabiya had been praising the Iraqi government and referring to the coalition as liberators and was ignoring mujahideen operations. If al-Arabiya did not stop airing stories that the insurgents classified as "procoalition," they would be attacked again.

I briefed Petraeus when I heard about the attack and started frantically calling Hassan and Ahmed and my other friends at the station. Petraeus asked me to write a letter expressing his condolences, which was hand-carried by Fahmy to al-Arabiya's blown-out Baghdad bureau. Hassan, Ahmed, and the Iraqi Peter Jennings fortunately all missed the attack.

It seemed we had hit a nerve. What we suspected could work to defeat the insurgents was working. We tapped into something that was reaching the Iraqi masses, and the insurgents didn't like it. They had been following al-Arabiya's reports, and they wanted to stop them. It was a similar tactic, just a lot more violent, that the coalition used when it was unhappy with a news group. If it didn't like what was being said, it shut it down. The coalition used political force to remove al-Jazeera from Iraq and tried to silence it; the insurgency used violence to silence al-Arabiya.

Why would the insurgency focus on al-Arabiya? The same reason the coalition focused on al-Jazeera. These two groups were effectively communicating to the Iraqi populace and impacting Iraqi perceptions. The insurgents knew al-Arabiya was valuable to our command and to the Iraqi forces, and they realized the information was having a noticeable impact on Iraqis. We were seamlessly providing information about Iraqi force development, and we didn't have U.S. fingerprints on it. Iraqi forces were the topic, and the stories were purely Arab and lacked an American government connection, and that threatened the bad guys.

The only bright point out of the attacks was the revelation that we had developed a system that worked. A sustained information flow into the Iraqi populace delivered by an Arab media network about Iraqi forces was the key to beat the insurgents. Their attack on al-Arabiya proved it, but somehow that escaped the *Mosquito*, which still categorized al-Arabiya as "anti-coalition."

I should note that the deaths of multiple Iraq Media Network employees are different. Iraqis, not just insurgents, and most Arabs, did not give any credibility to the Iraq Media Network. Their "reporters" were killed not because they were a viable communications threat to the insurgency, but because they were on the payroll of the coalition and considered colluders. Al-Arabiya's problems with the insurgency didn't begin until our third month of working with them. It was their content that drew insurgent fire, not their employer connections.

Fahmy set up a meeting with an al-Arabiya executive who was in Baghdad weeks later to hire a new station manager. I expressed my sorrow for the attacks on his company and told him I felt that the blood of his employees was on my hands.

"You can't be a journalist here without risk," he said with a British-tinged accent. But, he said, if the bombings continued, he might have to encourage his staff to lessen their coverage of the Iraqi forces. He had to protect his people, and in light of the bombing and continued threats, he was being forced to look around for new reporters now that some had resigned in fear or refused to work in Baghdad. Many reporters, he said truthfully, no longer wanted to cover the coalition, although Hassan, Ahmed, and the Iraqi Peter Jennings remained. The risk was not worth it. Sensing the relationship was slipping from me, I got desperate.

For months we had been working on the Iraqi *Cops* show, capturing raw footage but not really doing anything with it because we lacked editing and production capabilities. We had sporadically embedded guys from Fahmy's team with the Iraqi police (without knowledge of the ministry), and we had a few hours of footage of Iraqi cops on the job. I offered the footage and the show's concept to the al-Arabiya exec. It could be theirs exclusively. I explained how we gathered and captured the footage. Fahmy could deliver the unedited, raw footage to al-Arabiya so they could produce a pilot program. They could name it what they wanted, include what they wanted, and voice-over it how they wanted. We would do the ground work and collect the footage, and they would polish it by producing it and hiring a host.

In hindsight it was a silly proposal, considering I had a lot of problems getting Fahmy's team access to the Iraqi police. We had managed to sneak Fahmy's guys on ride-alongs with Iraqi cops, and they had walked the beat and gone on operations with the cops. But the footage was hard to get, thanks to an uncooperative Ministry of Interior. And most of our footage was pretty boring and uneventful. The bad guys usually just surrendered and were taken away without incident, unlike the reality law enforcement shows in the United States.

The exec wanted complete control of the footage, and I agreed. He said he did not want it to appear as if they were working for the Iraqi government or the coalition. It was important that they exercise a high degree of control over the footage and the show. If the show was well received by the populace, he might commit resources to it and ask his own crews to embed with the Iraqi police. He reluctantly agreed to take the idea back to his colleagues and develop a pilot. We aimed for a December 2004 production deadline.

After the bombings al-Arabiya only sporadically traveled with us, and soon it was only Ahmed who was showing up. He would travel with us and capture video and do interviews, but the stories would never air. Eventually, as the threats to al-Arabiya continued, al-Arabiya stopped responding to my invitations. The insurgents were successful in severing the relationship between al-Arabiya and our command. We lost our lone most effective communications channel to the Iraqi people.

I would lose touch with Hassan. I hired Ahmed as a cameraman for our Iraqi media team. He'd work with us for a few months, until the team was disbanded in 2005. He left Iraq, and last I heard he was in Jordan. The Iraqi Peter Jennings, whom I have intentionally not named, was almost killed by insurgents shortly after I left Iraq.

We would never regain the foothold we had in the Arab press, and the insurgents would deal our command a direct blow. I've never gotten over it. I don't like to lose, but more important I think daily about the people at al-Arabiya I got killed that day—a gardener, security guard, kitchen staff, and others. Sure, I had cracked the code to beat these fuckers, but at what price? Once again, I had not thought about the fallout from my actions, and now many were dead.

Al-Arabiya continued to be classified as "anti-coalition" for months that followed despite the fact that in the Arab world, even at the station itself, many Arabs thought they were too cozy with the coalition and with Allawi's government. Hell, the bad guys had blown them up for being a mouthpiece for the coalition, yet we still labeled them as bad guys.

The Arab media were not the enemy in Iraq. Sure, some Arab press groups were inclined to evoke emotions from their Arab audiences, and they fed into the whole Arab suffering line, but taking them on in a tit-for-tat manner resolved nothing. Trying to wrestle them into submission only strengthened their position in Arab society and worsened the American reputation. Detaining them was stupid. My team proved that the Arab press was more than willing to show progress in the development of Iraqi forces if progress was actually being made. The Arab media were willing to work with the coalition in any way, whether it was publishing pieces of our news releases or traveling with us to cover the Iraqi forces. The interest was there, but the coalition collectively never tapped into it.

The coalition also never tapped into the opportunity to speak to the Iraqis about collateral damage. It was widely seen throughout the Pan-Arab world, and within Iraqi culture it dominated many social circles and Iraqi media. If there was a barometer for the United States to use in gauging Iraqi disposition, this was a big one, and we seemed to miss the mark there too.

Jeffrey Ross wrote in a study on police violence that official reaction to an event determines societal posture: "If people believe that justice will be done, they are less likely to take matters into their own hands; for example, they will be less likely to join a protest group or take direct action."[2] In Iraq I think the same was true in regards to collateral damage. Had the U.S. military responded more appropriately and humanely, Iraqis would be less likely to join or support the insurgents. There had to be some level of "justice" that was served in these scenarios in the public's view.

Social scientists state that cultures struggle over events of violence but that one thing is certain: societal interpretations of the events can carry on for months, years, or decades. While I think the insurgency certainly helped turn Iraq upside down, U.S. collateral damage, coupled with U.S. unresponsiveness after the collateral-damage attacks, and reconstruction inaction both intensified the impact of the insurgency in Iraq. The U.S. government was its own worst enemy.

PAOs in Baghdad's Green Zone should have been aggressively managing information rather than reacting to it. They should have been busy trying to get Arab press talking about Iraq's security forces rather than worrying about getting a well-placed quote in *Time*. Small victories matter when fighting an insurgency, because collectively they become a strategic endeavor. The insurgent doesn't attack the counterinsurgent or host nation head-on because it will lose. Similarly, the coalition or counterinsurgent cannot take on the insurgent with broad-themed plans. It's like carpet bombing to get rid of a mole. Counterinsurgent PAOs must wage a communications war using host-nation media and host-nation officials and win tactical victories. The rhythm must be sustained at the lowest levels, attacking the insurgency from different angles with facts. PAOs applying effort from all sides yield victories.

American politicos and PAOs weren't the only ones who poorly treated the Arab press. Allawi, during his tenure as prime minister, ejected both al-Jazeera and al-Arabiya from Iraq, and he worked to have laws introduced to punish the media if they were critical of the government.

In an editorial for *Asharq al-Awsat* newspaper, an Iraqi writer wrote the following: "The Allawi government has lost its media campaign because Arab information media, especially the TV channels, are terrorist weapons giving a false view of Iraq. Another is the absence of the Iraqi national media, which would protect Iraqis against poisons of Arab and Iranian TV channels. Al-Iraqiya channel, which represents the government, is not supposed to represent the government, because the occupation had control over it from the beginning. The Iraqi people and the Iraqi government need a good lawyer to get back our al-Iraqiya TV channel from the occupation."

The writer was correct. Had we been a bit more creative in the execution of our communications strategies, we'd likely have been much more successful. Our mini campaign with al-Arabiya proved that we could succeed as counterinsurgents. I can only imagine the broad success we would have had across Iraq had PAOs engaged as we did.

The U.S. military counterinsurgency field manual says:

> Commanders should apply time, effort, and money to establish the proper combination of media outlets and communications to transmit the repetitive themes of host nation government accomplishments and insurgent violence against the populace. This might require counterinsurgency forces to be proactive, alerting media to news opportunities and perhaps providing transportation or other services to ensure proper coverage. Assisting in the establishment of effective host nation media is another important counterinsurgency requirement. A word of caution here: there can be no perception by the populace or the host nation media that the media is being manipulated by counterinsurgency or host nation forces. Even the slightest appearance of impropriety here can undermine the credibility of the counterinsurgency force and the host nation.

If this sounds familiar, it is because this is exactly what we did with al-Arabiya, and now Petraeus had formalized it in print.

Weeks after al-Arabiya stopped working with us, I received a phone call one night at the office. The male caller on the other end of the line said I should stop trying to spread lies to the Iraqis or something would happen to me. The person was Arab, spoke pretty good English, and sounded educated.

"You're a liar, al-Varez," he told me. He was pronouncing my name in the same Arabic-like way Salih's guys at the Ministry of Defense did. In seconds I thought it was probably a joke being played on me, but then I realized that my phone number was posted on the Internet, and it was also on hundreds of press releases we had sent out. It would be easy for anyone to reach me.

"Fuck you!" I told him. "Fuck you! You want me? You know where to find me, motherfucker!" I said. Yeah, I was a real badass, talking from a fortified compound with thousands of soldiers around me. It's not like I was standing in the middle of Baghdad, calling out the bad guys to come fight me. Truth was there was no way these guys could touch me, but I was pissed they had beaten me and angrier that our media-engagement plan had led to the deaths of innocent people from al-Arabiya. The blood of those dead al-Arabiya employees is forever on me. I hate those fuckers for what they did to my al-Arabiya friends. They had engaged me directly, and this time their sword had proved mightier than my pen.

"You're a liar. You will lose." He hung up, and when I tried to redial his number, I got an Arabic message that an interpreter told me said the caller couldn't be reached. It struck me that the caller told me that I would lose. He understood what I had been doing. He knew I was fighting him with information.

The insurgents had met me on my battlefield and won, but I took solace in the fact that we knew how to win the communications war if the coalition and the Iraqis would only give us the chance. I needed to convince the PAOs in the Green Zone to help us win it. I had succeeded as a counterinsurgent, but would our legions of corporate-style communicators listen?

The successes had come at a steep price, but I had kept a promise I made to the Arab news crew that I bumped for CNN months earlier on LZ Washington in order to get Jane Arraf on board the helicopter. It had been al-Arabiya that I removed off the aircraft months earlier, but while I was happy that I had settled an old account, the fact remains that I also helped get people killed. And I carry that load every day, and that is something I will never be able to settle.

9

AL-JAZEERA

November 2004 becomes the bloodiest month on record in Iraq
for U.S. troops. 1,429 are wounded, 141 are killed.
—U.S. Defense Department

PAOs can hold a grudge with the best of them, partly because when someone
from the press crosses them, it is done in a very public way for the world to
see. Missteps and misquotes are magnified in the professions of public relations and journalism. Erroneous, inaccurate, and unfavorable information
in print or on the airwaves reflects poorly on the military more broadly,
but it tinges the PAO's reputation, especially when he or she works directly
for a general officer or a presidential appointee in a highly visible agency
or command. It is the PAO's responsibility to ensure accurate information
is provided to reporters in an appropriate context, and sometimes, despite
the officer's very best efforts, reporters will file stories that make a military
communicator cringe.

Shortly after I arrived in Iraq I planned a press junket to Taji Military
Training Base. I asked the U.S. military advisers there to have demonstrations
for the media to showcase the training of Iraqi security forces and give the
press something to see. Prior to my arrival in Iraq the press hadn't really
been given a lot of access to them. I reserved two helicopters for members
of the international press corps, including a team from the *New York Times*.

The U.S. advisers planned a great day for the media. We watched Iraqi
sappers simulate breaching a building using explosive charges, Iraqis practiced marksmanship with different weapons on a firing range, and there were
two small-unit training exercises, one including a team of Iraqis entering

and clearing a room with unloaded weapons and the other a platoon-size element responding to an ambush.

I explained to the press, as did the advisers, that the Iraqi troops were merely practicing their individual movements during these scenarios. As trainers we wanted them to get accustomed to operating in an urban environment and operating as a team before we gave them ammunition and cut them loose to shoot targets in a live-fire collective scenario. Clearing buildings was much harder than just shooting at paper targets. We had to ensure the new trainees understood their individual responsibilities in relation to their team's movement before we gave them bullets.

A file cabinet set up by the advisers in one of the rooms would serve as a bad guy during the room-clearing training exercise. It was easier to place an object in a room and make it the target than to have an adviser stand there for hours at a time as the soldiers practiced the drill over and over again.

The Iraqis entered the room in picture-perfect formation, slinking smoothly through the door and around the jagged corners of the rooms they were clearing. They cleared and secured the room within a couple of minutes, and then an Iraqi soldier leveled his rifle on the file cabinet as a U.S. adviser explained that he had neutralized the threat as others cleared and secured the rest of the room.

The adviser explained the importance of training Iraqis for military operations in an urban terrain, operations they would likely be conducting in the coming months. The Iraqi soldiers were in their early stages of training, and this exercise best showed a critical skill they would later use that year in places such as Fallujah, Ramadi, Najaf, Samarra, and other hot spots throughout the country. Despite the explanations from me, from advisers, and even from Major General Eaton, who was commanding the training mission at the time, Jeffrey Gettleman, a *New York Times* reporter, filed a story that made the training of Iraqi security forces look amateurish.

In the article filed the day after the trip to Taji, Gettleman wrote that the Iraqis had stormed into the room and attacked "a very threatening looking file cabinet." He also wrote in the same story that the Iraqis were using "fake" weapons in their training, referring to simulated rocket-propelled grenade (RPG) launchers used in another exercise.[1] I wrote Gettleman an e-mail after I read his article, which for the most part was pretty fair, except for those two parts in the story that were sarcastic.

I had gone out of my way to ensure he and the others knew the context of the training scenarios. He and others had gotten unprecedented access to Iraqi soldiers, and I thought his word choice could have been better. At the time the training mission was being heavily criticized, and there were accusations swirling about inadequate funding and lack of equipment. Naturally, I would be sensitive to any language that might intensify those swirling rumors. While anyone can argue that using the word "fake" isn't unfair and can be considered accurate, I think he was editorializing a bit by saying the file cabinet appeared threatening. His word choices made the mission seem unprofessional, and the writing had a sarcastic, almost comical tone to it.

Gettleman's writing wasn't the only thing that surprised me. While at the weapons range Gettleman and his photographer asked U.S. advisers if they could fire the machine guns. Other journalists watched them in disbelief as they fired the machine guns and then posed for pictures like a couple of Rambos.

Gettleman's article could have better balanced everything he saw. He was told the trainees were new to the military and still learning how to maneuver and that for safety reasons we weren't using ammunition. He was also briefed about how it was common to build a training scenario around a static target, in this case a large file cabinet due to a lack of paper targets or mannequins. Militaries around the world train in dry-gun scenarios before troops are given ammo. All of these contextual details were excluded from his article. When I called him out about his word choice, Gettleman defended his choice of words.

He said he was trying to put a little energy into the story and that he was shocked his editors kept the "threatening looking file cabinet" phrase. As for fake RPG, Gettleman said he didn't know any other way to quickly refer to the weapon.

Gettleman also mentioned in his article rumors Iraqi soldiers had in April

2004 refused to fight, and he admitted that he was a little confused about how many Iraqis wanted to go and how many didn't and that he probably could have been clearer.

I was stunned by Gettleman's nonchalance about the article, but there wasn't anything I could do about it. Sure, I could bitch to his editor about it and retaliate against him, but instead I just made some professional observations about him and filed them away for future use.

My point in sharing the Gettleman story is that I tried very hard to ensure he and the other reporters that day understood what they were seeing, yet despite my efforts he saw and wrote what he wanted, and sometimes that happens in the public affairs business. I wouldn't have done anything differently that day except maybe listen to the advice of a coalition PAO who warned me not to invite Gettleman to Taji, but I gave him an opportunity nonetheless.

I never again asked Gettleman to come along with us on press trips, not because I disliked him or held a grudge; I just didn't have the time or energy to deal with someone like him. Just as the media have expectations of PAOs, I also have my expectations. I expect the media to give their full journalistic effort when I help them get stories. Otherwise, everyone is wasting their time. I expect reporters to be professional, ask real questions, and get a good story. I felt that our command and, more important, the international public deserved a little more than the effort Gettleman put into his story. I did not sever my ties with Gettleman's publication. Instead, we developed a very close relationship with another reporter from the *Times*, Dexter Filkins, who reported extensively on our program and traveled quite a bit with Petraeus.

I gave Gettleman's organization a second chance by engaging guys like Dexter and many others from the *Times*. If I had fixated on what Gettleman had done to the command and if I refused to work with the *Times* based on that one event, my mission would suffer, and, ultimately, the public would be uninformed because I was cutting off ties with a widely read newspaper. I couldn't shut down the lines of communication from the command to the public simply because of a reporter, but there are plenty of PAOs who told me they would have forever blacklisted the *Times* for what Gettleman did to me. There was plenty of press warfare being waged in Iraq, as many of my colleagues in Iraq and in Washington DC shackled the professional lives of reporters they felt had screwed them.

Public affairs people can be some of the grumpiest, bitchiest people on earth, and as a reporter, if you mess with them, you're marked for life. It's strange, considering the public relations profession should attract personalities that are outgoing, friendly, and receptive to communication and interpersonal interactions. But in more than twenty years in uniform, I've seen hundreds of PAOs enraged over "bad press." Every reporter and PAO has a story of a run-in. I've got many more and my Gettleman anecdote is very mild in comparison, but what's important to share here is that professionalism is paramount and military communicators often let their egos get in the way of their duties.

"Payback" is something that plagues the military public affairs community. There is little genuine respect between the military and the media, and most of that comes from the military side of the house. PAOs should expect reporters to be fair, but they shouldn't expect flowery, colorful reports all the time. It's unrealistic. There are plenty of good things that come around from having the press check underneath the hood of our bureaucracies to make sure things are working as the public was told they would work. PAOs should not perceive good, hard reportage as a personal attack.

I've sometimes tried to envision the fallout from the public affairs community if a Western news group profiled an insurgent in the same manner in which they did a U.S. soldier. In other words, what would happen if an insurgent was interviewed along with his family? What if the U.S. media told the story of his home life and painted his story as passionate, a man taking on a foreign force, in this case the U.S. military, because he truly believed the United States had no business being in Iraq? I can only imagine the panties that would get ruffled in public affairs offices worldwide if a major news anchor from the United States did something like that. From what I've seen done by my colleagues in the past, I can tell you that the network would have a hard time getting access to things for years to come or at least until the administration changed.

In October 2006 CNN domestically aired an insurgent-recorded video that showed U.S. soldiers getting fired upon by insurgent snipers. The video had aired on Pan-Arab satellite channels in the Middle East. The grainy footage showed U.S. soldiers getting stalked, and then CNN faded the video to black as an insurgent sniper shot a U.S. soldier. CNN never showed the soldier getting shot.

There was an almost instantaneous cry for retaliation from the PAO community, but joining those cries were the voices of the U.S. Congress. One lawmaker wrote Rumsfeld and wanted CNN's access to the U.S. military in Iraq pulled, while others stated they shouldn't be allowed to embed with the U.S. military again. U.S. leaders accused the cable network of helping spread enemy propaganda and being publicists for the insurgency. Rep. Duncan Hunter added disparagingly that CNN acted as a disinterested observer, which is precisely the role the media should take in their coverage. Hunter added that CNN didn't seem to care if the United States won in Iraq. That's an awfully big jump, but why should CNN care if the United States wins in Iraq? CNN isn't part of the U.S. military.

CNN's been around long enough to know how the U.S. military operates, and I can't imagine they thought they would air that video without any fallout, but in case they didn't know and in case reporters don't know how the military services operate, let me say this: if you screw over a PAO, you'll get yours. I don't subscribe to that unofficial policy, but that is the way it is all the way to the Pentagon.

It is passive aggression at its best. Phone calls from the alleged double-crossers will go unreturned because the voice-mail system "malfunctioned," or the reporter would be removed from media distribution lists "mistakenly" by a system glitch, keeping them in the dark about developing stories. E-mails would somehow not be received and be chocked up to "computer problems," and queries would get lost. It is a game that PAOs play to shut out media who have not played by their rules. I saw this in coalition dealings with al-Jazeera.

Al-Jazeera was launched in November 1996, and it quickly made a name for itself by filing reports that were known to be uncensored and independent.

It enflamed Arab governments throughout the Middle East by challenging the state-run status quo press posture. In the Arab world many countries still control what is being said in the press. Al-Jazeera fought to get unfiltered news to the Arab people and has done so quite well. According to the news channel, it has more than sixty bureaus all over the world and has 40 million viewers, who are primarily Muslim.

During my deployment to Iraq I was astonished to watch al-Jazeera push its quest to become a news superpower in the Arab regions to such an extent that its operation would manifest itself into the very definition of what the channel's name means in Arabic: "Island." But while the news channel alienated governments worldwide, especially that of the United States and the exile-heavy Iraqi government in Iraq, the mostly Western-trained al-Jazeera gained unsurpassed credibility with its Arab viewers, at least for a short period of time.

Al-Jazeera says that it is dedicated to objectivity, accuracy, and a passion for truth. Truth, its says, "will be the force that will drive us to raise thorny issues, to seize every opportunity for exclusive reporting, to take hold of unforgettable moments in history and to rekindle the willpower within every human being who strives for truth."[2] Well, not exactly. Al-Jazeera has done some things during its "exclusive reporting" that didn't rekindle anything in me but heartburn from the day-old hot dog I ate at the mess hall. One thing is certain: an interested individual's opinion of al-Jazeera is usually a passionate one, whether he is a U.S. soldier, a journalism purist, or an Arab national.

There is no doubt, though, that the U.S. government has made al-Jazeera a target of heavy-worded public criticism and some would suggest violent military action. U.S. officials branded al-Jazeera as information terrorists, and the U.S. Defense Department during the Bush administration blamed them for highlighting failures in Iraq. By doing so the U.S. government showed it was either ignorant and did not understand complex international communications or merely looking for a scapegoat for a botched military operation.

In 2003 the U.S. military launched a scathing communications campaign against al-Jazeera. That war of words was led by former U.S. secretary of defense Donald Rumsfeld all the way up to his resignation in November 2006, and it has further polarized the relationship between the military and the media. To put this in historical context, we should look at the press and the U.S. military's relationship.

The U.S. military and the press weren't bosom buddies during the Vietnam War, when U.S. military leaders blamed the war's unpopularity on an aggressive press corps bent on seeing the war fail. Famed correspondent Peter Arnett recounted in his 1994 book that the relationship was so bad that at one point, a U.S. Army military policeman unlawfully detained him at gunpoint when he was in Saigon. Arnett had been reporting independently from the battlefields but wasn't liked by military leaders because he didn't push their company line and was countering many of the PAO reports coming from Saigon (sound familiar?). He was also wandering around unescorted and getting both sides of the story. When Arnett complained to the Saigon information chief that deadly force had been threatened against him, the PAO smirked and told Arnett the military was going to charge him with assaulting the military policeman. Luckily for Arnett, there was an Associated Press photo of Arnett held by the weapon-brandishing soldier, so he had proof and the matter ended.

Several years into the mission in Iraq, the military public affairs community found it easy to return to the tired Vietnam-era arguments that the media were losing the war for them by focusing on all the bad and not the good. They took special exception with al-Jazeera. It is a relationship that has been souring for some time, long before the two ever had to share work space on the battlefield in Iraq. It started to get heated months before 9/11, when al-Jazeera aired an interview of Osama Bin Laden.

In early 2001 the United States didn't pay much attention to the fact that al-Jazeera was interviewing terrorists, mostly because al-Jazeera had little impact on the American world. Their news content didn't affect the insulated information environment in the United States. After 9/11 and the proliferation of the Web, things changed.

Western governments scrutinized al-Jazeera's relationship with the Taliban immediately post-9/11. Some politicos suggested that coded messages were being sent to al-Qaeda's soldiers via al-Jazeera's broadcasts after the channel aired Bin Laden's battle cry for Muslims to take up arms against the West in a holy war. Al-Jazeera then aired footage of Afghan demonstrators setting ablaze the U.S. Embassy in Kabul, Afghanistan.

Al-Jazeera vehemently defended its practices and fired back that a conflict has two sides and that the news channel had fairly given the United States and its allies the opportunity to speak about its new global War on Terror. The Taliban and al-Qaeda were the other side of that conflict, and journalistic standards dictated that both sides of the story be told, even if Bin Laden's interview angered many around the world.

In November 2001, as U.S. forces launched offensive operations in Afghanistan, the Kabul office of al-Jazeera was attacked after the Pentagon officially identified its bureau as an al-Qaeda facility. The U.S. military denied they knew it was a news bureau and used a missile to destroy the building. To date the U.S. government maintains that it believes it was an enemy target.

Airing the Bin Laden interview to a mostly Muslim audience is no different from when American networks interview followers from extremist Christian groups. Most Muslims do not believe in al-Qaeda's brand of Islam, no more than American Christians believe in the beliefs of extremist Christian groups, but the leaders of those organizations are doing things and preaching a philosophy that is due attention by the media, and as news consumers it is up to the public to determine its value. The networks are airing stories that will evoke emotions in viewers. We cannot serve as censors. The U.S. military seems to want the media to give it a soapbox, but nobody else is entitled to an opposing view. When the Arab media allow the bad guys to talk to the public and share their side of things, PAOs don't like it and the name-calling and finger-pointing begin.

Taking it a step further, PAOs definitely weren't fans of the language used by al-Jazeera in their reportage, but al-Jazeera was doing nothing more than trying to connect with its audience. It used language that embraced cultural and Arab national ties. PAOs didn't like it because the language enflamed Arab tempers, but in the United States when some newspapers reported that Westerners were beheaded or killed, they described the insurgents as "cold-blooded killers," "radical," or "Muslim extremists," or a news network could label the insurgents as "thugs." The closer a reporter was to U.S. forces, the less objective his or her language. Those who were embedded were ordinarily the worst violators. There was a definite "us" versus "them" tone in U.S. news stories about insurgents. Insurgents, Iraqis, and Arabs are dehumanized in most U.S. news stories, whereas the focus is ordinarily on the American plight.

It should come as no surprise, knowing that there are national ties that bond people, that al-Jazeera would report using similar language to evoke response from readers and viewers. In September 2004 it aired a story and said the "evil coalition kills more women and children in Fallujah." I never saw the al-Jazeera broadcast, but I did catch the analysis of the broadcast on a coalition media report. I asked Fahmy if he knew about it, and he did; he had seen the report the day before. In talking to Fahmy, who then read the analysis of the broadcast, he said that the coalition's translators were mistaken and misrepresenting the news story. A more accurate portrayal of the story, Fahmy said, was that al-Jazeera reported that the coalition attacked a Zarqawi meeting place in Fallujah and that the attacks had killed fifteen Iraqis and injured thirty. Medical sources from the city said that most injured in the "brutal attack" were women and children. Sources on the ground were classifying the attack as "brutal," not al-Jazeera. But for the sake of argument, considering U.S. media used language that was derogatory toward the insurgents, the U.S. military shouldn't have been upset if the Arab media were using the same language to describe the actions of American forces. Al-Jazeera, like the American media, understands its market, and those national ties attract viewers and readers.

Fahmy said that part of the problem with media analysis in Iraq was that Iraqi coalition contractors often gave their coalition managers slanted information because they weren't trained linguists. They were merely people who picked up English somewhere along the way under Hussein's rule, so translations could get mixed up. When PAOs, eager to pin something else on al-Jazeera, got excited and hounded coalition translators, the translators would often tell them what they knew they wanted to hear. Fahmy should know—he had done translations for the coalition at the press center.

As Operation Enduring Freedom in Afghanistan began, al-Jazeera, the only international news network with a bureau in Afghanistan, benefited from its proximity in the country and broadcast reports from the Afghanis' perspective. It showed the world what it was like to be on the receiving end of an American can of whoop-ass. As images of wounded Afghanis filled the television airways of the Middle East, accompanied by footage of Afghanis celebrating and supporting the Taliban, the U.S. government accused al-Jazeera of bias for Bin Laden's al-Qaeda and the Afghani government, the Taliban, which supported it.

Al-Jazeera continued to argue that while Bin Laden and the Taliban were given airtime, U.S. statements, briefings, and interviews had been given equal airtime. It noted that Rumsfeld as well as then U.S. national security adviser Condoleezza Rice were both interviewed by al-Jazeera. It also interviewed U.S. Air Force general Richard Myers, then the chairman of the Joint Chiefs of Staff, after 9/11.

During the 2001 Myers interview, al-Jazeera broached the topic of civilian deaths in Afghanistan at the hands of U.S. forces. Frustrated by an inability to control al-Jazeera, and now forced to deal publicly with images that had once been confined to the battlefield and seen only by soldiers, the U.S. military was taken aback and unprepared. Some PAO at the Pentagon should have studied footage of Middle Eastern news coverage, especially al-Jazeera's, which historically showed gory video of civilian casualties in fighting between Israel and Palestinians, to prepare military leaders for the realm they were about to enter as they began to fight the War on Terror. U.S. military leaders should have assumed al-Jazeera would do the same if the United States waged war in al-Jazeera's neck of the woods. Evocative video has always been a powerful journalism tool of al-Jazeera. Some might argue it doesn't show the end result of war or a direct product of it, but I argue it certainly shows a consequence of it and is part of the overall truth of war.

Pentagon leaders, backed into a corner, accused al-Jazeera of staging tragic scenes, going as far as saying that the Afghani casualties in the news videos were hired actors, women and children, paid to pose in videos recorded by al-Jazeera cameramen. U.S. officials also contended that al-Jazeera aired footage of dead civilians piled in warehouses that were not killed by U.S. personnel, killed instead by Taliban and al-Qaeda fighters.

"We plan very carefully, we have relatively sophisticated weapons that minimize civilian casualties, but in war we're going to have some. And we understand that. We regret that. It is a terrible tragedy, but I think it's the price that has to be paid to ensure that the world does not have any more 11 Septembers or events like that," Myers said. "To go back to your earlier point on the footage of some of the casualties," Myers continued. "Establishing ground truth in Afghanistan is very, very difficult. Every time there is an alleged incident of civilian casualties we go back and very carefully look to see what ground truth is. We know the Taliban have lied and exaggerated those casualties. We think they are very, very low. We regret every one of them because, again, they're the innocent bystanders."[3]

Myers told the reporter that the U.S. military was "not in the propaganda business" and that the U.S. military did not have estimates and didn't track the number of civilian casualties caused in operations in Afghanistan. He guessed that five or six targets might have been errant, but offered no number of civilian dead. Then how could he know the figures were low?

Here's the rub. In *Second Front: Censorship and Propaganda in the Gulf War*, author John R. MacArthur says that Hill & Knowlton, a politically connected public relations firm, was hired by Citizens for a Free Kuwait (wealthy Kuwaitis living in the United States), an organization that helped push the cause for U.S. intervention in Kuwait to expel Iraq's forces in the 1990s. The firm, with deep Republican connections to the White House, helped the organization present information to politicians on Capitol Hill to support Bush's call for war. Some of their projects included coaching Kuwaiti "witnesses" who testified at the United Nations and at the U.S. Congress about Iraqi atrocities. They also provided videos of Iraqis shooting people in Kuwait and photographs of dead people who had been gashed and apparently violently attacked.

Unfortunately, much of the products the public relations firm delivered were fabricated and not what they appeared to be. The witnesses used false identities in their testimonies and claimed to see things that never happened. One Kuwaiti girl spoke before a congressional committee that she had seen Iraqi soldiers kill babies. The girl happened to be the daughter of the Kuwaiti ambassador to the United States, and she wasn't even in Kuwait when Iraq invaded and was not identified as the daughter of the Kuwaiti ambassador when she spoke. The video that showed Iraqi soldiers executing men was actually a military execution. Iraqi soldiers were being shot for looting. As for the pictures, the "bodies" in the photos were mannequins, staged by the public relations firm. These are things Dick Cheney, then the secretary of defense, used to build his rationale for liberating Kuwait. Much of what the U.S. government accuses al-Jazeera of doing it has done itself. I should add that Hill & Knowlton is a firm where some career PAOs are sent to work in a military internship program called Training with Industry.

What the U.S. government hasn't done is sincerely acknowledge and address civilian casualties in its War on Terror. From a public relations perspective, that is a mistake, and the guys that pay the price for that mistake are grunts. Informed and educated people understand that armed conflict comes with a grisly degree of civilian bloodshed, especially in modern warfare, which is sometimes fought on the streets of cities in faraway places and not in remote jungles or wide-open battlefields.

Internationally, there is outrage when the U.S. military rains down death on civilians, and as Americans we felt the outrage firsthand when the United States was attacked on 9/11, an attack aimed at killing civilians. Sometimes it is an errant bomb and pilot error that kill innocent people, and sometimes the bomb hits its intended target but causes surrounding collateral damage. Other times the circumstances on the ground lead to misinformed decisions in the air, like the bombings in 2002 and 2004 of Afghani and Iraqi wedding parties. In both cases, U.S. reports said, civilians were firing weapons in the air, a popular cultural celebratory practice overseas, and U.S. aircraft opened fire on the crowds, assuming they were being fired upon. Even our successful, short Gulf War in the 1990s was estimated to have killed about one hundred thousand civilians in Iraq, even though the U.S. military made it seem as if we dropped bombs and didn't mess up a single thing other than intended targets.

As a career military officer I understand that bombs fall errant and that sometimes our warriors make mistakes or that things happen that are unplanned. It is our reaction to those events that I am concerned about. We're much too flippant about it.

I don't know who was providing public relations advice to our senior military leaders since the War on Terror kicked off, but it is not good to respond to collateral damage or deaths only after they're discovered by the media. There was a time, I suppose, when using words to counter words was acceptable. In imageless wars like World War II and Korea, the United States didn't have to worry about the effect of collateral damage because there were few images of human suffering leaving theater, unless of course it was human suffering caused by the Japanese, Germans, Chinese, or North Koreans, and then it managed to trickle back with the help of PAOs. Then the U.S. military could effectively counter reports of collateral damage by releasing a statement or by having an erudite battlefield general talk about what "our boys" were accomplishing.

During World War II the Allies dropped bombs all over Germany and Japan and killed hundreds of thousands of civilians. The bombings of Dresden and Hamburg, it has been argued, were not solely for military gain. They were also valuable cultural targets that could demoralize the Germans. The Allies were at war not just with governments but with the people of these nations. Around twenty-five thousand people were killed in Dresden alone. The point is that the U.S. military didn't have to defend its actions. There were very few, if any, reporters who covered the bombings, and most, if not all, simply went with the military's company line that the bombing of civilian targets was necessary because the targeted cities were military industrial targets. There was never a need to second-guess the U.S. military because we were fighting to prevent the Axis powers from taking over the world. There was a meaningful, deeper mission, and the entire nation, including its journalists, rallied around that cause. Vietnam, its causes, justifications, and engagements, changed how the military was viewed by the media and by the public, and we learned that our government had a bit of a dark side. We saw that they could offer versions of their truth.

War prior to Vietnam had been packaged nicely and presented to the American public. The United States bombed Cambodia and killed thousands of civilians, but the press was there to capture it. The American media didn't unjustifiably demonize U.S. troops or slant stories in such a way that they were antiwar or anti-American, but they did expose sensitive Americans to war on a regular basis. For the first time in U.S. history reporters would have unfettered access to the carnage caused by U.S. firepower, and many radio and television networks dutifully reported what they saw, which conflicted with what the government was reporting.

The U.S. military PAOs in Vietnam responded to the images of carnage by doing what it had always done, using words. It wasn't a good practice then, and it is certainly not a good practice now in the information age, when images can be shared with the world as quickly as events unfold. The U.S. military can no longer counter U.S.-caused collateral damage with mere words. The images are stronger than the spoken words. Myers's regretful words during the al-Jazeera interview mean nothing. They're just words. To the foreign community, they're dehumanizing coming from a guy wearing a coat and tie sitting in a climate-cooled office, thousands of miles away from the deaths. They are words that literally aren't even heard by the people they are trying to assuage.

The U.S. military has to get out of the sneaky habit of staying quiet when it does something wrong. It must break the news publicly as soon as possible and admit its mistakes. Errors are made worse when international news crews uncover the deaths. It stinks of My Lai. Moreover, not to be morbid, but it must try to keep a tally of civilian collateral deaths, especially when it is operating in an urban terrain. While labor intensive for some desk jockey, it is important in a war of perception, and it is important to track this metric to ensure we're trying to do it right and prevent mistakes from happening. Hell, every single unit in the Army tracks the number of accidents and injuries it has. Why can't the Army collectively track the number of civilians it has killed? There was plenty to keep track of in 2004–5.

We also need to shake the mind-set that being careful and more deliberate means we're bringing political correctness to the battlefield. That's not what this is about. Just like warriors have evolved, so must the tactics. If we were in the business of taking and holding real estate, that would be one thing, but taking, holding, and building is another mission completely, and to do that in this day and age, you need transparency or information will bite you in the ass.

In the fall of 2004 when U.S. forces launched operations in Samarra and air strikes in Fallujah, reports from Iraqi hospitals stated that there were mass civilian casualties. The Associated Press reported that residents in Samarra tried to bury their dead but were fired upon by U.S. soldiers, something the coalition denied, but an Iraqi ambulance driver confirmed that U.S. forces fired at him as he tried to rescue a wounded man. At the Samarra hospital, a reporter noted, were a wounded boy and girl whose pregnant mother had been killed, along with 69 others, dozens of whom were children and women; 160 others were wounded. There was no coalition commentary on the casualties.

Imagine if you are related to these people. What goes through your head if nobody explains anything to you? What assumptions are made? All you know is that the Americans killed your friends or family, and there is no explanation, just an apology you never hear. The U.S. military has immensely capable civil affairs forces, but what my friends in the information-operations community have told me is that there is very little projection on collateral-damage missions, and that should change because collateral damage has certainly gotten a lot of attention in our recent wars.

The American media developed an increasing interest in Iraqi casualties as more and more Iraqi civilians died in Iraq. In January 2005 the *New York Times* reported that five Iraqis had been shot by American soldiers after the detonation of a roadside bomb next to their convoy. When the reporter contacted the military spokesman in Baghdad, the *Times* wrote, he said he had no comment. A day later near Mosul a five-hundred-pound bomb was dropped on a house, killing five the U.S. military said. The Iraqi who owned the home said 14 died, seven of whom were children. The U.S.

military said it had hit the wrong building and issued a statement that expressed regret. An investigation would prove 13 died, including three kids and four women. Later that month the U.S. military would admit its forces accidentally killed a thirteen-year-old Iraqi girl and wounded a fourteen-year-old boy near Baqouba, thirty-five miles northeast of Baghdad, the Associated Press reported.

More widely, al-Jazeera's coverage of U.S. collateral damage fanned anti-Americanism throughout the Pan-Arab world. In another *New York Times* article published in December 2004, Abdel Sabour Shahin, a linguistics professor at Cairo University and a regular on al-Jazeera talk shows, said the Muslim world had to defend itself and that most foreigners in Iraq were fair game. When the reporter asked him if good Muslims should be chopping off heads, he replied, "When a missile hits a house it decapitates 30 or 40 residents and turns them to ash. Isn't there a need to compare the behavior of a person under siege and angry with those who are managing the instruments of war?"[4]

Similarly, Sheik Yousef Qaradawi, a Qatari cleric, was getting a lot of attention because of his encouragement of counterviolence on U.S. forces. His al-Jazeera show made him influential among Sunni Muslims. The commentary doesn't just show anger in the Muslim populace over collateral damage; it also shows that the ultraelitist in the Arab world were enraged and calling for retaliation against the Americans. This type of reaction was fueled by an American inability to manage the problem at the ground level. The U.S. military's response was very mechanical and insincere. Above all, it was happening way too often, and when that many mistakes are not addressed publicly, it breeds hatred. Qaradawi's recommendations proved Lippmann's herd theory, except it was the Pan-Arab world that was the herd and the Muslim clerics and educated Arabs were telling the rest of the herd what to think and what to do in response to the collateral-damage issue.

To illustrate how impactful remarks from societal leaders can be, I offer this anecdote. The coalition opened a sewage plant in September 2004 in the al-Amil sector of Baghdad. As the Americans arrived they gave the Iraqi children candy and interacted with them, and then a bomb exploded, killing thirty-five children. Al-Jazeera interviewed family members gathered to mourn their kids, and all of the families said that the Americans had lured the children to them because they knew there would be an attack and wanted to use them as human shields. One of the sources in the story said he was a cleric and had a son who died in the attack, and another was an Iraqi cop who said that celebrating the opening of a sewage plant that was already partially operating was wrong and that enticing the kids to interact with them was thoughtless. What strikes me is that violence had reached such a point that Iraqis were angrier at the fact that the Americans had mistakenly lured kids into a trap instead of being angry at the insurgents who had killed their kids.

Al-Jazeera was instrumental in bringing the story of collateral damage into the spotlight. They were persistent because they began to tell the story of collateral damage in 2001, a subject mentioned in U.S. media stories, but not given the kind of exposure that warranted a complete story. I spend all this time addressing collateral damage because along with lack of security, it was part of a dynamic, dangerous blend that eroded Iraqi public support for the coalition. Security and collateral damage both proved to be issues that were never appropriately addressed publicly in Iraq and ultimately led to the Iraqi public's acceptance of the insurgency, passively and actively, because Iraqis knew there was no security apparatus to protect them and that the U.S. forces were also killing Iraqis.

In her 2006 book Torie Clarke, the former Pentagon chief PAO, said that as 9/11 unfolded, "The best antidote to panic was information . . . as much as possible."[5] She's right, which makes me wonder why the Defense Department didn't see what was unfolding in Iraq as its forces failed to keep Iraqis safe, killed Iraqis, and then dismissed the civilian casualties. Iraqis were obviously in a panic, according to the Arab and Western media reports and U.S. surveys of 2003 and 2004. The situation had been brought to international attention by al-Jazeera, but the network was not the problem. The problem was the actual civilian deaths. They were widespread, and Iraq proved to be a complex battleground for U.S. forces where insurgents routinely blended in with civilians. Insurgents engaged U.S. forces in populated areas, pressing

U.S. soldiers to engage or die. But a complex scenario called for a sophisticated response, and I think the Pentagon could have done a much better job at this on the local community level with the Iraqis. Pressing palms goes a long way in that culture, but apologies and sincerity do too. Our role as PAOs is public relations, and we could have done much more in this regard and thought outside the box more. We could have gotten out from behind our desks and done some crisis communications on the ground instead of from the safety of the Green Zone.

If PAOs truly believed that al-Jazeera was staging its stories or doing things that were unethical, then the coalition should have politely and levelheadedly contacted editorial leaders at al-Jazeera, embraced them to try to get accurate information to them, and tried to continue to work with them after the initial reports of U.S. collateral damage. They should also have gotten information from them to try to locate the sites of collateral damage so they could visit the sites themselves and talk to the villagers and invite al-Jazeera to be there when they visit.

PAOs in charge on the ground in Iraq and in the Pentagon should have organized a special team of military communicators to engage and work with al-Jazeera and try to proactively manage collateral damage cases. I know there were "Arab media engagement teams" in Iraq, but whatever they did, they did ineffectively, because Iraqis were starving for information about their government. At the very least, PAOs leading the communications war should have recognized that a team was needed to liaise between the coalition and al-Jazeera.

In February 2003, weeks before the U.S. invasion of Iraq, al-Jazeera interviewed Defense Secretary Rumsfeld in Washington. Al-Jazeera's reporter Jamil Azer was polite but direct. He asked Rumsfeld if the looming war against Iraq was truly about weapons of mass destruction or more about ridding the world of Saddam. Rumsfeld replied that the planned invasion was about keeping Iraq free of weapons of mass destruction. But when Azer asked if no weapons were found, would Iraq be left alone, Rumsfeld got defensive.

"The United Nations resolution has found Iraq to be in material breach of their obligations under those resolutions. The Iraqi regime has not cooperated with the inspectors and the idea that the inspectors could come up and say that is just beyond imagination because the inspectors have said quite the contrary that in fact they're not cooperating. If Iraq were to do that obviously then they would have fulfilled the UN resolution," Rumsfeld said, but he never answered the question directly.[6]

Azer asked Rumsfeld what the U.S. plan was for the region if the United States did invade Iraq. Prophetically, Rumsfeld would offer a reply that would sadly reflect the root of the climate in Iraq after the U.S. invasion. "There is no master plan. We don't run around the world trying to figure out how other people ought to live. What we want is a peaceful region," Rumsfeld said.

The Rumsfeld interview showed the network was fair in giving high-level U.S. officials the opportunity to talk about operations in Iraq despite the bad blood between the Defense Department and al-Jazeera from Afghanistan.

The U.S. entered Iraq, and, similar to Afghanistan, al-Jazeera was one of the first news organizations on the ground in Iraq operating independently, with no U.S. military escort. The U.S. military credentials and embeds journalists on the battlefield for their own safety. That's what they say anyway, but military press credentials haven't prevented journalists from being killed on the battlefield in Iraq, and some Arab journalists have died from U.S. firepower. Most credentials are used as access badges and legitimize reporters, since PAOs issue the badges only once a series of documents are presented to them that validate the reporter as a legitimate journalist. This enables the media to enter military compounds and attend press briefings, conferences, and junkets. Credentialed media can also be embedded, but unescorted media on the battlefield run the risk of being killed. If they aren't with U.S. forces, they can be a part of the collateral damage and can be killed in firefights between U.S. forces and the bad guys. Reports vary, but there are estimates that indicate several hundred reporters have died in Iraq, and some of those were credentialed reporters operating sans U.S. military support or escort.

In addition to having unescorted reporters on the ground, al-Jazeera was also embedded with U.S. forces as Operation Iraqi Freedom kicked off and U.S. forces rolled across the border into Iraq. And like it had done in Afghanistan, al-Jazeera not only began to air stories from the U.S. perspective, but also captured footage of the U.S. invasion from an Iraqi perspective.

On March 23, 2003, al-Jazeera broadcast images of American prisoners of war (POWs) and dead U.S. soldiers who had been videotaped by Iraqi television and given to the satellite channel. On the tape captured U.S. soldiers are interrogated, and in other scenes dead U.S. soldiers lay strewn next to their convoy vehicles with visible wounds and pools of blood. Al-Jazeera aired the tape before the Defense Department could inform the soldiers' families that they were missing in action. The soldiers were part of a group from a U.S. Army convoy that took a wrong turn and got ambushed.

One of its more famous soldiers, Jessica Lynch, gained notoriety after the press incorrectly reported that she fought bravely in battle, some reporting that she expended every last bullet before being taken prisoner. Lynch later denied those tales and said she never said them. The military public relations branch never denied the stories were inaccurate or made any effort to correct the record.

In a press conference in March 2003 Lt. Gen. John Abizaid of the U.S. Army who would take command of U.S. Central Command later that year blasted an al-Jazeera reporter because his network had broadcast the images. "You're from al-Jazeera television and I'm very disappointed that you would betray . . . our service members, and I would ask others not to do that," Abizaid said at the briefing.[7]

I didn't understand then and I still don't understand now how al-Jazeera "betrayed" the U.S. prisoners. Videotaping prisoners may have been in bad taste, but it was done by Iraqi television and the tape was given to al-Jazeera. Even if al-Jazeera had taped the American prisoners and the dead U.S. soldiers, it legally and ethically did nothing wrong. It is a disinterested party to the conflict.

I recall the United States did the same thing in 1991's Gulf War. Thousands of Iraqi soldiers surrendered, and the U.S. military had no problem showing news video of surrendering and captured Iraqi soldiers in captivity. I remember one shot in particular where hundreds of Iraqis are sitting on the desert floor surrounded by barbed wire and guarded by rifle-toting U.S. troops; in all more than seventy-two thousand Iraqi prisoners were taken in three days. But in addition to the surrendering or captured Iraqis, there was also plenty of video showing U.S. weapons killing Iraqi soldiers in their tanks, in fighting positions, in convoys, you name it, including a video from an Apache gun camera cutting down Iraqi soldiers on foot that was reported on by the *Los Angeles Times* and painted a graphic picture of war. It was all like watching a video game.

Fast forward to Operation Iraqi Freedom and Abizaid's misguided accusations. In 2003 there was plenty of imagery and video of Iraqi soldiers circulating on the Internet and on news sites. Many were dead or captured. Why didn't the U.S. military go after the BBC, CNN, *Time*, or *Newsweek* and accuse them of unethical behavior? I saw images of British soldiers next to dead Iraqis on a BBC site. Did Abizaid's rules apply only to the other side? When Saddam was captured, he was paraded in front of a camera as a U.S. military medical officer inspected him in U.S. captivity. His trial and execution were recorded and aired on al-Jazeera. How is this different from video of our captured soldiers?

What about when a very dead and bloated Abu Musab al-Zarqawi, al-Qaeda's leader in Iraq, was photographed at his death so his picture could be shown worldwide and used in briefings? What about Saddam Hussein's sons? The Husseins and Zarqawi might as well have been deer tied to the hood of a car. They were American trophies, but where was the outrage then? The U.S. military condoned the broadcast and publishing of images showing captured, defeated, and dead Iraqis soldiers to the world in 2003. Why wouldn't it? It fortifies the message that the U.S. military will kick anyone's ass if it is messed with. It serves to deter, but also stirs the pot of nationalism stew back home. But again, in the information age, the U.S. military cannot get caught practicing what it preaches against, and the only way to do this is to execute its information operations cleanly. The U.S. message is undeniably that the only permissible battlefield images are those that benefit a U.S. communications agenda. Freedom of the press applies only when it serves the U.S. government, and that's no way to operate in a world made smaller by communications technology.

If the United States is committed to a free press and uses words like "democracy," "freedom," and "liberty" during its saber rattling to whip Americans into a prewar frenzy, then it must understand that internationally, media who doubt the U.S. government really goes to war purely because of those values will hold the United States accountable when it strays from those ideals. But they will also test the resolve of the nation to see if it truly believes in freedom of the press, or an Americanized version of it. That's what al-Jazeera did in Iraq and Afghanistan.

The U.S. government needs to put away the notion that images that show U.S. personnel when they're captured, wounded, killed, and seemingly vulnerable will not be broadcast. Admonishing the media that boldly does so is the wrong thing to do. As a former military communicator, I know the damage these videos and photographs do to the military's image. Instead of looking mighty, U.S. forces appear vulnerable, and they have a demoralizing impact on the troops. They also place doubt in the minds of Americans who have to watch their soldiers on television or see their pictures in publications. It's a type of psychological operation waged on the public's opinion and on their perception of the enemy. The enemy seems more capable, more barbaric than before, and doubts surface. Those doubts impact public opinion, and public opinion impacts presidential approval, and presidential approval impacts party politics, and so on and so on. The bottom line is that U.S. forces don't seem invincible, and while the Pentagon and elected leaders say that their concern is for the families, I don't buy it. If politicos care so much for military families, why do they continue to cut their benefits and give warriors lowest-bidder equipment? Their concern is purely political. Dead American GIs on television and in newspapers aren't good for politics. If U.S. military families were considered such a national treasure by politicos, servicemen and -women would be paid more and have better Veterans Administration care and wouldn't be thrown on the fire in wars that lack plans.

By airing the U.S. prisoner videos in 2003, al-Jazeera did nothing wrong; it simply reported a story from an opposing side. After scolding al-Jazeera, the U.S. military asked American news agencies to refrain from rebroadcasting the footage until the families of the dead and captured had been notified of the soldiers' status. The media complied. After a few days they aired still scenes of the dead taken from the videotape that ensured the dead weren't personally recognizable. Eventually, most U.S. news organizations realized the news value of the footage and aired it, but not its full version and only after the Pentagon informed the families.

American media cooperation was granted for several reasons. First, the soldiers in the video were American soldiers, and the American media, profit-oriented entities, would not risk alienating segments of its readers and viewers by broadcasting or publishing images that showed fellow Americans in this lowest of human conditions. While media managers used words like "ethical" and "responsible" to justify their reasons for not running the tape in its entirety, the truth is I'm sure many were eyeing the impact on their readership and viewership. Second, these were American soldiers, and the American media were linked to them through national ties. Remember that media experts Daniel C. Hallin and Todd Gitlin wrote, "The primary role of the media in wartime in the Anglo-American world has long been to maintain the ties of sentiment between soldiers in the field and the home front."[8] There are enduring cultural themes of community and national prowess that surface in the media during times of war. Had the American media aired the tape as al-Jazeera did, it would have imploded and hurt only itself. There would have been an American backlash because we do not have the stomach for that kind of thing.

What had started as a solid war-communications plan in Iraq, seven hundred embedded journalists, took a big hit when the captured U.S. soldiers video aired, and it seemed nobody in the public affairs arena was ready for it, mostly because the Pentagon public affairs team, then led by Torie Clarke, the secretary of defense for public affairs, was controlling the media through the embed process. By embedding the media the military controls the media and the Pentagon controls the message. What pours out of embedded reporters is purely pro-American when you consider what

Gitlin and Hallin mention and you combine that with reporter immobility. There's only one side of the story a reporter can offer, and that is the U.S. side, so while it seems the military is bending over backward to accommodate the press by inviting them on an embed, in truth they are controlling the message because they know reporters will only showcase U.S. soldiers in action. The American side of the story will be told. It is the only news angle the media has to offer. Every reporter I spoke with who has ever embedded with the U.S. military raved about American soldiers, their spirit, bravery, and ability to annihilate the enemy. The U.S. military, with few exceptions, has no better cheerleader than the American press corps when it goes to war.

Reporters share with their audience what they see firsthand on the battlefield. What they don't see, the battlefield gap, is often filled in by PAOs. As mentioned earlier, a reporter ordinarily will not physically confirm the number of enemy killed, nor will he or she check an area for collateral damage. That information comes from PAOs, and reporters ordinarily parrot the military's information. Most would think that's not a problem, considering the person that is filling that informational gap is a military officer and someone who should be trusted. Returning to the My Lai incident, the *New York Times*, in March 17, 1968, reported that U.S. forces had killed more than one hundred North Vietnamese soldiers in an operation to clear enemy forces from several cities. Journalists obviously were reporting what they had been told, not what they had seen, but had they had the ability to verify their facts, they would have learned the enemy deaths were really part of a civilian massacre at the hands of U.S. soldiers. They assumed government officials wouldn't lie.

Al-Jazeera removed the U.S. military's long-enjoyed fudge factor. In previous wars facts could be fudged a little and the details conveniently filled in by the military. The growth of media globally, particularly in the Middle East, changed all that for the armed forces. Based on how sloppily public affairs plans were executed, it seems nobody at the Pentagon took into consideration that foreign media might be wandering around on the battlefield, ready to show war from a different perspective. Nobody thought about the impact of informational immediacy and purity. They didn't think about it because PAOs spin wars; they don't win wars. They stir up public support and try to retain it and defend it. It's the wrong approach, and they should be more concerned with factual transparency, because lurking around every corner is a camera ready to offer the world the whole raw story. It's high time the U.S. military changes its one-dimensional approach to public affairs. It should stop selling war and push for a more open, more real approach in delivering its messages and managing information.

I'm not trying to be politically correct or be perceived as some wing nut who worries more about everyone else's rights than those of U.S. soldiers, but it makes the United States look incredibly incredulous when it doesn't practice what it preaches. I didn't like seeing U.S. soldiers on grainy videos scared shitless out of their minds or dead on the side of some remote Iraqi road. As a career soldier and as an officer it broke my heart to see them in this position. But they are serving the nation on a global stage, and while I admit it would have sucked for me to be captured and have my family learn of this by watching CNN, it is the nature of the business in today's modern military and a risk military leaders must assess and mitigate as part of operating in the information age.

The U.S. military cannot shut down an independent press or exert government action upon a free press simply because it doesn't like what it says or shows. What frightening precedence are we setting if our military powers prevent a free press from operating unilaterally? What type of government do we really have when military force is applied on the press? It is an American's right to boycott a news network if it does something a citizen thinks is unethical, but it is an American newspersons right (if not duty) to report the news, and we cannot allow those in power to forget that constitutionally rooted right.

The U.S. government understands the value of U.S. public opinion, and that is why the Bush administration tried to control the media's coverage of the war, ensuring that images of dead U.S. soldiers were not broadcast or published. They too used words to hide their real motives, saying words like "respect" and "privacy" to hide political motivations. They understood that the nation could not stomach seeing their young men and women dead on the battlefield or coming home in flag-draped caskets. But what the administration failed to understand is that the images aren't tolerated by the nation because the policies in Iraq were flawed. If there was sound and legitimate progress being made, the nation would grieve but accept that the service personnel died for a cause. There would be tangible progress to show for each drop of blood. Iraq lacked the "this for that" element that enables Americans to stomach military losses. In World War II Americans had tyranny as a motivator. As U.S. forces died killing Nazis and Japanese, Americans believed tyrannical ideologies were pushed away from their shores. As a nation we were convinced we were helping prevent genocide and oppression.

In Iraq there was a lot of misappropriation and mismanagement by American companies and two administrations. The connection of Iraq to al-Qaeda made before the U.S. invasion we all know is complete bullshit. In the aftermath of Desert Storm Americans accepted they might have been tricked a little bit into supporting the war, but they were willing to overlook it because the war was quick and had, militarily speaking, few casualties. Forget the one hundred thousand Iraqis who had been killed. America fared well. But in 2004 the revelation that Hussein wasn't as big a threat as he had been made out to be made Americans weary, and it made watching and counting the war dead come home that much harder. President Bush tried to tell the American public that preemption in Iraq was a sound strategy based on a number of factors, but the intelligence community refuted his points, and because his policy was flawed for invading and his occupation had been badly bungled, American support began to erode. The Bush administration then entered a panicked, reactionary communications path that has led the mission in Iraq to where it is today, on a reactive road with no destination. The Bush administration and the Iraqi government have violated media rights, suppressed the free press, imprisoned without cause or charge members of the media, and stemmed the flow of information to the public.

The Bush administration aggressively enforced a long-standing but little-imposed directive created long before the start of Operation Iraqi

Freedom that stipulates that repatriation of deceased U.S. soldiers will not be photographed and that ceremonies for dead returning military personnel will not be captured by media. The directive was, interestingly, a holdover from President George Herbert Walker Bush from 1991. The directive was created, I suppose, in the event war dead started pouring in during Desert Storm. Well into Operation Iraqi Freedom, Bush administration officials expressed outrage over photographs taken aboard a U.S. aircraft that showed several U.S. flag–draped coffins returning from Iraq. I've always felt that the Bush administration robbed the families of the fallen their chance to be embraced by the nation. Lawsuits by the media to gain access to the aircraft arriving at Dover Air Force Base were dismissed by U.S. courts. I think it is unconscionable that these leaders choose to use as public relations pawns families that have lost loved ones in operations supporting their nation, a nation that chooses not to recognize their sacrifices as they return to their native soil. The policy was reversed in 2009 by Barack Obama's administration.

U.S. military personnel serve under the flag of their country, and they wear the cloth of their nation when they fight its wars. U.S. sailors and Coast Guardsmen line the edges of their ships when they deploy and stand proudly as they pull away from port to serve in war. Soldiers, Marines, and airmen are celebrated as the nation sends them into harm's way from forts and bases. The very least the nation can do is embrace them and give them an appropriate ceremony when they return home after being killed in the nation's wars. Journalists can capture that return for all to see. There is no invasion of privacy if a soldier's casket is not individually identified, and, frankly, even if the flag-draped coffins were singled out and identified, it shows the sacrifice being made by our men and women in uniform. The only invasion of privacy comes when uninvited press attends the individual's graveside ceremony, an event that should be reserved for families.

However, graveside memorials better show the sacrifice at a more intimate level, and that is where the press should direct its focus, not as they arrive in Dover, Bush administration officials once said. Did I miss something here? What the fuck are they talking about? Why would a presidential administration ask the media to converge on a personal event like a funeral but chase them away from a very public place like a government military base? Here's why. Some slick communicator or staff weenie obviously thought that grieving families would better communicate to the American public the very personal sacrifices being endured by our military families. By recommending the media attend these individual funerals, the press would capture and convey that human cost at a very ground level, and American sentiment would be stirred and they'd rally around the flag. The stories would focus on the individual soldiers and their families and not the broader policy that led to their deaths. The local media would fit the individual into the community, humanize him, and show that a piece of that community was now lost. Throughout that city, county, locale, thousands would hear the family saying that their loved ones died for a good cause and doing what they believed in. Military families back their loved ones in uniform, and the administration knew that most American military families would not stand up and say their sons, daughters, husbands, wives, fathers, and mothers died in vain. I've traveled all over the United States, and media coverage of "a local hero" is always very reverent and respectful. By redirecting the media to the local level, it stirs grassroots support for the troops. Think about local media coverage when a service member dies. Isn't there always a family member saying how much that person will be missed and talking about their devotion to duty? These reports arouse people to support the troops.

If the media would have been allowed to photograph inside of the aircraft returning at Dover, they would see a cargo plane filled with the caskets of the fallen. Rather than show a solitary soldier being buried, the photo would show many dead, and there is a psychological impact when Americans see a steady flow of aircraft filled with war dead being ferried like cargo on a plane. Those who bring war dead home do an incredibly meaningful job, and they treat the fallen with deep respect and dignity. I have never understood how a flag-draped coffin becomes less private if shown on a plane instead of a cemetery. This was not an issue of family privacy, as the Bush administration argued. It was an issue of public opinion.

Interestingly, repatriations conducted by the Joint POW/MIA Accounting

Command (JPMAC) in Hawaii continued to be widely publicized and covered by the press during Operation Iraqi Freedom. Why is there no concern for their privacy? Is it because our war dead from past wars don't have a need for privacy since their wars are long over? Or is it that they gave up their right to privacy when they were abandoned by their country and left behind on foreign soil? Thankfully, we have a great team of professionals at the JPMAC that are bringing our guys home to our military families and they all deserve the attention commensurate with their sacrifices.

In 2005 the CPA's former senior media adviser Dorrance Smith wrote an editorial about al-Jazeera and the media for the *Wall Street Journal*. Smith, a former newsman, had worked for ABC News. Now he was part of a Defense Department movement so frustrated and paralyzed by a mismanaged Iraq foreign policy that it chose to lash out at the international media.

"While I was in Iraq in 2004, al-Jazeera was expelled from the country by the Iraqi Governing Council for violating international law. Numerous times they had advance knowledge of military actions against coalition forces. Instead of reporting to the authorities that it had been tipped off, al-Jazeera would pre-position a crew at the event site and wait for the attack, record it and rush it on air. This happened time after time, to the point where al-Jazeera was expelled from Iraq," Smith wrote.[9]

In this editorial Smith, the chief coalition communications strategist, suggests that al-Jazeera should take sides. Smith implies that it is acceptable for al-Jazeera news crews to suit up and embed with U.S. forces during the invasion and record military actions of coalition forces, which they did, but it is unacceptable for the news agency to present the U.S. enemy's side of the story and embed with insurgents. Smith says al-Jazeera should have tipped off coalition authorities because they had "advance knowledge" of attacks on coalition units, but, following that logic, then should al-Jazeera have tipped off the insurgents or Saddam's soldiers during the U.S. embeds since at the time they had advance knowledge of coalition operations in 2003? Is an American enemy automatically an enemy of the international press or, specifically in this case, the Arab press?

U.S. government PAOs needs to be mature enough to accept that the media can sit on both sides of the table and cover all sides of a story, as is expected by the public. If the United Nations issues some type of military or diplomatic edict, international journalists should not be subject to it. They are observers not just for one party, but for all. The U.S. government might have international law on its side as justifications for military action on another country, but the international press is not subject to those laws. There are no international treatises or rules that govern journalistic behavior when nations are at war. There is nothing that states anywhere that journalists must choose a side or serve only parties from the United Nations or some other organized multinational entity. Reporters should be free to roam, at their own peril, and report whatever they like. I'd like to know exactly what international law al-Jazeera violated? Was it the Don't-Put-U.S.-Enemies-on-Television law? Has someone actually written a law that says reporters worldwide are required to serve as intelligence sources?

When journalists embedded with U.S. forces in ground combat units, while they didn't have direct knowledge of the battle plan, they did know with certainty the guys they were with were going to kill people and that they would be along for the ride to see it. Similarly, when an al-Jazeera cameraman is told by an insurgent to stand at a particular corner and start recording when he sees an American convoy, how is that different from when a U.S. unit opens fire on an insurgent stronghold and embedded cameramen start recording? The problem isn't that al-Jazeera has taken sides; it hasn't. The problem is that there is a U.S. expectation that it should take sides, the U.S. side. There is a level of U.S. arrogance that believes that because we say this is a just cause, then everyone should join us, including the press.

The military ignorantly rebukes brave, bold, and independent press groups because it doesn't understand journalism fundamentals and doesn't understand how information, bad and good, can help it communicate its messages. The Defense Department accuses the media of reporting inaccurately, yet it floods the battlefield with incorrect information like stating that al-Jazeera violated international law.

War managers in Iraq told people what was happening in Iraq and argued that news groups like al-Jazeera were liars and inciting problems and impeding progress. On the contrary, organizations like al-Jazeera have helped the world get a better view of the war in Iraq. Early on the war seemed sanitized when I watched it on American media. Scenes of insurgent attacks showed the aftermath of the attack, but it was usually just smoldering metal or remnants of a building. The deaths were reported at the end of the story or broadcast, but they were not shown. Not a lot of emphasis was given to those killed, and it was reported as something that was expected in that part of the world.

If you watched the same story reported through al-Jazeera's lenses, the human drama would be quickly elevated. They showed mangled bodies, pools of blood in the streets, and crying family members. They would interview people, and the story would focus on the human devastation from the attack and not so much on the attack itself. Maybe because the Middle East has seen more violence in the region, its people are more desensitized to it, but there is no doubt that the Arab media don't filter violence for their people.

I remember sometime ago seeing footage from a gunfight between Palestinians and Israelis. A father and his twelve-year-old son were huddled amid a crossfire, and then the boy, Muhammad al-Durrah, went limp. Some believe Israeli troops killed him. It was pure agony to watch, but it brings into question the media's role in human events. According to Smith, the media has a responsibility to alter events by becoming one of the parties at conflict. In the case of the father and son, should the reporter from France 2 have saved them? Is the cameraman's role to capture the event or be a part of it?

American reporters must ask themselves in extremely difficult situations if they are purists of their professions. In wars they must determine whether they are journalists or American journalists. After all, if an American soldier once protected an embedded reporter in a firefight, will that same reporter allow an insurgent to kill the soldier or attack the U.S. unit he was embedded with if he is reporting from the insurgent perspective? Joe Galloway, a civilian reporter in Vietnam, was awarded the Bronze Star with a valor device for putting himself in danger as he helped wounded U.S. soldiers in the Ia Drang Valley in Vietnam. It is a tough call to make, but one that must be left up to the reporter.

Whether on the front lines or domestically, reporters must decide if a human life is worth more than the human story. If a building is burning and it is obvious there are people still inside because they are hanging off ledges and screaming for help out of windows that are billowing smoke and flames, does the reporter have an obligation to fulfill his role as an observer and record the event, or does he drop his notepad and camera, rush the building, and help those inside?

Based on al-Jazeera's coverage of Arabs, Americans, Palestinians, Israelis, you name it, it seems they are inclined to capture the event. I'm certain human life has its value to al-Jazeera crews, and I know from speaking to many war-weary cameramen that combat coverage takes its toll on the soul, regardless of ethnicity or nationality, but in these traumatic human events, they understand that their role is not to interfere but only to capture the events of human lives.

On 9/11 American reporters overwhelmingly showed they too are true journalists, as they captured some of the most dramatic and unforgettable images ever captured by cameras: people leaping to their deaths from the World Trade Center towers. In performing their duties as journalists, the cameramen helped document a ghastly day in U.S. history, and their products would humanize the anguish felt in New York City and the nation. Their roles as witnesses for the world can and will be argued by the journalism and communications academe, but what they shared globally speaks loudly. Their work at ground level that day was extraordinary as they documented the despair, bravery, hopelessness, hopefulness, and mayhem of 9/11.

What is noteworthy about al-Jazeera, regardless of how a person might feel about it, is that it executed its duties consistently. It reported from a U.S. vantage point and gave the coalition a forum, allowing them to disseminate their talking points to the Arab world. Fairly, al-Jazeera then reported from the side of the insurgents and gave them a forum to speak out about their cause, in essence delivering their talking points. Some of my public affairs counterparts in Iraq argued that al-Jazeera granted self-proclaimed Arab analysts the time to rant about anticoalition commentary and that, coupled with the insurgent videos, caused things to go badly in Iraq. I countered that just as the self-proclaimed Arab analysts were given time, the coalition did have equal time and could have had politicos on al-Jazeera to disprove points raised by the analysts. They could have pushed Iraqi leaders to be on al-Jazeera. Instead, they virtually ignored the network, argued with them, and engaged them only when they felt compelled to disprove their stories. Had they been smart, the coalition would have worked with Iraqi officials to ensure they saturated al-Jazeera's airways with their presence. The insurgents and angry Arabs got plenty of face time in front of al-Jazeera's mics, and look what it got them. They made the greatest country in the world look like liars, hypocrites, and cruel occupiers. Obviously, somebody inside al-Qaeda understands media-engagement campaigns.

Al-Jazeera, I'm certain, would have shown progress in Iraq if it had truly happened, but massive explosions throughout the country are hard to ignore compared to the opening of a new hospital in a rural city. Violence will always have a place in the headlines so long as it occurs. The Iraqi government could have tried to make the insurgent attacks second-tier headlines by providing real results and showing progress was being made to secure Iraq or had government officials inciting outrage from the populace over the constant civilian death toll.

The insurgents understood that a sustained media presence works. At the height of the conflict in Iraq before the surge, each day there was a news story about a bombing, an IED attack, a sniper killing, or a missile attack. The insurgents ensured that every single day, the international press corps had something violent to show the world about the U.S. occupation of Iraq. Did this impact international support for America in Iraq? You bet—and the damage isn't limited to foreign soils. Americans grew sick of the war in Iraq and the constant flow of bad news. So does a constant flow of information work? It worked effectively for the bad guys.

Another tired U.S. Defense Department argument is that U.S. soldiers do good work but will get coverage from the media only when they do something bad. I've never found that to be true, but, again, it is hard to overlook fifty dead people in a marketplace when it competes with the refurbishment of an Iraqi ministry. PAOs argued that they tried to get good news out, but

I've seen firsthand that their efforts were no more than passively sending a press release to a reporter. That type of media-engagement posture in an insurgency won't get good news out.

For the sake of this argument, it is hard to overlook a soldier who rapes, murders, and tortures a noncombatant. The story has news value and shouldn't be overlooked because a bed of daisies is blooming next to a soccer field built for Iraqi kids by U.S. soldiers. As I said earlier, news groups are businesses, and in order for these businesses to make money, conflict needs to be present in its content, much like the movies, books, and games Americans consume each year. Otherwise, people don't watch, read, or listen. It is a sad but true fact of human nature, and the press shouldn't be blamed. If I were an editor, I'd always place the highest value on human life, and when it is lost it would certainly have high precedence in my news-value matrices. This doesn't mean that there is something wrong with the media, but as humans we are interested in things that preserve or threaten our mortality, and that is just a part of our human fabric.

Some of the so-called bad news in Iraq covered by al-Jazeera has included incidents of collateral deaths at the hands of coalition forces, and I don't want to make light of that because those deaths are significant to those Iraqis who no longer have a loved one thanks to U.S. missiles, artillery rounds, or a nervous GI with a rifle. But the truth is that the coalition does not intentionally plant bombs in marketplaces and apartments in hopes of killing civilians with no tactical value, but it does sometimes kill innocent people around the strike zones of precision munitions and writes those losses off, as professional warriors are often expected to do in the military culture. Publicly, that's a bad move, especially when a nation spends $3 million on a laser-guided "smart bomb" that is meant to limit damage around the target area yet blows the living shit out of a family eating dinner next door to some bad guys.

After Operation Desert Storm, when precision-guided munitions were publicly praised after being widely used all over Iraq, the U.S. Air Force reported that 70 percent of the eighty-eight thousand tons of bombs dropped in Iraq missed their targets because it had used only a small percentage,

7 percent to be exact, of smart bombs, wrote Bruce Cumings in his book *War and Television*.[10]

Al-Jazeera was one of the first, if not the first, news agencies in Iraq to try to keep the coalition honest. As U.S. forces hunted Saddam and fought the remaining elements of his regime in early 2003, al-Jazeera began to broadcast images of U.S. collateral damage in Iraq. It didn't mince words and would ask rhetorical questions like "Is this what democracy in Iraq looks like?" as they showed dead civilians in the streets. This further incensed the U.S. leadership and PAOs. Al-Jazeera offered the world the perspective of what it was like to be an Iraqi being invaded. It was exceptional coverage, but, again, it showed the unfiltered and unvarnished version of U.S. military action.

There were many examples in Iraq of U.S. military might gone awry. Some Iraqi deaths are attributable to legitimate mistakes, where soldiers were placed in a situation where they had to decide if they would live or die. It's hard to make those calls unless you're the guy on the ground, and in most cases those are legitimate mistakes. But there are other cases where the damage was simply a reckless disregard for human life and Iraqi personal property, and in those cases there was little U.S. action to punish offenders and settle with the Iraqis.

Al-Jazeera didn't discriminate, whether intentionally or not. Iraqi civilian deaths were shown for the world to see. Instead of launching highly visible investigations for each incident and sending out a team to do some public relations damage control, that is, have a U.S. commander on the ground meet with grieving families and pay money to help them bury the family or rebuild the edifice that was destroyed and follow up with those families until they got back on their feet from their losses, within hours coalition spokesmen would often say that forces acted within the rules of engagement. The deaths were "regrettable," and, like warriors, the U.S. military would move on.

The U.S. military cannot take responsibility for collateral damage from behind a podium. It must do so publicly at the site of the accident, and it must provide emotional, monetary, spiritual, and physical restitution. I'm not offering war-fighting or operational advice. I am making recommendations that will help eliminate perceptions that Americans are uncaring savages. When Americans mistakenly kill someone's family member, they create victims. When they do nothing about it, they create enemies. Would it be a heavy lift and a cumbersome process? You bet, but it would help prevent the climate we have today.

Al-Jazeera showed the true face of war, and when they did it scared the hell out of the Pentagon. Underneath all the flag waving and yellow ribbons behind U.S. wars lies the very nasty business of delivering death, and that was something that the national audience was not prepared to see. Collectively, the nation likes to see U.S. forces kicking ass, but it doesn't like to see its forces doing things wrong, even if they are mistakes.

I'm a life member of several veterans groups, and I've had the privilege to befriend many veterans from World War II. Many told me that what they saw during the war was so appalling that they never wanted to speak of the war to anyone again. That is why the "Greatest Generation" came home and prospered. They didn't want to relive the atrocities they had witnessed on the battlefields; they simply wanted to move on and share those memories with blokes like me who sat atop barstools and hovered over tall beers in smoky bars. They didn't share the misery with their family because their war, like all wars before them, was barbaric. These guys liberated the world from tyranny and then went about their business. While the world patted their backs and put them on pedestals, they knew what they had seen was the very worst mankind could offer.

I found it refreshing to see how candidly Steven Spielberg presented U.S. soldiers in his film *Saving Private Ryan*. In one scene after scaling cliff walls under an incessant barrage of German small-arms and artillery fire, two U.S. soldiers shoot two surrendering German soldiers. Would I have done the same thing after surviving that hellish gauntlet? Probably. I can't jump on my high horse and talk about restraint from the comfort of my home, but having served in Iraq and knowing what I know about myself, there is a good chance I'd probably put a round in each of them. But that scene does show that the World War II generation had seen its share of horror and also committed its share of indiscretions too. While it is comfortable for the world to sit back and judge today's warriors, nobody knows what they're capable of doing under intense, life-threatening stress unless they are put in the very real, very savage scenarios known only to our nation's war fighters. It's easy to armchair quarterback. It's harder to face and control those instincts that have driven us to survive since long before there were laws that civilized mankind. Killing is a survival instinct, and in war it is a part of the mission statement and overall objective of the Army. When threatened most humans react. Most soldiers are incredibly decent human beings who come from the civil sector. They are a cross-section of our society, but every now and then we will have a few that stray and the military deals with them.

Let's face it, al-Jazeera gave the world something it was not ready to see, but it wasn't anything new. What al-Jazeera brought to the world was the cold truth that has been known to soldiers since armed conflict began and has been confined to the dark places of their souls. In fact, the United States killed more than two hundred thousand Japanese when it dropped two atomic bombs on the cities of Nagasaki and Hiroshima, but those horrific images were never widely publicly shared with the American public, and instead the massive loss of life was molded into a nationalistic purpose, a necessary means to an end. As I mentioned earlier, the United States went to war against an entire nation then, not just its government, and the men who killed civilians in World War II did so in official capacities. As long as there are people on earth, we will always debate whether dropping the bomb on Japan was justified. I wasn't alive and I can't judge, but as a military officer I will say that it got their attention and the Japanese quit fucking with us.

"We know that al-Jazeera has a pattern of playing propaganda, over and over and over again. What they do is, when a bomb goes down, they grab some children and women and pretend that the bomb hit the women and the children. And it seems to me that it's up to all of us to try to tell the truth, to say what we know, to say what we don't know, and recognize that we are dealing with people that are perfectly willing to lie to the world to attempt to further their case, until ultimately they are caught lying and they lose their credibility, and one would think it wouldn't take very long for that to happen," Rumsfeld said in the 2004 movie *Control Room*.[11]

If the Defense Department had proof that al-Jazeera was lying, why didn't it show it? Why didn't it go down to the bomb's target area with al-Arabiya or another news crew willing to make al-Jazeera look like liars and disprove them? Why didn't it physically discredit them? Why did it fight a visual argument with words?

Al-Jazeera went looking for story angles because the coalition didn't work with them. While the coalition accused al-Jazeera of favoring the terrorists, it did nothing to ensure al-Jazeera was proactively given information to offer a coalition perspective to stories from Iraq in hopes it would better balance its reportage. Without active, sustained coalition engagement, the network had little choice but to offer what appeared to the world to be one side of the story, the insurgent's side.

In 2003 the United States attacked the Baghdad office of al-Jazeera. The attack killed al-Jazeera reporter Tareq Ayyoub, a very popular and well-known Jordanian journalist. Reports on the incident vary. Everyone has a version of the truth, but most agree, including U.S. forces, that a U.S. missile struck the station's Baghdad bureau, located in a residential neighborhood. The United States says it was targeting an electric generator outside the building and responding to enemy fire in the area. Al-Jazeera maintains it never fired any weapons from their building, and people on the ground all said there was no gunfire in the area to support U.S. claims.

What is agreed upon is that a U.S. aircraft launched an air-to-surface missile near Ayyoub's position, killing him. If U.S. pilots said that there was gunfire in the area, then the United States should support pilot claims by releasing gun-camera footage from the aircraft or the cockpit recordings of the crew's interaction with command-and-control elements. If U.S. forces assert that the airmen engaged a legitimate target, using rules of engagement, then let's see it. That will lay the issue to rest. As a PAO that's what I'd do, and that would silence al-Jazeera in a minute and discredit them, unless of course the footage shows no such enemy activity. In that case then it's up to the pilots to explain why they fired, and, again, if within the rules of engagement, there should be no problem with a public explanation and accountability inquiry.

Ironically and sadly, the U.S. military had days before been given the exact grid coordinates of al-Jazeera's Baghdad bureau, which lay smack in the middle of an area filled with Iraqi government buildings targeted by the coalition. Al-Jazeera was basically saying, "We're in here. Don't shoot us." The coordinates were given by al-Jazeera to the Defense Department. Yet the building was still attacked. Also under fire that day was Abu Dhabi TV, and their journalists were also wounded in the attack, despite having a large sign on their building that said "Abu Dhabi TV." The day before the missile attack al-Jazeera journalists said they were fired upon by U.S. forces as they traveled from a press briefing held by the Iraqi Ministry of Information in Baghdad. Al-Jazeera said its car was clearly marked as press.

The Republican Palace was attacked many times during my tour. Once, an insurgent mortar team managed to kill two people in an attack. In one of those attacks, within a couple of hours, video of the attackers was released to the press. The attackers had been locked in by U.S. hardware, and the entire attack was captured by U.S. unmanned aerial vehicles (UAVs) flying overhead, which followed the attackers to their home. Within minutes after the attack U.S. forces apprehended them. All of it was captured on video.

Releasing a tape like this deters would-be bad guys, but it also shows the public that these thugs are vulnerable and can be captured and killed. Furthermore, as U.S. forces come into neighborhoods, tearing down doors and shooting people, it shows cause. I've never quite figured out why we release UAV footage like the mortar-team apprehension but not the gun-camera footage of missions that led to collateral deaths.

Remember the death of al-Arabiya reporter al-Tomaizi I mentioned in another chapter? A look into al-Tomaizi's 2004 death revealed information that conflicted with what the U.S. military had offered. Iraqis I spoke to told me that once the fighting had subsided between the U.S. forces and the insurgents, unarmed civilians came out to celebrate near and atop the burning U.S. Bradley vehicle. It was mob-induced frenzy not much different from the drunken college crowds that riot in U.S. college towns.

Overhead in Baghdad as the young men celebrated the insurgents' trophy (the burning Bradley), a U.S. Apache attack helicopter circled the crowd.

Al-Tomaizi stood in front of the wreckage and began to record a report that would eventually be broadcast throughout the Middle East. The story showed Iraqis celebrating a successful insurgent strike on Americans. As al-Tomaizi tried to sign off and end his report, a U.S. helicopter fired a missile at the Bradley, and it exploded behind him. His cries were captured by his cameraman as he told the Arab world he was dying. He died at the scene moments later. His cameraman and more than sixty people were wounded. A total of thirteen people were killed in the missile strike.

A U.S. spokesperson said that the aircrews fired on the crowd because they received gunfire from the mob. Several videotapes from the scene showed celebrating Iraqis but did not capture the sound of gunfire, nor did the footage from several cameras reveal anyone carrying a weapon, much less shooting at the helicopters. If al-Arabiya, considered to be anticoalition like their competitor al-Jazeera, was known to videotape attacks on the coalition, wouldn't it have recorded the mob's attack on the U.S. helicopters or the IED attack that crippled the Bradley? Wouldn't the cameras have been fixated on the gunmen shooting at the helicopters that were the targets? The only thing that al-Arabiya's and Reuters' footage showed was U.S. helicopters attacking an unarmed crowd sympathetic to the insurgents.

As the video of the attack circulated globally, a press center spokesman told the Associated Press that the U.S. helicopters fired on the vehicles to protect the technology and weapons of the Bradley and prevent it from falling into enemy hands. This contradicted previous U.S. statements that said the pilots fired on the crowd because of ground fire.

I've never flown over a battlefield with bullets and bombs and all sorts of shit happening below me as I try to squeeze a multimillion-dollar aircraft in between buildings filled with innocent noncombatants, so I won't try to armchair quarterback the attack on the Bradley. It's a tough job those pilots have, but only the pilots know why they killed al-Tomaizi and why they fired on the Bradley and on the crowd. Videotape from Reuters and al-Arabiya shows there was no attack from the crowd or from the area of the Bradley on the ground. But if press center personnel said the pilots fired to protect the technology, it is a violation of the Fourth Geneva Convention, because soldiers cannot attack civilians. I suspect the coalition argued that those on the Bradley were combatants, but, as I mentioned, there were no weapons on the scene, so how was it determined that those killed were combatants? Moreover, why wasn't the gun-camera footage released to support the coalition's comments and remove any doubt that the pilots did the right thing? There has been no release by the U.S. military of the thermographic video captured by the Apaches that killed al-Tomaizi, nor has there been any release of the pilots' cockpit voice tapes. My only guess is that the U.S. military was protecting the platform's technology and someone made the call to fire based on the fact that insurgent flags were being waved atop the Bradley. But the protection of that technology came at a high cost that likely will never be measured. How many more Iraqis did we entrench in hatred toward the United States that day? How many more sworn enemies did we make in order to keep our tools a secret?

There have been many Arab journalists killed by U.S. forces and many more captured and detained simply for reporting from the battlefield. In all, more than 150 journalists have been killed in Iraq since 2003, according to the Committee to Protect Journalists (CPJ). It is the worst fatality record for the profession in any war, and 2004 was the bloodiest year for the profession in recent decades. The bulk belonged to al-Arabiya and al-Jazeera. Some reporters were held for several years by U.S. forces with no charges issued against them, such as Bilal Hussein, an Associated Press photographer who won the Pulitzer Prize for Breaking News Photography when he photographed four insurgents firing a mortar and small arms in Fallujah in November 2004. Hussein was held captive by the coalition for two years and released in 2008.

I understand that the U.S. military cannot guarantee the safety of reporters who are roaming freely about the battlefield, especially when they are embedded with insurgent forces. As a soldier I would certainly find it hard not to shoot a weapon if I had the enemy in my sights and could kill several of them but a reporter was nearby. But would U.S. forces behave the same way if the reporter on the other side were Tom Brokaw? In other words, if it was Brokaw who was reporting from the Bradley vehicle and not al-Tomaizi, would the U.S. aircrew have fired? I doubt it. For the sake of argument, let's say they didn't even see al-Tomaizi. Again, if it was Brokaw who was killed or some other Western journalist, wouldn't there be some serious reckoning or answers to all these questions I'm posing? Al-Tomaizi's death simply doesn't warrant an explanation, and that is the crux of the problem. Because he was a member of the Arab media, he simply doesn't matter, and that is really fucked up. He is written off as the cost of doing business.

I have reviewed samplings of al-Jazeera's video coverage during 2004–5 and read their translated Web content. What stood out the most, what made the reports troubling, was the misery captured by al-Jazeera. While it was troubling to see blame cast on U.S. forces, unfortunately, much of it was true, and at its core that's what angered U.S. leaders. The U.S. military was doing the best it could to fight an insurgency in an urban environment, but in some cases it was a bull in a china shop and al-Jazeera had been there to capture that side of the story.

Almost a year after being suspended in September 2003 for filling Iraq's airways with reportage that the coalition said disrupted progress, al-Jazeera was ordered by the Interim Iraqi Government to close its doors in August 2004 and a month later learned the ban was indefinite. Al-Jazeera continued to report about Iraq using stringers and news services to file its stories about Iraq. In 2004, with al-Jazeera shut down and al-Arabiya left in shambles after attacks and crippling sanctions against it by the Iraqi government, the lone media group left at the top was al-Iraqiya. Al-Iraqiya had been running a distant third after al-Jazeera and al-Arabiya since it was created months earlier. The coalition at long last had an Arab news network it could control, the U.S.-funded al-Iraqiya, a station part of the Iraqi Media Network, run by the Harris Corporation. U.S. officials wasted no time in surveying Iraqis. Who were they watching? Iraqis, according to the officials, responded overwhelmingly: al-Iraqiya. Who else was there?

A 2006 Iraqi law was created and states that journalists cannot ridicule the government or its officials. Since the law was implemented in 2006, dozens of journalists have been charged and jailed. Sadly, the Iraqi media caved into the political pressure, and many news agencies signed documents stating they agreed to abide by the law and not use inflammatory language in their reports. The law forbids them from interviewing victims of insurgent attacks or U.S. attacks, and they cannot use video or pictures of attacks in their stories.

Al-Jazeera critics say that the network has failed to scrutinize its own host nation as a state news agency, a solid conclusion considering the U.S. and Qatari governments worked together to support operations in Iraq. The U.S. military had personnel working in Qatar, and the small nation was a hub of recreational activity for U.S. soldiers who took R&R there from 2002 through 2011. This story gets overlooked by al-Jazeera, and I often wonder why insurgents didn't attack Qatar or al-Jazeera because it's funded by a government that supports U.S. troops politically. It seems odd to me.

There is no doubt that al-Jazeera's goal was never to be a state medium but rather to be a regional or Arab national news phenomenon. While it can be effectively argued that reports of collateral damage alone can't inspire anti-American feelings, reports that Americans intentionally target civilians can stir those emotions. I don't think al-Jazeera did this type of dirty reporting intentionally. Arab suffering was just an important story line, and al-Jazeera gained viewers by showcasing the Arab plight.

"Successful leaders engage the media, create positive relationships, and help the media tell the story. Otherwise the media develops a story of its own that may not be as accurate and may not include the counterinsurgent force perspective," Petraeus's counterinsurgency field manual reads. Amen. Can I get a witness?

American PAOs lost their battle with al-Jazeera. The network emerged victorious with their audience intact and their viewer base growing and their operation expanding. They have even lured away high-caliber American reporters, and they are a legitimate international news source, competing with the BBC and CNN. They now have websites in several languages and an English version of their broadcast. In early 2011, six years after having been expelled, al-Jazeera was back in Iraq. I guess time will tell if the new Iraqi government will tolerate government criticism.

Ultimately, the network accomplished what it set out to do in Iraq.

According to a 2003 Congressional Research Service report, many of al-Jazeera's reporters were drawn to work for the network because they believed American coverage of Operation Desert Storm was "not even handed in that it paid insufficient attention to topics of interest to Arab audiences, such as the plight of Iraqi civilians during the conflict."[12] The network would certainly even the playing field in 2003's Operation Iraqi Freedom when its programming of the war was called the "War against Iraq."

Clarke, the former Pentagon spokesperson, I think brings up a great point in her 2006 book. She admits that the best course of action in dealing with bad news is to be transparent and tackle the issues head-on, but she reveals what I perceive might have led to her departure from the Defense Department. "If you've got a pig on your hands—which is to say, a tough story—no lipstick can be laid on thick enough to cover up that fact. Smart communicators acknowledge that fact; smarter ones embrace it. Because once you figure out you can't put lipstick on a pig, what you've really learned is far more powerful: you've learned not to produce a pig in the first place. Smart communicators know they can't talk their way out of dumb decisions."[13]

Iraq was a big fucking pig. Maybe that's why the Defense Department went through six assistant secretaries of defense for public affairs during Operation Iraqi Freedom—and they left us with nothing but a stick of lipstick.

10

FALLUJAH

Nearly 500 U.S. troops are wounded in action in Iraq during a one-week period in November 2004.
—U.S. Defense Department

I woke early the morning of November 10, 2004, after a few mortar rounds exploded nearby and jarred me from a light sleep. The insurgents and a U.S. Marine Corps artillery unit at Camp Fallujah had been lobbing mortar rounds and artillery at each other since I arrived at the forward camp the previous day.

Using some high-speed technology, the Marines could detect and lock the position of the enemy mortar team and then almost instantly fire a salvo at their position. My guess is that the insurgents lost a few mortar teams this way by taking on the artillerymen until they finally got smart and would launch their mortars and then flee in trucks. I had seen a video before coming to Fallujah that the insurgents released where they set up the mortar and quickly fired a few rounds and then left the scene but also left a video camera to record what happened next. Within a minute the Marines' artillery rained down all over the position, knocking over the camera. A while later the insurgents returned and picked up their camera while it still recorded and anything that was still functional in the mortar kit. I suspect they released the video to prove they could dodge high-tech weaponry.

I staggered sleepily in the morning darkness to a portable building nearby that had showers, sinks, and toilets. The Marines at the artillery battery were stirring to life, answering the insurgents' morning mortar call with a barrage of big gunfire. In between the blasts I could hear singing from the latrine. As I got closer I recognized the song. When I opened the door dozens of Marines were singing "Happy Birthday" at the top of their lungs as they shaved, sat on toilets, stood in front of urinals, took showers, or stood naked drying themselves after their showers. It was the Marine Corps' birthday, and they were serenading themselves as the artillery kept an unsteady beat for them just meters from us.

By the time I finished shaving and getting my uniform on, the morning's mortar melody and heavy artillery thumping had subsided. It was wonderfully quiet around the camp, except for the sounds of groaning and humming generators nearby. There were no insects chirping, no birds singing, which for a Florida boy was surreal, but at least there was the silence and I was thankful for that. Those I had traveled with were still asleep, and our duty day wouldn't start for more than an hour, so I decided to call my wife, Rosie.

I had submitted paperwork for R&R leave, and it had been approved. I was slated to go home mid-November for two weeks. It was a decision I wrestled with for quite some time, but I knew I was fast approaching burnout. My ordinary intolerance for stupidity was running down. If anyone did anything remotely stupid, I was in their face telling them about it, and oftentimes those stupid people were senior to me, so I knew it was a matter of time before I put my foot in my mouth and got into trouble.

Rosie knew I was likely coming home for Thanksgiving, but my deployment to Fallujah might throw a wrench into those plans and I needed to let her know. I had done a very good job of keeping Rosie disconnected from the war. My blog was an extension of my professional persona, so while it offered personal and professional reflections, it didn't address the fears, frustrations, and anger I was experiencing. In my weekly call to Rosie I would talk momentarily to my son, Duncan, who was a little more than two years old and not really keen on phone calls, and then I would spend the next few minutes getting information out of Rosie. I wanted her to talk to me about home: what she was doing, where she had gone that day, what she had seen, what things looked like, who she had seen in the neighborhood. I wanted to talk about something other than the war, but as I spent more time in Iraq, the deluge of professional frustration would spill over into our personal conversations simply because she would ask, "How was your week?" I knew it was time to get away from the eighteen-hour days. I often felt like I had no skin, like I was just this raw piece of flesh walking around with absolutely nothing to lose.

I had done a great job of convincing Rosie I was in no danger. The dangers were there but very small. Our greatest threat was IEDs, but because most of the places we had to travel to in Iraq were far away and we usually dragged a press entourage along with us, it wasn't feasible to travel by convoy. During my entire tour in Iraq I only went on a few dozen convoys, some of the most memorable with Jalal Talabani through Kurdistan's Sulaymaniyah, where people ran out to see us and waved at us as they picnicked on hillsides or celebrated weddings at the city's overlooks. Okay, they probably were waving at their president, Talabani, and not us, but it still felt nice to see a stable region in Iraq and see happy, thriving Iraqis who welcomed us with open arms.

I traveled by air mostly, and I logged a lot of hours up in the air in Black Hawks. While there had been some helicopters and cargo planes shot down by insurgent missiles, the threat, again, was very small for a traveler like me. For aircrews who flew all the time, that threat increased, but for someone like me who was up in the air every few days, I didn't feel like it was dangerous. As for the mortars, rockets, and bombs directed at the Green Zone, those were a daily occurrence. Some days it would be just one, and other days it was several, some days rockets, other days mortars; they even threw in suicide bombers to keep it interesting. It was an insurgent potluck.

In the time I was there from 2004 to 2005, the Republican Palace was hit three times, twice when we still worked there and the third time after we had moved to Phoenix Base. The third attack killed two people at the contracting office. Phoenix Base had been hit twice that I knew of, once as it was being built. A mortar round landed directly atop it and shattered windows throughout the compound and damaged one of the buildings. The second attack hit directly over several staff sections after we had moved into the compound, and the inertia of the round buried it into our roof, but luckily it didn't explode. I got a real kick out of some of our Marines who decided to play cowboy and were up on the roof with a rope, trying to dislodge the thing. It never exploded.

A Kurdish compound near us had been hit, and a few soldiers were killed. The rest of the enemy rounds fell angrily to earth all around the Green Zone, usually doing nothing more than just causing property damage. Soldiers once discovered an IED in the Green Zone, and a suicide bomber walked into a Green Zone restaurant and blew himself up. Minutes later one of his buddies did the same thing at an outdoor bazaar and vaporized several Americans (one guy was never found). A kidnapping plot had also been discovered whereby several Iraqi Green Zone workers were going to kidnap a U.S. government official and his assistant in a parking lot in the Green Zone, and after that we were no longer allowed to walk alone in the evening. If we were getting attacked every day, several times per day, and fewer than a dozen had died and been injured in Green Zone attacks during my tour, that meant that the indirect-fire attacks were effective about 1.25 percent of the time, which I thought were pretty good odds that I'd stay safe and in one piece. Baghdad was only as bad as a person thought it was, and knowing how bad things were for soldiers outside the walls of the Green Zone, I knew we had it made in comparison. There were soldiers who had it much worse.

Guys like me took excursions into the war, and when we were done doing what we needed to do we returned to the safety of the Green Zone. The only soldiers under real combat stress in the Green Zone, in my opinion, were the medical crews at the combat hospital who every day courageously fought the insurgents on their emergency room tables by trying to fix broken soldiers and those guarding the Green Zone who daily kept the bad guys at bay. Our small threat didn't stop melodramatic fools from calling home and telling their loved ones about how dangerous Iraq was, although many at Camp Liberty and at the Green Zone spent their entire tours living behind the high blast walls. They convinced themselves and others that they lived a dangerous and precarious existence. I know of many Green Zone–stationed soldiers who were awarded combat badges and are now being treated for post-traumatic stress disorder and never left the Green Zone. Everyone is different, I suppose, and an explosion within three hundred meters of two soldiers might make one a psychiatric patient for life and the other will not be emotionally impacted at all. It's all perspective, and reactions to the elements of war are managed differently by us all.

Rosie faced an intense media campaign back home. Each day the television, radio, and newspapers were filled with constant reports of violence in Iraq. When reports surfaced about attacks in Baghdad, there was an assumption I was right there in the middle of it. Although the explosions outside the gates of the Green Zone might have rattled our compound, I assured her I hadn't heard anything and that it was probably on the other side of town. When the suicide bombers hit the Green Zone Café and the Haji Mart, I told her we were blocks from there and that we were safely in our compound. I didn't tell her those two places were two U.S. hot spots to buy stuff and grab a meal that I had been to numerous times. And I certainly didn't worry her with stories about the mortar rounds and rockets. One morning, in fact, as I was talking to her and getting into my truck at the palace's parking lot, I heard a mortar round launch nearby.

"Honey, hey, let me call you right back," I told her calmly, and as I hung up I ran into a bunker I was parked next to. The round screeched in seconds later and exploded nearby at the landing zone, wounding an American soldier. Once medical personnel responded and things were all clear, I called her back. She asked me what happened, and because I lied I can't recall what I told her, but I think it was that I had run into someone I needed to talk to about an issue and it couldn't wait.

My point is that she had enough to worry about back home, raising a kid on her own, running her business, and trying to stay sane in between my sporadic phone calls while the media painted an honest but ugly picture of Iraq. I tried to downplay the image of what she saw on television as much as possible because I knew the truth and I wasn't being overly sensitive. What we experienced at the Green Zone was what all noncombatant staffers experienced in all of our nation's previous wars, indirect fire, no more, no less. The dangerous jobs were filled by infantrymen and other soldiers out on the streets every day. I love my wife, so why worry her?

Not all guys thought like me, and I would often hear Green Zone soldiers telling their loved ones about the danger they were in although they sat behind a desk all day. I never understood why they wanted to worry their families. It seemed like there was a lot of exaggeration going on, and I don't understand why. I saw an article published by the Georgia News Service in which one of the U.S. spokesmen in the Green Zone said he was the target of a sniper attack, and then he talked in detail about all of the dangers in the Green Zone. The man has a family, wife, and kids. Why on earth would he share that kind of information? I know my wife could have managed it if I had told her about the risks I faced, and maybe this PAO's wife managed it well too, but why worry her? Military spouses are put through enough when their soldiers deploy, but like I've said before, everyone is different. I simply could not see that the Green Zone was so dangerous and that being a spokesman inside the Green Zone could be so harrowing. I guess working with some of the people in our command gave me a different perspective. Nobody I knew shared stories like that about themselves, and I walked among badasses in our command. They were naturally modest and brave, and they downplayed their actions. We had many soldiers who earned awards for valor in combat (including the Distinguished Service Cross, the second-highest award for valor in the U.S. military). Two men in my unit were killed while I was there. Our guys were reluctant to tell their stories even to us as military journalists, so I suppose it is hard for me to look at people with desk jobs through those same lenses when I worked with genuine heroes. I simply could not see the heroics of spending an entire year behind a desk in the Green Zone.

After my return Rosie saw residual reflexive reactions every now and then. Once after I completed my tour a severe thunderstorm was approaching our home, so I walked out the front door to bring in the U.S. flag before it started raining. Over my neighbor's house, toward the western horizon, thunder rumbled, and occasional flashes of lightning whitened the landscape. As I turned my back and started walking back inside the house, a lightning bolt struck within a few yards of the house, and the energy exploded loudly.

Instinctually, I dove from the front door into the living room, where Rosie was seated. I flew about ten feet and looked like a baseball player sliding into home, arms extended, my body completely horizontal to the ground. I landed on a rug, flattened against the floor. She smiled. "Are you okay?" We both enjoyed a hearty laugh. As the months passed I'd tell her more about my experiences in Iraq, and at one point as I shared a story with her about a mortar attack at Taji where I had thrown Radhi over my shoulder and ran with him to safety as rounds fell behind us, she smacked me in the arm, covered her mouth, and said "You're such a jerk!" as she wrapped herself around me and hugged me. I should note that I told her about that event only because I had to go and see an orthopedic doctor because I had torn ligaments in my knee while carrying Radhi.

Back to my story, in Fallujah there was a lull in the artillery, so I took a gamble and called Rosie. She needed to know that I might not make it back for R&R because I was deployed forward. But most of all she needed to know I was there because the battle was getting ready to start and I would be reporting from there, so if she didn't hear it from me, she'd read it in the blog or on Defense Department news articles and learn that I was in Fallujah. She needed to hear it from me in the proper context. I wanted her to know I was safe.

The phone rang, and when I heard her voice I was instantly happy. Calling her was like feeling the warmth of the sun break through the clouds on an overcast day. She would warm my cold soul. I would many times get a lump in my throat. Our conversation went something like this.

"Hey, cutie, how are you?" I said.

"I'm good. I miss you. How are you?" she replied.

"Good, I miss you too. Listen, I wanted to tell you—"

Boom! A Marine howitzer blasted out a round in the background, just meters from me. It was deafeningly loud, and I almost jumped out of my boots.

"What the hell was that?" Rosie said excitedly.

Shit, I thought. No escaping the truth now. I was maybe fifty feet from the big gun when it went off, and I could now barely hear her. I thought they were taking a break from firing. I thought wrong.

"Honey, I'm in Fallujah," I told her.

"You're where?" she said sternly.

For six months I had dodged the war when it came to Rosie, but there was no escaping it now. The battery started to fire again, and I spent the next few minutes explaining to her that the sounds were Marine artillery rounds firing at the city, several kilometers away. The enemy wasn't firing at us, not right then anyway, and she had nothing to worry about.

"Okay. You know we support you. Do what you have to do and come home to me when you can," she said. Her strength was amazing, I thought. I'd later learn that she too had her own secrets. Truth was she was worried about me and acted strong for me so I could focus on my job. She'd spent many a night glued to the television set, watching hours of reports about the violence in Iraq. Our neighbor tattled on her, saying that she saw the television burning through the window in the middle of the night every day that I was gone.

Two days earlier before I arrived at Camp Fallujah, a U.S. Army officer who served as an adviser with the Iraqi joint headquarters contacted me and said he needed my help. The lieutenant colonel told me he was heading to Fallujah. Offensive operations were getting ready to kick off there, and he and another U.S. officer would be traveling to Camp Fallujah, on the outskirts of the city, escorting the Iraqi ground-forces commander for the operation, Iraqi Army major general Abdul Qader Mohammed Jassim al-Mifarji.

Abdul Qader had been promoted and not only appointed the ground-forces commander of the Iraqi forces for the operation but made the chief of the Iraqi Army. The colonel said he needed assistance with managing the general's communications, and he thought I would be a good press adviser for him. There were no PAOs going to Fallujah to help the Iraqi general. There would be press in Fallujah and ample media opportunities, and the colonel needed my help. I was more than happy to assist, so I let Petraeus know I would be gone for a short spell.

After getting asked to go to Fallujah I thought about how useful Sabeeh would have been in this scenario. Had the coalition public affairs community helped train Iraqis and mentor them in public affairs, or given us the resources to do so, Sabeeh would be traveling to Fallujah with me to put an Iraqi face on the operation in the restive city. It would be him, not me, whispering in the general's ear, and he would be talking to the media.

I also thought about all of the Iraqis the Defense Information School cadre claimed to have trained. Where were they? Why weren't they coming with me? The school's commandant said they had been given a good foundation to do their duties, but if they had been prepared, then why weren't they going to Fallujah? As it was there was no uniformed Iraqi military PAO to escort the Iraqi general.

After arriving Abdul Qader received a briefing from a U.S. Marine Corps Jordanian-born colonel who spoke some Arabic. The colonel briefed the general about what was happening and shared plans for the battle. As he did behind him a large map of the city was alive with electronic activity, as colored symbols representing Iraqi and coalition forces moved about the screen like a video game. One of the screens carried a live video feed from an unmanned aerial vehicle above the battlefield. It followed insurgents as they ran from coalition forces and hid. Some were engaged and killed as we watched, while others were captured, thanks to the eye in the sky. As I sat and listened to the colonel brief Abdul Qader, who was snacking on grapes, dates, and some other assorted fruits, I started to realize that Abdul Qader didn't know what the hell was going on and hadn't been involved in the planning of the operation.

He asked silly questions. "Which direction are they going to attack from? How many Iraqi soldiers are on the ground? What is their objective?"

This guy was being labeled by the coalition as the "ground-forces commander" for the Iraqi Army in Fallujah, but it was all a sham. He didn't know shit. He was the ground-forces commander by virtue of the fact that he was the highest-ranking Iraqi officer in Fallujah, but he wasn't commanding troops, nor was he leading them in battle. He didn't know what was going on, which Iraqi units were fighting, what their roles would be, nothing! He learned about the operation as I learned about it, from the U.S. Marine colonel.

Abdul Qader had no tactical or strategic input into the operation whatsoever. He was, in essence, a spectator, somebody sent to Fallujah to put an Iraqi face on things there. As the battle waged he was not managing the war. He was not controlling Iraqi forces, their maneuvers, their actions. He wasn't even in communications with Iraqi units. He didn't even have a weapon, but he and his aides did bring some nice blankets and pillows with them for their sleepover.

Fallujah's battle was being controlled and executed by a U.S. Marine Corps three-star general and his battle staff. The U.S. military was again stretching the truth. The coalition was trying to lead the media and the public to believe that the Iraqis had key roles in Fallujah, but most who fought or served there told me the Iraqis had a very minor role and were not involved with planning. I would have preferred Abdul Qader be identified as an Iraqi military spokesman so he could respond to questions that were uniquely Iraqi in nature, but to label him as a commander during the ground offensive was a very long stretch.

Publicly, the mission was given an Iraqi name, al-Fajr, or New Dawn, despite only a small Iraqi military presence of about twenty-five hundred Iraqi soldiers, compared to twelve thousand coalition personnel. It kept its U.S. code name, and to those coalition troops who were there it was known as Operation Phantom Fury. It was the U.S. military's bloodiest battle during its time in Iraq.

Iraqi soldiers who participated in the battle, I'd later learn, were predominantly devoted to clean up missions after the coalition had done the bulk of the heavy fighting. The Iraqis mostly were used to sweep up the town after U.S. forces had cleared it, which was still dangerous, but nowhere near as dangerous as the initial assault, U.S. soldiers told me. There was one Iraqi battalion that was part of the main assault along with its advisers. There were Iraqi units that operated independently, maneuvering into the city and providing security at checkpoints. The Thirty-Sixth Commandos did take the city's hospital on their own, U.S. officials contend. Some Iraqi forces ran into resistance and some died, but that was an infinitesimal amount (most reports say about six Iraqis were killed compared to more than fifty

U.S. soldiers killed during the first ten days of fighting). Overall, the Iraqis were performing as well as could be expected, and to ensure they grew confident and did not fail operationally they were given sectors in the city that were not high risk. They were organized and equipped and operating at a level the Iraqi military had never before seen. I don't want to take away the importance of this operation from an Iraqi perspective. This operation was a huge shot of confidence for Iraq's forces, and they performed admirably, but what was being presented by the coalition simply was not true.

I spent a good part of my day collecting facts from the battlefield and confirming them with the operations colonel who was briefing Abdul Qader. I wrote some talking points and short remarks for the general's press conference. We had decided to have a press briefing at the operations center, and Abdul Qader would offer some remarks but take no questions. That had been my recommendation to Abdul Qader, which luckily had been supported by the Iraqi government. I wanted Abdul Qader to speak to the press and brief them about what was happening, but I didn't want him answering questions yet. Many Western reporters were asking about Iraqi desertion rates, which was overshadowing the fact that many Iraqis had shown up for a fight. The Iraqis were doing well on their operations, and I wanted their success stories flowing into the press for a day or so before being tinged with data about Iraqi desertions, which, from what I knew, were minimal.

I wrote a very brief statement that spoke to the more than three hundred thousand Iraqis who had fled Fallujah. I wanted them to know that the battle wasn't against them, but rather against those who had set roots into their communities without their consent. I wanted Abdul Qader to ensure he spoke to the families of the fallen, offering condolences in his remarks up front, a standard military communications protocol. I wanted him to calm the worries of Fallujans by addressing the fact that vital services would be reestablished once they returned to their city.

The general talked to a small group of press and did well the night before the battle started. He didn't take questions, and everything had gone as I had hoped. He got some key messages out, and he was humble and, more important, grateful for his troops. I even managed to get him to mention the fallen forty-nine briefly. The quiet counsel I had provided was working well, and I even managed to get his hair under control, which Petraeus had warned me about.

On the second day of the battle Lessel sent information forward to the Marine PAOs at Camp Fallujah, stating that he wanted a full press conference, complete with a question-and-answer period. Things were about to change. He also wanted plenty of Western press there. I didn't get it. He wouldn't assert himself like this in Baghdad and encourage the Iraqis to talk to media, but now he was excited about having Abdul Qader talk and he wanted Western press to interview him. What the hell had changed in a month? Why did he want to put the general in the media's crosshairs? Days earlier he was telling me to relax and give the Iraqis time to get their public affairs in order, and he allowed the cancellation of the joint Iraqi Ministries of Defense and Interior press conferences by the Iraqis. Weeks earlier he was telling me to wait on al-Shaalan's media plan. Where was all this poorly timed urgency coming from? The American media would rip Abdul Qader apart. I thought his prolonged exposure to the media might show his lack of knowledge on the operation, and it would damage his credibility.

Abdul Qader could effectively reach out to a small group of Arab press, but we had to keep the press briefing intimate and manageable since he had limited knowledge of the operation. We could get information out to the Arab press and show that the Iraqi military was involved in the operation, but if we opened it up to Western press they would start asking too many questions and expose that he was nothing more than a talking head and not a true commander. I did not want to lie, but I didn't think it was a good idea to show him for what he really was, a spectator. If I could pass him along as a spokesperson, I would. Hell, we had several of those in Baghdad, and they weren't in charge of anything other than just offering up overly massaged talking points. We could certainly offer up an Iraqi to do the same.

To add to the problem there would be a live satellite feed from Fallujah to the States. I made some calls back to Baghdad and told Petraeus what was unfolding. I tried to stop the press conference, but it was already locked and we would move forward with it. I would have to work quickly with Abdul Qader and spend the next few hours preparing him for the American media. I stayed hopeful until I saw a fellow Army Reserve officer I knew from Baghdad arrive at the operations center.

The U.S. Army Reserve lieutenant colonel arrived in Fallujah on our second day, lugging his belongings in plastic grocery shopping bags. I met him in Baghdad weeks earlier before he surfaced at Camp Fallujah. He was an older officer who looked like an Iraqi military officer. He was a really nice guy, funny, and he told me some hilarious stories about his animal practice back in the States. He was a veterinarian.

This guy was assigned by Lessel to be a special adviser for senior leaders at the Iraqi Ministry of Defense. He was an Iraqi who had fled his native country decades earlier and moved to the United States, where he was raised and educated and where he established his veterinary practice and later joined the Army Reserve. When Saddam was ousted by the coalition, much to his credit this man felt compelled to serve in his former nation and returned to the Army Reserve ranks and picked up where he had left off, as a veterinarian.

Prior to his deployment to Fallujah I had sat in meetings with him alongside of Radhi, who spoke exceptional and articulate English. Radhi would cringe as the guy translated for Iraqi officials, and he would often interject and correct him as he was stumbling his way through a translation.

"No, that is not what was said," Radhi would say disgustedly, as the Army Reservist tried to interpret from Arabic to English. Or he would question the officer's choice of Arabic words as he translated from English to Arabic. "That is not what the American said, Colonel," Radhi would angrily say. "You're changing the meaning of his words completely," and then Radhi would jump in and finish the translation.

"Steve, who is this man?" Radhi asked me at one point. "He is horrible. He doesn't speak proper Arabic."

It made no sense to install anyone as a special adviser at the Ministry of Defense, considering we already had Radhi in place. Radhi could best offer us cultural advice as it pertained to public affairs. Any Iraqi in the ministry could do the job better because they were Iraqis and because they had been a part of the culture in previous years and not connected to it merely by genes.

When I saw the veterinarian in Fallujah I knew things would derail, and I wondered if Lessel or the lieutenant colonel had already bent Abdul Qader's ear with his advice. That afternoon before the press conference I handed Abdul Qader some talking points and said, "Here are some remarks for you, sir. These are remarks I've heard you say in other conversations since our arrival, so I took the liberty of writing them down, organizing them for you, in the event you'd like to use them."

I recommended we sit down and do a question-and-answer prep session so he could get his brain thinking how he would answer questions. Abdul Qader didn't look at the talking points I had placed in front of him and then slowly raised his eyes to me as I sat across from him.

"Thank you," Abdul Qader told me, as the veterinarian sat next to him and translated my remarks. Abdul Qader didn't even look at the list, and he slid it over to the vet. He would not look at them and told the veterinarian to tell me that he did not require preparation.

"Sir, I am simply offering you sound bites, based on professional experience, on points I think the media will want covered in your speeches. That is my job. It is my role with our command and the reason General Petraeus sent me here," I replied.

"I know what to do, and say," Abdul Qader replied.

Then the animal doctor jumped in. "He's good, Steve. He knows what to do. He doesn't need all this," he said. "He's a general! This guy fought in tanks!" he exclaimed, and he repeated the comment to Abdul Qader, who nodded in agreement and refused to look at me.

I pushed back a little and asked that Abdul Qader at least look at my materials for that night's press briefing. Abdul Qader pushed them back at me across the table and said, "No, thank you."

I thought to myself, you are a stupid, fucking, wiry-haired son of a goat.

I lobbied the vet and got the remarks in front of the general's eyes, and they made some changes to the document, but Abdul Qader was still refusing to prepare for the media's questions. I had intentionally kept the bombast out of the statement, but the vet and the general felt it was important to inflate the language. They gave it some "Iraqi flavor," as the vet put it, and they planned to use some of the statement as opening remarks.

I didn't want to push my luck, but I explained one last time that talking points were a common practice for military generals; they were merely facts from the operation that I had bulleted for him to use and that they shouldn't be emotional and include flowery language. The coalition PAOs were planning a question-and-answer period with the press, so question-and-answer drills should be conducted. It would prepare Abdul Qader to effectively answer questions at briefings. It would prevent stumbling and cue responses already learned. Abdul Qader had tuned me out. The vet insisted the general was ready.

That night as the final details were falling into place, I watched everything come together. I had been in Fallujah a few days, and we had some good smaller-scale success so far with the press. I had been unable to get an Arab news crew into the city with Abdul Qader, but my press releases with some quotes I attributed to him, coupled with some limited press engagement, were getting information out of the battlefield. I was the only Defense Department reporter feeding news back to the Pentagon almost immediately as it happened. Radhi at the Ministry of Defense was under the radar, feeding information to select Arab media, and Jared and the U.S. Navy journalist were working hard to get news out back at Phoenix Base through military channels. Things were going smoothly, and Radhi said the Iraqi media coverage so far painted Iraqi forces in a good light.

An hour or so before the press briefing, there was a small commotion that entered the press conference area. It was Lessel. He brought along reporters on his excursion to Fallujah. He came in shaking hands and smiling like a rock star. The veterinarian rushed over to see him, and they smiled, joked, and smacked each other on the back. I sat in the back of the room, far away from it all.

Lessel made his way around the room and eventually walked back toward me. As the noise in the room increased, I entered a type of fog. I was so tired and zoned out that I missed this, because as Lessel walked away one of the Marines standing nearby was smiling at me.

"Sir, I can't believe you just did that!"

"What?" I asked him.

"He was trying to shake your hand, and you just stared at him," he said. "You left him hanging."

I don't remember any of it, but as the Marine continued to talk I could feel the fog envelop me again as I watched Lessel's gaggle make its way around the center. People walked up to me and talked, but I could not hear them.

That evening Abdul Qader stepped into the press conference as I suspected, unprepared, and he stumbled his way through most of his remarks. Much of it was inaudible. The first question was an operational question directed at Abdul Qader, and the Army Reserve veterinarian struggled to translate it, only to be followed by Abdul Qader, who stammered to piece together a response. The Marine Corps general jumped into the fray and fielded the question. In fact, he took most of the questions.

The Army Reserve veterinarian stood in front of the cameras and microphones alongside Abdul Qader and tried to understand the questions posed by Arab reporters. He appeared uneasy and unsure as he searched for the words to use. Several times a man from Allawi's office stepped in and answered questions as the vet searched for words. More than a few times the man interjected for Abdul Qader, providing needed clarity in the translation.

I had planned for Abdul Qader to humbly compliment his forces and inform the Arab press in a modest fashion about what his forces were doing in Fallujah. I wanted him to talk to all Iraqis, but specifically to Fallujans, but now he was standing in front of a larger press pool of mostly Western press, with a live feed back to the Pentagon press pool that was also asking questions, stumbling to find answers to questions on a topic he knew little about. The Iraqis looked like chumps. With my plan we didn't need an interpreter, and Abdul Qader could have directly briefed the Arab media, given his statement, and walked away. Now we needed to lean on an interpreter who wasn't performing that well. What's worse, the interpreter was wearing his U.S. Army uniform—so much for the Iraqi face.

After the briefing the vet came over, and Lessel patted his back and firmly and happily shook his hand. Lessel told him that he was proud of the work he had done in Fallujah thus far in preparing Abdul Qader. At that moment I decided it was time to head home.

Fallujah was an interesting side trip on a journey of communications failure in Iraq. The coalition thrust an Iraqi into the limelight but overshadowed him by changing the informational dynamics of an Iraqi officer interacting with his nation's press corps. Ironically, while the coalition pushed to put an Iraqi face on Fallujah, they should have worked harder to put an Iraqi face on its military. Most of the Iraqi soldiers I spoke to in Fallujah didn't know who the hell Abdul Qader was, which showed a desperate need for internal communications in the Iraqi Army, something else we had been pushing to accomplish by encouraging the Iraqi military's command information magazine, *Jundi*, which had been shut down by the minister of defense.

The only footage I saw of Iraqi forces in action in Fallujah was a poorly shot video of Iraqi Special Forces raising an Iraqi flag at the Fallujah hospital in a staged scene reminiscent of the Marines on Iwo Jima. Coalition PAOs showed it at the press conference, and one of the media guys who had come with Lessel said aloud, "Wow, that's cheesy." It was embarrassing.

The Iraqi military would continue to be faceless and lack a voice. While we had waited months for a chance to get an Iraqi face out there, somehow that opportunity eluded us again. I spent four days in Fallujah, and it was just another side trip to disappointment. As soon as I could, I packed my ruck and got out.

I caught a ride on a helicopter filled with people from my command who had flown down to tour Fallujah. I was tired and simply wanted to go home. I sat down, closed my eyes, and strapped myself in. I could feel the emotion overtaking me, and I surrendered to it completely because I knew in a couple of days, I would be home in the arms of my wife. Across from me war tourists from my command talked excitedly about what they had seen in the city. They were staff guys rotating in and out of the battle to ensure everyone on their team got a battlefield trinket and the chance to say they had been to Fallujah. In the distance barely audible over the whupping sound of the rotator blades, the artillery started to beat its deadly rhythm. I felt myself being lifted off the ground, and after a few minutes of some aggressive flying I opened my eyes and noticed the aircrew was older than the young-buck flyers who had been ferrying me around Iraq for the past few months. They were well into their late fifties and sixties and had a lot of rank.

We flew out of Fallujah with the same sounds that greeted me when I arrived there. Explosions bellowed in the distance, and smoke plumes rose from the horizon in the city. As we took to the sky our two helicopters flew much tighter than I'd ever flown before; there was a tension, a fury, but maybe it was just me. We were also going much faster and climbing up and over power lines much more aggressively than we had ever done in my months there. As we approached the landing at the Green Zone, these guys made the Black Hawks fall out of the sky and then touched down so softly I couldn't even tell we had landed. They were incredible pilots, and the flight home was the highlight of my diversion to Fallujah.

It turned out all the crew members on this mission from Fallujah on these two Black Hawk helicopters had been pilots, gunners, and crew chiefs on helicopters in Vietnam. They were from different units, but they had banded together and flew some missions in and out of Fallujah that day as a way of celebrating their Vietnam War heritage. I wished PAOs had that type of unity. It was a flight I will never forget, in part due to the great aviators I had the privilege to fly with, but mostly I will remember it because it was the beginning of my journey home, albeit for a few short weeks, a respite from the visionless landscape of Iraq. I was more than happy to get the fuck out of there.

In June 2006, as I read my daily dose of news about Iraq in my home, I read a short article and almost spit my coffee. Iraqi prime minister Nouri al-Maliki had appointed new ministers. I looked carefully at the Associated Press photo. A man with frizzy hair stood next to a podium as he was introduced by al-Maliki. It was Abdul Qader. He had been appointed Iraq's minister of defense, a position he held until 2010. Abdul Qader was later prohibited from running for office because Iraqis alleged he still has ties to Iraq's Ba'ath Party. He was not reappointed as defense minister.

11

PUBLIC AFFAIRS

503 Americans are killed in the latter part of 2004. It becomes the bloodiest period in Iraq up to that point since the war started in 2003.

—U.S. Defense Department

The U.S. Army lieutenant colonel sat next to me in the computer lab at the Defense Information School at Fort Meade, Maryland, noisily clicking his computer's mouse and releasing audible signs of frustration every three or four seconds.

"Damn it," he said, sighing just loud enough for me to hear him, his fat fingers continuing their poking of the computer keyboard and the mouse. A few seconds lapsed. "Shit," he continued.

After about five minutes of softly spoken profanity and a repertoire of snorts, grunts, and sniffs, I finally caved in and leaned over to him. "Sir, do you need some help?" I asked him.

"I don't know shit about computers," the middle-aged officer told me. He was a military combat engineer by trade and had seen his share of deployments, but as a field-grade officer the Army never required him to have basic technical skills, and many professionals, including many in the U.S. military in 2000, were starting to realize that computers were not just a passing phase but something that was here to stay.

"Let me take a look, sir," I told him. We had been given a simple exercise by our instructors in the public affairs officers' course. We had to write a press release, but the colonel didn't even know how to open Microsoft Word to begin writing his press release. "Sir, you have to open Word first before you can do this," I told him.

"Yeah, I know. I just appreciate your helping me," he said. I knew he was embarrassed, but I thought to myself that he had no business being a PAO if he didn't know how to use a word-processing program. I recommended he stay later and use the tutorials available in the lab to help him learn more about the program. Later that evening I saw him at a social mixer for students at the all-ranks club.

"Thanks for the help today, Lieutenant," he told me.

"Did you do the tutorials, sir?" I asked him.

"Fuck no," he said. "I hate computers."

Days later he was once again struggling with the computers, only this time we were asked to build a Web page. Despite having step-by-step instructions on how to create, save, and publish the page, he couldn't do it. This time another young officer helped him along, but it was apparent the colonel had no computer skills whatsoever.

A few days later he couldn't figure out how to use the spell-check function in Word, something he desperately needed. He couldn't spell everyday English words and couldn't figure out how to remove the squiggly red line from underneath his poorly spelled words.

After a few weeks at the school he knew how to turn on the computer, but not much else. He graduated from the PAO course, qualifying him as a PAO in the U.S. military. He would later command a public affairs unit that deployed to the Balkans, and he would be given the public affairs equivalent of a battalion command.

Sadly, many U.S. Army PAOs are carbon copies of this officer. The bulk have spent their careers in other fields—flying helicopters, managing supply inventories, working in human resources, or other fields like finance—but a very small minority actually studied communications in college and entered the Army with the intention of serving as military communicators and professionally tracking as a communicator.

The U.S. Navy, Air Force, and Marine Corps all have specially dedicated career fields designated for PAOs. These services seek out officer recruits who have studied or are studying public relations, journalism, or mass communications, and they lure them into the ranks, commission them as officers, and send them to the Defense Information School to become PAOs, where their civilian education is augmented by what is in essence military public relations familiarization training, or a military PR primer.

Throughout their careers some military PAOs are given the opportunity to participate in programs like Training with Industry, where a military officer is allowed to work in a civilian public relations environment or with a media organization, but only a handful get selected to participate in that program. Others are also allowed to pursue graduate degrees, but these are the exceptions, not the rule, and the military's training of PAOs is more geared toward corporate public relations, more marketing oriented, than it is centered on international mass communications, where it should be, to tackle today's ideological and perception wars. Instead, that job is left up to information- and psychological-operations personnel, professions that can lie to publics to change societal conditions. I'm not sure that's a sound practice when we're trying to change conditions for the long haul. We're trying to change a generational thought pattern, not change minds to win some tactical victory. While I think that information-operations personnel certainly add a ton of value to any mission, I think if we are trying to change perceptions, educate, and inform people, that can be done only by meaningful factual engagement of native populaces through local media and civic and religious leaders, and that job needs to fall on PAOs.

All services except for the Army commission young people as PAOs and have made professional-development career paths for them to progress professionally throughout their careers. A person in those services can remain a PAO their entire career and serve as a military communicator at various levels. As they progress in rank, so does their professional responsibility. But there is little opportunity for advanced military communications training for most after they attend their qualifying course unless they pursue an advanced degree on their own, a challenge in a military that keeps its people moving. For most Army PAOs in particular, once these officers receive their basic PAO training at Fort Meade, there is little meaningful educational opportunity in communications for them to explore as they advance in rank. Again, the program is corporate style and marketing centric.

The U.S. Army does not recognize public affairs as a professional field, but sees it only as a functional area. In layman's terms that means that the Army thinks that public affairs is a function and not a specialized career field; in other words, any square peg can be inserted into the round hole. Most PAO billets in the U.S. Army are branch immaterial slots, meaning the Army believes that any Army officer can carry out the function of a PAO so long as they attend a short training course in military public relations. It matters not if you're a logistician, finance officer, or infantryman. Imagine a corporate setting where accountants are managing corporate communications or public relations is being run by computer techs after they receive a short course in public relations. That's what the U.S. Army is doing. I attended the PAO course with Army nurses, pilots, supply guys, personnel officers, infantrymen, and military policemen, just to name a few. The Army didn't have a baseline educational standard. All it required was that someone have an Army officer commission, and usually it required officers to have completed their basic branch-development training, which means most of these folks will enter the field as captains and with a few years of military service under their belts.

Despite the fact that former secretary of defense Rumsfeld and others in the Defense Department have acknowledged the importance of timely and knowledgeable communications, Army public affairs is still not its own professional branch, complete with stringent entry requirements and an educational path that teaches military communicators how to effectively do their jobs as they progress in rank.

I think undergraduate and graduate training in mass communications and public relations is a good foundation for domestic PAOs, but the war in Iraq and the larger global War on Terror changed what the military should require to make officers qualified PAOs. The U.S. military needs PAOs to objectively examine the impact of media in the Middle East and understand the role sociological and cultural dimensions bring to the relationship between news groups and news consumers. The military needs professionals who understand how cultures use mass communications and how they consume news. The services should be looking at people with impeccable professional credentials the caliber of lawyers, doctors, and chaplains. It needs experts in mass communications or international relations, not spokespersons who can regurgitate overly edited statements to the media. PAOs must be gifted researchers and practitioners who understand whom they are trying to reach. They must be students of culture.

The Department of Defense Joint Course in Communications at the University of Oklahoma was a graduate-level program in which PAOs gathered and in cohorts worked on communications issues currently facing the military services. From afar the program sounded impressive, and many of the students I've talked to who have attended the program raved about it. I do not doubt that the school offered a good corporate or domestic public relations program, but, again, that's not what is needed now. A closer look at the joint course reveals that projects were corporate oriented; not one of them involved international mass communications or a study of al-Jazeera or any other terror group's communications programs, despite the fact the military is at war on many fronts and has squared off with this news agency and is combating these groups on the battlefield. No papers, in fact, examine the Arab media. Why isn't the PAO force looking across the ocean and studying foreign media? Mostly, it is because the foreign press is never truly analyzed by PAOs. PAOs are oriented toward peddling the war effort back home. PAOs have always been considered part of the marketing arm of the armed forces, and this has to change.

The United States is at war, but the academic papers written by participants in this program and others mostly dealt with corporate crisis communication instead of dealing with communication in an international conflict. Papers covered racial discrimination lawsuits at Denny's, NASA after shuttle disasters, and Union Carbide's factory explosion. Other papers analyzed the relationship between the media and the military, an overanalyzed, tired topic. An interesting point in this last paper, when journalists were asked what they thought of PAOs, most journalists claimed to be smarter and considered themselves better than most PAOs. A few papers did examine the media's role in war, but overall it was nothing of substance and the research supported the military's age-old argument: the press and the military don't get along. Why does the military continue to beat that dead horse?

To illustrate how desperately the country needs professional international communicators to help it run its strategic communications, I offer this anecdote. Clarke, the Pentagon's former top communicator, admitted in her book that she sought the advice of top corporate leaders to find out how they "sell" their products overseas. That's a problem. We should not be in the business of selling anything, especially war. She then turned her focus on a man outside of the Pentagon to try to get fresh ideas in engaging the Arab world. He explained to her that Arab youth did not believe that their musicians and entertainers were liked in the United States. He recommended (and she liked the idea) of assembling Arab performers to tour the United States and Europe. A filmmaker would accompany them and make a documentary, and this would look favorable in the Arab world and have a positive impact on Arab youth. Clarke wanted to fund this project with Defense Department dollars as a way to reach out to the Arab street. When she couldn't get the funding for it at the Defense Department, she tried the State Department. Luckily for U.S. taxpayers, she was unsuccessful there too. Where did she get this idea? She got her communications advice from the former manager of the rock group the Police.

How did she think this would help the U.S. military in the long run? I don't see the connection, but is it clear now why we have lost the communications war? PAOs have to stop thinking like cheap marketers and salesmen. As for the band idea, I've still not figured out that one, but that was the ranking military PAO's solution to reach out and talk to the Arab media, sponsoring an Arab band's tour. We just dropped a five-hundred-pound bomb on your neighborhood, but please note that we're sponsoring a tour of an Arab band, so please excuse our dust. What the hell? For the record, let me state that I know plenty of Iraqis with teenage kids, and guess who they are listening to: American hip-hop artists.

Many PAOs argue that my concepts are simply "not what we do!" They say that information operations officers are responsible for the more strategic objectives. That way of thinking needs to change, and PAOs should petition to reengineer their career fields. Information operations officers are allowed to misinform in the execution of their duties in order to mislead the enemy. On the battlefield this serves a valuable purpose, but they are also tasked with disseminating information through those same channels. Although they often do so with little detection back to the source, it still presents a problem of having a government entity lying to an audience and then giving them information they are expected to receive as factual. It's a contradiction that can be avoided if PAOs are allowed to control the factual strategic communications objectives. That responsibility has to be given to professional communicators, and a professional communicator is not made by the Defense Information School or by any other U.S. military public affairs training course. Communicators and students of mass communications are built in academic institutions around the globe just as doctors, lawyers, and other professionals are made.

Information operators use information to gain information superiority in support of military operations. Information operations links operational security, psychological operations, deception, electronic warfare, and physical destruction with civil and public affairs capabilities. And that's my point: officers who are allowed to deceive to make operational gains should not be in control of working with public opinion. Publicly, the masses will question the credibility of the communications source if the deception is detected, and then all credibility suffers. There is too much at risk. PAOs must deal in fact, not fiction, and PAOs must be transparent purveyors of truth and fact.

But while all the military branches, including the Department of Homeland Security's U.S. Coast Guard, attend training at the Defense Information School, the differences between Army PAOs with their sister services' counterparts are glaring. Most PAOs in other branches outside the Army have four years of communications academic training and internships under their belts by the time they arrive at Fort Meade as commissioned officers, and some might have graduate degrees. They are proficient in the use of language and have likely already worked or interned at public relations firms, newspapers, or news stations. They know how to write news copy, understand the news industry, and have a good grasp of communications, and they are keenly aware of technological trends that impact the industry. Because they are recent graduates, they are atop the latest developments in the field and understand the emerging issues and practices of the profession.

Naturally, many of these recent grads are well versed in communications theory, and some understand the complex social dynamics of mass communications. Because the bulk are young, they have frightening skills with emerging technologies and social media, as well as fresh approaches to things. But aside from knowledge, these young men and women should be valued because their professors have likely performed case studies and conducted comparative analysis on theories of mass communications and passed that information on to them, and much of that research is valuable when applied to missions like the war in Iraq. Some of it, in fact, is directly related to the war in Iraq, but the training fundamentals these students receive as undergraduates is still very marketing oriented, and few have studied American mass media and its role in U.S. wars, and fewer understand the role of the press during armed conflict. Most PAOs are soldiers, airmen, Marines, and sailors first, meaning their allegiance is to promoting goodwill toward their services. They are not specialists in using information with foreign and domestic media to support military operations, and that is an abysmal shortcoming. They do not know how to use information to gain and hold territory.

Many Army PAOs entering the public affairs field when I was still a PAO lacked the undergraduate preparation in communications. That's not to say that all Army PAOs lacked a communications or public relations background, but overwhelmingly most did not have it. For many in the Army, the training they receive at the Defense Information School is the only public affairs training they will receive in their entire careers. The Army trusts its communication programs with personnel who have either attended the two-week reserve-component PAO course or the two-month PAO course. That may have once been considered adequate training for a mission that is marketing oriented, but now that the U.S. Army and the Defense Department are engulfed in a global war on terror, the training and preparation of U.S. military public affairs forces are grossly substandard, lack originality and strategic vision, and teach defensive and reactionary tactics.

The core problem with the public affairs field in the U.S. Army is that it fails to nurture career professional communicators who can operate internationally and communicate with a global audience. An Army officer assigned to be a PAO can still excel in his career field as long as he fulfills the requirements. For example, an infantry officer turned PAO can still be promoted even though he's not serving in the infantry, as long as he fulfills the requirements for promotion within his career field. He has no promotion prerequisites as a PAO to fulfill in order to get promoted. In other words, he does not need to earn a master's degree in communications or public relations. He is also not required to return to the Defense Information School for further training. Hell, when I was in the Army Reserve I knew a command sergeant major who held the top enlisted leadership position in a public affairs battalion, meaning he was the leader of all military journalists and broadcasters in the unit, including several units that fell under his unit's command and control, and he never attended any type of public affairs training. What would happen if he was mobilized and sent downrange to work with media?

Still, training in its current form is not the answer. Military public affairs training provides its officers with opportunities to socialize and share war stories, but it does not encourage serious intellectual thinking, critical analysis, or original research. Public affairs in the U.S. military is an administrative function more than a strategic element, and no matter what senior leaders might be preaching publicly, it is bullshit. Public affairs is an afterthought behind most closed doors, and most commanders associate PAOs with publicity. And that is flawed and antiquated thinking.

PAOs sit on a commanding general's special staff. They are part of a group of officers who provide counsel to generals, as do staff professionals for law and medicine. The advice is, of course, delivered by terminally trained officers who are doctors and lawyers, but PAOs are the only staffers on a general's staff with little, if any, rigorous professional training in their field. Even the chaplains require goddamn theological training.

The U.S. Army's public affairs mission is a domestically oriented undertaking with obsolete plans and objectives. Similarly, the Defense Department public affairs community suffers from the same strain of ineffectiveness. Much like the U.S. military's counterinsurgency manual that in 2006 received an overdue facelift from my old boss Petraeus, who coauthored the new manual, the public affairs doctrine for the U.S. armed forces also needs a revamp. The U.S. Army needs a fundamental overhaul in its approach to training and developing a viable PAO corps that will be able to perform the missions of a modern army in the information age.

For starters at Fort Meade there needs to be a faculty shakeup. The military relies too much on instructors with field experience, and while that has its benefits, it has hurt the services in the communications field. Ideas outside the institution are rarely entertained, and the doctrine is considered a perfect jewel that nobody wants to tamper with and everyone protects. Emerging trends like social media have been embraced, but at its core the Defense Information School is still preparing corporate-style communicators. I've always felt that the school would be better served if it hired civilian professors from academe to teach courses in current international mass communication instead of trying to teach a career officer how to use a publishing software program. And what I mean is hiring people with legitimate academic credentials, doctorates who are experts in international mass communications or international relations and not contractors who once attended DINFOS and were PAOs themselves.

Considering the position U.S. forces are now in with the War on Terror, wouldn't it have been better to teach U.S. PAOs how to communicate globally using current technologies and foreign media than how to write a press release or create a Web page? The absence of communications theory and philosophy in military public affairs training is grossly evident as we slog along years into the War on Terror, a war on ideologies and perceptions. We are hated now more than ever, it seems. PAOs have never received preparation on the use of factual information through tactical and strategic mediums to achieve objectives in a global forum. However, they are trained how to avoid questions, control information, and inject talking points, and they assume a defensive posture the minute they walk out the doors of the Defense Information School and begin their careers in public information. They spend their careers repelling media and public queries rather than launching aggressive information campaigns (using good and bad information) that keep a global audience informed. PAOs thrive on controlling information and situations, and when they are at war they are given a lot of license to withhold information and restrict media in the name of operational security.

In January 2005 at Taji Military Training Base, I shuttled about fifty reporters to the base, along with Allawi's PAO Al. There would be a massive pass and review of Iraqi military hardware and army personnel as Iraq celebrated Iraqi Army Day with a parade and a ceremony. The review stand would be filled with Iraqi dignitaries and coalition VIPs. The event had been bumped back about an hour at the last minute, I suspect to throw off insurgent attacks since the prime minister, commanding general of coalition forces, the U.S. ambassador, and others were attending. Just as we arrived on the parade field and began to tell the press where to set up, we came under rocket and mortar-round fire. Interestingly, the rounds hit directly on our position. Hundreds of people scrambled for cover in buildings as windows shattered and debris flew. We scurried the press into a building, and during the chaos I turned around when I reached the relative safety of the building with all of the reporters and saw Radhi out in the open, slowly walking with his crutch as fast as he could toward us. The rounds and rockets rained down. In a second we made eye contact, and he looked directly at me and I started running toward him.

"Steve, help me!" he yelled.

I ran to Radhi, picked him up over my shoulder, and ran with him off the parade grounds as more rounds came in around us. It seemed as if I was running a hundred yards with him, but in fact it was only a few meters. Once we reached a building I set him down with the help of some Marines.

"I'm sorry I left you, man," I told Radhi. "I forgot."

In an instinctual reaction I had run for cover along with everyone else, and I had forgotten Radhi couldn't run on his own. I didn't know how to finish the sentence. Radhi simply embraced me tightly and repeated, "Thank you, brother, thank you," and we held onto each other for a few seconds as glass continued to shatter and the concussions from the rounds reverberated against our souls. As the shelling slowed I went back across the parade field with an Iraqi named Mustafa, from the Ministry of Defense. We helped evacuate some wounded Iraqis, and then I went back to the press pool, which was back at the building with Radhi.

Immediately, everyone suspected someone from the Iraqi military had become a turncoat and given the grid coordinates for the attack. The media began to record the chaotic aftermath as people ran around and tended to the injured, smoke and dust in the air, and fresh smoking craters in the ground. Once I knew the press and my team were uninjured, I was stopped by Ben Gilbert from National Public Radio (NPR). We had developed an odd relationship: every time we worked together, something bad happened. Months earlier Ben was with me when the Green Zone Café and the Haji Mart, popular American hot spots inside the Green Zone, were attacked by suicide bombers, just blocks from our compound. The media wanted to access the sites but weren't allowed by the coalition. Luckily, before I knew of the restrictions, I drove Ben by there, and he had a firsthand look at the carnage that killed several people. He was the first reporter to see the attacks firsthand just minutes after they happened. I felt it was important for him to see the challenges we faced, even inside the Green Zone. Others would tell me that it showed Ben that the coalition was weak. I simply felt it showed him the truth. As we drove away from the Green Zone bombings, coalition PAOs from the press center arrived on scene, and we both got a chuckle as we drove right past them.

After the attacks at Taji Ben grabbed his recorder and microphone and said he wanted to talk about the attack. Before he turned it on I explained to him that if he broadcast an interview about the attack, the insurgents would know they had been successful in hitting us and would be able to again: set up their weapons exactly as they had that morning and fire at Taji again. He understood and felt it was important to tell the story of what happened that morning. Winded from running around during the attack and from lugging Radhi across the parade field, I did an interview with Ben about one minute after we evacuated the wounded, puffing on a cigarette Ben had given me as I paused to listen to his questions. It was my job, and there was no reason to prevent Ben from telling the story. Several yards from me Al, the PAO from Prime Minister Allawi's office, was yelling at reporters. He and his assistant were pulling videotapes out of video cameras and pulling memory cards out of digital cameras. As soon as I finished the interview with Ben, I approached Al.

"Al, what are you doing?" I asked him.

"I told them not to videotape the attack, and they did," he replied.

"I know you'd prefer not to have this out, but they have a right to do this," I said as I lured him away from the reporters, who were agitated and yelling at him.

"They'll do what they're told, or we won't work with them, Steve!" he said sternly, and he returned to the angry mob, which was now sequestered underneath a gazebo.

Other Arab journalists protested Al's actions to me and pleaded with me to convince him to change his mind. I explained I had already talked to him, and while I didn't agree with his actions, Iraq was a sovereign nation and could do what it wanted. I couldn't control Al. Many of the reporters grew angrier at me, and some even said that the Americans controlled the Iraqis when it was convenient for them.

Seconds later, once the tapes were rounded up, Al began to rip cell phones out of the hands of reporters trying to file stories with their bureaus telephonically. There was no way the story would get out. Allawi's office was determined to suppress it. While the Americans told the world they were bringing democracy to Iraq, it was plainly obvious that they had not taught Iraqis the importance of a free press; then again, the Americans hadn't set a great example for the Iraqis. Americans had tried to control al-Jazeera and were instrumental in kicking them out of the country, and they had shut down al-Arabiya too. They also tried to change the tone of Iraqi news coverage by bribing Iraqi reporters to write more positive stories. No surprise the Iraqi government PAOs followed the example they were given, but it wasn't a stretch from the way they ordinarily operate. Arabs weren't known for having independent media organizations; that phenomenon had started only within the past decade with al-Jazeera.

The media had a right to report the story, and we had a responsibility as government officials to answer their questions and help them get the story out, but rather than embracing openness the Iraqis censored the press, which is something the U.S. military often does. While in Iraq there were numerous reporters who told me their cameras had been taken away or they had been detained by U.S. troops. Nearly all of the reporters who got their gear confiscated were Arabs, but some were from the West. Most were never offered good reasons for why they were censored.

Collectively, the services need to be more open, more frank, and proactive. Information—bad, good, indifferent—must go out at lightning speed. The military owes that to the public it works for, and it owes it to the press who watches what the government does for the people. Concepts like this are hard to grasp by most public affairs types, who find themselves striving for the approval of their commanding generals and political appointees. They claim they are loyal to their leaders, but PAOs get so caught up in being "team players" that they forget they work for a grander team, the American people. Their officer commissions are granted by the people, not their bosses, but few remember this, and most operate as if they are in some type of mafia, loyal only to the military and not the American people they are sworn to defend.

Most of the Army PAOs I ran into in Iraq were one-dimensional thinkers. They had the typical with-us-or-against-us mentality often found in military ranks, and most couldn't conceptualize communication strategies that called for even the slightest bit of ingenuity. They were Cold War relics, and they had infected their junior officers with the same tired strategies and vision of the pre–information age days. Unfortunately, while universities created some immensely bright communicators and they joined the ranks of the Air Force, Navy, Marine Corps, and Coast Guard, many young, bright officers were disillusioned when they discovered the reality that awaited them in the ranks.

The public affairs community is about whom you know, not what you know. Officers are too focused on doing what is right for their careers, not what is right for the mission. They build their networks, not their knowledge base. In Iraq there was no shortage of public affairs people getting their tickets punched and planning their follow-on assignments by playing their cards right. The public affairs community needed officers with courage to stand up and redirect war managers and explain that the communications piece of the operation was broken and that strategies weren't sound. But that didn't happen and wouldn't happen, because some didn't know what the hell they were doing and those who knew did not have the balls to say anything, or if they said anything were silenced.

Many PAOs do as they're told by clueless commanders who don't emphasize communications because they don't understand the value of communications in military operations. I have been pretty fortunate to have had several receptive bosses who let me run my teams and operations as I saw fit and stayed out of the way. But if the PAO does not know the mission inside and out, and does not earn the trust and respect of the commander he serves by displaying a knack for strategic or tactical communications execution, then he will be run over in war. Battlefield commanders have millions of things to worry about, and the last thing they need to deal with is an uninformed, insecure, and indecisive officer who doesn't inspire and demand confidence.

It is inconceivable that nobody from the public affairs community at the highest levels was not examining, studying, and planning a communications contingency plan for implementation in the Middle East beyond assembling an Arab band to tour the United States. The minute the USS Cole was bombed, someone at the Pentagon public affairs shop should have formed a team and launched the planning of a multiprong approach that would be implemented, depending on scenarios. This way, as war plans are drawn up, the communication plans are inserted into the battle plan and snapped on. PAOs have plenty of open-source information resources they can use. The Arab media's products were available for examination, but nobody took a look at them to devise a plan on how to carefully proceed. Nobody examined the Arab media culture before the U.S. military stepped into Iraq. If they did, they never told us, because we all rolled into Iraq making stuff up as we went along. It was fucking pathetic.

To fight today's wars requires PAOs to be strategic visionaries who understand global cultures and mass communications. They need to be well versed in U.S. foreign affairs and more broadly in international relations. They must understand their audiences and their environments. The most successful soldiers on the battlefield historically have always been the ones who understand their enemies and the nations where they wage war.

In November 2001, as U.S. troops deployed to Afghanistan, they were unleashed to do what they had been practicing to do for hundreds of years; kill the enemy. PAOs were also unleashed to do what they had previously trained to do. They tightly controlled the media as the operation was launched. PAOs soon discovered that al-Jazeera, running freely around the battlefield, broadcasting images that countered U.S. claims of a problem-free invasion and showed unhappy Afghanis and collateral damage, was a problem they had not prepared for. The public affairs plan should have incorporated civil affairs personnel who could immediately respond to areas of unrest, with an embedded news crew, to try to offer support, whether financial or emotional or both, that the United States didn't intentionally try to kill innocent people. Public affairs officers should be redesignated and made a part of the civil affairs field or vice versa because they should be working with local and national publics on the battlefield. In the future their professional role should involve more foreign public interaction. Instead of being proactive, the United States wrote off the Afghani deaths and enflamed anti-American views. Apologies for the deaths were uttered to reporters in the Pentagon press pool, not to Afghanis on the ground.

Imagine an innocent Afghani on the ground who maybe doesn't like the Taliban, but the Taliban never physically harmed his family. Suddenly, a bomb is dropped by a U.S. warplane that kills his family and destroys his home, and the Afghani knows it is a U.S. plane. The Afghani will of course be distraught, but as days and months pass, nobody from the U.S. military approaches him to apologize for the damage and the deaths or to offer reparations. He becomes angry, and he spreads word of his misfortune to others. The Taliban fans embers of anger by helping him, while pointing out the Americans have done nothing for him other than kill his family and destroy his home. With nothing left to live for, or lose, the guy becomes an insurgent. The people Americans tried to liberate and help become their sworn enemy. Sounds pretty basic, but this stuff happens, and this is how our enemy grows.

What I'm recommending isn't implausible. War is a messy business and shit happens. Bombs are errantly dropped, overstressed soldiers mistakenly engage noncombatants, mistakes are made, but what the U.S. military does in response to the messes it creates is important. The regret for the bombing is communicated to the wrong audience, not the man who is the victim. The victims on the ground need to be told there will be help with burial of their loved ones or reconstruction of their homes and compensation for their losses. There needs to be sustained interpersonal communication between the U.S. military and the victim. Some guy at the Pentagon should not express sadness to a room filled with Pentagon press people who don't give a crap that Ahmed's family is dead. If this seems labor intensive, it is, and I guarantee that we would be more careful if we were practicing accountability. The U.S. military can't fight this battle any other way than by winning the information war one person at a time. This is combat community relations and outreach, and PAOs and, more important, their commanders must embrace that this new way of doing business must happen soon. PAOs must show goodwill and represent the military on the ground and not from a press center, in a press release, or from a podium. PAOs must get out into the battlefield in America's wars and handle a crisis on the ground, as they do domestically, and interact with the global populace, wherever that may be, and ensure that the proper image and message of the U.S. military are shown and expressed. They must earn their title, public affairs officers, and that can't be done when fat asses are sitting behind a desk safely behind high blast walls in an overly protected place like the Green Zone. The U.S. government can either invest in this preventative type of operational mission, or it will pay as it is now doing with the lives of its service personnel or through the prolonged fiscal support of veterans who are wounded in combat.

PAOs have never been part of the mechanism to win wars, and that thinking also needs to change. Maneuver forces and their support branches all contribute to an effort, but PAOs have never been a part of that effort overseas. Their sole role is keeping the public's interest in the war, and their success is gauged upon their reactions to scenarios created by maneuver forces. If done correctly, I am saying, PAOs can create scenarios that help maneuver elements. For example, as I've mentioned a lot, what would have been the outcome of a sustained media engagement by the Iraqi government that showcased their security forces' development? Had the Iraqis successfully communicated with their people and let them know forces were securing the streets, backed by U.S. forces, and that there were resources being deployed to keep order, Iraq would have been much different after 2003, but communicated information is a lie if it is not backed up by action. Action makes it fact. PAOs can't say something is happening if it is not. I once read the words of a PAO in a newspaper that said that U.S. military forces had broken the cycle of violence in Iraq. Yet every day for more than ten years I have read the stories of insurgent bombings where hundreds of Iraqis have been killed.

Imagine if information was used in such a way that a populace rejects an insurgent presence and helps the coalition. Instead of a coalition patrol coming into a sector and getting attacked, it is able to use actionable intelligence and capture or kill the insurgent threat, thanks to information that was put out by PAOs that caused information to flow back to the maneuver elements.

In Iraq public affairs was disjointed, at best, and varied depending on the region, but while tactical considerations should be taken into account, the overall strategic communications goal must be kept in everyone's sights. Tactical operations should not only fulfill unit goals, but also fulfill strategic visions of offices like STRATCOM. PAOs in Iraq were loosely tied together by documents know as PAGs, or public affairs guidance, that would advise PAOs what the folks at STRATCOM or the Pentagon were thinking. The documents focused too much on generalities and of course offered talking points and messages. It was no wonder reporters were frustrated because PAOs on different ends of a map would say the same thing to very different events. In response to a press query about civilian deaths at the hands of U.S. soldiers, a PAO might say, "It's unfortunate and we regret the loss of life, but the path to democracy isn't an easy one." Hundreds of miles away another reporter might be interviewing a general who is commenting on Iraqi female police officers being abused by their fellow male officers, and the general might comment, "It's unfortunate that things like that have to happen, but the road to democracy isn't easy." While the messages are successfully inserted into the media and communicated, and they're uniform, the information stops there. It is disposable communication, and readers, listeners, and viewers consume it and discard it. I've never heard intelligent news consumers saying things like "the road to democracy isn't easy" as they talk around the water cooler. It is disposable sincerity and a foolish waste of an opportunity to talk to millions in a meaningful manner.

PAOs operate in a change-the-message world. They reinterpret facts and reconfigure the truth, and that is why so many in the media disrespect PAOs. It is also why there is so much sparring between the government and the media. My job in Iraq wasn't to mask problems. The profession of military public relations must move away from the dirty practices of masking the truth. We are purveyors of truth, and we should not become stewards of flawed policies. My job, I felt, wasn't to garner American public support as our public affairs mission dictated. It was to tell the international audience the story of Iraq's forces (including Americans), using transparency in delivery.

Media manipulation must be dropped as a U.S. military public affairs tactic. The U.S. military must embrace the truth, no matter how ugly, and work not to change facts but to change the conditions that create the fact. Let's not try to counter a flood of reports with media engagement that paints things in a different light. We shouldn't spin it to win it. Had PAOs embraced transparency, maybe the problems the U.S. military faced in Iraq would have been addressed sooner. Maybe we all wouldn't have had to live a lie in Iraq, supporting an administration that was saying everything was fine when it was not. Had PAOs embraced the problems and helped communicate those instead of tales of joy and harmony, maybe the policies would have been changed and the impact would have been better.

The problem with PAOs is that they are a public relations arm in uniform for presidential administrations. Generals are too. They become slaves to secretaries of defense and their services, and they are pressured by the administration to improve the public opinion of the war. They only want to hear good news coming out of Iraq instead of the real news, which can, because of its nature, paint a dismal picture. In order to prevent this type of abuse, the Defense Department should hire a permanent civil servant who does not change with administrations. This office would serve as a protector of the military's ability to speak its mind without executive pressure or influence. It would give unvarnished reports to Congress about operations in places like Iraq and protect PAOs and service members who speak factually about operations on the ground. We need something stronger than the Government Accountability Office or a special investigator. I think it's ironic that Clarke mentions in her book that the facts, no matter how bad, should never be disguised as anything but what they are, yet during my Iraq tour PAOs every day tried to paint the war with a broad brush to try to appease a Pentagon that wouldn't hear the truth, all while they blamed the media for not covering the good we were doing there.

And as an advocate of combat community relations, each PAO must realize that interpersonal connectivity matters. As public relations professionals, we should be actively interacting with our forces, with the local populace, and with reporters. On one of my first of many flights to Taji Military Training Base, I sat next to the open door in a Black Hawk, and as we whisked along at rooftop level I waved at Iraqis as we flew over them. As they heard us approaching they would run out of their homes to look up and wave at us. If we were flying early in the morning, many of them were still asleep atop their homes, as some Iraqis slept on their roofs to stay cool and we startled them as we zoomed past them, but I'd smile and exaggerate my waves to ensure they saw me. They always waved back enthusiastically and happily. I don't know why I did that. I guess it is a habit for me. When

I see low-flying helicopters I always wave and try to get the crew to wave back, so I didn't have some master plan behind the friendly gesture.

A photographer for *Newsweek* watched me do this for the twenty-five-minute flight.

"That's great airborne PR," he said as we finished the flight. He thought it was cool that I spent the entire flight waving at everyone. I hadn't thought about it, but every single person I waved to waved back, and while maybe it was a small thing to do, I think it was better than simply flying over everyone, looking down at them and scaring the shit out of them.

A few months after my "airborne public relations" operation, we released a declassified intelligence report revealing the thoughts of a would-be terrorist. A young Saudi had been captured and interrogated by Iraqi forces. He said he had grown disillusioned as an insurgent because of the lies of the insurgency's leaders. Insurgents had told him that U.S. soldiers intentionally killed Iraqi civilians.

Weeks prior to his arrest, angry and with this fact still in his head, the prisoner said he prepared to attack U.S. soldiers, despite never having seen a U.S. soldier. What he discovered was that some U.S. soldiers were friendly with the populace, and that day they brought toys for Iraqi kids. At one point, prepared to detonate a device against a U.S. patrol, the Saudi said a U.S. soldier smiled and waved at him. He waved back and decided not to engage the Americans. Lesson: little things matter. Somewhere there is one lucky soldier who doesn't realize that waving at an Arab that day made a difference and saved his life, the lives of other soldiers, and the lives of a number of children.

When I've told some of my PAO friends about how we should work with civil affairs and have accountability teams, some of my buddies argue that channels like al-Jazeera would turn an accountability story into something negative. My response to that is that the death of civilians, like other things that happen in war, *is* something negative, and it can't be spun. The sooner it is dealt with, the quicker channels like al-Jazeera can't sensationalize the stories. When U.S. personnel initially deny a problem, it gives the issue a life of its own. It later resurfaces again, only this time another official claims the news group fabricated the story, and later there are additional accusations leveled at the news agency. Before the services realize it, the story has been kept alive for weeks by U.S. officials when it should have been resolved within twenty-four hours. Bad news doesn't get better with time like wine; it spoils like milk.

Reacting to collateral damage immediately also sends a message to the troops that care needs to be taken in executing the mission. When senior officials dismiss collateral deaths without much effort and review, it sends nonverbal messages to field soldiers that killing innocent people can be written off, and it gives derelict soldiers wiggle room to hide behind rules of engagement to vent frustrations or commit crimes. Addressing the deaths immediately would tell all parties involved that it is wrong and will be dealt with and that lies and cover-ups aren't the way the U.S. military does business. Accountability would be a great instrument and compass heading.

One of the big problems I've always had with the military is that there is an assumption made that if a person has rank, they are somehow capable of performing at a given level. Sort of like a doctor: if a person holds a medical degree, there would be an expectation that the doctor could diagnose basic ailments. This wasn't the case when it came to PAOs in Iraq.

There were false assumptions in Iraq. The U.S. military believed that if a person was a lieutenant colonel or a colonel and worked in public affairs, they knew what they were doing. There is an expectation in the military: if a person is senior in rank, they will know what to do. There is credibility in rank. Pretenses like that work in most fields. In aviation most pilots at that rank have often accumulated thousands of hours of flight time. They know their jobs and their aircraft inside and out. Military lawyers too have often had so much military law exposure and training by the time they reach the colonel ranks that they can help draft complex international policies and directives, as many did in Iraq. This isn't the case in public affairs.

My wife has a standing joke. "They Army won't trust a PAO to fly a helicopter. Why would they trust communications to an aviator?"

While a joke, it reflects the reality of the Army. The Army is convinced that it can slide any officer into a PAO billet with minimal training. There was a time when that probably worked for the Army. All they needed to do was train someone to stand in front of a microphone and teach them the formulaic responses so often heard. Anyone can be taught to market or sell something. It's a mentality that has carried public relations in the Army for decades.

The U.S. military, with hundreds of PAOs in Iraq, most with college degrees and many who were senior in rank, lost the information war to an unsophisticated, uneducated, less technically capable enemy with much less money, manpower, and resources. We've spent millions of dollars, yet the enemy achieved success with video cameras and social media. Their success is due to their use of what is already in place. Terrorists utilize the cultural communications infrastructure and do not rely on elements of their own force to sell their messages via the media. That task is accomplished by their marketing of CDs and DVDs. They communicate using Arab media. If PAOs want to win this war, they must master this skill. Otherwise, the U.S. military will continue to lose because the strength of its messages is not being heard or felt in the Arab world. If PAOs are to win the communications war against terrorists, they must become information guerrillas and deploy counterinsurgent communications techniques. If they want to win over a populace, they have to talk to it.

Domestically, there are ample examples of how cultures and societies react when they see a perceived outsider inflict violence on one of their own, like the 1991 Rodney King beating videos and the 1992 riots that followed. The four police officers charged in King's beating were acquitted of charges, which sparked riots in Los Angeles. The video showed King, an African American, on the ground, getting beaten by the police. For African Americans the video made it hard to stomach the lack of punishment and accountability by the judicial system and the Los Angeles Police Department after the trial.

Brian Martin, of Australia's University of Wollongong School of Social Sciences, Media, and Communication, published a paper in *Critical Criminology* that spoke about the King tapes and offered information that could be paralleled to the U.S. military in Iraq. In his paper Martin states that there are five principles that authorities use to inhibit what he calls the "backfire effect," that is, the attack on King by police, which "recoiled adversely on the attackers."[1] The King beating hurt the Los Angeles police in the long run. Similarly, I postulate, collateral damage has hurt the U.S. military significantly in Iraq because PAOs and U.S. military leaders use the same tactics to inhibit the backfire effect. The principles are as follows: cover up the attack, devalue the target, reinterpret the events, give the appearance of justice, and use intimidation and bribery. The U.S. military has done all of these things in Iraq. While I was deployed they did not mention collateral damage unless it was first uncovered by the press or unless it happened in a very public place. If discovered, they offered condolences far removed from the scene in order to devalue the target by not showing death and damage and referring to the event as "collateral damage" and by saying that military personnel engaged the target because they themselves were engaged (like the accidental bombings of wedding parties). They reinterpret the events. When they announced that an investigation showed soldiers used rules of engagement, they showed justice because it illustrated that the military reviewed itself to ensure rules were followed. And last, when they bribed local media to write positive stories about U.S. forces, they committed the final principle to avoid backfire, bribery.

"Challengers can augment the backfire effect by countering these five methods of inhibition, for example exposing the attack," Martin writes.[2] Al-Jazeera did just that by showing the world their news footage. Another important item to note in Martin's paper is his recognition that government organizations control their public destinies. "In the conventional social science view of the news, the 'official dominance model,' officials are the primary definer of events."[3] This is the case with the U.S. military in Iraq in cases of collateral damage, prison abuse, Haditha killings, and other blunders. Al-Jazeera and the Arab press challenge this convention and remove the control from officials. By allowing al-Jazeera to uncover mistakes, the U.S. government loses its informational dominance and is forced to react.

According to Martin, Gene Sharp, a nonviolence researcher, coined the phrase "political jiu-jitsu," a term taken from the sport of jiu-jitsu, where the opponent's strength and force are used against him. Political jiu-jitsu, Martin wrote, is when "violence used against nonviolent opponents generates outrage and rebounds against the aggressor. The attack can lead to great support for the challengers among third parties, among some members of the attacker group, and among what Sharp calls the 'grievance group,' namely those with potential affinity with the target of the attack."[4]

This is Iraq in a nutshell, and the insurgents used informational jiu-jitsu to help their cause. Al-Jazeera's coverage of collateral damage caused outrage in the Pan-Arab world, in Sharp's terms the third party. The grievance group, in this case the Iraqis, naturally felt emotionally and culturally bound to side with their own citizens since the Americans were trying to inhibit the backfire of their attacks. Ultimately, the ones who win the informational struggle are the insurgents, because more Iraqis and Arabs become supportive or tolerant of them as challengers to the attack, despite the fact that the attack wouldn't have occurred had the U.S. forces not been protecting themselves against the insurgents or actively hunting them. The Iraqis then counter that the insurgents wouldn't be there if the U.S. forces weren't there in the first place. The ethnic and cultural ties prevail because the Americans tried to prevent the backfire.

If some African Americans responded with such unrestrained outrage to the King police beatings, wouldn't it be logical to assume that if Arabs, or any other nationality for that matter, saw American military might gone awry, they too would react negatively? The point is that images from King's attacks stirred incredible outrage from Americans. The unchecked violence and lack of accountability caused public rage. An educated person might deduce that military violence, if perceived as misdirected, might have the same fallout overseas. If errors go unexplained, assumptions might be made. But Pentagon PAOs aren't thinking like this because they are marketers, not social scientists. The Defense Department didn't have true communicators in important roles when it went to war. It had people who weren't students of the communications discipline or analytical about their approach to military communications.

At the helm of the Pentagon's communications team was a politico with political communications experience. Naturally, Clarke's policies and plans would satisfy political personnel, but they would be tremendously inadequate to prevent the deaths of U.S. soldiers on the ground, and they would not win hearts and minds in the Arab world, only the hearts and minds of those in her party.

Famed British soldier and Arab expert T. E. Lawrence stated that the importance of the press in the Arab world was almost as important as weapons, and if information was impeded, the insurgents would successfully root themselves in a culture. "The printing press is the greatest weapon in the armory of the modern commander."[5] As a counterinsurgent Lawrence knew it then, but we failed to recognize it in 2003.

It didn't bother me that we couldn't convince some PAOs in Iraq that communication was linked to violence. We knew we were dealing with a not-so-bright bunch that had at its core a very close-minded and intellectually unsophisticated people who were incapable of thinking beyond press releases. Most simply felt that the only way to win in Iraq was through firepower and that the flawed policies implemented early after the invasion were to blame. What bothered me was that the public affairs community's inaction caused further American bloodshed. Today more than ever I believe that the PAO community shares in the blame for the war's failure, and every last drop of American and Iraqi blood spilled in Iraq is on the hands of every single PAO who served there, including me. The public affairs community did too little, too late, and the inaction of PAOs at the highest levels and in critical roles in Iraq caused the climate on the streets that led to the deaths of U.S. soldiers and Iraqis.

Interestingly and surprisingly, many of the concepts that my team argued in Iraq between 2004 and 2005 are included in the 2006 counterinsurgency field manual drafted by the U.S. military two years after we broached them in Iraq to our public affairs colleagues. I find it humorous how many PAOs suddenly became disciples of what we preached in 2004 simply because Petraeus penned the manual and put his stamp on it. It is what we had been saying all along. It reads:

Effective commanders directly engage in a dialogue with the media and communicate IO (information operation) themes. With the proliferation of sophisticated communication technologies throughout the global information environment, the nature of media coverage has a significant impact on COIN [counterinsurgency] operations at all echelons. Civilian and military media coverage influences the perceptions of the political leaders and public in the host nation, the United States, and throughout the international community. The media directly influence the support of key audiences for COIN forces, the execution of their operations, and the opposing insurgency. Recognition of this influence creates a war of perceptions between insurgents and COIN forces that is conducted continuously through the communications media. The media are a permanent part of the information environment and effective media/ public affairs operations are critical to successful military operations.

Note that last sentence that says public affairs operations are critical to successful military operations. I wonder where the naysaying PAOs are these days. I wonder how they feel now that the military has clearly stated that public affairs is critical to the military mission overseas during war. The manual continues: "Every aspect of a military operation is subject to immediate scrutiny. Well planned, properly coordinated, and clearly expressed IO significantly clear the fog of war and improve the effectiveness and morale of coin forces, the will of the U.S. public, and the support of the HN (host nation) people for their government. The right messages can reduce misinformation, distractions, confusion, uncertainty, and other factors that cause public distress and undermine the COIN effort. Constructive and transparent information enhances understanding and support for continuing operations against the insurgency."

The Defense Department obviously knows it is falling short but recognizes the need to do more with PAOs, but dumping money into the problem won't resolve it. It needs to change its doctrine and approach. In 2005 and 2006 the Defense Department awarded hefty contracts to civilian companies and spent more than $120 million to improve the way it executed public affairs in Iraq. Nothing has shown that these contractors helped the military with interpersonal interactions with Iraqis or reaching out through Arab media engagement.

In February 2006 Rumsfeld admitted in a speech that the War on Terror is unlike any other war the nation has fought. "Some of the most important battles are being fought not on the ground, but in newsrooms around the world. We are fighting a battle where the survival of our free way of life is at stake and the center of gravity of that struggle is not simply on the battlefield overseas; it's a test of wills, and it will be won or lost with our publics, and with the publics of other nations," Rumsfeld said.[6]

While contracts are being awarded and new PAO teams are being organized, fundamentally the target audience is still the problem. Money and reorganization will not solve the problems made by a misaimed message. It is important for the Defense Department to hone its engagement skills and move beyond tired public relations tactics. They need to focus on their audience and the medium they are using to reach that audience. While the Defense Department said that the Joint Chiefs in 2004 "determined that serious issues and challenges existed in military public affairs" and that there were no "clearly defined roles for strategic communications," military communicators are still developing and employing solutions that don't address the problems. I'm certain that the Joint Public Affairs Support Element created in 2006 to improve PAO operations can add value in disaster-relief missions or in other domestic scenarios, but the element will bring no value to a complex insurgency and counterinsurgency communications unless it has a training cell that will prepare host-nation PAOs and teach them to engage their local media and regional media. The element will not succeed in communicating to local nationals while deployed during a counterinsurgency unless they train and mentor, for an extended period, host-nation PAOs and help them engage in a sustained media campaign. And it cannot train foreign people to do these things unless the team itself first receives training on the impact of global communications and they become students and masters of international mass media communications. The U.S. government can form all the teams and units it wants, but short of training and mentoring PAOs and engaging the media, nothing else will work.

PAOs should also be organized into teams, not joint support elements or public affairs detachments that can support communication operations in specific theaters. The U.S. military has regionalized commands that perform military operations in the Pacific region, the Middle East, and Latin America, as well as other areas. The reserve system is also broken down into regional support commands. The U.S. Army has Special Forces or Green Berets that have military occupational specialties like demolition-, medical-, or weapons-trained personnel trained in cultures and languages of specific regions. Using elements from all these commands and units, the PAO community should restructure its forces.

The Green Berets are known to be immersed in language and cultural training. This should be the case with PAOs too. As PAOs try to communicate with international audiences, it would be an enormous benefit to have a communicator who understands regional communications. Public affairs detachments should be reorganized into public affairs teams that specialize in performing international, tactical, and strategic public relations operations within an assigned region. For example, teams could be assigned to work in the Middle East; North, South, and Central Americas; Africa; Asia; and European and Pacific theaters. Each region would have its own set of standards and training needed to become qualified based on their geographic area. Obviously, a communicator in the Middle East would require much different training than a communicator on a U.S. team. Each team would have professional military communicators who are experts in local languages and knowledgeable of the region's history and culture. They would be best qualified to determine the types of communication strategies to deploy because they would understand the culture. We need to move away from the U.S. corporate PAO culture that is expected to fit all situations overseas.

To ensure military service and regional team interoperability, a joint element could be stood up to manage the regional teams since terrorism is a global problem. This entity could liaise, for example, a team in Iraq and a team in the Philippines because al-Qaeda has roots in both the Pacific and Middle Eastern fronts.

Instead of sending troops to train with industry in the United States and get worthless corporate experience, the U.S. military could send an officer to work with the Arab media or the media of a given culture, if the press were willing, to learn how they could better serve the media's informational needs and learn how audiences think. Instead of a communications course at the University of Oklahoma, PAOs could attend communication courses at the University of Cairo (if it is safe) or Sorbonne to learn how others outside of U.S. borders think, process information, and use the media. Being armed with that knowledge makes the military communicator more dynamic, more robust, and a better purveyor of what international news consumers need. The communicator becomes an adaptable, fluid officer fueled by the communications energy in his region, and he or she should be given a new title, like global affairs officer. Some might say this is unreasonable, but is it? The U.S. military already has language and cultural trainers. All it would have to do is open its training to PAOs and then restructure the teams accordingly. With a robust curriculum of several years to endure to obtain qualifications, most of the PAOs who attended a two-week or two-month shake-and-bake course and were drawn by the glitzy media duties would haul ass, and good riddance to them—they are dead weight. If it were harder to become a PAO and if the role focused more on long-term strategic gains and less on the glamour and being seen on Capitol Hill or rubbing elbows with news personalities, the field would attract better officers, not the glorified media coordinators it has today. It would draw intellectuals, not just those in love with themselves or those who like seeing themselves on camera or seeing their names in print. We need smart people, not people who like to talk about how many times they are quoted in the press.

Will this happen? Likely not, but the failure of PAOs has gotten the attention of many senior leaders. It was during 2004–5 that Rumsfeld publicly recognized the public affairs failure in Iraq, although nobody was ever formally assigned any blame. I wonder how many PAOs got high-profile medals, evaluations, and promotions from their war tours, despite the widespread failure of the PAO community in Iraq and the loss of the communications war.

Since our command was the exit strategy, U.S. military PAO leaders could have asked the PAO community in Baghdad to unite around our efforts, but instead it seemed everything they directed countered what we were trying to do. When I asked STRATCOM, the press center, CENTCOM, the Pentagon, and everyone else for help, I expected them as senior PAO leaders to help me look for the manpower we needed to help the president give our mission the thrust he stated was needed.

When PAO leaders I was in Baghdad with left Iraq in 2005, they never once during their tours saw the Iraqi face so many had waited for. The Iraqi military stayed quiet for months, and violence surged. Public support for the war back home eroded, and the media continued to report violence steadily throughout 2004–5. Who is to blame for this? Multinational Force Iraq PAOs? PAOs at CENTCOM? PAOs at the Defense Department? Maybe a combination of all three of them? Were they decorated for their duties? You bet, and handsomely, but for what? For creating conditions that led to erosion of public support? For creating conditions that led to lagging public opinion? For passively contributing to the development of an insurgency on the ground?

I'm certain the PAO community during 2004–5 has lauded all sorts of communications milestones. They likely touted the thousands of media interviews they managed, the thousands of media queries they answered, the thousands of journalists they processed and supported in theater, and their involvement in significant events such as elections or transfer of authority. I know a lot of PAOs liked to tell people they were the most-quoted authority on the war in Iraq. But when you look beyond the numbers, what did they achieve? Did Iraqis ever tell their story? Did American public opinion of the war stay high or plummet? Did the insurgency entrench itself and kill and injure thousands of our troops? To me it looks like those who are patting themselves on the back are avoiding the fact that they didn't do a very good job as public relations people. More directly stated, they are spinning their own accomplishments to reflect something more than what they really accomplished, which was absolutely nothing. I'm sure all of the colonels and generals who served there during that time have stuck their chests out nice and far when they got their "combat" awards. I hope they eventually shoulder some of the blame for what they did, or in this case didn't do, in Iraq. I hope they carry that load like I do every day.

Clarke admits in her 2006 book that a nation cannot have successful ongoing military operations without public support. Clarke assumed correctly in her book that the more the public saw U.S. military personnel in action, the more they would support their military forces. But if this theory is applicable in the United States, did her team recognize that it could also be applicable in Iraq? Did she realize that Iraqis would benefit from seeing their forces routinely or hearing about them frequently?

One guy who understood the importance of a steady drumbeat of communications was Mohammed Saeed al-Sahhaf, Saddam's minister of information. I had a picture of him tacked up on one of the walls of our office, along with one of his many quotes underneath it. He's a colorful guy, most likely remembered as the man who stood before an international press corps and insisted that the coalition had not entered Iraq in 2003.

"Their infidels are committing suicide by the hundreds on the gates of Baghdad. Be assured, Baghdad is safe, protected," al-Sahhaf told the press in the early hours of Operation Iraqi Freedom.

This guy was easy to use as a punch line. He was obviously either misinformed or bordering on delusional, but he was also incredibly inept at working with information. He was a propagandist at best, and everyone in the press knew better than to believe anything he said. But at least he tried.

Al-Sahhaf and Saddam, based on experience, would try to deceive Iraqis and the world, so it was a good idea that the Pentagon embedded hundreds of journalists with U.S. military units at the onset of the war to counter al-Sahhaf's efforts.

Al-Sahhaf, a little old man, had maintained an aggressive propaganda machine and had managed to help Saddam keep a very tight rein over Iraq for decades, and despite being ridiculed by the rest of the world, and by my team, he led an information network that struck fear in the heart of Iraqis for decades. That's not to imply that al-Sahhaf's communications plan was good or sophisticated, or that it even convinced many Iraqis of his lies, but his authoritarian method worked.

When I'd walk to the mess hall past the massive blown-out, dusty remnants of Saddam's Ministry of Information in Baghdad, I often thought of al-Sahhaf and how he and Saddam had managed to keep their nation in line for decades using lies and threats. Comical as al-Sahhaf was, the longer I served in Iraq, the more parallels I began to see between his machine and the coalition public affairs community, two groups I would never have compared had I not been in Iraq to see their similarities myself.

The coalition public affairs community was certainly more polished and refined than al-Sahhaf, but the tactics used by both Saddam's former Iraqi PAO and the coalition's PAOs were strikingly similar in their crudeness and ineffectiveness in time of crisis in Iraq. They mirrored each other more than most in military communications would probably admit.

As coalition troops rolled into Baghdad, al-Sahhaf told the world that coalition troops were dying in droves, comments disproved by embedded journalists. He was considered a liar and a lunatic by the international community as quickly as he spoke his words, but internally to his Iraqi audience al-Sahhaf remained defiant, and many in Iraq believed him because they had little evidence to contest what he was saying. That would obviously change as U.S. M-1 tanks rumbled through the center of Baghdad and Iraqis saw for themselves that Americans were not committing suicide at the city's gates but instead were actively sweeping through the Iraqi capital looking for a fight.

Radio Baghdad, a station owned by Uday Hussein, Saddam's now very dead son, played patriotic music and glorified Saddam in the days following the U.S. invasion until it was finally shut down. Although Saddam was successful in spreading his own version of the truth during his dictatorship, he remained in power largely because Iraqis knew that he would crush anyone who opposed him. He could tell the press whatever he wanted, and it would go unchecked and unchallenged. Al-Sahhaf and Saddam had a firm grasp on the Iraqi press corps, I was told by Iraqi news people during my time in Iraq. Saddam would not have a free press in his nation, but neither would the coalition.

The CPA and the U.S. military did try to control the Iraqi press despite liberating Iraq in the name of freedom and democracy. As they tried to assert control over free Arab press in Iraq and curb what they called "anti-American" news content, the coalition unknowingly created communications parallels that made them almost as suffocating to the Arab press corps as Saddam's government. The media took notice of the manner in which PAOs worked with the Arab press, but Rumsfeld also took notice and became an outspoken critic of PAOs and publicly threw PAOs under the bus.

In 2006 Rumsfeld wrote in an editorial for the *Los Angeles Times*:

> The standard U.S. government public affairs operation was designed primarily to respond to individual requests for information. It tends to be reactive, rather than proactive, and it operates for the most part on an eight-hour, five-days-a-week basis, while world events—and our enemies—are operating 24/7 across every time zone. That is an unacceptably dangerous deficiency. . . . In some cases, military public affairs officials have had little communications training and little, if any, grounding in the importance of timing, rapid response and the realities of digital and broadcast media. Let there be no doubt that the longer it takes to put a strategic communications framework into place, the more we can be certain that the vacuum will be filled by the enemy and by hostile news sources who most assuredly will not paint an accurate picture of what is actually taking place.[7]

The scary thing is that despite this nasty public revelation by the Defense Department's senior man, PAOs with little communications training were allowed to continue to train Iraqi communicators and, worse yet, given control of the strategic communications effort that they had abysmally failed to operate effectively. Why didn't the department take note of this in 2004 when our team was telling them these things? Couldn't they see the signs? I was merely a captain, by their standards, and I saw the deficiency. Why did it take a defense secretary two more years to figure out this shit?

Moreover, why didn't anything change in the communications arena by the latter part of 2006 once he made this announcement? Why is everything still, for the most part, the same? Years have lapsed since Rumsfeld wrote the editorial acknowledging shortcomings with military PAOs and since he left the department, yet even after his resignation nothing significant has been done to alter the approach other than hire more contractors to do what military PAOs should be doing. The U.S. military is investing in companies rather than investing in educating its own force of communicators. Sure, there have been some changes, but not in the way in which it impacts the environment on the ground.

I think it is erroneous to say or imply that the insurgency was smart or ambitious enough to topple public opinion and support for the war in the United States. Insurgent messages were not meant to target Americans, but rather they were directed at Arabs to rise up in a holy war against the Americans and their allies. Insurgents issued battle cries for Muslims to fight against U.S. occupiers, but the insurgents' steady, violent, and well-documented campaign certainly had a residual impact on many Americans; sagging public support for operations in Iraq is evidence of this. The insurgents accomplished more than they expected using modern media, and their success in swaying American public opinion doesn't show their skill as communicators; rather, it directly reflects the value of globally deploying modern communications platforms in a counterinsurgency. The insurgency wanted to kill Americans and as a by-product make their mission in Iraq fail. They got both objectives done with the help of al-Jazeera, which wasn't engaged by U.S. PAOs, who declared it the sworn enemy of the U.S. and Iraqi governments.

It's ironic that U.S. support for the war hit rock bottom, considering that the public affairs community's sole focus while I was in Iraq was to communicate and engage with the Western press and convince the American people that everything in Iraq was hunky-dory. They worked doggedly to preserve a positive U.S. public opinion. They entered the Iraq war with the mind-set that they would showcase the U.S. military's success in Iraq through the media and in the process garner public support for the war. PAOs couldn't even manage to achieve their assigned mission, much less what I thought their mission should be. History now shows us this. It's undeniable.

While the coalition public affairs community had many flaws—such as inexperienced, young, unprofessional CPA PAOs; conventional one-dimensional military flacks; and no clear and flexible outline of the public affairs way ahead for strategic communications in Iraq—it wasn't these elements that solely led to the communications failure in Iraq. The core problem with all things related to public affairs in Iraq was the tone at the top that trickled down to the public affairs operators on the ground, more than six thousand miles away, in Mesopotamia.

The mission of the U.S. military's public affairs branches is to fulfill the services' obligation to keep the American people and the service personnel informed. They also help establish conditions that lead to confidence in America's military and its readiness to conduct operations in peacetime, conflict, and war. Maybe that needs tweaking now.

The U.S. Defense Department's Principles of Information states: "It is Department of Defense policy to make available timely and accurate information so that the public, the Congress, and the news media may assess and understand the facts about national security and defense strategy." Nowhere in public affairs mission statements does it state that military PAOs are charged with the stewardship of U.S. public opinion. Furthermore, it says nothing about the military's role in swaying political public opinion, but that is how PAOs were used in Iraq and on the home front. The mission of the military public affairs community is to inform the public, and if the United States is fighting a global war on terror, that public must include the Arab audience.

According to William M. Hammond, who authored *The Military and the Media, 1968-1973* for the U.S. Army's Center of Military History, PAOs in the Vietnam War for the first time ever became involved in helping administrations with public opinion. It would be a role they would never shake. "Where in earlier wars the president and his party had conducted most of the public relations, in Vietnam the military rather than the political sector came to bear heavy responsibility for the effort," Hammond wrote.

"[President Lyndon] Johnson relied on [Gen. William] Westmoreland and his public affairs officers to justify his efforts and to endorse his claims of progress."[8] In Iraq good news was the only news that Washington wanted to hear, and when the PAO community couldn't make that happen, Washington blamed the press.

In the fall of 2006 the Defense Department launched a wasteful public relations campaign called "Why We Serve." The program's director said it was an effort to help the American people understand why U.S. service personnel serve their country, since the U.S. military could not rely on the international press to tell their story. The idea, officials said, originated, you guessed it, with Rumsfeld and Gen. Peter Pace of the U.S. Marine, chairman of the Joint Chiefs of Staff. Both men felt it was important for military people to communicate with Americans by sending them into their hometowns to talk about the war. Translation: this is a grassroots program to gain public support for the war, which leads to improved poll ratings and presidential approval ratings—you get the picture. Public surveys continue to show the U.S. military is highly respected over elected officials, year after year. The services don't need a campaign to win public support. They have it. U.S. troops are supported by the American public. Americans have a problem with the war managers, not soldiers. Why We Serve was part of another public relations money pit known as America Supports You, a Defense Department program that showcased American public support for military personnel and their families.

I know quite a bit about the programs because as a reservist, prior to my mobilization, I was assigned as a military reporter to the Office of the Assistant Secretary of Defense, Public Affairs. I wrote for all Defense Department websites, including Defense Link, America Supports You, Defend America, Defense Transformation, and the specialty sites created for special events like Women's History Month.

After 9/11 the Defense Department identified a need to garner support for the troops as they fought the War on Terror. Despite having a website dedicated to military news, the military felt it was important to spend more money on a dedicated program that would provide news about the War on Terror. Frankly, I didn't see the point. News from the War on Terror, if presented factually without all of the puffy, fluffy language known to military public relations writers, would stand on its own. Dedicated sites weren't needed.

The push for dedicated programs and sites was managed by Allison Barber, a political appointee with a background in elementary schools and nonprofits. Barber will likely best be remembered as the woman who in 2005 coached servicemen and -women in Iraq on what many media groups would label as a staged teleconference between President Bush and U.S. personnel. It was an embarrassing moment for the public affairs community, and it showed that the public affairs community would do anything to align itself to support administration war goals.

The money spent on trying to convince Americans to support the war could have been better spent by channeling it into communications programs in stability and security operations and providing Iraqis with a secure environment. It could have been spent on public relations operations in Iraq, to try to convince the Iraqi populace of the alleged strides being made in Iraq.

But the few times the public affairs community has tried to think outside the box, it has been disastrously out of ethical bounds. The Defense Department paid the Lincoln Group $37.3 million for three contracts between October 2004 and September 2006 to buy article space in Iraqi newspapers to counter insurgent propaganda. I can't imagine the fallout domestically if the Pentagon tried to buy positive press in the *New York Times* or *Washington Post*.

Rumsfeld admitted that the U.S. military command, U.S. Embassy, and the Iraqi government had sought "nontraditional means to provide accurate information to the Iraqi people." Rumsfeld argued, "Yet this has been portrayed as inappropriate: for example, the allegations of 'buying news.' The resulting explosion of critical media stories then causes all activity, all initiative, to stop. Even worse, it leads to a 'chilling effect' among those who are asked to serve in the military public affairs field."[9]

I don't know what the fuck Rumsfeld was talking about. I never suffered from a chilling effect because I never tried to bribe reporters to write good news, nor did I pay anyone to place my command articles in their publications. Rumsfeld said the media was being manipulated by the disinformation of insurgents and that the press was inaccurately portraying U.S. soldiers who served in Iraq. PAOs, he added, were afraid to do their jobs because no matter how hard they tried, the press would always report that things were horrible in Iraq. What a bunch of crybaby bullshit. We were back in the Vietnam War.

PAOs have always been used to push agendas, and most in military communications won't readily admit that fact. They have helped administrations push their politics nationally and at the state level. After the first Gulf War author John R. MacArthur wrote in his book *Second Front: Censorship and Propaganda in the Gulf War* that the George H. W. Bush administration wanted to manage information in such a way that it supported the political goals of the administration and avoided mistakes from Vietnam. Years later Bush's son would want the same thing, and his top defense leaders worked hard to heavily engage the Western press.

The public affairs community in Iraq seemed content spinning its wheels and, like Iraqis, getting theirs. It was a great place to earn top-notch credentials. Public affairs staffers got to work with the media's leading news personalities: Brokaw, Williams, Amanpour, Rather, Jennings, and others. Where else could public relations people get this kind of experience? Postwar résumés were stuffed with impeccable press experience filled with these big names, despite the fact that the media interaction might not have accomplished anything more in the long run than producing a great picture PAOs could use as a conversation piece. PAOs could say, and show, that they worked with the biggest names in news, that they had helped with some historical events in Iraq, but had they done anything more than just manage the logistics of an event or of an interview? It wasn't the PAOs who were talking to the heavy hitters of the press. PAOs weren't being interviewed by Dan Rather or Peter Jennings; it was U.S. generals. Is this what the military expects its PAO colonels and lieutenant colonels in public affairs to do? Coordinate interviews? Where's the challenge? Why are taxpayers paying high-ranking military officers six figures to do secretarial work? It's not like these officers are the subjects of these interviews, and it's not like they're guiding the public affairs mission. What exactly are they doing? When a spokesperson in Iraq bragged that he was the most-quoted person in the war, it gives a false image of that person. Truth is the person is answering questions from media cards that were compiled by PAOs in STRATCOM or the Pentagon, compiled from PAOs out in operational commands who wrote the questions and answers for the media cards. The person is merely reading answers from cards that were created to field media questions. Where is the skill in that? Repeating comments someone else has written doesn't take skill. PAOs have media cards they can use so they can deliver mindless responses to the press. So when someone would call about an attack, there was already a response formulated. It is robotic and insincere and requires no skill. It serves a purpose, but it shouldn't be a strategy, certainly not one people boast about.

"The enemy is so much better at communicating," Rumsfeld was quoted in an Associated Press report published August 29, 2006. "I wish we were better at countering that, because the constant drumbeat of things they say—all of which are not true—is harmful. It's cumulative. And it does weaken people's will and lessen their determination, and raise questions in their minds as to whether the cost is worth it," he said.[10] I'll ask again, if we were bad at something and he knew it, why didn't he fix what was wrong within his department?

In the Associated Press article he states that the insurgency has managed to sway the opinion of the American public, but nowhere in his comments does he address or even recognize the importance or significance of securing the Arab and Iraqi public trust or opinion. His department's focus continues to be the American audience. There was little thorough introspection by Rumsfeld, and while he implicitly blames the public affairs community and also blames the media for the current climate, he does little to remedy the situation and shoulders none of the blame.

In the 2006 Rumsfeld editorial for the *Los Angeles Times*, he said that media database research shows a huge disparity in the media's coverage of the U.S. military. "Consider that a database search of the nation's leading newspapers turns up 10 times as many mentions of one of the soldiers punished for misconduct at Abu Ghraib than of Sgt. 1st Class Paul Ray Smith, the first recipient of the Medal of Honor in the global war on terror," Rumsfeld wrote.[11]

It is awful that Rumsfeld has to stoop so low and use the memory of a fallen soldier to try to make his case. Smith fought and died in Iraq. His actions were incredibly brave and recognized by the U.S. military, but what Rumsfeld doesn't understand is that the story of Smith's death and subsequent award of the Medal of Honor has a limited shelf life in the news industry. It has immense historical and cultural value for us as a nation, but professionally speaking, the report of the tragic death of Smith and his award of the Medal of Honor has limited news value.

The presentation of the medal to Smith's widow and all of the ceremonies that followed had news value for a prescribed period of time. The news media cannot continue to talk about Smith because there are no new developments in the story. He fought bravely, died in battle, was recognized with the Medal of Honor, and nothing follows. The story is over for the press. That's not to imply that Smith is forgotten or overlooked. He's not. He is a historical figure now and one of our American heroes. But once the nation's media has profiled him, the family he left behind, and the eventual award of the medal, what's left to report? In later years maybe the story can be revisited, a follow-up with the family five years without their father, for example, but the story cannot be continuously told. There is nothing new to report. The story has a limited shelf life in the news industry, and while that sounds callous, I am merely stating what is known to most reporters.

Misconduct by soldiers at Abu Ghraib, as an example, has a more protracted news shelf life. First, there are allegations, and those whistle-blower allegations and leaks will make the headlines. Then there are investigations that will also make the news pages. Then come arrests and charges. All of those developments make the headlines. After investigations are complete come the hearings, and then charges are filed and that certainly has news value. Military trials follow that are covered from opening through closing remarks. The news story finally culminates once all of the U.S. soldiers involved go to trial. More headlines follow, and then comes the verdict stage, which is followed by, guess what, more headlines. Then comes sentencing for their crimes, and then comes their release from prison or parole.

We repeat these same stories over and over for each individual who gets charged, goes through a trial, serves time, and gets released. We endure the same sordid stories as the legal cycle repeats itself for each defendant. Naturally, there will be more stories, and we're not even including profiles that are done of the brave guy who blew the whistle on these abusive assholes. The story can take months if not years to play out in the media.

My point is that the story would be in the media's crosshairs for a longer duration than Smith's Medal of Honor ceremony, which happened in a single day. But even as Smith's story unfolded, the media covered it. As his heroism became known, it was reported that Smith had been "recommended" for the Medal of Honor. Smith's award of the medal was the culmination. Rumsfeld expects Smith to receive some protracted press attention, but the news industry does not work this way. If there is nothing new to report about Smith's heroism, then Smith doesn't need to be revisited in the press, unlike Abu Ghraib, where the story developed dynamically, with more facts coming to light as time passed, requiring the press to report on updates and developments to the story. Rummy just seems like he's trying to get the military to hate the media, and if that was his goal, it worked. A lot of military people despise the press, and it's no wonder when their leader is talking like this.

Rumsfeld's editorial shows more of the core problem. He is naive to expect a news story with limited shelf life to continue to get coverage over a prolonged newsworthy event that unfolds over the course of several years. Moreover, it shows a clear lack of understanding of how the press functions and makes decisions. Smith's heroics are certainly worthy of a lot of press coverage, but they will not sustain a time test. Enduring news will dominate, and the prison scandal was something that evolved in the press over a spectrum of time. Smith's story was packaged, presented, and reported, and the news agencies moved on. Similarly, once the abuse trials were over, the media moved on with that story too. It is the nature of the news industry, and Rumsfeld's comparisons are off base. It is troubling that a man in his position would present such an off-the-mark editorial.

There is an expectation in the military public affairs community that good news be given a chance. Military public relations folks constantly bitch about the press being "liberal" and "biased," but the truth is that the military expects reporters to show the good but never the bad, and when you've got the ranking Defense Department civilian military leader writing nonsensical commentaries, it's no wonder the PAO corps is out of touch too.

I've always strived to have reporters file fair and accurate stories and have avoided the stress found in seeking information utopia; that place exists only within our own ranks when we deploy and employ military writers. Some PAOs talk about how they just expect fair reporting, but they wouldn't know fair reporting if it bit them on the ass.

"A lesson we should have learned in the 1960s and 1970s is that when governments, including our own, become desperate over a failing policy, they are tempted into that historic folly of nations, self-delusion," Ben Bagdikian wrote in MacArthur's book. "The more frustrated the leader becomes, the more the leader is likely to see subordinates who report bad news as disloyal or not sufficiently zealous about the official enterprise. Bad news is filtered out before it reaches the top. Official channels of information become corrupted. In the end, as always, the propagandist government becomes the victim of its own propaganda."[12]

I personally saw some great things in Iraq that showed progress: schools opened and kids flocked to them to learn, towns prospered with U.S. aid as commerce proliferated, technology scattered and connectivity in the once dark country flourished, and women began to crawl out from underneath the male-dominated culture of old Iraq. There were good things happening in Iraq, but they were often shadowed by the powerful sensational bombings of the day, and the public affairs community never understood that they couldn't silence the sound of an explosion. The insurgents had something to show, the coalition had something to say, and I've always said that public affairs is 95 percent about showing the press something and 5 percent is about telling them about it. The coalition brought computer keyboards to a video fight and lost.

Had I been a news reporter in Iraq, odds are good I probably would have had a stringer floating around most cities, waiting to record something. If an insurgent attack happened, I could deploy that cameraman and have him tape the violence; it is news, after all. But if I'm sitting in a news bureau and I get an e-mailed news release from the press center or a coalition PAO, how can I possibly show this on television? If a PAO calls me to tell me about something, how can I use that? If the coalition isn't showing me anything because they're waiting on the Iraqis to talk and they're not getting me anything, guess what story I'm airing? If I am in the business of showing the news, how does a press center news release with all sorts of misspellings and factual errors in it help me show anything to my viewers? How can I take that as credible? If I'm in radio, how does this help me?

For the sake of argument, though, let's say there is a lot of good happening in Iraq. Wouldn't the media tell those stories if they were truly happening? Does the U.S. Defense Department honestly believe that there is a vast conspiracy against U.S. men and women in uniform? Is this why CNN auctioned a humvee to benefit a wounded-warrior nonprofit organization? Or why they have a military salute on one of their morning programs? Does the Defense Department believe that everyone in the media simply ignores or walks by good stories and hunts down the bad stuff? The press, I am 100 percent convinced, would have reported on progress in Iraq if some were truly there to report. They would sniff out the good stories, much like how they sniffed out the bad. It is ridiculous to think that CNN, NBC, CBS, and others conspire against the U.S. military. When we offered the press stories of progress involving Iraqi security forces, they covered it fairly and accurately.

In 2004, shortly after Iraq's transfer of authority, Multinational Force Iraq began cutting back support for press junkets. Ordinarily, I could request air support as the chief of public affairs, and the coalition would support it. I could request two to four Black Hawk helicopters and ferry media around Iraq, but once Casey assumed command of Multinational Force Iraq, acquiring air support and even ground transportation to move the media around on the battlefield became arduous.

I would be required to obtain my commanding general's endorsement before submitting the transportation requests, and Casey's office, I was told by our transportation team, was reviewing every request and allotting only a handful of air-support requests per general officer. They said Casey's office had labeled media-support missions low priority. Naturally, there was an inclination by our command not to stir things up, so I reduced the command's media-engagement profile after Casey silenced Petraeus and put press on our command's logistics missions whenever I could find empty seats. Otherwise, the press would never leave their news bureaus and cover the progress being made by Iraqi forces. I think Casey was trying to keep the Americans off the television and out of the papers because we had entered the so-called Iraqi-face period. But as I've said, the Iraqis weren't talking. So if Casey is having his forces in Iraq avoid the media and expecting the Iraqis to take the lead, and he's making it hard for the media to get out by not allowing transportation to be allocated for press trips, how can Rumsfeld argue that the media were only reporting bad news and not the good news? How can the press cover the good news when it isn't allowed to see it?

Needless to say, I was frustrated. I had a charismatic boss who was great with the press. I had capable and willing Iraqi PAO counterparts in the Ministries of Defense and Interior, but the directives of the commanding general of coalition forces in Iraq were getting in the way of our progress. At the end of my proverbial rope, I tied a knot and sent Petraeus a lengthy note one evening.

I explained that I knew he wanted to wait to engage the media and that I regretted not having the foresight to predict the fallout from the *Newsweek* cover, but he could not disappear because it was bad for the mission. I explained I was watching us lose a great deal of real estate on the information hill that we took when he arrived. I told him I did not think the PAO community collectively had its act together and that we were missing a lot of opportunities.

I told him about an idea that I shared with Slavonic: that we should have a coalition PAO forum for Iraq and bring PAOs to Iraq to meet and discuss ways to improve business, so we could get on the same sheet of music.

Interestingly, that would turn into an event that I think was held in Qatar, but although it was my idea I was not allowed to attend because I was too junior in rank, despite the fact that I was one of only a handful of chiefs of public affairs in Iraq serving the multinational commands.

I told him that it was hard to be the exit strategy and watch all of the missed opportunities and that we needed to give a television newsmagazine a look-see at our operations from the ground up and talk about training, equipping, and mentoring the Iraqis. We needed something big to get us back on the map. Above all, we could have the Iraqi leadership meet with the reporters. They would be the thrust. We could highlight both police and military sides and also host the Arab press equivalent at the same time. Al-Arabiya, I explained, had been more than fair to us. I explained I could always advise Lessel and Slavonic to recommend to Casey that we be granted the opportunity to host *60 Minutes*. I told him that it would not seem like it's coming from him and that it would be the recommendation of a lowly O-3 who is making observations about the press posture and public opinion.

I warned him that when the insurgents had the international podium for as long as they did, opinions would shift, and the press would too, in this case unfavorably. Little did I know how prophetic my words would be. My goal was to use the domestic engagement obsession of public affairs against them. I still wanted to put a face on the U.S. mission in Iraq for those back home, and *60 Minutes* might help me do that. But I also wanted to reach out in the same manner to Iraqis, and al-Arabiya had plenty of news shows that I could engage to do that. I would run the idea up the flagpole to Slavonic and Lessel.

Petraeus told me that I had been persuasive as usual, and he told me to ask Slavonic or Lessel to recommend the *60 Minutes* pitch to Casey. He added that he wanted me to keep his fingerprints off it.

We would never do the *60 Minutes* show. We were stuck in the mud. I couldn't engage with Petraeus, and I couldn't get the Iraqis to talk because the coalition was giving them enough rope to hang themselves and allowing them to take their sweet-ass time to engage the press.

In October 2004 Washington-based writer James Lacey penned an article that caused another stink in the public affairs community but best reflects the climate in public affairs during that time: "Who's Responsible for Losing the Media War in Iraq?" In the editorial Lacey accused the public affairs community of many things. Lacey bravely stated the obvious and went on record shouting what many reporters had been saying under their breaths in fear of payback.

"The reason the military is losing the war in the media is because it has almost totally failed to engage, and where it has engaged, it has been with a mind-boggling degree of ineptitude," Lacey wrote. "It is a strange circumstance indeed when virtually every senior officer agrees that the media can make or break national policy, but no more than a handful can name the top military journalist for *The Washington Post, The New York Times*, or *The Wall Street Journal*. Thousands of officers who spend countless hours learning every facet of their profession do not spend one iota of their time understanding or learning to engage with a strategic force that can make or break their best efforts," Lacey wrote.[13]

Lacey was a former military officer who was trying to get some good news out in Iraq. He admitted in his article that he had tried to counter the bad news cycle developing in Iraq in 2004. And despite being an insider, he found the system mazelike and filled with hacks.

> Even with knowledge of how the military works, I still found virtually my every attempt to get information from PAOs to be akin to getting water from a stone. Many times I sat looking at the phone in disbelief at some answer or non-answer a PAO had given me. Too often, I hung up the phone and thought to myself, if the Secretary of Defense only knew how one of his PAOs was treating a man about to write a column for national distribution. Sometimes, I had to sit back and count off the reasons I should not just start writing mean little articles about the military.

Lacey also wrote what many reporters felt and had communicated to me, especially those in the Arab press. They were not being engaged and could cover only limited stories trapped inside their news bureaus.

The PAO process needs to be radically rebuilt. Critical to accomplishing this is reversing the passive mind-set of the PAO community such that it ceases being a filter for information and becomes actively engaged in making sure information gets out the door. There is no reason PAOs should be sitting back waiting for journalist inquiries or requests for interviews. Every day they should be out executing an aggressive media plan to get the military story in front of the public. This has to go beyond the sterility of a periodic press release or press briefing. It means spending every day trying to get important stories into the hands of journalists or facilitating stories already in the works.

Lacey's most powerful and telling paragraph about the press experience in Iraq with the public affairs community is best reflected in this excerpt:

So, when I called the PAOs at the CPA to work out some access for my return to Iraq, I was stupefied by the response. My offer, which was given to half a dozen civilian and military public affairs folks over the course of 20 or 30 calls was pretty extraordinary. At a time when everyone in Iraq was screaming that the media were failing to cover the military's accomplishments, I said I wanted to tell the country what was going right. If given the right access, I told them, I probably could get the cover of a major newsweekly several times over the course of a couple of months. In addition, I had several national opinion magazines lined up that would publish all I could send them. I also was in conversations with producers of a network TV news magazine, and they were interested in doing a piece along the same positive lines. Finally, I reminded these public affairs people that *Time* and CNN were owned by the same company and that I probably would be able to get substantial air time during what I expected to be an extended stay in Iraq. I was coming to Iraq to look for the news the rest of the media were missing. In short, I had an agenda that correlated exactly with the military's and the CPA's, but no one wanted to be bothered. Excuses about it being a hectic period should fall on deaf ears. At one point, I asked for access to Paul Bremer, civil administrator for Iraq, and was told I would have to get in line behind 250 other requests for the same thing. I reminded that PAO what I was bringing to the table and that it was ludicrous I should be placed in line behind a request from the Podunk Gazette. He hung up on me.

Rajiv Chandrasekaran, a reporter who visited our command a few times during his days with the *Washington Post Foreign Service*, wrote a revealing article on June 20, 2004, that offered insight into the public affairs community. He expressed to me prior to that article how poorly he had been treated by the public affairs community in Iraq, so it came as no surprise when I read his piece in which he turned the cannons on public affairs. Rajiv would go on to write a lengthy three-part series about the U.S. occupation in Iraq that was fair but justifiably critical, and he would later release a book, in 2006.

The other major conflict within the occupation bureaucracy has set the legions of young staff members chosen for their loyalty to the Bush administration against older, more liberal diplomats from the State Department and the British Foreign Office. Several of the diplomats said they regarded the young staffers as inexperienced and eager to pad their résumés during three-month tours.

These diplomats singled out the Office of Strategic Communications as unsuccessful in its efforts to disseminate information to Iraqis. Instead of creating an all-news television station that would compete with other Arab broadcasters that the CPA deemed anti-occupation, the communications office, with several employees straight from Republican staff jobs on Capitol Hill, set up a channel that aired children's programs and Egyptian cooking shows.

"It didn't put any effort into communicating with the Iraqi people," a British CPA official said. "STRATCOM viewed its job as helping Bush to win his next election."[14]

The military in addition to the U.S. government, if it is to regain the press and public trust, must invest in hiring and retaining professional communicators. The U.S. Army must develop a full career track for Army communicators.

The reality is that Army public affairs will continue to get leftovers from other career fields. I have seen guys who can't spell and can barely operate a computer given control of press operations and be charged with engaging international media. Pilots who have gotten too fat to fit into their aircraft should not be given the controls of an even mightier weapon, information. Unskilled communicators who backed into public affairs should not be given the critical mission of communicating in the global information environment. Rank does not equal knowledge or experience in public affairs, but in a rank-structured environment, sometimes that's all people see.

In late 2004 Petraeus was asked by the Office of the Secretary of Defense, Public Affairs, to write an editorial for the *Washington Post* during his media-blackout period. The piece was penned and published with the concurrence and review of Rumsfeld's public affairs staff. In addition, Casey, who had shut him down, personally reviewed the document and gave his permission for the editorial, given that the request had come from Rummy's team. The opinion piece, in my view, was reactionary and spawned because of Petraeus's noticeable silence as the media looked for stories on their own. Where once there was a flow of information to the press about our exit-strategy mission, now there was silence. Casey's press ban on Petraeus was having some fallout, and instead of being engaged with news from our command, the press was finding news to fill the void.

When Petraeus's editorial was published I got an e-mail from Washington DC from a fellow PAO. He had been copied in an e-mail, and he wanted to share it with me. It seemed some PAOs at the Army's Office of the Chief, Public Affairs, and at the Office of the Assistant Secretary of Defense, Public Affairs, were cranky. One lieutenant colonel, an Army officer at the Pentagon's public affairs office, wrote another officer at the Defense Department's press operations center. The press center director, these PAOs said in this e-mail, had told them that I had been freelancing and not coordinating with his press center and that I was acting like I was wearing Petraeus's stars on my collar. They said that I believed I could operate solo, and they referred to me as a young captain. As a guy into his forties, likely as old if not older than some of these light colonels, I was flattered that they thought I looked young enough to be considered a young captain.

The PAO went on to say that neither the press center nor the Army's public affairs office knew of Petraeus's opinion piece prior to publication, and they recommended somebody tweak me.

Our command had coordinated and cleared the editorial through our chain of command that ran from Casey through Central Command to Rumsfeld's office. This did not, however, suffice for these two Pentagon colonels and the press center director in Baghdad, none of whom were in our chain of command and all of whom were at command levels far lower than ours. These PAOs did not need to be informed because this was not an Army communications issue within their purview, so they were wrong. Second, the truth was that all three officers' superiors had been informed and knew about it, but the superiors didn't deem it necessary to inform the light colonels at the Pentagon or in Baghdad about the editorial. Information, as we often joke, was given on a need-to-know basis, and these PAOs didn't need to know because ultimately in this issue, they didn't matter. Had they had a need to know, I'm sure the information would have trickled down from above to their level.

They were reading way too much into things, and I think they were projecting a bit. I never intended to slight them, and truth be told I never had the time to sit around and pick apart someone's actions like they were doing to me. I knew that the right people had been informed about the op-ed, and we pressed forward. It isn't like I sat around and thought of ways to be difficult, and I hope their sensitive feelings are not hurt when they learn that I really did not give them that much thought. It was a very raw type of existence for me and Jared, and we hoped that our peers would be supportive of the fact that we were busting our asses doing the work of twelve people with two. We hoped that because we did not get the support we requested from PAOs in Baghdad, Tampa, Qatar, and Washington DC that we would at least get a level of understanding, but even compassion seemed elusive. As I mentioned earlier, if they lacked the ability to give us some of their manpower, they could have tried to help us get manpower from other sources, given we were the exit strategy. In my opinion, good leaders assume a role of servant leaders, but people are people and commissioned officers are no exception, and many will show very human flaws. I've certainly got mine.

Frankly, once I got a good compass heading on our mission after a few weeks in country and multiple unfulfilled requests for support, and I figured out what elements and people added value to our execution, I did not think about the press center or any other overly bureaucratic support organization very often because I was too busy trying to fulfill our mission and working around all of the obstacles that had been set along our path. Unlike the press center director and Pentagon officers, we traveled all over the country and to neighboring nations to tell our story, by land, by air, and even by sea. We were all over the place, and we did not have time or energy to sit around and be negative.

I said it then, and it is worth repeating, if PAOs didn't like the way I behaved or if it ruffled feathers, I didn't then, and still don't, give a fuck. If they wanted to armchair quarterback from the safety and comfort of the press center and lob their judgments across the ocean all the way from the Pentagon, they were welcome to do that, and I handled their criticism and comments just like I always did: I used their assessments of me as rectal wipes.

I was a prior enlisted officer, a mustang, as we're often called, with more than a decade in the enlisted ranks, so my objective wasn't to climb the ranks. My career didn't hinge on riding someone's coattails or affixing myself to a popular general. I never wanted to retire as a colonel. It wasn't a career goal. I had nothing to lose, so in the execution of my mission I would ask politely once, and if I couldn't get what I needed, then I simply went through the obstacle. In fact, Petraeus asked me to stay in Baghdad and extend my tour with him, and I politely declined.

My team and I saw how inefficient the press center was and the reputation they had built. When I first arrived we tried to work with them, and we leaned on them to distribute our press releases. We soon noticed that their releases had a lot of errors, and I don't mean simple things like a misspelling or a random comma. A press release, for example, might have a headline that mentions a particular operational success, but the press release's body was about something completely different. When the press center would catch the mistake, they would then issue a recall for the e-mail with the error-filled press release. They would make changes and then send it out again with a complete set of different errors. Sometimes the e-mail subject lines did not match the e-mail subjects; sometimes there was nothing attached or included in the e-mail. My point is there wasn't a lot of attention to detail or oversight being given by the press center leadership to the press releases, and I had heard comments from the media about their sloppy work. In addition, they were notorious for moving slowly. When I explained the climate to my chief of staff, he recommended we work directly with the media and not use the press center, so that's what I did. That was our option and prerogative, but I didn't do this unilaterally. I sought out the opinion of my chief, and together we decided what was best for our command. The press center doesn't get a vote. They are a support element.

When we needed photography equipment, they loaned us the worst equipment they had, despite having newer functional equipment that sat there for most of the tour. A sergeant I used to work with in the States prior to deploying told me that the equipment belonged to a unit that did not want to loan it to me because they feared we would lose it or damage it, so new functional equipment sat there and went unused, and we went out and spent more money. The Iraqi media team also sat around with no gear to use for months, although there was equipment nearby ready to use. They rejected our requests to loan us personnel, and when we tried to get the press center to find work space for the Iraqi media team and to give them access to press conferences, they did not help us. After several months of no cooperation, naturally I moved forward without them.

I was our command's chief communicator, and that meant I was also responsible for our reputation's management. As the chief of public affairs, it was my prerogative to determine whether I would accept the press center's support. We initially asked for it because we were desperate, but based on what we saw and heard, we happily distanced ourselves from them and worked around them. The press center was a support element that helped

PAOs do their jobs, no more, no less. A press center director has no authority over any PAOs in the combined or combatant commands that are out actually executing the mission. A press center director's job is to help tell the story of the work the rest of us were doing by sending press releases and hosting press conferences. The director is not a spokesperson at a press conference; that duty falls to the chief spokesperson, guys like Lessel, Kimmitt, and, if needed, Slavonic. We opted to instead tell that story directly to the press and cut out the middleman. Furthermore, a press center director is in charge of what I consider to be a logistical hub. They are merely an extension of our staffs, and the soldiers in their centers belong to other units commanded by other officers, so the press center director isn't really in command or in charge of anything. When a person is a director of a press center, that means they are the point person for media logistics, nothing more. Strategy and execution, plans, and operations for communications all come from elsewhere. We had no need for the press center and all the extra stuff attached to them, so we bought our own gear, founded our own newspaper and website, acquired our own transportation, hired our own PAO teams, and moved out.

I was able to run circles around disruptive elements because, above all, Petraeus was immensely supportive of me. Credit also goes to Col. Pete Henry, my chief of staff, who would step in and rip these PAOs a new asshole anytime they fucked with me. He would often encourage me to ignore them and to work around them to get the job done.

Colonel Henry would go on to write in my evaluation from the war that I was a "captain in colonel's garb," and Petraeus would write on my evaluation that I was the "best PAO in theater," so with that kind of appreciation and validation, I didn't focus too much on people who talked behind my back, especially PAOs who avoided telling me to my face about how I was flying "solo" or "freelancing." I gave them plenty of opportunities to "tweak" me, but somehow, despite my many visits to the press center, calls to the Pentagon, and e-mail interactions with all of them, I was never tweaked.

Colonel Henry more than once reminded PAOs in Baghdad who I worked for, and he had no problem reminding anyone who fucked with me that I worked for a lieutenant general, not lieutenant colonels, and that type of territorial pissing will certainly set off most people. I loved it. He basically, professionally, told them all to fuck off, and that got things rolling down a rocky road for me, but I didn't care. I had the respect of my general and his staff, great teams of advisers in the field, and Jared in my corner with sponge and bucket, so I didn't need much else.

I should note that I didn't just take the advice of the chief of staff. Prior to deciding to work directly with the press, I spoke with Slavonic and asked him if the other three-star commands in Iraq had to distribute their press releases through the press center, and he said they weren't required to send their releases to the press center. Slavonic repeated what Kimmitt had said, that the press center was "there to help, but not serve as something that is a requirement."

Toward the end of my tour Petraeus was asked by the Defense Department to do a press conference via video with the Pentagon press corps. I had gone ahead of time to ensure the press center had everything lined up. As Petraeus walked into the room, he was swarmed by PAOs who wanted to rub elbows with him. They sidled up to him like a rock star. It was embarrassing. Petraeus looked beyond the crowd and made eye contact with me as the small herd, which included the press center director and Lessel, tried to talk to him. He ignored them and focused on me.

"We ready, Steve?" Petraeus asked me.

"Yes, sir," I said, as I looked him over one last time and pulled some hanging strings off his uniform. I think Petraeus knew that I was getting the shit kicked out of me by senior PAOs in Baghdad and in Washington DC. I never complained to him. He had other things to worry about, and my interpersonal affairs weren't something he should concern himself with. The chief of staff knew, though, and maybe he had conveyed something to Petraeus.

Petraeus sipped some water and finally looked at all the PAOs who had swarmed around him. He smiled and then he looked at me and pointed. "Here's the best PAO in the military," he said as I backed away from him. Petraeus wasn't shy about laying the compliments on me or on anyone who did good work for him. Petraeus would tell me several times during our time together that I was the best PAO he had ever worked with in the Army, and now, apparently, in all the services, according to his latest public display of affection. I was deeply flattered, because to me no single military person had understood military public affairs like Gen. David H. Petraeus. And while I knew part of him was just busting their balls, I knew deep down inside he truly meant it.

"Steve, we've got to get you promoted. When do you put on major?" he said, smiling.

"I'll retire before I make major, sir," I replied with a smile. At this point in my tour I was ready to distance myself from the military and my chosen profession within it. I did eventually make major and retire at that rank.

"You need more rank because you're doing a lot more than any of these guys in here, I can tell you," Petraeus said, smirking as he jabbed at the PAOs around him.

I smiled and said nothing.

With the comment the PAOs all stopped their clamoring and quietly dispersed and took their seats to watch the briefing. It was as if he had thrown a verbal grenade in the middle of the group. In sum, a three-star general had just told the ranking PAO in Iraq, the coalition spokesperson, the press center director, and a bunch of other field-grade PAOs that I was doing much more and much better work than they were doing, and I was only a captain.

I later thanked Petraeus for taking up for me in front of those officers, and he replied, "You get what you earn, Steve."

In Iraq my fight was not only against the insurgents' communications campaign, but also against my PAO peers. The Defense Department press operations team, the Army's public affairs staff, the Combined Press Information Center, STRATCOM in Baghdad, and the public affairs shop at U.S. Central Command all failed miserably to focus on what needed to be done. U.S. military PAOs failed to support us, despite the significance of our mission, but I hope they all realize that they weren't hurting me by not helping. Instead, they were hurting our mission and, ultimately, our war fighters on the ground, and I find that unforgivable.

The military public affairs community needs to trust its operators and their leaders to effectively manage their communications campaigns. The U.S. military needs to empower people on the tactical level to make decisions because they are the ones who know the issues from the ground level. The tactical PAO should establish from the forward area what will be done with his or her respective command. Once they engage the press, the rest of the community should follow and not vice versa. Strategically, organizations like STRATCOM and the press information center should serve the commands with actual missions by supporting them with personnel and media logistics and by providing the strategic unity of effort. Overarching enduring themes and messages should come from places like STRATCOM, but that should be the extent of the relationship. STRATCOM should not manage communications plans for tactical units based on some fuzzy definition of cohesion of message or unity of effort. Uniformity didn't matter in Iraq because the battlefield differs from region to region. Cookie-cutter communication tactics can't be applied, and communications management should start from the ground up and not top to bottom.

Public relations is important to the military, and the Defense Department sees that information and knowledge are connected to violence and public opinion. Otherwise, they wouldn't have paid the Rendon Group $6 million to manage communications in Iraq, they wouldn't have invested nearly $96 million for U.S. contractors to run the Iraqi Media Network, and they wouldn't have paid $112 million to the Lincoln Group to manage Defense Department information operations and strategic communications efforts.

Doctrinally speaking, we also need to train all of our soldiers, starting in basic training and then through advanced individual training, regardless of their profession, that they are all PAOs and they are all ambassadors of their services. We need to give them intensive blocks of instruction on mass communications so they understand that their actions domestically and abroad impact the reputation of the U.S. military and, more widely, the United States.

The Defense Science Board published a report in September 2004 that said, "Strategic communication is not the problem, but it is a problem. Strategic communication is a vital component of U.S. national security. It is in crisis, and it must be transformed with strength of purpose that matches our commitment

to diplomacy, defense, intelligence, law enforcement, and homeland security. . . .
Thus our challenge is to transcend Cold War clichés, to seek out new and creative responses—especially in the realm of strategic communication—and to do so most urgently, because at this moment it is the enemy that has the advantage."

The massive public affairs failure in Iraq is a convergence of errors years in the making, and the remedy can be only a full-suite reconstructive approach to communications on the battlefield. U.S. military public affairs must be gutted and reconfigured, refitted and redesigned.

STRATCOM in Iraq didn't see itself as an organization in crisis, even though it was labeled that way by the Defense Science Board. I remember in September 2004, the same month the science board filed the report, a particularly violent month for the coalition in Iraq, I was in STRATCOM's office in the Republican Palace in the Green Zone when I looked down on a desk and saw a stack of glossy eight-by-ten-inch photos of Lessel with his autograph on them.

Everyone recognized that STRATCOM or, more broadly, military PAOs were failing in Iraq, but the community itself was so insulated within the Green Zone that it couldn't see that the international press corps and the world longed for information and waited for answers to questions that were never heard. Seeing Lessel's pictures made me realize that those who were drawn to the public affairs community to work in the ostentatious world of the media could cross the line and in their own minds become the celebrities they often saw on television. By seeing themselves too much on television or seeing their names too much in print, they lived in a whimsical world, and their personalities, not the mission, became important in their lives. I'm not sure why there was a stack of autographed pictures of Lessel, and I'm not sure who would want a signed picture of him.

Al-Sahhaf, the seemingly crazy former Iraqi minister of information, said three things at the onset of Operation Iraqi Freedom that have stuck with me despite how comical they were at the time. He spoke them as coalition forces poured into Iraq. "We have placed them in a quagmire from which they can never emerge except dead. Washington has thrown their soldiers on the fire. I speak better English than this villain Bush."

Maybe he's not as crazy as he seemed. He seems to have gotten a lot correct.

12

WESTERN MEDIA

70 percent of Americans think U.S. security gains have come at an "unacceptable" cost in military casualties. This led 56 percent to conclude that, given the cost, the conflict in Iraq was "not worth fighting," the first time a decisive majority of people have reached this conclusion.

—*Washington Post*–ABC News poll, December 2004

A gunfight between insurgents and U.S. soldiers had broken out on a vicious little stretch of road in Baghdad. It was something that happened nearly every day. The gunfire had become part of the daily sounds of Baghdad, much like birds singing in trees back home. Explosions bellowed deeply, while automatic weapons fire seemed to keep a tympanic, snare drum–like beat. Minutes earlier it had been quiet at Phoenix Base, the place we affectionately dubbed "Mortar Manor," where our command was headquartered inside the Green Zone; it was aptly named because the area was a well-known impact zone for insurgent mortar fire.

I was in my last ninety days, a two-digit midget, as it is known, and my attitude after nearly a year of mobilization to the war zone dealing with the idiocy of PAOs had worn me thin. I had a short fuse and was frustrated at the lack of progress the coalition had made, but I was determined to finish my tour strong, get across the finish line, and go home.

"Hey, Steve, we've got a problem. I need you to come with me!" a security contractor said, bursting into my office.

In Iraq you never want a security person to tell you there's a problem, especially with a raging gun battle nearby. I donned my helmet and flak vest and headed toward one of the corners of our compound, following the contractor. As we approached a security tower along the perimeter, he grimaced and pointed up toward the tower.

"Can you please get him down from there?"

I looked up, and covering the battle raging over the nearby walls was Geraldo Rivera. He was visiting our command and was scheduled to interview Petraeus that morning. It was Rivera's second visit to our command during my tour, and I had left him earlier under what I thought was the watchful eye of a fellow officer whom I had detailed to help Geraldo set up his equipment. When the fighting broke out, Rivera and his cameraman wanted to record the action but lacked a good vantage point, so they climbed up the tower, which had been evacuated by security guards. When I looked up, Geraldo was directing the cameraman what to record.

"Hey!" I shouted. "Can you please get down from there?" I said over the din of the fight. The two ignored me and continued to capture the action. At one point Geraldo stepped in front of the camera and began to report with the gunfire as his backdrop. The weapons reports bounced off of buildings and made their way throughout the alleys and streets, traveling quickly all around us.

"They need to get down," the contractor told me.

"Okay," I said, smiling. I redirected my comments to Geraldo. "Hey, man, please don't make me come up there," I shouted to Rivera.

"We're almost done, Captain," Geraldo said excitedly. I wasn't too urgent about getting him down because I understood what he was recording was great footage for a newsman. But I had to convince the security contractors I meant business, so I complained to him from the ground.

Over the noise of the gunfire I continued to shout. "What's Fox News going to say if you guys get killed on my watch, in our compound? C'mon, get down from there, please."

Geraldo and his cameraman kept telling me they were "almost done" for about another two minutes. By then a small group of soldiers had gathered around and were watching Geraldo in action. I stalled as long as I could to let him get some footage, and then I climbed up the ladder and onto the tower, where the noise from the fighting was a lot louder.

"Guys, I'm really too short for this shit. What are you going to tell my wife if I buy the farm? We really have to get down," I said, smiling.

Geraldo smiled a big toothy grin from underneath his famous mustache. "Okay, we're done here," he said, patting me on the back as we all climbed down.

"Please don't do that again," I told Geraldo, motioning with my head to our security officer. He just smiled. I wasn't angry at the guy, but I was legitimately concerned they might get shot. I really liked Geraldo, and I didn't want to see anything happen to the guy. While there was a slim chance he would take a round directly, there was a better chance that one of those rounds could ricochet and hit him.

Geraldo later that day had a nice interview with Petraeus on his patio and didn't kiss him this time, as he had done on his previous visit. The first time he visited our command in 2004, Geraldo greeted Petraeus with the double-peck cheek kiss so common in the Arab and European world, right to left. I think he wanted to do the triple-peck, but Petraeus pulled away. Maybe the mustache tickled him. But how many men can say they kissed Dave Petraeus?

This time Geraldo surprised Petraeus not with a kiss but with a recorded message from Petraeus's wife, Holly. Geraldo had recorded it at a black-tie function in the States that he attended with Mrs. Petraeus. As the video played on a small video monitor and Petraeus watched his wife appear onscreen, the cameraman started to point his camera at Petraeus, who was watching his wife intently. He wanted to capture Petraeus's reaction since he was visibly moved to see his wife. When Geraldo saw the cameraman lifting the camera to aim it at Petraeus, he looked at him and disapprovingly shook his head softly. The cameraman put the camera down as Mrs. Petraeus finished her message and said, "We miss you. Come home soon."

Geraldo smiled at Petraeus excitedly, and it was apparent he had been containing the excitement for weeks and thousands of miles. He was beaming.

Visibly moved and surprised, Petraeus said, "I'm just a soldier, and like anyone else, I want to go home too," and he thanked Geraldo for the personal message. Geraldo could have captured the tender moment on tape and later shown it on Fox News, but instead he did the decent thing and let a spouse and her soldier keep an intimate moment personal and private.

Geraldo had earned an unjust reputation in PAO circles because they accused him of giving away unit positions and plans of attack in Iraq in 2003, which from what I was told were mostly overreactions by sensitive military officers. Service personnel loved Geraldo, and he spent nearly two hours getting his picture taken with damn near everyone who worked at Phoenix Base, including Iraqis who didn't know who the hell he was. The first time he visited us in 2004, as Petraeus arrived, Geraldo and his brother Craig threw us a pizza party and sat around and bullshitted with us for a long time. I've got nothing but love for the guy.

It was refreshing dealing with nationally recognized journalists because they didn't really have anything to prove and weren't aspiring to do too much more than get a good story. Back in the States I had worked with a lot of local reporters from different cities across the country, and they tended to be more confrontational and operated with the premise that as a government communicator, I was always telling them half the story and hiding something. Can't say I blame them.

To my surprise I was shocked by how seemingly low maintenance most network news personalities were when they visited. Tom Brokaw, for example, was as blue collar as you can get. He was truly a man's man. Soldiers felt comfortable around him as he released a few carefully placed raw expletives that seemed manlier coming from his deep, regularly eloquent voice. On television he told viewers about the world, but in Iraq he could have passed for just another soldier, wiping the sweat from his brow, bitching about the heat, and drinking as much water as he could stomach. When he talked to soldiers about the enemy, he used colorful words when referring to them, and he shook enough GI hands to develop carpal tunnel syndrome. He was gracious, but as he maneuvered around the training sites, there was an inner strength to him that made him gigantic yet humble enough to still come up to me and say, "Captain, thanks for going through all this for us. I know you dealt with a lot of bullshit to make this happen."

I smiled at him as he looked me straight in the eyes and locked his hand in mine as he firmly shook it. That would be Brokaw's final trip to Baghdad as anchor of NBC News. As he interacted with people, he was actively listening. As he walked around and looked at the training we were showing him, I could tell he was trying to soak everything in, a last adventure in Iraq with people he obviously admired dearly: U.S. soldiers.

Petraeus gave him some extraordinary background on the training mission, and the two were connected at the hip for the entire day. I knew that our story was in good hands and that Brokaw would do a great job sharing what he had learned from us with the American people.

When I heard Rumsfeld blame the media for the climate in Iraq, I think about my press interactions in Iraq. The overwhelming majority of my media interactions in Iraq were positive engagements. Fair and accurate stories were broadcast or published most of the time, and I discovered the press understood the challenges I faced. I never found any merit to things stated by Rumsfeld or any PAO about the Western media.

Christiane Amanpour, I found, had a very strong personality and exuded as much confidence as Brokaw, only in person her strong femininity threw me off balance, something not visible in her on-camera, safari shirt–wearing persona. She also visited our command a couple of times and each time greeted us with kisses and hugs. She was definitely all woman, but there was an inner being she showed that told me she'd kick a person's ass in a New York minute if she needed to. She was worldly and had seen a lot, and I could feel that by talking to her. There were anchors and then there were correspondents, and there was no doubt that the latter of the two were always a bit edgier. I learned from some of Christiane's colleagues that CNN staffers regularly referred to her as the "queen," not to her face, though, or I suspect she'd put a royal bitch slap onto their knavish faces. Some crew members at CNN viewed her as a prima donna, but from my interactions with her during my tour I found her to be extraordinarily friendly, hassle free, intelligent, and polite. As with Brokaw, I could tell she was a professional, but underneath was an immensely tactile reporter in touch with her surroundings and her story. She was someone who could get texture and offer that to viewers.

Anderson Cooper, whom I had been e-mailing back and forth about all things Iraq before he came to Baghdad, was slated to meet with Petraeus for about an hour in the summer of 2004. I was surprised to hear from Cooper when I picked him up the day of his interview that Amanpour would be joining him.

"Whoa, I didn't plan for that," I told him. "I'd love to accommodate her, but all the general has is an hour, and you're it, my friend," I told him. Cooper said he knew we couldn't give him more time, and he'd let her cut into his interview window.

"Like I have a choice," Cooper said jokingly, taking it all in stride. The day of the interview, Amanpour showed up at the last minute and cut into 75 percent of Cooper's time and spoke with Petraeus on background with no cameras. There was no doubt Amanpour was queen bee for CNN overseas. Cooper got to talk to Petraeus for about fifteen minutes on camera, not exactly the deep interview he was after with Petraeus, but back then I think Cooper understood his place in the organization, and his rise at CNN shows he played his cards right.

Anderson had the spirit of an extreme sports junkie churning violently underneath his calm, well-coifed exterior. While in Baghdad Anderson routinely checked with me to see if there were any missions he could go out on with us. We didn't have much going on at the time, as we were still training the Iraqis in garrison, but one day Anderson told me he had found something and was going "on a mission." He had fallen upon some soldiers going out into the Red Zone. He saddled up and went out on a convoy. When he returned I asked how his trip had gone.

"Boring," he said. "Nothing happened," he added. He looked disgusted.

"What do you mean?" I said. "You guys went out, delivered water, and you made it back safe and sound. That sounds like a good thing," I said.

"You know what I mean, Steve, I mean, you know, nothing happened," Anderson said. He was so frustrated he could barely talk, but he was good-natured about it. He wanted to get into the "shit," as we called it, and was looking for a story. Years later I ran into him in Moore, Oklahoma. I was there as part of a corporate public relations disaster team, and he was there covering the story. He is a really nice, energetic guy.

In a candid conversation with Amanpour and Cooper in Baghdad in 2004, I asked them to confirm rumors I heard about strained relations between the media and PAOs. Cooper said he hadn't had too much trouble with PAOs, but he also admitted having limited interaction with them, since he was rarely in Baghdad. Amanpour was the more animated of the two. She felt PAOs treated the press disrespectfully, as if they were "stupid children."

"They're always on message. You know what they're telling you is shit," she said. She complained that the military tried to control the press too much, and she said she found it refreshing to speak to someone frankly, as she had just done with Petraeus, who didn't give her "bullshit," adding, "That's what we need more of here."

Days later I received an e-mail that had some pictures of Amanpour that had been taken by a U.S. military photographer. The CPA on June 28, 2004, transferred authority of Iraq to the Interim Iraqi Government two days before schedule, as Bremer fled out a back door. PAOs asked reporters to be at the press center for a very important event, but they did not reveal what was scheduled to happen. As reporters showed up, cameras, phones, and recording devices were confiscated by PAOs. Then Bremer announced that the CPA was no more and Iraq was a sovereign nation. Amanpour, according to those in the room, began to complain and asked for her electronic devices so she could file a report, and she was immediately rejected. When she got up to leave, insisting she be allowed to file a story, ignoring the demands of the military officers in the room, she was confronted by a security guard, who encouraged her to calm down.

PAOs and the coalition argued that the restrictive steps were necessary to keep an element of surprise and to prevent the insurgents from attacking and foiling plans for the transfer. That's bullshit. The CPA could have easily allowed cameras in the room and stipulated that reports would be delayed for thirty minutes or so for operational security reasons. We embargoed information all the time, and we could have done it again.

Pictures of Amanpour at the transfer of authority spoke loudly of her disgust with the PAO community. She was shocked. Her mouth was wide open in disbelief in every picture. I find it interesting that a U.S. photographer would train his camera lens on her and not on the actual announcement. Even more interesting was how the PAO community circulated these pictures so quickly within its ranks and how many people chimed in and offered jabs when they replied to all in the e-mail. In 2006 on CNN *Presents*, Amanpour would say:

> We witness this very, very short ceremony, very bland, very short; there were some smiles. When it was over, well, of course, as a journalist, you think, wow, this is great, off we go. We've got the exclusive. Let's see who can get the news out first. So of course we ran for our phones and our walkie-talkies to see that they had disappeared. And I remember running for my phone. I was body blocked by a huge former Navy SEAL, now bodyguard to any of these new officials, and I mean almost knocked to the floor, and I went ballistic. I mean, I just went nuts. I said, "But we need our phones. We're journalists. you brought us here to tell the story." Such was the paranoia, such was the fear, because of this incredibly insecure situation that they just—they wanted to hold on to this news for several hours. Well, after a lot of, you know, to and fro and back and forth, we finally got our equipment back and we got the news out.[1]

Peter Jennings was scheduled to talk to Petraeus the day authority was transferred to Iraq. His producer, a real nice guy named Vinnie, had been easy to work with, and I was looking forward to getting another big name knocked off my very long list of interviews I had Petraeus scheduled to do. Petraeus's press calendar during June 2004, prior to Casey's media blackout, was a full plate. I often joked with him that I had him on "three-a-days," where he would do media interviews in the morning, afternoon, and early evening six times per week. It was an important time.

I got a call from Vinnie early that morning. The CPA had invited Jennings, like Amanpour and others, to a location for a secret event. Vinnie didn't know if he should cancel Jennings's trip to Taji and his later interview with Petraeus or attend the coalition's secretive press function. He probed me to see if I knew something, but I knew nothing (PAOs expected coordination from my team, but they didn't coordinate crap with us—nobody had told me about the transfer). He thought about it for a few minutes out loud and made the decision. He would divide his crew: one camera would go with Jennings to the convention center, and the other would travel with Vinnie to Taji to capture footage of Iraqi Army training and record interviews with Iraqis and their U.S. advisers. The interview with Petraeus would be canceled, and the advisers at Taji, expecting Vinnie and Petraeus, would get only me, Vinnie, and a cameraman.

I was pissed. A lot went into planning a press dog-and-pony show. The advisers on the ground had to practice training scenarios with the Iraqis and then ensure everyone was in inspection order because Petraeus would be there as well. They'd have to arrange for ground transportation, beverages, and lunch. I had to arrange for air support to travel to Taji by helicopter (two Black Hawks), and we had to move things around on the general's schedule to accommodate the visit. There were a lot of moving parts. I knew the advisers would be let down if Jennings wasn't there. We would travel with only about seven people out of an original party of twenty-two that day. It was a waste of resources.

I called Petraeus and told him what had happened, and he was flexible about it and filled his time with work. I traveled to Taji with Vinnie sans the general, and we went through the motions for Vinnie and the cameraman. Shortly after we touched down at Taji, a U.S. Marine colonel yelled in my ear as the Black Hawks readied for takeoff after dropping us off. The Iraqis were sovereign. The coalition had transferred authority while we were in the air. I shouted the news to Vinnie. Vinnie responded as expected.

"Fuck! God damn it!"

He immediately started calling his bureau on his satellite phone. We now knew what Jennings had attended at the convention center, and Vinnie was less than thrilled about being at Taji with me and missing a big story. He got some good interviews, some great information, and some good footage, so the trip wasn't a wash for him. Later, he asked if Jennings could still interview Petraeus, and despite a very busy schedule Petraeus squeezed him in later that evening and moved some stuff on his calendar. I told Vinnie that Jennings would have to be punctual. Petraeus was trying to be accommodating, but he was busy. Jennings and Vinnie's crew would have to be efficient, in and out, because of other schedule demands. Vinnie assured me they would be on time and quick.

Jennings would be more than an hour late. My phone was busy that early evening. I was on the phone with Vinnie, with Petraeus's aides, trying to make the interview happen. I finally told Vinnie if they weren't at the palace in fifteen minutes, Petraeus had to move on. About twenty minutes later I got a call from Vinnie at the entrance of the palace grounds. He said they had been delayed by security officers but were on their way. I ran down to the checkpoint to help them. Jared had picked them up and driven them to the palace, and I could tell something was eating him. He had this look on his face like he could go on a tristate killing spree. I introduced myself to Jennings and noticed when he shook my hand that his grip was limp and he didn't look at me. I greeted Vinnie with a glare, and I said, "Okay, let's go. General's waiting." I tried to hustle them onto the palace grounds and up to Petraeus's office. I was urgent, and I was tired of explaining to the boss why Jennings was not there, as I had promised.

Unlike other anchors who showed up wearing cargo-pocket pants and safari shirts and vests, Jennings wore slacks and a remarkably crisp blue shirt that had no visible sweat marks on it, despite the fact that it was more than one hundred degrees that day in Baghdad. Draped across his forearm was his blazer. The guy looked flawless. As Jennings moved along it was obvious he was in no rush and didn't take kindly to my rushing him.

"Please follow me. The general has been waiting for you and was disappointed he didn't get to see you this morning," I said, and before I knew it I was about fifteen paces in front of Jennings. I stopped and turned around to see Jennings moving slowly and smoothly as onlookers gawked at him, almost as if he was arriving at a movie premiere in Hollywood and he was the star. It wasn't hard to miss him. He looked exactly the same on television as he did in person, and he was almost ornamental while he walked on the dirty grounds of the palace.

Two American contractors approached him and shook his hand, and he paid more attention to them than he did when he met me. They asked him to pose for a picture. I stayed quiet as he agreed and posed with one of them. The other said, "I just have to run back to my trailer and get my camera. Can you please wait here?" the man said in a southern drawl, and before I could say anything, he sprinted off as his buddy stalled Jennings, who seemed more than happy to wait and chat.

"We really can't do this. He has an appointment with General Petraeus," I told the contractor, but before I could finish, Jennings interrupted me.

"Surely the general will understand the delay. We're nothing without our viewers in this business, and this is the least I can do," Jennings said.

"He's waited for you all day," I said. "Surely you understand he's busy and has waited long enough."

I understood he was trying to be nice, but it wasn't the right time. He could have easily told the guy to be in that spot in an hour, but instead he felt it was okay to make people wait. At that time Jared said "Jesus Christ!" aloud, pushed Jennings into the contractor and posed them, whipped out his personal camera, took two quick pictures, and gave the contractor his e-mail address and said, "Write me and I'll send you the pictures. Now let's go!" and held out his arm to point the way for Jennings. Jennings quickened his step this time, as Jared herded him from behind to ensure there would be no more fan encounters. As he walked into the palace, I noticed some sweat stains on his shirt. I guess Jared made him nervous, and that made me smile. I could not have been paired up with a better sergeant. Petraeus would have to wait even longer as the crew set up the lights and cameras for the interview.

Later, Vinnie would apologize for the tardiness and tell me Jennings really wasn't a difficult guy and that he wasn't as stuffy and high maintenance as we thought he was. Sure he wasn't, I thought. But it didn't matter to me because Jennings had his face time with Petraeus, and if I ever worked with him again, I would buffer in an extra hour to ensure the general wouldn't have to wait. As it turns out, Jennings would die of cancer months later, and he would never revisit our command. In hindsight, maybe his attentiveness to his fans was his way of saying good-bye.

The big three anchors (Tom Brokaw from NBC, Dan Rather from CBS, and Peter Jennings from ABC) would visit our command during my tour on what would be their final trips to Baghdad as anchors. The most memorable, I think, was Dan Rather. Rather interviewed Petraeus in June 2004 and later before the Iraqi elections in 2005. Both times he and Petraeus sat down before the interviews and had long unrecorded conversations about a multitude of topics as the crews set up. They connected, it seemed, on some intellectual level, but I think it was that each man found the other fascinating. Each of them was at the top of his profession, both old soldiers in their own right, and they genuinely enjoyed each other's company.

Rather's first words to me were "Captain, very nice to meet you. Thanks for having us, and thank you for your service." Like Brokaw, he looked me square in the eye and gave me a handshake as firm as a lumberjack's. Unlike Brokaw, I detected a bit of sorrow in Rather's eyes, and maybe it was a result of all that he had seen in his many years in journalism reporting from all over the world; maybe it was because I knew Rather had covered some tough stories in his day. It seemed his eyes had seen a lot, but around soldiers they were grandfatherly and beamed, and he shared smiles with everyone he encountered.

As he walked through the palace in 2004, he shook more hands than a presidential candidate and thanked every single person in uniform for their service. He asked many where they were from and seemed to know a little something about every city and every town, and he offered personal anecdotes to some about his time in their locales as he kept moving. Many soldiers were surprised that he knew about certain restaurants or places where only locals gathered. There was no hiding the fact that he liked soldiers.

Rather, though supportive of U.S. troops, was no wimpy newsman. He had heard before arriving in Baghdad that insurgents were infiltrating the ranks of the Iraqi police and army. It was one of the many things he wanted to talk about with Petraeus. His producer, Andy Clarke, was kind enough to tip me off about Rather's plan. During the interview, Andy told us, Rather intended to pull an Iraqi police uniform from a coat bag after questioning Petraeus about the vetting process of Iraqi police. He and his team had bought the uniform in an Iraqi market. He wanted to get Petraeus's reaction on camera. Andy said he told me because we had been really nice to him and the crew and he didn't want to ambush us.

Minutes before the interview I looked over the general's appearance, and we talked about how to respond to the uniform issue. As I checked his grooming I thought aloud about Rather's plan, and the general remained silent.

"Simply because a person can get an Iraqi police uniform doesn't mean that our vetting process is flawed," I said. "In the United States anyone can buy military uniforms or police uniforms and outfit themselves to look like military or paramilitary forces, sir," I said. "It doesn't mean you can infiltrate the army. It just means you can look like a soldier."

I added that we had security measures in place with our new vetting, such as identification cards and emerging biometric technology that helped prevent phony cops from getting into the ranks. "Okay, that's good stuff," Petraeus said, and when he did the interview, he used the talking points I had offered and the uniform was a nonissue.

On his second visit, this time to Phoenix Base, when he wrapped up his interview with Petraeus, Rather could have easily left the compound and killed time somewhere else, but instead he walked around our compound and poked his head into rooms and offices, where soldiers greeted him with smiles, open arms, back slaps, and happy handshakes. Again, he thanked every last one of them, and lines formed as soldiers waited to get their pictures taken with him. It was like kids waiting to see Santa in a mall.

Months later Rather would resign as the anchor for CBS News after twenty-four years amid criticism over a story he did about President Bush's National Guard service. Media critics and his own beloved CBS News, an institution he had helped build into a news superpower in his forty-three years with the organization, were dragging Rather over the coals. Rather said he made a judgment mistake and apologized in 2004.

As controversy swirled around Rather and more and more of his peers seemed to be beating up on him over the Bush story, Petraeus asked me for Rather's e-mail address. He wanted to send him a note and express his appreciation for Rather as people were "piling up on him," Petraeus said.

Rather's last broadcast as anchor for CBS was March 9, 2005. I was surprised and deeply moved when Rather addressed service personnel as he signed off for his last time. "To our soldiers, sailors, airmen, and Marines in dangerous places . . . courage."[2]

The majority of my tour in Iraq wasn't filled with a lot of press frustration like my PAO counterparts faced. I suspect we had a pleasant working environment because we operated with truth as our heading. We didn't have to sit around and think of ways to twist and spin things. Our media relations activities were overwhelmingly successful because we didn't try to bullshit our way around these exceedingly bright people. Things weren't always perfect, and there were some media folks who certainly rubbed me the wrong way, but we worked together to try to inform their audiences as best we could.

A good friend and frequent visitor was *Washington Post* columnist Dave Ignatius, who more than once was a fly on the wall in our command. He attended our staff meetings and traveled with Petraeus as he met with sheikhs, police chiefs, military commanders, and other Iraqi leaders. What I enjoyed most about Dave was his ability to shake off his refined, groomed, and manicured outer shell and become this gruff, cussing, Hemingway-like correspondent who could blend in with foreign dignitaries or a group of grab-assing U.S. privates. Dave would encourage me to write a book about Iraq after reading my blog and some of my op-eds. No trip to Iraq was complete for Dave unless he spent a few days embedded with us.

After Brokaw retired his replacement, Brian Williams, also visited us before the 2005 Iraqi elections. Williams was tall and personable, and, like Jennings, he looked the same in person as he did on television. He interviewed Petraeus on a concrete bench outside in the cool winter air under a bright-blue sky. I encouraged soldiers to watch instead of chasing them away. It was the best public affairs training I could ever ask for, as enlisted and commissioned members of our command quietly sat by and watched Williams and Petraeus chat. While some PAOs with their behind-the-velvet-rope demeanors might discourage the crowd, I welcomed it. It was a great learning experience for soldiers and a phenomenal way to get military personnel to rethink their attitudes toward the media.

Williams left our compound and headed to another interview in the Green Zone. Hours after the interview an enraged Williams called me. He was supposed to fly out of the Green Zone via helicopter to Baghdad International Airport, where he would fly to Jordan to do his *Nightly News* broadcast from Amman that evening. He and his team arrived at the landing zone, only to learn that there were no flight arrangements made for him. He was stuck in Baghdad. He called me because he had called everyone in the public affairs community, and nobody seemed willing or able to help him. When we had parted ways earlier, I told Williams, "If you ever run into any brick walls, give me a call." I had no idea it would be a few hours later.

"Captain, I hit a brick wall," he said. "I am stuck here in Baghdad, and I need to be in Jordan by tonight. They told me I had transportation, and now these guys say there's no more air travel!" It was refreshing to see a calm, cool, collected guy like Williams blowing a gasket. It made me realize that everyone is human, no matter how in control they may seem. Williams wasn't mad at me; he was simply mad.

"Can you please help us?" he pleaded.

"Let me see what I can do. I'll call you back, Brian," I told him.

I made some calls and got some things rolling. I told Brian that he would hear from someone within ten minutes, and if he didn't to call me back and I'd reengage. Five minutes later he called me back. He had gotten a helicopter that would be picking them up soon. They were on their way to Jordan.

"Thanks, Captain. We owe you one!" Brian said. "Stay safe," he said. The next day I watched his broadcast from Jordan from the previous day. As he spoke in his nasally voice, he was as cool as the evening air, and little did most people realize how much Brian had hustled around that day to bring them the news. It seemed effortless and seamless.

While many in the Defense Department and even more on the right wing criticize the media, I believe they did a good job, given the circumstances, reporting on the war in Iraq. They had limited mobility and could tell the story only from either their news bureaus or the vantage point as an embedded journalist with U.S. forces. Wandering out into the streets was suicidal. Those with larger budgets could hire Iraqi stringers to get the interviews and footage off the streets of Iraq, and some still braved the streets to try to tell the story of Iraq under U.S. occupation, but Iraq was a dangerous place to wander freely as a reporter.

I had the privilege to work with some great reporters in Iraq. Deb Amos from NPR, Vivienne Walt from *Time* (although initially our relationship started off rather rocky), Martha Raddatz from ABC News, Jane Arraf from CNN, Dexter Filkins from the *New York Times*, Greg Jaffe with the *Wall Street Journal*, Steve Komarow from USA *Today*, Jim Krane from the Associated Press, Bing West and Fouad Ajami (both authors), Dana Lewis, Brett Baier, Oliver North, Scott Rutter from Fox News, and the list goes on and on. They were always focused on getting a good story, learning as much as they could about our mission, and getting their facts right. I do not understand how the media can be blamed for anything in Iraq.

Ned Parker wrote for Agence France Presse, produced great pieces about our command, and was a reporter who actively worked stories on the ground for his mostly European audience. Initially, Petraeus did not want to do the interview based on his past experiences with AFP, but I talked him into it and he agreed to the interview.

Petraeus often referred to our mission, training Iraqi security forces, as a cattle drive. He likened the mission to the famous Remington painting where ranch hands are riding horses in driving rain underneath lightning-filled skies, driving a herd of cattle home. The comparison was that our mission was hard and that we needed to be resolute and be comfortable in chaos, but some had thought that he was comparing the Iraqis to cattle, so I recommended he lay off the analogy. In addition, I felt some Europeans didn't like or understand the American cowboy spirit. Using the analogy in the States on an audience who had knowledge of the cowboy heritage was okay, but to reach out to Europeans in a cowboy context, especially since a cowboy was then in the Oval Office and not too well liked overseas, I thought was a bad idea.

The next day Petraeus started getting passionate as he spoke to Ned. I always knew Petraeus liked someone when he started talking with hands and smiled and joked. He felt comfortable with Ned, and I knew what would be next. During the interview Petraeus told Ned that the mission often reminded him of a stampede.

"Ah, shit, here we go," I said under my breath. Petraeus walked over to a large conference table in his office and motioned for Ned to join him. He unrolled a print that was in his office and spread it out on the table. He began to explain to Ned how the mission was reminiscent of a cattle drive.

"We've got all these forces working against us," Petraeus said. "It's like these poor guys riding tough through the storm, under lightning, rain coming in sideways," he said, pointing to the Remington print of cowboys on the stampede.

Ned asked for clarification. "Sir, do you think the Iraqis are cattle?"

Oh, crap! I was screaming at the top of my mind. Boss, shut up, shut up! He not only had said what he shouldn't have, but also gave Ned a visual aid. This was bad.

Petraeus explained that the coalition and the Iraqis were the ranch hands and that the mission in Iraq was the cattle. They represented the fight against the insurgency. I could see the lightbulb go on in Ned's head. Petraeus had educated him.

The next day Ned published his article, and in it he tactfully presented Petraeus's stampede analogy. Petraeus was very happy with the article, which included, he noted, the cowboy analogy. I gave up trying to get Petraeus to stop using the analogy, and once Ned's article was published I told Petraeus that while I had concerns about the analogy, it looked like all's well that ends well. I had worried about it for nothing.

In hindsight, I suppose Petraeus was right: we were running with a herd, Lippmann's herd, trying to get an uncontrollable situation under control and get Iraq to where it wanted and needed to be. The bad weather around us on the drive was the violent climate that had loomed over us like a dark cloud and worn us down but didn't deter us. Despite the deaths of Iraqi soldiers and some of our advisers, we kept driving on, around the setbacks and through the violence. We took chances and found strength in each other.

Weeks later as I prepared to complete my tour, Petraeus called me into his office and presented me with a token of his appreciation. He wrote:

"For Capt. Steve Alvarez, Phoenix PAO Extraordinaire and one of the *great* outriders in the Mesopotamian Stampede. Thanks for your awesome work! Air Assault! Dave Petraeus, LTG, U.S. Army (Phoenix 6)." It was the Remington print he had used in his analogies when he spoke with the press.

It now sits on my wall in my home office as a quiet reminder that I don't know everything and as testament to the long, hard trail we rode in Iraq. I look at that print a lot these days as across the ocean Iraq continues its painful drive to democracy.

For my part, I'm glad the trail is over. And like true outriders at the end of their trails, I went unceremoniously out to pasture, happy to have the love of a good woman waiting for me and content when my lips tasted their first sip of whiskey in months. It had been a long, hard, dusty ride indeed, but at the end of this ride there was no sunset waiting for me to ride into, no happy trails. My trail would end, but the Iraqis' is yet to begin. I hope the Iraqis do what we did when they're at the end of their ropes: tie a knot and hold on.

I'm still sore from all my time in the saddle, and some days I sit on my porch and look off at a fading sun and wonder if the herd will ever be brought home.

EPILOGUE

A lot has transpired since I left Iraq. Bin Laden was killed in a raid. In 2015 it was revealed that the Central Intelligence Agency (CIA) had managed a secretive program that purchased chemical weapons in Iraq during my tour. It appears that there were in fact weapons of mass destruction in Iraq. Saddam Hussein was captured, tried, and executed. I could not help but wonder as I watched the grainy video of his hanging how far he had fallen out of grace from the time when the United States considered him a friend, a time when Rumsfeld went to Iraq and shook hands with him in a show of friendship that was captured by cameras.

Even though Petraeus asked me to stay on board and continue to be his PAO in Iraq, I declined the offer. While flattered, I was ready to get back home and retire. I could have easily done what so many did and latched on to him and made a nice career for myself, but the truth was I wasn't interested in being a PAO anymore. I was more interested in being a dad and husband. I packed my stuff and headed home in the spring of 2005. I never told Petraeus about all of the challenges that were placed upon our team by PAOs, some of whom he went on to work with later in his career. I wonder how surprised he will be to learn about all the crap we got from people who were supposed to be on our side. I've intentionally not mentioned some of their names in this book because seeing their names on these pages would be a shit stain, a dirty skid mark on what I think is a book that can help future PAOs who do not toe the line. I don't want to soil it.

Jared Zabaldo left the Army Reserve. He went on to become a very successful businessman in Portland, Oregon. He married, had kids, and is enjoying a wonderful life. We keep in touch, and we have seen each other a few times in recent years. He was, in my opinion, the hardest-working military journalist to ever wear the uniform in Iraq, and he deserves endless kudos not just because of his body of work in Iraq, but because he put up with my bullshit for nearly a year. No other person in public affairs worked harder than Jared. I would go to war with him any day. There is no one I'd rather share a foxhole with than the Great Zabaldo. Nobody comes close.

In more than twenty years of service, I have led a squad and a section as a sergeant, a platoon as a lieutenant, several staffs as a captain, a battalion's subordinate units as a major, and a detachment as a commander, and none of the folks I served with, zero, managed to rise to challenges the way Jared did. Given the high caliber of some of the people I've served with, Jared left an impression on me, and after serving with him my expectations were too high. My standards were rigorous, to say the least. He had set the bar so high that nobody could reach it, and knowing there were people out there like him, I simply chose not to adjust my expectations. The Army Reserve fucked up by letting him go. He was no ordinary soldier.

Radhi Badhir continued his fight within the Iraqi Ministry of Defense. We kept in touch for several years. There was a short period of time when other Iraqi friends told me he had been killed. Years ago I heard he was alive and still working at the Ministry of Defense. Recently, a contact at the Ministry of Defense told me he was no longer there but at another ministry. I often think of how I used to have to hold him up whenever we were around helicopters. The prop wash would knock him over, and he'd lean up against me. That image is burned into my mind. I miss him, and my hope is that one day I will see him again. For now he is on my desk, framed in a picture, my arm around him, and we are both smiling for the camera for an image we know will be used to reminisce and stir melancholy. A large brass plaque he gave me is on my office wall, and he signed the back of it in Arabic with his title, media relations director. I have thought that he did that as a way of telling me, without saying it, not to forget him, who he was and what he did.

Fahmy has not been heard from by anyone on the Iraqi media team since 2005. I do not know where he is or if he is alive.

Assad, my interpreter, came to the United States in 2008 after I helped him earn a visa under a special U.S. government program for translators and interpreters. Petraeus wrote him a letter of support, at my request. He lived with me and my family in Florida for several weeks until he found work as an Arab role player in Indiana, helping train deploying soldiers. Later, he worked for an online shoe company. He returned to Iraq for an arranged marriage, and I last heard from him in 2014. He was in Basra, and he said conditions in Iraq were bad.

Al, Allawi's press secretary, works for the U.S. State Department in Iraq.

Lieutenant General Petraeus was promoted in 2007 and got his fourth star. He returned to Iraq as the commanding general of Multinational Force Iraq and quickly improved conditions on the ground. Petraeus later went on to become the commanding general of U.S. Central Command and was later given the job to lead operations in Afghanistan before he retired to take over as the director of the Central Intelligence Agency. Not sure why, but I often think of walking him into a helicopter for one of my many press trips and giving him a quick rundown about the trip, who was on it, and what member of the media would get the headset on the helicopter (he liked to talk to media as they flew). He would sit next to the window on the right side of the helicopter, and as his bird would gently lift off the ground, I would salute him and feel this deep satisfaction inside.

I think of those moments when I think of him. I last heard from him in 2014. I wrote him a short note, and true to form he responded within minutes while riding a train somewhere in the Northeast. The last time I had reached out to him prior to 2014 was when he fell from grace during the Paula Broadwell scandal. I offered him some unsolicited reputation-management advice, but he chose a surprisingly silent path. I also expressed my disappointment, but like he had done with Dan Rather, I learned from that and tried to show some grace. Not to sound cliché, but nobody is perfect, and I know that more than anyone. He remains the best officer I have ever served under, and, like Jared, no one else comes close. He elevated the expectations I had of subsequent leaders, and that did not work out for me because they all fell woefully short. In hindsight I have learned that it was unfair and unrealistic of me to think all officers could be of his caliber. I was screwed the minute I decided to return to active duty in 2007 because I had served with Jared and Petraeus. Naturally, nobody would compare. I should have retired, but I'm glad I served for a few more years. After I retired from the military I have come to terms with holding others to such high standards and expectations. In working with people I still struggle with that sometimes. Not long ago I sent a youth coach an e-mail regarding something about one of my sons, and I didn't hear from him for weeks. I followed up with several e-mails and heard nothing. Weeks later he would tell me about how busy he was, and he apologized for not replying to me. The former director of the CIA can e-mail me a reply in less than five minutes, but somehow a salesman can't make the time. That bar has been set high.

Rear Admiral Slavonic retired from the Naval Reserve in 2005. He has authored several books on leadership and works for a U.S. senator.

Brigadier General Kimmitt retired from the U.S. Army in 2006 and became the deputy assistant secretary of defense for Near Eastern and South Asian affairs. He later became a defense consultant.

Brigadier General Lessel became the U.S. Air Force's director of communication. He was later promoted to major general and became the director, plans, requirements, and programs, at headquarters of the Air Education and Training Command, Randolph Air Force Base, Texas. He retired as a two-star general.

Former Iraqi defense minister Hazim al-Shaalan and twenty-six other former Iraqi officials from the U.S.-backed government of former Iraqi prime minister Ayad Allawi in 2005 had warrants issued for their arrests. More than $1 billion is missing, and al-Shaalan left Iraq. In addition, twenty-three former Iraqi ministry officials are being sought for arrest. The Iraqi government is trying to lift al-Shaalan's immunity and is seeking extradition of the former minister of defense.

Salih's whereabouts are unknown. An Iraqi friend who worked with him says he has not known about Salih's fate for eight years. He is no longer at the Ministry of Defense.

Dan Senor, the CPA's spokesman, went on to become a Fox News analyst and a columnist.

Colonel Morganthaler retired from the Army Reserve and became the Illinois governor's deputy chief of staff, public safety, and later served as a Homeland Security adviser for former Illinois governor Rod Blagojevich, who is now in jail. She also made an unsuccessful run for Congress, owned a business that helps organizations prepare for disasters, and most recently authored a book about leadership. The book refers to her as a military trailblazer.

The Army Reserve major I replaced at the Iraqi training mission returned to Iraq as a public affairs detachment commander. He was promoted to lieutenant colonel and subsequently given high-profile public affairs missions.

Major General Eaton became an outspoken critic of Rumsfeld and the administration. He blamed them for bad handling of the Iraq war after he retired.

Colonel Bell, the former commandant of the Defense Information School who came to Iraq to teach Iraqi PAOs how to do their jobs, retired from the Army. One of the achievements highlighted when he retired was his establishment of mobile training teams sent overseas.

In 2006 and for several years the U.S. Defense Department identified my blog as the first-ever official U.S. military blog. Now somebody at the Defense Department added a caveat, stating it was the first official military blog published by a daily newspaper, but it doesn't matter. Anyone can research this and see that what I published was the first U.S. military blog, even if it wasn't hosted by the Defense Department. When officers write for publication as representatives of their services, they are writing in an official capacity. My blog was no different, and that is why it was officially the first U.S. military blog. It is still what I consider to be the first official military blog since I was the first military official to ever write one as part of my official duties. That fact will always remain. History can't be changed, even if words are changed online.

In January 2006 the Ministry of Defense created a show called *Iraqi Protector* that was broadcast weekly on al-Iraqiya (the coalition-funded network). The show was the very concept we had tried to push for two years earlier with the Ministry of Interior, and I couldn't help but think that the coalition had intentionally obstructed our progress on this show just so the contracted Iraqi Media Network could manage it and charge U.S. taxpayers for it. The producer was killed four months after it aired, and the show met a similar demise.

At least two hundred thousand Iraqi civilians have been killed since the war in Iraq began in 2003, according to the British independent Iraq Body Count program, which uses Iraqi and U.S. officials, media and government reports, eyewitnesses, family members, local officials, mortuaries, medics, nongovernmental organizations, and a multitude of other sources to collect its data.

According to the IBC, between 2003 and 2005 37 percent of all deaths in Iraq were caused by U.S. forces, as opposed to 9 percent caused by insurgents. A staggering 36 percent were killed in postinvasion criminal violence. More than half of the Iraqi deaths were caused by explosive devices; of that figure 64 percent of the deaths were caused by air strikes. The U.S. military, to date, has kept true to its statements issued by Rumsfeld and retired general Tommy Franks, the architect of Operation Iraqi Freedom. Both men said that the U.S. military didn't "do body counts." Yet while the number of U.S. military dead was painstakingly tallied each day until the U.S. pullout in 2011, 4,493 as of February 2015, a confirmed and accurate number of Iraqi civilian casualties, insurgent dead, and Iraqi security forces casualties is yet to be provided by any U.S. administration or by the Iraqi government. Most nongovernmental organizations say a true number of Iraq war dead will never be tallied because many deaths go unreported, and in some cases entire families have been killed.

A 2006 Johns Hopkins University study states that 655,000 Iraqis have been killed since U.S. forces arrived in Iraq in 2003, a testament to the failed U.S. policy there and a reflection of the horrid human conditions in Iraq. Other studies estimate at least 6,200 members of Iraq's security forces have died since 2005, and many suspect that number is far larger. I have also seen estimates stating that more than 1 million Iraqis have been killed. Someday we might know.

Retired U.S. Army general George Casey led the U.S. mission in Iraq from 2004 to 2007. According to the Defense Department, the total number of U.S. dead in Iraq almost doubled in 2004, the year Casey took over, rising from 486 U.S. dead in 2003 to 848 in 2004. Duty in Iraq during 2004, the year I was there, was particularly bloody and saw more than 8,000 soldiers injured; it remains the second-worst year on record for U.S. military injuries and deaths in Iraq.

Soldiers executing Casey's plans and policies in Iraq have deluged military hospitals, and former defense secretary Robert Gates nominated Casey to be chief of staff for the Army, a position he entered after leaving Iraq. The Senate confirmed Casey 83–14, and the same people who overlooked Casey's policies in Iraq voted for him to lead the Army. I took solace in the fact that it was Petraeus, not Casey, who turned things around in Iraq and made it safer, albeit for a short time.

Donald Rumsfeld resigned from office, fighting with the media on his way out. He wrote a memoir in 2011 and a book about leadership in 2013.

In late 2006 the Iraq Study Group reported in its report a chilling fact that harked back to the Vietnam War.

In addition, there is significant underreporting of the violence in Iraq. The standard for recording attacks acts as a filter to keep events out of reports and databases. A murder of an Iraqi is not necessarily counted as an attack. If we cannot determine the source of a sectarian attack, that assault does not make it into the database. A roadside bomb or a rocket or mortar attack that doesn't hurt U.S. personnel doesn't count. For example, on one day in July 2006 there were 93 attacks or significant acts of violence reported. Yet a careful review of the reports for that single day brought to light 1,100 acts of violence. Good policy is difficult to make when information is systematically collected in a way that minimizes its discrepancy with policy goals.

It seems I was right: somehow only the good news was floating up and out of Iraq, and the U.S. military had somehow become a sausage grinder for the truth.

As for me, I came home and began a one-man campaign to alienate many around me (including Jared and other friends from the war). I wanted to distance myself from the war, forget it, but at the same time I felt like I could talk only to those who had been over there. I had held in a lot of emotions during my twelve-month mobilization, and I was overtired, overemotional, and frustrated. I found it hard to interact with people and discovered I had a very low tolerance for those not associated with the military and, more specifically, for those not connected to Iraq. It seemed everyone wanted to offer me their opinion on the war, as if I needed to hear it, as if I wanted to hear it.

Imagine putting your ass on the line for something, for what you believe is a greater good, and having someone marginalize it because of their politics. The only person who has earned the right to say anything to me, right, wrong, or indifferent, is my wife. She has earned that right as a military spouse, and she can state any opinion because she has endured more than a decade of sleepless nights, lonely days, and missed anniversaries, birthdays, and holidays, all so I could serve.

When I got back I bought an antique truck I tinkered with and a shiny new boat. I lost myself under the hood of that old truck, enjoying the control I had over it, finally able to fix something that was broken and pouring myself into something that had been neglected and needed attention.

In the colorful waters of the Florida Keys I looked for answers and for the calm I had once known. I fished the depths, hoping to catch some of the mysteries that swam underneath my boat in the emerald and blue waters below me. I fished and a lot of times came up with an empty hook.

I did a lot of remodeling in our home and tore up the yard more times than I can remember, trying to get something to grow. I planted shrubs, trees, and sod in efforts to get stuff to grow around me.

I took a year off and tried to get reacquainted with my family and with myself. While many PAOs came home and celebrated their tours, I came home empty, feeling like I could have done more, should have done more. I guess I was a sore loser. I felt like I had been beaten by the bad guys, and I felt betrayed by my own military because I was unsuccessful in Iraq. Very much like running in that mortar attack, I felt alone, and the strength and deep purpose I had found serving in Iraq against all sorts of crazy odds were now absent. Domestic life in the suburbs seemed trivial.

For the first few months after I returned I penned a lot of editorials for the *Orlando Sentinel* about the war in Iraq. I criticized the war's management and tried to advocate better policies, pay, and health care for our soldiers. Most of my op-eds went against the company's (Army's) grain, but I found there was catharsis in the writing.

Before I left Iraq I was accepted to the University of Florida's doctoral program in mass communications, thanks in part to a glowing recommendation letter from Petraeus. I wanted to take all I had learned in Iraq and somehow share it through research, but my graduate school entrance-exam scores weren't great, and despite my hope to be conditionally admitted, I was asked to retake the test and achieve better scores by the department chair in order to gain full admission. Every year loads of athletes are let into colleges on special admissions programs because they can run fast, throw a ball, or perform some athletic feat. If the University of Florida was willing to admit athletes using special conditions but did not want to give me that same option, fuck them. I had a master's degree and I had served my country, and all I was asking for was a chance to be conditionally admitted and the chance to prove myself, but I suppose standards are standards. I made one trip to Gainesville, and that was it. I pulled out of the program before I even started.

In 2006, unable to deal with the bitterness in my head, I locked myself up in a condo on the Florida coast and wrote this book. The first draft was painful to write. I had gotten a lot off my chest. The military had been my family for decades as a young man. I grew up in the ranks, and I was writing some ugly things about the way the services conducted themselves that did not make me feel good. When I finished I then tucked the draft away for about a year and pulled it out in 2007 and edited it.

That same year I returned to active duty for the Army Reserve, feeling compelled to try to fix things that I thought were broken in the Army PAO field, and I put the draft away yet again, but my frustrations grew. I was immensely intolerant of most officers, I was impatient with most soldiers, and I found the Stateside full-time military reserve to be appallingly inefficient, unprofessional, and unpolished.

In 2010, after twenty-four years of service on active duty, in the Guard and Reserve components, in both the officer and enlisted ranks, in two branches of service, I dropped my retirement papers. There was no traditional retirement ceremony. No retirement medal or accolade. I was so sick of it I simply asked the military for my retirement orders and left just as quietly as I had come into the ranks, right after high school.

On this my tenth year after returning home from Iraq, I have finally mustered the courage to edit, rewrite, reedit, and publish this manuscript in hopes someone might read it and carry my lessons learned forward and change the way the military manages its communications programs. We are in a fight for hearts and minds, and that requires more than just fancy words and messages. We need to do more.

In 2006 the Army's public affairs field was realigned into the Maneuver, Fires, and Effects functional category. The Army says that public affairs now has a "complementary role to civil affairs, special operations forces and associated roles with psychological operations and information operations," bringing a profession that deals in facts closer to professions that deal with battlefield misinformation and propaganda. Furthermore, the Army has stated in its realignment of PAOs that in order for captains to be promoted to major in the public affairs field, a field-grade rank, the Army does not require the officer have experience as a PAO. In order for PAOs to be promoted to full colonel, they must now have only forty-eight months of experience as PAOs. It still matters not if the person is an educated communicator.

In November 2006 the Iraqi government formed a special team that monitors news coverage in Iraq. The Associated Press reported that it was established by the Iraqi Interior Ministry. The Iraqi government now threatens legal action against any journalist who does not report as the Ministry of Interior dictates. This directive is coming from a ministry that had secret prisons at its buildings (which the U.S. military did not know about but discovered in November 2005), has thousands of weapons missing, has wasted millions of dollars, and continues to have issues with corruption.

The Committee to Protect Journalists says that more than one hundred journalists have been killed in Iraq since 2003. Insurgent action is responsible for more than seventy of these deaths (includes crossfire, suicide bombings, and murders), while the U.S. military is responsible for the rest of the deaths. The CPJ says it has not found evidence to conclude that U.S. troops targeted journalists in these cases. Iraqi armed forces during the U.S. invasion killed three, and Iraqi armed forces, post–U.S. invasion, have killed one reporter. Eight others have unconfirmed sources. Iraqi journalists make up the largest group of dead reporters, with more than seventy-five, followed by Europeans with eleven, other Arab countries with three, and the United States with two. The rest are from other nations.

I left Iraq in April 2005 aboard a U.S. Air Force C-130, the same way I entered the violent nation. We boarded the ass end of the C-130 as an aircrew played Toby Keith's "Courtesy of the Red, White, and Blue" over the aircraft intercom speakers. An American flag hung overhead inside the plane as we passed underneath, and the crew chiefs shook our hands and patted us on the back. I was happy, sad, confused, deliberate, but more than anything, I was ready to go home to my family.

As the aircraft lifted off Iraqi soil, it jerked violently skyward and then banked sharply. I left Iraq with a platoon of Marines, and we all howled as the plane jerked us to and fro. We smiled and screamed as the engines roared loudly and carried us farther and farther away from the din of the battles waging below us throughout war-torn Mesopotamia.

The U.S. military left Iraq in 2011. In 2014 U.S. troops were sent back to help combat extremists, and a steady flow of U.S. personnel continues to trickle back into the country.

I don't regret serving in Iraq, but I do regret that I couldn't do more to prevent the deaths of coalition personnel and Iraqis. I especially regret that we entered a nation, turned it upside down, and hauled ass. I regret that we've not been able to help the Iraqis as we promised we would, but I also know that much of that is on the shoulders of the Iraqis themselves. They are a soup sandwich, placing everything in front of nationalism, and that will forever keep them looking back and not forward. But I remain proud of the men and women I served with in Iraq, those select few who gave everything they could to make Iraq a safer and better place. Those who disgrace the uniform and did little to improve things in Iraq, knew then, and know now, how I feel about them. I often think of the hundreds of Iraqis I came to know, and I wonder if they are still alive. I wonder if they still believe, as I do, that democracy will truly come someday to their nation. There are some days I wish we would just pull out and let that whole region deal with the mess themselves. I never have consistent emotions about Iraq.

My quiet moments spent reflecting on the war are all filled with a profound helplessness, knowing what could have been. I see the landscape, the faces. I hear the sounds. I smell its scents. I taste it. And all of those who fell during my watch seem to follow me. Ghosts I've never met, they follow me and linger over my shoulder. I am never alone in solitude. Even now, as I type this sentence, more than ten years after returning home, they are looking over my shoulder and whispering for me to get it right. I carry that with me. I think part of my duty is to carry that responsibility. That's what officers do, and it isn't debilitating. On the contrary, it is a propellant. I would be remiss in my duties if I looked the other way and allowed all that transpired to occur again. This book isn't about calling people out. This is all about ensuring it doesn't happen again and that we learn from mistakes. Doing the right thing in this case means writing this book, and if I affix an ugly legacy to my time in Iraq, then so be it. It is a small price to pay for setting a record straight, and if this is the one story I can successfully tell from Iraq that will have lasting, meaningful impact and possibly change some conditions, then it is worth it. Still, despite all of the setbacks, my heart is full of incredible memories of teamwork, esprit de corps, brotherhood, and how we faced up to challenges. More than anything I remember how we stuck together and how together we were stuck. And in that misery I was never alone. I am proud to have served there with my brothers and sisters.

I remain an early riser, despite having hung up my boots years ago, and I wake in the predawn hours and think about the melodic chants of muezzins echoing in the distance amid a fiery orange morning horizon when they called Muslims to prayer from the minarets. I hear nothing, and there is only a serene silence, the very thing I wished for in Iraq.

The silence is peaceful, but my mind is anything but at peace.

NOTES

3. IRAQI FACE

1. CPA, *An Historic Review of* CPA *Accomplishments, Baghdad, Iraq*, 2, 32, 14.
2. CPA, CPA *Accomplishments, Baghdad, Iraq*, 28.
3. CPA, CPA *Accomplishments, Baghdad, Iraq*, 14, 15.
4. CPA, CPA *Accomplishments, Baghdad, Iraq*, 14, 12.
5. Gallup poll results from May 2004, http://www.gallup.com/poll/1633/iraq.aspx.
6. W. Lance Bennett and David L. Paletz, eds., *Taken by Storm* (Chicago: University of Chicago Press, 1994), 161.
7. Daniel C. Hallin, *The Uncensored War* (Berkeley: University of California Press, 1989), x.
8. *Report of the Defense Science Board Task Force on Strategic Communication* (Washington DC: U.S. Department of Defense, September 2004), 41.

4. BLOG OF WAR

1. Author's blog, *Dispatches from Iraq, Orlando Sentinel*, July 4, 2004.
2. Tori Clarke, *Lipstick on a Pig* (New York: Free Press, 2006), 124.
3. Donald Rumsfeld speech at the Council on Foreign Relations, http://www.defense.gov/Speeches/Speech.aspx?SpeechID=27.
4. *Report of the Defense Science Board Task Force*, 27.

7. TRAINING THE IRAQI MINISTRIES

1. Edward Wong, "Iraq's Prime Minister Faults U.S. Military in Massacre," *New York Times*, October 27, 2004, http://www.nytimes.com/2004/10/27/international/middleeast/27iraq.html?_r=0.

8. ARAB MEDIA

1. From T. E. Lawrence's principles of insurgency, *Seven Pillars of Wisdom* (privately published, 1922).
2. Jeffrey Ross, "A Process Model of Public Police Violence," *Criminal Justice Policy Review* 7, no. 1 (1995).

9. AL-JAZEERA

1. Jeffrey Gettleman, "The Reach of War: Counterinsurgency," *New York Times*, June 4, 2004.
2. Al-Jazeera's English-language website, http://america.aljazeera.com /?utm_source=aje&utm_medium=redirect.
3. Al-Jazeera interview of Gen. Richard Myers in 2001, posted on the Defense Department's website: http://www.defense.gov/Transcripts/Transcript .aspx?TranscriptID=2290.
4. Neil MacFarquhar, "Muslims Scholars Increasingly Debate Unholy War," *New York Times*, December 10, 2004.
5. Clarke, *Lipstick on a Pig*, 222.
6. Al-Jazeera interview of Donald Rumsfeld in 2003, transcript posted on the Defense Department's website: http://www.defense.gov/transcripts/transcript .aspx?transcriptid=1946.
7. Jim Garamone, comments of Lt. Gen. John Abizaid in response to an al-Jazeera reporter's question, posted on Defense Department website: http://www.defense .gov/news/newsarticle.aspx?id=29243.
8. Bennett and Paletz, *Taken by Storm*, 161.
9. Dorrance Smith, "The Enemy on Our Airwaves," *Wall Street Journal*, April 25, 2005.
10. Bruce Cumings, *War and Television* (London: Verso, 1992).
11. Donald Rumsfeld quote in *Control Room* documentary (2004).
12. "The al-Jazeera News Network: Opportunity or Challenge for U.S. Foreign Policy in the Middle East?," CRS *Report for Congress*, July 23, 2003, CRS-2, http://fpc .state.gov/documents/organization/23002.pdf.
13. Clarke, *Lipstick on a Pig*, 233.

11. PUBLIC AFFAIRS

1. Brian Martin, "The Beating of Rodney King: The Dynamics of Backfire," *Critical Criminology* 13, no. 3 (2005): 307–26.
2. Martin, "Beating of Rodney King," 3.
3. Martin, "Beating of Rodney King," 3.
4. Martin, "Beating of Rodney King," 4.
5. Lawrence, *Seven Pillars of Wisdom*.
6. Sgt. Sara Woods, "U.S. Must Outdo Terrorists in Opinion Battle," February 18, 2006, http://www.defense.gov/news/newsarticle.aspx?id=14819.
7. Donald Rumsfeld, "War in the Information Age," *Los Angeles Times*, February 23, 2006.
8. William M. Hammond, *The Military and the Media, 1968–1973* (Washington DC: U.S. Army Center of Military History, 1996).
9. Rumsfeld, "War in the Information Age."
10. Robert Burns, "Rumsfeld: Terrorists Manipulating Media," Associated Press, August 29, 2006.

11. Rumsfeld, "War in the Information Age."

12. John R. MacArthur, *Second Front: Censorship and Propaganda in the Gulf War* (Berkeley: University of California Press, 1992), xiv.

13. James Lacey, "Who's Responsible for Losing the Media War in Iraq?," in *U.S. Navy Proceedings* (Annapolis MD: Naval Institute, 2004).

14. Rajiv Chandrasekaran, "Mistakes Loom Large as Handover Nears," *Washington Post*, June 20, 2004.

12. WESTERN MEDIA

1. *CNN Presents*, January 26, 2006, http://transcripts.cnn.com/TRANSCRIPTS/0601/29/cp.01.html.

2. Dan Rather, CBS News broadcast, March 9, 2005.